SAILING DIRECTIONS

for the

SOUTH and WEST COASTS of IRELAND

First published (South and Southwest Coasts) 1930
Second Edition 1946
Third Edition (South and West Coasts) 1962
Fourth Edition 1966
Fifth Edition 1974
Sixth Edition 1983
Seventh Edition 1990
Eighth Edition 1993
Reprinted with amendments to October 1996
Ninth Edition 1999
Tenth Edition 2001
Eleventh Edition 2006
Twelfth Edition 2008

© Irish Cruising Club Publications Ltd.

Irish Cruising Club Publications also publishes a companion volume *Sailing Directions for the East and North Coasts of Ireland.* Both volumes are available from booksellers and chandlers. A list of stockists in Ireland is published on the ICC website, www.irishcruisingclub.com.

In Great Britain both volumes may also be obtained from:

Imray, Laurie, Norie & Wilson Ltd
Wych House
The Broadway
St Ives
Huntingdon
Cambridgeshire PE17 4BT.

Telephone +44 (0)1480 462114, fax +44 (0)1480 496109, e-mail ilnw@imray.com.

Plans © Irish Cruising Club Publications Ltd. The plans contained in these Sailing Directions are not to be used for navigation. They are intended to assist the user to relate more readily to the text and should always be used with the latest up-to-date navigational charts.

Aerial photographs © Kevin Dwyer and other photographs © Geraldine Hennigan except where separately acknowledged.

ISBN Number 978 0 9558 199 2 6

Printed by W & G Baird Ltd, Greystone Press, Antrim, Northern Ireland BT41 2RS

SAILING DIRECTIONS

for the

SOUTH and WEST COASTS of IRELAND

Information gathered by members of the Irish Cruising Club, supplemented
by the contributions of many others who sail, live and work around the coast of Ireland.

Norman Kean

Editor

with a foreword by Willy Ker
Editor, *Faroe, Iceland and Greenland*
RCC Pilotage Foundation

What joy to sail the crested sea and watch the waves beat white upon the Irish shore!

Saint Columba, 563 AD

Foreword

When we started to cruise the West Coast of Ireland over thirty years ago, we bought a copy of the 1974 edition of the ICC Sailing Directions. Over the years, this well-thumbed copy has served us well, guiding us into many of the superb anchorages of this truly remarkable coast. I saw no need to buy another, until I was persuaded some years ago to get the then latest edition. It was a revelation, with very clear plans and excellent aerial photographs. The latter are invaluable, particularly to anyone new to the area. Thankfully there are still the same old down-to-earth instructions. I was, however, surprised; but, in a perverse way, pleased to find that one of my favourites had been omitted. It is virtually land-locked and I have lain there at anchor, secure in a F9 and the pub is not too far away! I fear that it will not remain a secret now, although you may have to look on the ICC web-site to find it!

While pinned down by bad weather in Kilrush on the Shannon recently, I decided to visit an anchorage in the Fergus River described in the 'pilot'. The route is quite tricky, through winding muddy channels and when I had successfully dropped and set my anchor, I called Veronica, my wife, on the 'mobile' with the words; "I am in Paradise"- much to her surprise and consternation! This anchorage would be unremarkable but for its history and it is this pervading sense of history which makes cruising the west coast so very special for me. Sail amongst the little islands that fill the head of Clew Bay and climb Croagh Patrick for a bird's eye view. The history of Ireland starts here, for these are the drumlins (a name which Ireland has given to the world of geographers) which were left when the ice retreated after the last Ice Age. 'Fast forward' to the Iron Age and anchor in Portmurvy on the north side of Inishmore, to walk up and marvel at the huge fort of Dun Aengus. Land, if you can, on Skellig Michael and climb up to feel the presence of the early Christian monks among the oratories and beehive huts. The history of the turbulent times of the Middle Ages is everywhere, as well as the Elizabethan Period and the 'Commonwealth' - some, perhaps best forgotten. Modern navigators are spoilt, of course, with GPS and radar, as well as forward looking echo-sounders; but 'the rocks don't move' they say and when the barometer drops like a stone or the visibility closes down, it is to the Sailing Directions we turn for comfort and guidance. It is as well, then, to have the latest edition.

As the editor of a 'pilot' myself, I know both pleasure and the pain of producing Sailing Directions. How much one is indebted to the number of sailors and others who have contributed in the past and continue to find the time after a busy cruise to feed back new information. Keep it up; we all depend on you!

Willy Ker

Editor, *Faroe, Iceland and Greenland*, Royal Cruising Club Pilotage Foundatiion

Front cover: Galley Head

Frontispiece: the Old Head of Kinsale

Contents

Preface

Harry Donegan

Wallace Clark

Sailing Directions for the South and South West Coasts of Ireland were first compiled by Harry Donegan, a founder member of the Irish Cruising Club, and were published (for the use of Club members) in 1930. They were revised in 1946 by his son, Harry Junior, and for the first time offered for sale to the public. Paul Campbell, Bob Berridge, Roger Bourke and Wallace Clark then expanded the Directions to include the west coast, and our knowledge of the tidal streams on the west coast, in particular, owes much to Wallace's efforts. The third edition, this time covering the South and West Coasts, was published in 1962. Over the following 44 years the book went through a further eight editions, with new information provided by recreational sailors (ICC members and non-members alike), professional seafarers, Government agencies and many others. The ICC was a pioneer in the use of aerial photographs as an aid to navigation.

For the present edition, the south and south-west coasts, and many areas on the west, were revisited by sea between 2006 and 2008, and photographs were taken at sea level, to illustrate transits, harbour approaches and dangers. Contributions were received from amateur and professional mariners, and harbour engineers. Information on facilities, navigational aids and shoreside amenities has once again been brought up to date. The use of plans and charts has been standardised throughout the book, and many of the plans have been redrawn. Appropriately sited waypoints have been provided for ports, harbours and anchorages, and where possible these are marked on the plans. In some places the traditional visual transits have become ambiguous or indistinguishable (or were unavoidably poor to begin with) and in these cases we have instead provided safe clearing latitude or longitude lines or waypoints for many of the dangers. All but the most stalwart traditionalists use satellite positioning in this way, and the practice is sensible and seamanlike. Nevertheless, a clear visual transit is still the best position line, and many of these have been photographed for this edition. The layout and design of the book have been improved, to minimise its bulk and to ensure that as far as possible the text, plans and photographs of each place are on the same or facing pages.

Aerial photographs (including 60 new ones) are by Kevin Dwyer, and sea-level photographs by Geraldine Hennigan, unless individually acknowledged.

Acknowledgements

Thanks are due to the staff of the UK Hydrographic Office in Taunton, especially Roger Millard, hydrographer responsible for the charts of Ireland, and to the staff of the Commissioners of Irish Lights in Dun Laoghaire, especially Tim Ryan, Inspector of Local Navigational Aids; to harbourmasters Alan Coghlan and Redmond Gillen, harbour engineers Richard Browne and Robert Tackaberry, and also to Tommy Arundel, Arthur Baker, Paddy Barry, Brendan Bradley, Peter Bramah, Paul Bryans, Leo Conway, Jarlath Cunnane, Dave Cush, Dominic Daly, Paraic de Bhaldraithe, Peter and Susan Gray, Simon Nelson and Ed Wheeler. Without their diverse and vital contributions, this edition could not have been produced. Thanks also to John Clementson, whose sterling efforts make important updates accessible on the website.

Kevin Dwyer's beautiful aerial photographs have become a keynote feature of these Directions and an important aid to navigation. The present edition includes many spectacular new ones, including those below and opposite. Kevin has prudent views about flying over water in a single-engined aircraft, but he does it with great enthusiasm (despite himself) in the interests of safe navigation for those of us confined to sea level; and for that, and for his immense skill with his camera, we are duly grateful. Sea-level photographs are by Geraldine Hennigan, who also proof-read and checked the entire volume, and for all of that, and for continuing to put up with her husband the Editor, she has my heartfelt thanks.

Norman Kean   October 2008

Barry's Cove, Co.Cork

Bofin Harbour, Inishbofin, Co.Galway

Important Information

Please read this and the introduction which follows before using this book as an aid to navigation. The information which follows is essential to a proper understanding of the book and to the safety of your yacht and crew.

WARNING

The Flag Officers and Members of the Irish Cruising Club, and the Editor, together with Irish Cruising Club Publications Ltd and its Directors and Members draw the special attention of purchasers and readers of this volume of Sailing Directions to the following. Coastal cruising, just like passage-making or any other activity upon the sea, carries inherent risks. Such risks are increased by the passage of time as channels vary, conspicuous objects are repainted or become obscured, and many other changes occur. It is impracticable to check all of the information contained in this volume on a continuous basis. The publishers assume no obligation to amend or update this publication. This volume is intended as an aid to recreational sailing and cruising, to be used by skilled, competent and prudent sailors in conjunction with up-to-date cartographic, textual, mechanical and electronic aids and equipment. Whilst all reasonable care has been exercised in its compilation and editing, it is not warranted to be completely accurate nor error-free in every respect, nor is it practicable for it to be so. The above-mentioned persons do not accept any liability or responsibility for any loss, damage or injury to property or persons arising or allegedly arising out of any error, inaccuracy, mis-statement in or omission from these Sailing Directions.

Additions and Corrections

Additions and corrections are welcome and may be sent to the Editor at Burren, Kilbrittain, Co.Cork, phone +353 23 46891, e-mail sailxanadu@gmail.com. Amendments and updates are published on the Irish Cruising Club website, www.irishcruisingclub.com.

Sheep's Head light, Co. Cork (p107)

Summer Cove, Kinsale (p60)

Introduction

The south and west coasts of Ireland are among the finest cruising grounds in the world, blessed with wonderful and varied scenery and warmed by the North Atlantic Drift. The south coast is 130 miles by sea from Land's End, 250 miles from the north coast of France or the Clyde, and a long day's sail of 60 miles from Dublin or Milford Haven. It can claim to be the cradle of yachting as a sport, and is the setting for several of its most prestigious events. The west coast is wild, remote and spectacular, and yet only 48 hours' sailing from England, France, Scotland or the Irish Sea.

This book is primarily aimed at the recreational sailor, with a vessel in the range 6 to 18 metres in length, having a draft of 2.4m or less, a reliable engine and an echosounder, probably GPS but not necessarily radar.

PORTS AND HARBOURS

From the bustle of the historic cities to the stark and lonely grandeur of the remoter islands, the south and west coasts of Ireland have the full range of ports, harbours and anchorages. There are several fine marinas, but this cruising ground most richly rewards those who are confident in using good anchors and can deal with the rise and fall of the tide alongside an old stone pier. Many places are accessible by day and night in all weathers, but many can only be reached in daylight and a few only in specific weather conditions. Access to most places is free of tidal restrictions. There are numerous small piers and jetties, old and new, some with deep water and some drying. In recent years many of the older piers have been renovated and extended, but not all of these improvements have been reflected on the Admiralty charts.

The coast is for the most part cliffbound, with splendid sandy bays and long, sheltered inlets, and is breathtakingly beautiful in every inch of its length.

TOWNS AND VILLAGES

The major population centres are the cities of Waterford, Cork, Limerick and Galway but the towns of New Ross, Dungarvan, Youghal, Cobh, Kinsale, Skibbereen, Bantry, Castletownbere, Cahersiveen, Dingle, Kilrush, Clifden, Westport,

Belmullet, Sligo, Donegal and Killybegs are all locally pre-eminent, and many smaller villages are significant as well. The beauty of the scenery, the relaxed pace of life, and increasing prosperity have encouraged a building boom all around the coast, with a parallel improvement in facilities, services and infrastructure everywhere.

Of the islands, 23 have permanent populations, including Sherkin (106), Heir Island (24), Cape Clear (125), Long Island (5), Bere Island (187), Whiddy (22), Dursey (6), the Aran Islands of Inishmore (824), Inishmaan (154) and Inisheer (247), Inishbofin (199), Inishturk (58), Clare Island (136), Inishlyre (7), Inishbiggle (24), Aranmore (522) and

Durrus (p107)

Inishfree Upper (9). Although frequently described as Ireland's largest island, Achill (2500) is linked to the mainland by a bridge, as are Valentia (700), Great Island in Cork Harbour and many of the islands on the south coast of Connemara. There are many others with seasonal or occasional residents, including Great Blasket, with its one faithful inhabitant who returns every summer.

WEATHER

The famously capricious Irish weather is, in general, free of extremes. The climate is maritime, and is characterised by the passage of Atlantic depressions, with rapidly changing weather conditions. A typical depression produces lowering clouds and a rising southeast wind, followed by more-or-less continuous rain and a gradual veer to the south or southwest. The passage of the cold front is often quite sudden, with a clearance to showers and an abrupt veer in the wind to west or northwest. This may all happen within twelve hours and be followed by a day or two of moderating winds and sunshine as a ridge of high pressure passes, before the cycle begins again. But equally, an anticyclone can dominate for days or weeks at a time and the weather can be glorious, with cloudless skies, warm sunshine and limitless visibility. Statistically, summer winds blow from the west and southwest about 40% of the time. The mean daytime temperature is about 18°C in June, July and August, and the coast of Kerry gets about 100 mm of rain per month. Fog is relatively uncommon, averaging one or two days in the month. The one predictable feature is unpredictability, at least more than a few days ahead; but that said, it must be declared that weather forecasts, from both Irish and British Met services, are extremely accurate and reliable. The Irish sea-area forecasts are regularly broadcast by the Coastguard on VHF and by local and national radio stations, and Irish and British forecasts are both transmitted on Navtex. More specific details of weather forecast sources are listed

The swell can run high on these coasts. West Calf and Cape Clear Islands (Chapter 2)

cause the seas to break. No hard and fast guidance can be given about when these hazards may be approached and when they must be avoided, but if in doubt stay well clear. Such a rock will often form "blind breakers", the sea rising into a steep pinnacle before subsiding without actually breaking. These are usually clear from leeward but hard to see from the windward side. A big breaker offshore in a heavy swell is a tremendous spectacle.

in Appendix 3.

A typical two weeks' summer cruise can be expected to include a day weatherbound somewhere, but it is also common to find yachts held up for days at the east end of the south coast waiting for a persistent west or southwest wind to change in their favour. If crossing from England or France it is often wise to make landfall further west, so as to have options if the weather does not co-operate. The best way to be weatherproof, so to speak, is to start at Baltimore, from where a cruise can be shaped almost regardless of wind direction.

Severe storms are unusual in summer, but do happen, the infamous Fastnet Race storm of August 1979 being perhaps the best-known. The sea state in winds of force 9 and 10 can be awesome and dangerous, especially close to the salient points and in wind-over-tide conditions. East of Cape Clear, the worst swell comes with south and southeast gales; north of Cape Clear, southwest and west do the most damage. On the west coast, a swell is rarely absent, and may become high and persistent if a deep depression passes within several hundred miles. The swell – particularly in combination with a tidal set – may raise steep and breaking seas in quite deep water; for example the Barret Shoals, northwest of Slyne Head, have 22m of water but must be avoided in heavy weather. There are many so-called "breakers" on the coast – rocks with anything from a metre to 10 metres of water, or even more, which

The seawater surface temperature offshore rises from 12°C in May to 16°C in September, and in the recesses of the longer inlets may reach 20°C or more in a warm summer. Daylight hours are long in summer; at the solstice the sun rises over Cork at 0510 and sets at 2155.

TIDES

Tidal information is based on the Admiralty Tide Tables, and other information is based on the Irish Coast Pilot. It is published with permission of HM Stationery Office.

The tidal rise and fall averages 4m at springs and 2·5m at neaps, and is remarkably uniform all around the south and west coasts, the range being slightly greater in the upper reaches of the estuaries and at Galway. There is an amphidromic point close to the east coast 25 miles north of Carnsore Point, which has the effect of reducing the range at Rosslare to 1·6m at springs and 0·6m at neaps. All round these coasts, spring high tides occur morning and evening,

Numbers indicate the area covered in each chapter

and neap high tides around midday and midnight. There are no anomalous tides; the tidal curves are everywhere more or less sinusoidal, so the rule of twelfths can be applied.

The main flood stream divides west of the Kenmare River, and flows north on the west coast and east on the south coast. Tidal streams are noticeable but for the most part not very strong, and the only tidal gate is the Bull's Mouth, at the north end of Achill Sound. The strongest tides are naturally around the headlands and in narrow channels, with spring rates of about 2 knots at most headlands, 3 to 4 knots in some of the narrow channels and 5 knots or more at the Bull's Mouth. Strong and persistent winds may increase the rate of the streams by up to half a knot and the duration of flow or ebb by as much as an hour.

Details of tidal streams are given in Appendix 4 and throughout the text.

NAVIGATIONAL AIDS

The coastal marks throughout Ireland are maintained by the Commissioners of Irish Lights, and harbour marks by harbour authorities, marina owners or the County Councils. In some places privately- or locally-maintained marks exist, and these are described wherever they are considered reliable. IALA System A (red to port) is used in Ireland, and the standard of provision and maintenance is very high. The principal lights are on the Tuskar Rock, Hook

Irish Lights Vessel Granuaile

Head, Mine Head, the Old Head of Kinsale, Galley Head, the Fastnet Rock, Mizen Head, Sheep's Head, the Bull, the Great Skellig, Tearaght, Loop Head, Eeragh, Slyne Head, Black Rock, Eagle Island, Rathlin O'Birne, Aranmore and Tory Island. The conventional direction of lateral buoyage changes at the Bull Rock, northwest of Dursey. The power and the range of the major lights are being reduced, but not so as to concern the recreational sailor.

The most significant recent advance has been the introduction of AIS (Automatic Identification Systems), for which transmitters are compulsory on large commercial vessels but are also being fitted to certain lighthouses and buoys. While AIS transmitters are, at the time of writing, rare on leisure craft, small AIS receivers are readily available and inexpensive. AIS transmitters on lighthouses and buoys are identified in the text.

Characteristics of lights and buoys are described using the same standard abbreviations as in the Admiralty List of Lights. Arcs of visibility are expressed from seaward.

CHARTS

Seven Admiralty or four Imray charts, on scales between 1:150,000 and 1:200,000, cover the coast and are useful for planning purposes and

passagemaking. On some parts of the south coast there are, in fact, no larger-scale charts. For cruising the coast, the largest-scale charts are almost always essential, both for safety and for the fullest enjoyment of the experience. The few exceptions are some of the large-scale harbour plans. The coast from Waterford Harbour to Bantry Bay is comprehensively covered by two Small Craft Folios. The Imray charts offer an economical and convenient alternative on part of the south coast, but west of Galley Head and north of Cape Clear, the Admiralty charts or Folios are indispensible. The text gives more specific advice, and Appendix 1 gives a complete listing of Admiralty and Imray products for the area.

The standard chartplotter packages include all the largest-scale information, but bear in mind when using chartplotters that the data displayed is never any better than that on the paper charts, and that only a hairsbreadth fuse stands between the navigator and the loss of this vital information. Always carry the paper charts as a backup.

Much of the coast of Ireland has not been surveyed since the mid-19th century, and many of the charts are still based, at least in part, on the old data. This includes Imray as well as Admiralty charts, and the chartplotter products directed at the leisure market. Satellite-derived positions are more accurate than the charted data in many places, and the UK Hydrographic Office has issued a standard caution to the effect that reliance should not be placed upon satellite-derived positions in relation to several of the charts of the Irish coast *(see Appendix 1 for details)*. This situation is being addressed urgently. Ireland is now a member of the International Hydrographic Organisation and there is to be an Irish Hydrographic Office

The Kowloon Bridge *buoy off the Stags in West Cork, marking the largest wreck in Irish waters (p76)*

6

(although Ireland has no plans to print its own charts). The Irish Marine Institute is undertaking a major survey project of the inshore waters.

Getting all of this on to the charts will take several years. In the meantime, the standard advice to the prudent navigator applies with full force in the waters around Ireland. Keep a good look out, maintain good traditional pilotage, and do not place undue reliance upon GPS when in close proximity to the coast or charted dangers. In certain places where the published charts are known to be seriously inaccurate, these Directions point this out.

To landward, the Ordnance Survey maps are excellent and up-to-date, and provide detail not only for exploration ashore but landmark-spotting from seaward. On the smaller scale the 1:250,000 scale Holiday Map is recommended. For intimate details of the land, including the minor road network and locations of hundreds of antiquities, the 1:50,000 scale Discovery Series is excellent.

PILOTAGE

A clear and unambiguous visual transit is the best position line. On this coast, the traditional ones are specified on the Admiralty charts, but many of them are no longer clear or were never clear to begin with. Many of the better transits have been photographed, but for many dangers, safe clearing latitudes, longitudes or waypoints have been provided. Waypoints are given for ports, anchorages and those channels where GPS is more than usually helpful. Where the waypoint symbol appears beside the position data in the text, the position will be found on the appropriate plan, marked with the same symbol. They are identified by two-letter abbreviations, which should be self-explanatory. These points or position lines should always be cross-checked on the chart.

The plans are intended to illustrate the text, and should not be used for navigation; that is to say that they do not necessarily show all the dangers, and that bearings, courses, clearing lines and positions should not be taken from them unless these are specified in figures.

Depths and heights on the plans are in metres, and the plans are oriented north-south (true). Depths are reduced to Lowest Astronomical Tide. Bearings quoted in the text and on the plans refer to true North. Magnetic variation in the region is approximately 5°W (2008), decreasing 11' annually. These Directions run from south-east to north-west. To avoid needless repetition of descriptive material, they sometimes require the reader to skip to the next section or paragraph to find the approach to a harbour from the other direction, and the reader sailing from northwest to southeast will inevitably be flipping back and forward occasionally.

Baltimore (p77)

ANCHORAGE, MOORING & BERTHING

In most places on this coast, anchorage, where it is available, is free. Good ground tackle is essential, and that includes an ample scope of chain as opposed to all-rope or a nominal length of chain next to the anchor. In most places the holding ground is good. Weed and kelp may occasionally be a problem, and care must be taken to ensure that the anchor is well bedded in and not merely hooked in the weed. This involves going astern on the anchor, gently at first but then more and more forcefully until full astern, while keeping an eye on a transit on the beam. Lift and re-lay if not satisfied.

There are marinas at Kilmore Quay, Waterford, New Ross, Crosshaven, East Ferry, Kinsale, Lawrence Cove, Cahersiveen, Dingle, Fenit, Kilrush and Galway, and more modest pontoon facilities at Dungarvan, Courtmacsherry, Baltimore, Sherkin, Foynes and Sligo. Many of the harbours described have proposals for marina developments, and at the time of writing (2008) a marina is under construction at Knightstown, Valentia Island. Where other projects seem likely to be realised within the next few years, they are mentioned so that the intending visitor may check the latest information on the ICC website, www.irishcruisingclub.com. Visitors' moorings are maintained in certain places by the County Councils and private businesses. The Council moorings are usually designed for 15 tonnes displacement and are equipped with large rigid yellow buoys which may or may not have pickup ropes attached. There may be a charge for the use of visitors' moorings; if so the details are often on a tag attached to the buoy. These Directions cannot give any assurances about the condition of these moorings, and visitors use them entirely at their own risk. Bear in mind also that many yacht insurance policies place the onus for checking visitors' moorings on the user.

Piers and harbours may charge dues for visitors; when they do, a typical level is €10 or €15 per night. Marina charges are generally but not always higher than this.

In the following pages, when an anchorage is

Kinsale Yacht Club marina welcomes hundreds of visiting yachts each year

8

described as being sheltered (or not) from certain wind directions, the sense is always clockwise, so for example "W to NE" means "W through N to NE". A "mile" is the nautical mile of ten cables or 1,854 metres. Distances on land are specified in kilometres.

PASSAGEMAKING

On most parts of this coast harbours and anchorages are closely spaced, but there are no good harbours on the west coast of County Clare, and the popular option for those not wishing to explore the Shannon estuary is the 75-mile direct passage from the Blaskets or Smerwick to the Aran Islands or further to the mainland coast of Connemara. The crossing is straightforward and most yachts can make it in a long day's sail.

The beaten track also leads 55 to 75 miles direct across the mouth of Donegal Bay, from Portnafrankagh or Broad Haven to Teelin, Church Pool or Aran Sound; this is a pity, since Donegal Bay offers many attractive ports of call.

A table of distances around the coast is given in Appendix 5.

SAILING ROUND IRELAND

Many each year prove to themselves that Ireland is indeed an island. The circumnavigation fits comfortably into a summer holiday, two weeks being a little tight, three giving more time to explore, and beyond that, the more the better. Clockwise or anticlockwise is a matter of personal preference, as of course is the choice of which areas to explore and which to leave for next time. A major factor, naturally, is the weather. Bear in mind that on the west and north coasts, strong winds raise an enduring and often heavy swell, whereas on the south coast, and particularly on the east coast, light winds bring calm seas.

RADIO COMMUNICATIONS AND SEARCH & RESCUE

The Irish Coastguard has its Marine Rescue Coordination Centre in Dublin, and Sub-Centres at Valentia Island and Malin Head. These three stations maintain constant listening watch on VHF. Valentia and Malin Head also listen on MF and are Navtex stations. There are also ten subsidiary transmitters, each with its own station name. The Coastguard stations provide regular weather forecasts, navigational warnings and traffic lists, and coordinate search and rescue. The RNLI has all-weather lifeboat stations at Rosslare, Kilmore Quay, Dunmore East, Ballycotton, Courtmacsherry, Baltimore, Castletownbere, Valentia, Fenit, Kilronan, Achill Island, Ballyglass and Aranmore. Kilmore Quay and Baltimore have 17-knot Tyne lifeboats, and the others 25-knot Severns or Trents. Inshore lifeboats are stationed at Fethard, Tramore, Helvick, Youghal, Crosshaven, Kinsale, Kilrush, Galway, Clifden, Westport, Sligo and Bundoran. There are affiliated local inshore rescue services at

The Shannon Coastguard helicopter lands on the sand at low tide, Courtmacsherry (p63)

West and Rushbrooke), in Berehaven (between Castletownbere and Bere Island and from Pontoon Pier to Lawrence Cove), from Reenard Point to Valentia, across the Shannon between Killimer and Tarbert, and from Burtonport to Aranmore. Passenger ferries sail from Baltimore to Sherkin and Cape Clear, from Galway, Rossaveal and Doolin to the Aran Islands and from Bunbeg to Tory Island. Ferries also run from Schull to Cape Clear, Cunnamore Pier to Heir Island, Bantry to Whiddy Island, Cleggan to Inishbofin and Inishturk and Roonagh Quay to Clare Island. Tourist boats take day-trippers from the mainland to the Skelligs, the Blaskets and Garnish Island. Dursey Island is unique in being served not by boat but by a cable car.

Tramore, Bunmahon, Schull, Bantry, Derrynane, Ballybunion and Kilkee. Airborne rescue is provided by Coastguard helicopters based at Shannon and Waterford, supported by the Irish Air Corps from Baldonnel near Dublin and Finner, Co. Donegal, and by the Royal Air Force from bases near Belfast and in Cornwall.

Details of Coastguard Radio stations are given in Appendix 3.

COMMERCIAL SHIPPING

There are Traffic Separation Schemes off the Tuskar and Fastnet Rocks, in which the usual International Rules apply. Rosslare Europort is the busiest passenger port in Ireland, Waterford has a large container terminal, and Cork is a major international port with constant traffic in oil and chemical tankers, container ships, passenger ferries and general cargo ships. Cork is also the headquarters of the Irish Naval Service, with nine patrol vessels based at Haulbowline Island. Foynes, in the Shannon estuary, is a major cargo port. Crude oil tankers, including some very large ones, use Whiddy Island terminal in Bantry Bay. Cargo vessels also visit New Ross, Youghal, Kinsale, Fenit, Limerick, Galway, Sligo and Killybegs, and visiting cruise ships may be seen in Cork and in the large inlets of the southwest. Coastwise shipping traffic is constant if not heavy on the south coast, but light on the west.

There are small car ferries in Waterford Harbour (between Ballyhack and Passage East and across King's Channel), in Cork Harbour (between Passage

FISHING

The fishing industry in Ireland and the UK is undergoing inexorable decline, but fishing is still important. In fishing harbours yachts are rightly expected to accord priority to fishing

Herons are numerous, and can be shrewd opportunists

Castletownbere is the principal whitefish port in Ireland (p110)

vessels and their requirements. The major ports are Killybegs, Castletownbere, Dunmore East, Rossaveal, Dingle, Kilmore Quay and Union Hall, but Crosshaven, Kinsale and Baltimore also have significant fleets.

The principal fishery close inshore is for shellfish – lobsters, crabs and prawns – and pot markers are met almost everywhere. These are usually orange plastic buoys, but dan buoys with black flags are also used. They generally mark the ends of a long string of pots on the bottom. It is normally safe to pass within a boat's length of a buoy, but beware of floating ropes, especially when two buoys are tied in tandem to cope with a fast tidal stream. Don't sail between them.

Rope culture of mussels in Roaringwater Bay

Sea angling is a thriving tourist business in many places; the boats often work to a regular timetable and the skippers appreciate having their normal berths left available. In return, they are often the handiest source of wonderfully fresh fish.

Drift netting for salmon is prohibited in Ireland and the UK. Avoiding the nets used to be a major preoccupation of yachtsmen, but it may now be assumed that a buoy offshore marks shellfish pots.

Fish farming is carried out in many places on this coast. Locations of many fish farms are noted in the text, but these can change at short notice, so a good lookout is required. Fish farms are usually, but not always, marked by yellow buoys with flashing yellow lights. Parallel rows of buoys – usually grey or blue plastic barrels – indicate rope culture of mussels. There are shellfish beds in some places, with oysters and scallops cultivated, where anchoring and running aground are frowned upon.

It is often convenient to raft up with fishing boats in harbour, but if doing this, a little courtesy and common sense are the key, as are good fenders and a willingness to keep antisocial hours. If in doubt, consult the harbourmasters for guidance. In many places, facilities for yachts and fishing boats are well segregated anyway.

Salmon cages in Bantry Bay

and small sharks. Grey and common seals are widespread, and otters are often seen along the shore.

Vast numbers of seabirds nest around the south and west coasts. These include the various species of gulls and terns, kittiwakes, guillemots, razorbills, cormorants and shags; and the now-ubiquitous fulmar, which fifty years ago was very rare. The Little Skellig

DIVING

The coast is liberally strewn with wrecks, some ancient, many casualties of the great 20th-century wars, and the largest of all, the giant ore carrier *Kowloon Bridge*, which foundered on the Stags off Toe Head in 1986, with her cargo of 169,000 tonnes of iron ore. These wrecks are a magnet for divers, and diving boats, usually large rigid inflatables, are commonly seen. They display the blue and white International Code flag A, and should be given a wide berth. Baltimore is a major centre for this activity. Unauthorised salvage of artefacts from wrecks more than 100 years old is illegal in Ireland.

is one of the world's largest gannetries. About 180,000 pairs of storm petrels – a third of the world population – nest on the offshore islands, which also have huge colonies of Manx shearwaters. The birds only come ashore after dark, so many visitors (and predators!) are unaware of their presence, but rafts of them may be met at sea. There are several large puffin colonies. Puffins are easiest to observe on Skellig Michael, where they are very tame, but they disperse to sea in July. Cape Clear Island has a noted bird observatory.

WILDLIFE

Whales and dolphins are common around Ireland, and the minke and pilot whale, the common Atlantic dolphin and the harbour porpoise are often seen. Bottlenose dolphins and fin whales are rarer, as are basking sharks. Humpback whales have visited the coast in recent years, normally late in the season. Sunfish are becoming more common, and leatherback turtles are sometimes reported. Jellyfish sometimes occur in huge numbers (and may even block engine cooling intakes) and at other times are nowhere to be seen – nobody knows why. The harmless moon jelly is the commonest but the compass jellyfish and the stinging lion's mane are also seen. Sea anglers catch mackerel, pollack, whiting, ling, cod, haddock, dogfish, congers

Mute swans (above); and (right) a bottlenose dolphin, common seals and a little egret

Schull (p93)

In the estuaries herons, egrets, oystercatchers and curlews abound, and waders arrive for the winter. Ireland is, in general, blessed in its freedom from aggressive and venomous creatures of all sizes, only partly thanks to Saint Patrick and his fine work on the snake population, now (as is well known) zero. There are few if any mosquitoes, even in a warm summer, and the south coast is mercifully free of that scourge of Scotland, the midge.

PLACE NAMES

Almost all the place names on this coast are derived from Irish Gaelic, and their English transliterations may be variable in spelling or usage. Many charted names are plainly misspelt, such as "Skull" for Schull, Co. Cork, and some have two equally valid spellings, such as Cahersiveen/Caherciveen (Co. Kerry). This can lead to confusion. It appears to be a uniquely Irish phenomenon, and it probably dates back to the original Ordnance Survey of Ireland in the 1830's. It must be assumed that the authorities whom the surveyors of the time consulted – probably the landowners or clergymen – had individualistic opinions on the matter. Be

that as it may, the Admiralty charts usually (but not always) follow the OS spelling. Where this is locally regarded as incorrect, the text uses the local name but refers to the charted name, for example "Rossaveal (Rossaveel on the chart)".

Many places have two distinct names, for example Garinish and Illnacullen, which refer to the same island, while many names occur more than once. There are two Inishbofins, three Inishturks, at least three Gar(i)nishes and seven Horse Islands. Sometimes the chart gives a place one name and the OS map another.

Appendix 7 lists many of the placename elements, with their Gaelic derivations and English translations.

(or "Castletown Bearhaven" on the charts)

Dingle has a large supermarket not far from the quayside (p160)

SUPPLIES

Availability of supplies of all kinds is detailed in the text. There are at least small shops of some kind in most villages, and for a major restock, Dungarvan, Castletownbere and Dingle offer perhaps the best combination of convenience by sea and proximity to the supermarket, while Youghal, Kinsale, Unionhall, Baltimore, Schull, Bantry, Kilrush and Galway come a close second. There are some very capable boatyards, but large chandleries only in Cork, Skibbereen and Killybegs. There are sailmakers in Crosshaven, Kinsale, Schull and Sligo. Fuel is not hard to come by, but in the remoter places may require a little forethought. It remains legal in Ireland for leisure craft to use marked (untaxed/agri/tractor) diesel, which is dyed green. Tankers, and all marina and harbourside pumps, dispense green diesel. In general, in the text, this is what is meant by "diesel". However leisure craft must pay an additional 32 cents per litre in tax, in respect of all marked diesel used for propulsion. The self-declaration must be made and the extra tax remitted direct to the Revenue Commissioners by March 1 of the year following purchase. As from 2009, yachtsmen are strongly advised to retain on board all receipts and tax documents for fuel, which may be subject to Customs audit. Petrol (gasoline) is only available at roadside filling stations, all of which sell taxed (road) diesel as well. Some of them also have a green diesel pump, and most of them sell bottled gas (propane or butane). Gas may pose problems of compatibility of fittings. If all else fails, the Irish standard fittings (which differ from the British ones) are easily bought. Camping Gaz, while expensive, can be obtained in many places.

PUBS AND RESTAURANTS

Ireland is legendary for the warmth of its welcome, and nowhere is this more marked than in its pubs, of which there are thousands. The pub is the local meeting-place where the best *craic* is often to be found. This Irish term, which derives from English but has developed to the point where it has no longer a direct English translation, describes the mix of conversation, banter, jokes, ribbing, argument and laughter that has made the Irish pub and its customers a worldwide success story. It is in the pub that the curiosity of the island is seen in its highest form – "are you on holiday?" is not a straight question but an invitation to share your life story and your opinions, and in return to have the questioner reciprocate.

Equally, the quality of restaurants is outstanding. It would be a full-time job to stay current with the phone numbers, let alone the merits of individual establishments, so this book does not

attempt it – the cruising sailor should carry an up-to-date tourist guide book as well and make full use of the tourist information facilities listed.

WASTE DISPOSAL
Dumping of any waste overboard in Irish waters is forbidden by law. Waste disposal facilities in ports and harbours may be on the scanty side, and any opportunity to use a recycling facility should be seized. The law does not, however, require holding tanks for sewage on yachts, and in consequence there are very few pumpout stations. Most marinas and harbours prohibit the use of on-board heads while in port, and it is only common courtesy to use the facilities on shore.

COMMUNICATIONS
Mobile phone signal is available in most places up to five miles offshore, but there are still some blank spots both afloat and ashore. In emergency, it may be assumed that every house, shop and pub has a telephone anyway. The foregoing is not meant to suggest that the mobile phone is a satisfactory means of communicating distress at sea; there is no substitute for marine VHF. Wi-fi with associated voice-over-Internet service is rapidly becoming standard in marinas, although the user may have to subscribe to the provider; and Internet access is (formally or informally) available in most places.

CUSTOMS AND IMMIGRATION
For most yachts arriving from other EU countries there is normally no requirement to report to Customs, and there are no passport formalities between the UK and Ireland. However the authorities are vigilant, their major preoccupations being drugs, firearms, illegal immigrants and the protection of Ireland's vital farming industry from illicit or diseased plants and animals. For an official statement of the requirements, see Appendix 2.

GETTING THERE
These parts of Ireland can be reached by road or rail from Dublin or points north or south, and more directly by ferries from England, Wales and France, or flights to the airports at Dublin, Waterford, Cork, Farranfore (Kerry), Shannon (Clare), Galway, Inishmore (Aran Islands), Knock (Mayo), Sligo, Carrickfin (Donegal) and Derry. Rosslare, Waterford, Cork, Tralee, Limerick, Galway, Westport and Sligo have train connections with Dublin, and bus services are widespread and comprehensive. Car rental offices tend to be concentrated in the cities, at the airports and at Rosslare Harbour. There is a dense network of minor roads, and almost every mainland anchorage is reachable by road. To get to and around Ireland, as anywhere else, consult the Internet.

The authorities are well equipped for maritime operations

Sneem (p143)

Adrigole (p115)

Chapter 1

Rosslare to Cork Harbour

Crosshaven

The south-east corner of Ireland can be a surprisingly challenging place for a yacht. The coast near Carnsore Point is unimposing, but the strong tides, offshore rocks and lack of good landmarks make for tricky pilotage, and convenient and accessible harbours are few. The ferry port of Rosslare offers reasonable anchorage in its bay and the possibility of a temporary alongside berth. The charming village of Kilmore Quay with its busy marina, a few miles west of Carnsore Point, is often the most convenient first port of call for a yacht arriving from south-west England or from France. West of the Saltee Islands, the picture changes as the coast rises in bold cliffs, with a succession of broad bays, fine natural harbours, and few dangers offshore. Waterford Harbour was well known to the Vikings of the 10th century, and was the scene of the first Norman invasion of Ireland in 1177. Between there and Dungarvan is the "copper coast", where the

metal ore was once mined from the sandstone cliffs. To the west lie Ardmore, Youghal and Ballycotton Bays and the great natural harbour of Cork.

Charts

The small-craft folios SC5621 and 5622 cover the whole of this section in full detail. In terms of individual charts, AC2049 Old Head of Kinsale to Tuskar Rock, or Imray's C57 analogously titled, cover almost all of it. AC1787 Carnsore Point to Wicklow Head or the larger-scale AC1772 Rosslare Europort and Wexford is needed for Rosslare. For exploring the Saltee Islands, AC2740 is essential. AC2046 is necessary for the Rivers Suir and Barrow above Duncannon Bar. The large-scale charts AC2071 and 2017 are optional. The 1:50,000-scale AC1765 Old Head of Kinsale to Power Head is useful, but AC1777 Port of Cork, Lower Harbour is better for Crosshaven. AC1773, Port of Cork,

sectors show inshore to N and NW and over Holden's Bed to the E.

Ballygeary, pole bn Oc WR 1·7s 7m 4M, R shore –152°, W 152°–200°, W(unintens) 200°–205°. Shows red to W, white to N, unintensified white close to the breakwater end.

Rosslare buoy, SHM QG

Traffic Separation Scheme

There is a TSS E and S of the Tuskar Rock. The S- and W-bound lane is 3 to 6M from the lighthouse, and the E- and N-bound lane 8 to 11M from the lighthouse. The lanes should be crossed at right angles, or as nearly as possible. Yachts rounding the Tuskar should use the inshore traffic zone, between the TSS and the rock. The South Shear is the main channel for ships approaching the port of Rosslare.

Tuskar Rock

The Tuskar should be given a berth of 5 cables on its E, N and W sides, more in heavy weather. On the S side, South Rock buoy should be left on the proper hand.

ROSSLARE

⊕ *RL* 52°15'·5N 6°20'·8W
AC1787, 1772, SC5621·15, Imray C61 and Plan
Rosslare Harbour lies opposite the southern end of the sandbanks which parallel the Irish coast from Dublin southwards. There is anchorage in the bay to the W. The harbour is sheltered from NE through S to SW but exposed from WNW to N. Very large conventional and fast ferries sail to Fishguard, Pembroke Dock, Roscoff and Cherbourg, and the harbour is also a busy RoRo cargo port. With recent heightened concerns on transport security, the Port Area is required to comply with the International Ship and Port Facility Code, which may mean restricted or prohibited access to the harbour. Subject to these provisos, it is possible for a yacht to be accommodated alongside the quay on the SW side, by permission of the HM.

Directions

From the E (South Shear Channel) leave the Tuskar light 2M to port, South Long, South Holdens and West Holdens buoys to starboard and Splaugh and Calmines buoys to port. Identify the breakwater light, and give the breakwater end a wide berth to allow space for ferries leaving. **From the S**, leave the Tuskar light 1M to starboard, then Splaugh to port and South Holdens to starboard as above. **From the N** (North Shear Channel), leave West Long and West Holdens buoys to port, then identify the breakwater light.

Anchorage

Anchorage is available to the W of the harbour entrance, in 3m, sand, staying well out of the way of the ship channel and clear of moorings. Anchorage is prohibited within 5 cables to the N and E, and 3 cables to the W, of the breakwater head. Somewhat subject to swell.

Harbour

For an alongside berth, permission must be obtained from the Port Operations tower; call Rosslare Harbour VHF Channel 14 or phone 05391 57929 or 087 232 0251. The SW quay has 3 to 5m. The RoRo berths on the central pier and the breakwater must not be obstructed. The harbour is managed by Iarnród Éireann (Irish Railways).

Facilities

For mechanical and electrical repairs, check with the Port Operations tower. Filling stations, shops, pubs, restaurants, hotels. Train, bus and ferry connections, car rental. RNLI all-weather lifeboat station.

Carrick Rock Perch from the N - Carnsore Point wind farm beyond

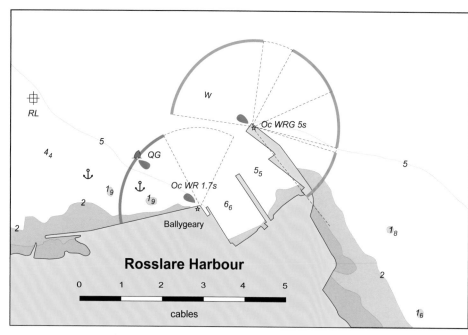

RL

Oc WRG 5s

QG

Oc WR 1.7s

Ballygeary

Rosslare Harbour

0   1   2   3   4   5

cables

ROSSLARE TO THE SALTEES AND KILMORE QUAY

SC5621, AC1787, 2049, 2740,Imray C57

In settled weather, the waters around Carnsore Point can be like a millpond, but in adverse conditions the combination of wind over tide and the irregular bottom can throw up tumultuous seas. The Saltee Islands, S of Kilmore Quay, are surrounded by dangerous rocks, and this, combined with the low-lying and relatively featureless nature of the mainland coast here, makes for an area to be avoided in heavy weather or poor visibility. The main ship channel passes outside the Coningbeg buoy, 9M offshore, but with careful pilotage a yacht can pass between or north of the Saltees in any reasonable weather. The classic route is across St Patrick's Bridge, a gravel bar between the Little Saltee and the shore, with 2·4m at LAT and buoyed in summer. Saltee Sound, between the Great and Little Saltees, has 7m but is unmarked. There is deep water south of the Great Saltee, but the approach passes close to the dangerous Bore and Brandies Rocks.

Landfall from the S and SE

Approaching the SE corner of Ireland from Land's End or the Bristol Channel, most yachts are likely to make their first call at Kilmore Quay or Dunmore East, and the natural course is to leave Coningbeg and the Saltee Islands to starboard, thus avoiding the complications of negotiating the Saltees at the end of a long and possibly tiring passage. All the approach options are described below.

Tides

Streams run at up to 3 kn at springs between Carnsore Point and Greenore Point, and through Salt-ee Sound, and can reach 4·5 kn over St Patrick's Bridge; elsewhere at 1·5 to 2·5 kn, turning N and E at −0110 Cobh and S and W at +0510 Cobh. Over St Patrick's Bridge the E-going stream starts at −0250 Cobh. S of the Saltees the streams are rotatory clockwise. The N and E stream begins N at −0100 Cobh, reaches its greatest rate of 1·7 kn (springs) to the ENE at +0200 Cobh, and ends SE. The S and W stream begins S at +0530 Cobh, reaches 1·9 kn (springs) W by S at −0355 Cobh, and ends NW. Slack water lasts about an hour. There are ripples near and over all the shoals. In heavy weather there are overfalls S and E of the Saltees, and steep and dangerous breakers on The Bailies, between the Tuskar Rock and Carnsore Point.

Constant (Great Saltee) +0014 Cobh, MHWS 3·8m, MHWN 2·9m.

Dangers

S of Rosslare and W of the Tuskar:

Splaugh Rock (extensive reef drying 0·3m), 6 cables SE of Greenore Point

Whilkeen Rock (dries 2·5m), 4 cables offshore 2M SSW of Greenore Point

Collough Rock (awash at LWS), 5 cables NE of Fundale Rock and 5 cables E of Crossfintan Point

The Bailies, 9 to 12m, 1M NE of Collough Rock

Fundale Rock (dries 1·2m), the outer end of a reef extending 5 cables SE from Crossfintan Point

Between Carnsore Point and the Saltees:

The Barrels (dry 1·5m), 1·5M SW by S of Carnsore Point

Nether Rock (5m), 2 cables NW of the Barrels

Black Rock (2m high), 2·5 M SW by W of Carnsore Point

Tercheen (dries at LW), 2 cables N of Black Rock

A **dangerous wreck** 2 cables N of Tercheen

Long Bohur (4m), and **Short Bohur** (7·3m), 1.5M E of Little Saltee

The Bore (5·5m), 1M S of Long Bohur

The Brandies (dry 0·9 and 2·5m), 1·5M SE of Great Saltee

Around and between the Saltees:

Coningbeg Rock (dries 2·8m), 2·5M SSW of Great Saltee.

Coningmore Rocks (4m high), 1·5M NE of

Coningbeg Rock and 1·5M S of Great Saltee

Red Bank (7·9m), 1.4M W of Coningmore Rocks, breaks in heavy weather

Whitty Rock (awash at LAT) and **Power's Rock** (0·3m) 3 cables NW of Great Saltee, and **Shoal Rock** (0·9m) 2 cables S of it.

Sebber Bridge (0·6m to 4m) boulder spit extending 7 cables N from Great Saltee

Galgee Rock (dries), 1 cable S of Little Saltee

Murroch's Rock (awash at LAT), 5 cables NW of Little Saltee

Unnamed rock (awash at LAT), 3 cables W of Little Saltee

Jackeen Rock (1·5m) 8 cables W of Little Saltee

Goose Rock (dries 2·6m), 1 cable W of Little Saltee

Forlorn Rock, 1·5m, 7 cables SW of Kilmore Quay

St Patrick's Bridge, 52°09'·2N 6°34'·9W, gravel bar with 2·4m in mid-channel, between Little Saltee and the shore SE of Kilmore Quay.

Lights and Marks

Splaugh buoy, PHM Fl(2) R 6s

Calmines buoy, PHM Fl R 3s

Carne Pier, metal col Fl R 3s 6m 4M

Fundale Rock buoy, PHM Fl(2) R 10s, 2 cables SE of the rock

Carnsore Point, wind farm of 14 conspicuous turbines close inland of the point

Barrels buoy, E Card Q(3) 10s, 1M SE of the rocks

Coningbeg buoy, S Card Q(6) + LFl 15s 9M, Racon (G), AIS, 9 cables S of Coningbeg Rock

Bore Rocks buoy, E Card Q(3) 10s, AIS, 8 cables SE of The Bore

Red Bank buoy, W Card VQ(9) 10s, AIS, 2.6M W of Coningmore Rock

St Patrick's Bridge buoys SHM, Fl G 6s, and PHM, Fl R 6s, both these marks about 3 cables to the E of the bar. Conventional buoyage direction N and E. On station 1st April to 12th Sept

Kilmore Quay fairway buoy, RWVS Iso 10s (this buoy is also on the line for St Patrick's Bridge)

Kilmore Quay breakwater end, Q RG 7m 5M, R 269°–354°, G 354°–003°, R 003°–077° shows green over approach channel from S (including, further S, between Murroch's Rock and Little Saltee), red elsewhere

Kilmore Quay leading lights 008°, Oc 4s 6M, white with red stripe on grey concrete columns, front 3m, rear 6m.

Experimental buoys

A position 7 cables S of Black Rock and 2M W of the Barrels E Card buoy is used by the Irish Lights as a test location for experimental buoys. At the time of writing (2008) there is a yellow pillar buoy, Fl(4) Y 10s, on station. This buoy is of no navigational significance. Check www.cil.ie for the latest information.

Offshore weather buoy

Buoy M5, yellow, Fl(5) Y 20s, is moored 33M S of the Coningbeg Rock at 51°41'·4N 5°25'·5W

Directions – Rosslare to Kilmore Quay – inshore passage

The passage between the Bailies and Collough Rock is 1M wide, and the passage between the Bailies and the Tuskar is 2M wide. In settled weather the inshore passage may be taken close E of the Calmines, Splaugh and Fundale Rocks buoys, staying E of the line between Fundale and Splaugh buoys to clear Collough Rock. The red perch on Carrick Rock may be left half a cable to starboard, but beware then of the Calmines shoal and a shallow patch N of it. There are several short cuts: Black Rock just visible S of Carnsore Point 239° leads safely between Fundale Rock and its buoy, and also SE of Collough Rock, while a course of due S towards Fundale buoy on longitude 6°20'·2W leads between Collough Rock and the shore. The tall white mast among the trees masking Ballytrent House, in line with Whilkeen Rock 340°, clears Collough Rock to the NE.

Carnsore Point is clean, and in calm weather it may

Ballytrent mast and Whilkeen Rock in line clears Collough Rock

be given a berth of one cable. It may be identified in moderate to good visibility by its conspicuous wind farm. Once round the point, identify Black Rock to the SW and steer due W to leave it 7 cables to port. Identify the buoys on St Patrick's Bridge and steer to pass midway between them. The buoys are positioned 3 cables E of the Bar; if entering Kilmore Quay, hold the W'ly course to the fairway buoy, when the leading marks line up 008°. If the buoys are not on station, hold mid-channel between the Little Saltee and the shore until well over the bar and in deeper water.

Anchorage

Anchorage in winds between SW and NNW may be found in St Margaret's Bay, between Carnsore Point and Greenore Point. This is a useful and comfortable anchorage in strong NW winds, when Rosslare is exposed. There is a small drying pier at Carne (Carna on the charts), on the S side of the bay. **From the N**, from a position 2 cables SE of Whilkeen Rock, steer towards the pier. Anchor 2 to 3 cables NE of the pier in 3 to 4m, sand. **From the S**, pass close to Fundale buoy and from it steer due N to pass inside Collough Rock. When Carne pier bears 250°, turn in to the bay, steering NW. The pier is unsuitable as an alongside berth, and rocks extend 20m beyond the pier head. Shop, pub and restaurant at Carne.

Anchorage is also available in Ballytrent Bay, to the N.

Directions – Rosslare to Kilmore Quay – offshore

In rough conditions, steer SE from the Splaugh buoy for a mile, then turn S, leaving the overfalls on The Bailies well to starboard. Give Carnsore Point a berth of 3M, and leave the Barrels buoy to starboard. In N'ly weather it should then be practicable to cross St Patrick's Bridge, leaving Black Rock to starboard. The safest option is always to head out to sea round the Coningbeg buoy, but in moderate conditions St Patrick's Bridge and Saltee Sound are passable, and with careful navigation a course close S of the Great Saltee can be taken except in heavy

weather and wind over tide.

For Saltee Sound, steer from the Barrels buoy for the N end of Little Saltee, keeping it on a bearing of not more than 270° to pass 4 cables N of Long Bohur - in other words, make good due west, and do not let the tide carry you south. When the top of Great Saltee bears 237° (waypoint ⊕*LB*, 52°08'·5N 6°32'·9W), turn on to this course to leave the S point of Little Saltee 4 cables to starboard. Keeping this distance from Little Saltee to avoid Galgee Rock, Goose Rock and the unnamed rock W of the island, skirt the island until heading 330°, then hold this course for 4 cables through the Sound to clear Sebber Bridge. When the S end of Little Saltee bears 110° (from waypoint ⊕*LS*, 52°08'·15N 6°36'·0W), identify the Kilmore Quay fairway buoy, W of St Patrick's Bridge and steer towards it, passing E of Jackeen and Murroch's Rocks. (If the buoy is not on station, steer 022° from waypoint *LS*).

For the passage outside Great Saltee, pass 4 cables N of Long Bohur as above, then steer 225° to leave the Brandies 1M to port and the E sides of both the islands 4 cables to starboard. Do not alter course to starboard until 5 cables S of Great Saltee (waypoint ⊕*GS*, 52°06'·0N 6°36'·9W). Once round, and W of 6°38'W, and if heading for Kilmore Quay, steer 000° until the breakwater bears 037°. Note that a direct course from the Bore Rocks buoy to close S of the Great Saltee passes dangerously close to the Brandies.

In bad weather and darkness or fog the safest option is to stay south of the Coningbeg buoy (clearing waypoint 52°03'·0N 6°38'·6W).

Directions – passage from W to E between or outside the Saltees

Refer to the above directions for the passage from E to W. In settled conditions, the directions for St Patrick's Bridge and Carnsore Point may, as it were, be reversed. For the passage of Saltee Sound from the W, approach with the summit of Little Saltee bearing 095°. When the E tip of Great Saltee bears 185° (at waypoint ⊕*LS*, 52°08'·15N 6°36'·0W), turn to starboard and steer 150° through the sound.

Carne Pier

Rounding the S point of Little Saltee, steer NE, giving the island a berth of 4 cables until its N point is well abeam, then turn due E for the Barrels buoy, 7·5M to the E.

For the passage outside Great Saltee, give the S end of the island a berth of 4 cables, then keep this distance off while rounding the island and steer to leave Little Saltee 4 cables to port as well. When the N end of Little Saltee is well abeam, turn E for the Barrels buoy.

Approach to Kilmore Quay and Dunmore East from offshore to the S

From a position close W of the Coningbeg buoy, a course of 350° leads 3 cables W of the Coningbeg Rock. If the rock can be clearly identified when abeam (it usually shows, or breaks) it is then safe to turn on to a course of 010°, which leads 5 cables E of Red Bank. and 4 cables W of Great Saltee. The safest approach to Kilmore Quay is then to stay on this course until clear well N of Little Saltee, leaving Jackeen Rock and Murroch's Rock to starboard. Then steer towards the fairway buoy W of St Patrick's Bridge until the leading beacons for Kilmore Quay are identified. For Dunmore East, a course of 292° leads from the Coningbeg buoy to Hook Head.

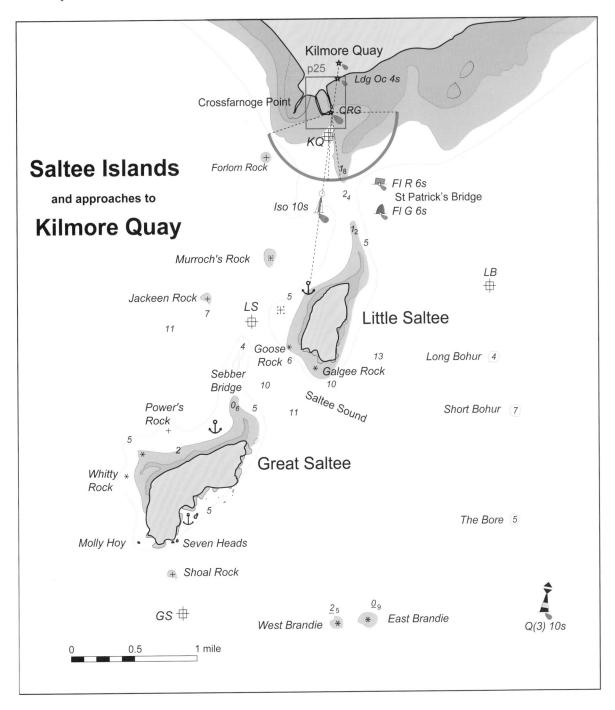

Kilmore Quay from the SW

KILMORE QUAY

⊕*KQ*   52°10'N 6°35'·1W, *AC2049, 2740, SC5621.16, Imray C57 and Plan*

Kilmore Quay (Kilmore on the charts) is a busy fishing harbour but has a good marina and welcomes yachts. The approach to the harbour, through a channel dredged to 1·9m, has little room for error. In winds of F6 and above between SE and SW, or in a heavy swell, particularly near LW, Dunmore East, at the mouth of Waterford Harbour, 15M to the W, offers a safer option to the stranger.

Directions

From the E, after passing the buoys on St Patrick's Bridge, hold the W'ly course to the fairway buoy, which is on the leading line for Kilmore Quay. Steer in on the line of the leading beacons 008° until the harbour entrance is abeam, then turn in. Be alert for traffic coming out as the entrance is only 20m wide. The dredged channel to Kilmore Quay is narrow

and subject to strong cross tides; care must be taken to stay on the leading line. The charted transits on Ballyteige Castle are no longer of use since the castle is obscured from seaward by new buildings in Kilmore Quay village.

From Saltee Sound, refer to the above directions for *Rosslare to Kilmore Quay – offshore.* **From the W,** the church building at Kilmore Quay provides the most prominent landmark, while the leading beacons are initially obscured by the pier. Give the shore at Crossfarnoge Point a berth of 5 cables to clear Forlorn Rock, then identify the fairway buoy.

Marina

The harbour, managed by Wexford County Council, has 4·4m alongside the E pier and 2·4m alongside the W pier, and contains a 60-berth marina with least depth 2·4m. The marina is very busy in summer and it is advisable to make contact in advance; VHF Ch 16 and 9, phone 05391 29955, e-mail hmkilmore@eircom.net.

Approach to Kilmore Quay from the S; breakwater end and leading beacons centre R, church centre

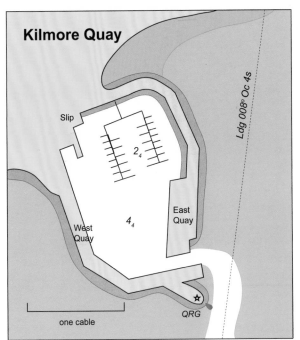

Kilmore Quay

Slip

2₄

West
Quay   4₄   East
Quay

Ldg 008° Oc 4s

☆
QRG

one cable

to the Admiralty's usual high standard. The charts display a caution to the effect that positions differ by varying amounts from those on the smaller scale charts. Certain rocks, notably the Seven Heads and the rocks 3 cables NE of them, are shown as drying but in fact stand well above HW. The offset between AC2740 and WGS84 datum is officially unknown; this offset varies over the area of the chart and may be as much as a cable, the sense being as usual, i.e. GPS positions must be adjusted E and S before plotting on the chart. In any case, when navigating at close quarters around the Saltees, allow an extra cable of margin for GPS error, and do not depend upon chartplotters.

Be that as it may, the islands are a fascinating place to explore in good weather, home to several hundred species of birds, and offer reasonable temporary anchorages.

Kilmore Quay entrance

Anchorage

In settled conditions or moderate winds between NE and S, anchorage is available off the NW shore of Little Saltee in 4m, sand and boulders; and also off the N shore of Great Saltee, N of the buildings, in 2 to 4m, sand. In settled conditions with no swell, the bay (with 3·4m on the chart) on the SE side of Great Saltee 3 cables N of the Seven Heads Rocks provides an attractive temporary anchorage. The

Facilities

Water, pumpout and shore power on the pontoons; CCTV security. Diesel in cans; shops, pubs, restaurants, chandlery. Buses to Wexford. Bicycle hire. Taxis 087 912 2259. Repairs, Marindus Engineering 05391 29794. Doctor. RNLI all-weather lifeboat station.

SALTEE ISLANDS

⊕*LS* 52°08'·15N 6°36'W, *AC2740, SC5621·16*
The islands are privately owned, and Little Saltee is farmed, although neither is permanently inhabited. The somewhat eccentric owners of Great Saltee request that when they are in residence (as indicated by the standard of the Prince of the Saltees, flown from the flagstaff), visitors vacate the island by 1630 each day.

The pilotage of the islands is tricky, and is complicated by four factors: the strong tidal streams, the numerous dangerous rocks, the lack of good transits, and the fact that the charting of the islands (in 1847) was evidently not up

THE SALTEE ISLANDS
AND THE WATERS SURROUNDING THEM ARE AN ABSO-
-LUTE POSSESSION OF THE PRINCE OF THE SALTEES
AND HIS HEIRS.
NO MAN OR ASSEMBLY OF MEN HAS ANY RIGHT
WHATSOEVER TO INTERFERE IN THE AFFAIRS OF THE
SALTEE ISLANDS.
ALL DECISIONS AFFECTING THE ISLANDS ARE
MADE BY THE PRINCE OF THE SALTEES AND HIS
HEIRS, BOTH OF THE MALE AND FEMALE LINE.
ANY DECISION NOT UNANIMOUS CAN BE
BROUGHT BEFORE "THE ABSENT TWELVE"
AND THEIR DECISION IS FINAL.
THE "ABSENT TWELVE" WILL CONSIST OF
TWELVE FISHERMEN ONLY, WHO CAN COME FROM
ANY PART OF THE EARTH.
ALL PEOPLE, YOUNG AND OLD, ARE WELCOME
TO COME, SEE AND ENJOY THE ISLANDS, AND
LEAVE THEM AS THEY FOUND THEM FOR THE
UNBORN GENERATIONS TO COME, SEE
AND ENJOY.

MICHAEL THE FIRST

Plaque overlooking the N anchorage, Great Saltee

The anchorage on the SE side of Great Saltee

rocks on the E side of the bay, shown on the charts as drying but in fact 2m high, provide a landmark for entry *(see photograph)*. The Seven Heads rocks, to the SW, also stand well above HW.

KILMORE QUAY TO DUNMORE EAST
AC2049, 2740, 2046, Imray C57

Heading W from Kilmore Quay, do not turn for Hook Head until 5 cables S of the harbour, in order to avoid Forlorn Rock. Apart from that there are no dangers on the direct passage across Ballyteige Bay and the mouth of Waterford Harbour, and Hook Head is clean and steep-to. There is a cluster of islets and a few rocks in the bay, close inshore E of Baginbun Head. Fethard-on-Sea, in Bannow Bay to the NW, has limited facilities, but Dunmore East is a significant fishing port and sailing centre, accessible in all weathers by day or night, and a popular call for yachts cruising the coast.

Tides
E of Hook Head the tides set E and W, turning E at –0050 Cobh and W at +0553 Cobh. The spring rate is 1 to 1·5 kn, increasing to 2 kn or more near the Saltees and Hook Head. S of Hook Head is the Tower race, with overfalls extending several miles to the W on the W-going stream in fresh winds between SE and W. Close W of Hook Head, the ebb stream from Waterford Harbour runs S at up to 3 kn at springs. Off the entrance to Waterford Harbour the E-going stream begins at –0120 Cobh and the W-going at +0450 Cobh. Constant (Dunmore East) +0005 Cobh, MHWS 4·1m, MHWN 3·1m, ML 2·2m.

Dangers
Forlorn Rock, 1·5m, 4 cables SW of Crossfarnoge Point

Keeragh Islands, two islets 6m high, 6 cables offshore in Ballyteige Bay

George Rock, 1·2m, between the Keeragh Islands and the shore

Selskar Rock (dries 2m) 3 cables SW of Clammers Point at the E end of Bannow Bay

Selskar Shoal, 0·3m, 3 cables WSW of Selskar Rock

Brecaun Bridge, 1·7m, reef extending 3 cables offshore, 1·5M NE of Hook Head

Wreck 2 cables offshore, 5 cables NW of Hook Head.

Lights and Marks
Baginbun Head, tower, unlit

Hook Head, white tower with black bands, Fl 3s 46m 23M, Horn (2) 45s, Racon (K) 10M

Waterford buoy, PHM Fl(3) R 10s, 1.5M E of Dunmore East

Dunmore East, E pier head, grey tower Fl WR 8s 13m W17M R13M, W 225°–310°, R 310°–004°, shows red to S and SE over Hook Head, white to E over the estuary

Dunmore East, E breakwater, red pole beacon Fl R 2s 6m 4M

Dunmore East, W wharf, green pole beacon Fl G 2s 6m 4M.

Fethard-on-Sea
52°11'·5N 6°48'·5W

Anchorage is available in settled conditions or offshore winds in Bannow Bay, N of Baginbun Head, which is identifiable by its conspicuous tower. The village of Fethard-on-Sea lies 1M N of Baginbun Head, and has a tiny drying harbour close NW of Ingard Point. **From the E,** stay close to Ingard Point to avoid Selskar Shoal. **From the W,** give Baginbun Head a berth of 2 cables to clear the drying reefs on its E side. Anchor in 2 to 3m, sand, NW of Ingard Point. Fethard harbour may offer a convenient dinghy landing. The harbour wall carries two memorials: one to the bombardment of the harbour by two British frigates during the rebellion of 1798, and the other to the five who were drowned when a sea angling boat from Fethard sank off the coast in 2002.

Shops, PO and pubs at Fethard village, 3 km.

Hook Head from the SE

Hook Head

In settled weather, particularly with a fair tide, it is safe to pass within a cable of the shore at Hook Head, but in adverse conditions, especially with wind over tide, it is advisable to give the Hook a berth of a mile or more, particularly at night. Hook Head has the oldest lighthouse in Ireland and possibly even in the world. The 12m-diameter tower was built by the earliest Norman overlords in Ireland in the late 12th century, and it replaced a beacon dating from 700 years before that. The short light structure now surmounting the Norman tower dates from 1864.

DUNMORE EAST

⊕*DE* 52°09'·1N 6°59'·3W
AC2049 2046, Imray C57

Dunmore East is one of Ireland's principal fishing ports. The harbour is deep and sheltered, but very busy with fishing boats. However, the bays within 5 cables to the N of the harbour are fringed by high cliffs and provide anchorage well sheltered from winds between S and NE. **From the E** and Hook Head, identify the breakwater at Dunmore East, bearing about 315°, and steer for it. At night, stay in the red sector of the harbour light until well clear to

Dunmore East from the N

the W of Hook Head, then come N and approach in the white sector of the light. **From the W**, give the coast a berth of 4 cables to clear Falskirt Rock (2M W) and Robin Redbreast Rock (5 cables SW).

Harbour

If intending to enter the harbour, call the HM first on VHF Ch 16 or 14 for permission. At night, note that the breakwater extends 0.5 cable to the NW of the powerful sectored light. When rounding the breakwater end, be alert for traffic leaving. The harbour has at least 2m at LAT everywhere but give the breakwater extension a berth of at least 50m on either side. The N'most berth on the E pier is the fuel berth and must be left free when not fuelling. Follow instructions from the HM if available, or raft up with permission to a fishing boat at the E pier. The S and NW sides of the harbour have constant fishing boat traffic. The harbour is managed by the Department of Communications, Energy and Natural Resources; HM phone 051 383166.

Anchorage

The best anchorage is under the cliffs in the SE-facing bay 3 cables N of the harbour, in 3 to 5m, sand. A mooring may be available in the bay close NW of the harbour mouth. Both these bays are subject to swell in strong winds from S or SE, particularly on the ebb tide in the estuary.

Facilities

Diesel and water by hose on the E pier; phone the Fishermen's Co-operative 051 383790 for diesel. Filling station 1·5 km on the Waterford road. Shops, pubs, restaurants, PO. Small chandlery. RNLI all-weather lifeboat station. Waterford Harbour Sailing Club (051 383230) has its clubhouse at the harbour; showers available. Waterford airport, 8 km.

WATERFORD HARBOUR AND NEW ROSS
AC2046, Imray C57

Waterford (45,000) on the River Suir is the oldest city in Ireland, starting as a Viking settlement in 914

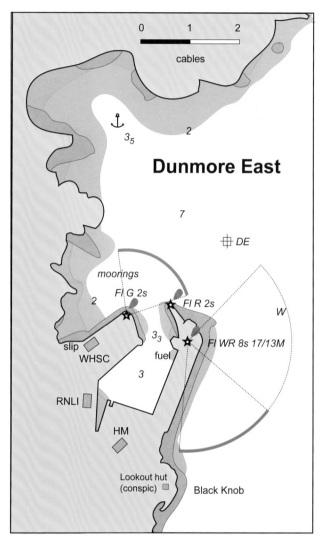

and becoming the country's first Norman stronghold in the 12th century. Best-known today for its beautiful glassware, Waterford is also a considerable general cargo and container port, but there is a convenient small marina in the river. The city has many fine buildings reflecting its long and eventful history. Its name in English is derived from the Old Norse *Vatre-fjord*, "sea inlet"; the Irish name *Port Lairge* is older and unrelated. The River Suir is a well-marked deepwater ship channel leading 10M from seaward to the port of Waterford.

Dunmore East harbour

The River Barrow, tributary to the Suir, is spanned at its mouth by an opening railway bridge and is navigable with a least depth of 2m and good marks and lights for 10M upstream to the town of New Ross. The replica Famine emigrant ship *Dunbrody* is moored here as a museum, and there is a marina.

Tides

Inside the entrance the flood begins at –0425 Cobh and the ebb at +0045 Cobh, with a spring rate off Creadan Head of 2·5 to 3 kn, less in mid-channel. Close inshore between Creadan Head and Portally Head the flood commences an hour earlier. There is a ripple on the ebb off Portally Head where the tides meet. Tidal streams are strong in the rivers, reaching 2 to 3 knots at the narrow points, the ebb often being stronger than the flood.

Dangers

The area on the W side from Creadan Head N to Passage East is an extensive sandbank, part of which dries, and Duncannon Spit, which also dries, extends 7 cables SSE from Duncannon Point. Apart from these and the shallows in some of the bays further upstream, there are few unexpected dangers in the rivers, and the main hazard is commercial traffic. N of Cheek Point and E of Little Island, there are groynes at right angles to the shore, and the submerged remains of fish traps. There are several obstructions with less than 1m on the E bank of the Barrow close S of New Ross. A cable area 4 cables wide crosses the estuary from Duncannon. Anchoring is prohibited here, and also between Cheek Point and Kilmokea Point.

The River Suir and Waterford from the W; Waterford Bridge foreground, Little Island and King's Channel upper L

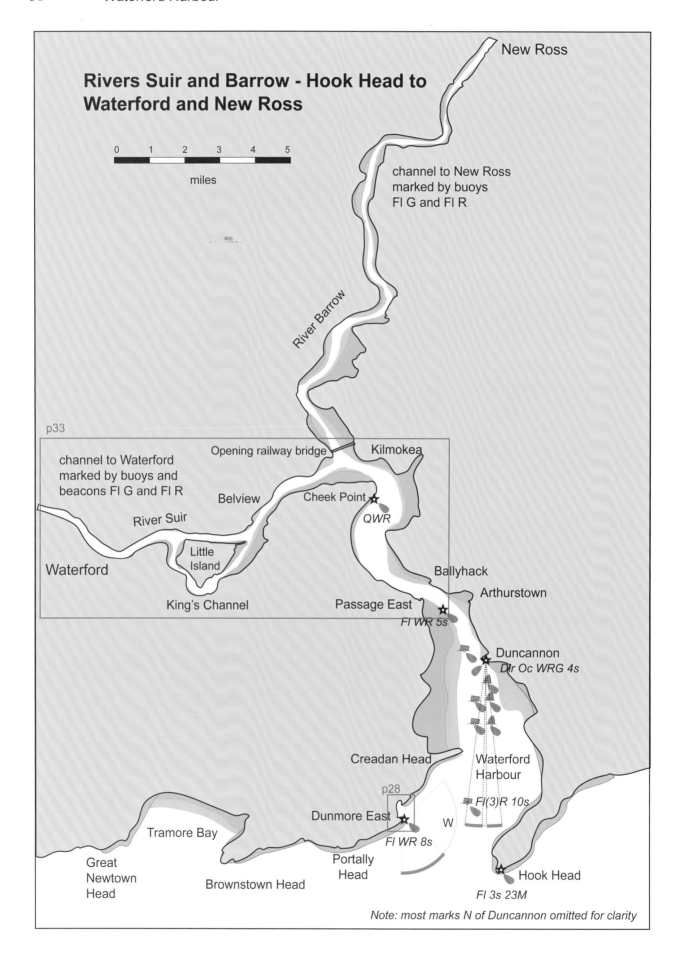

Rivers Suir and Barrow - Hook Head to Waterford and New Ross

New Ross

0 1 2 3 4 5

miles

channel to New Ross
marked by buoys
Fl G and Fl R

River Barrow

p33

Opening railway bridge   Kilmokea

channel to Waterford
marked by buoys and
beacons Fl G and Fl R

Belview   Cheek Point
                                    ☆
River Suir   *QWR*

Little
Island   Ballyhack

Waterford   Arthurstown

King's Channel   Passage East
                                    ☆
                              Fl WR 5s

                                        Duncannon
                                        Dir Oc WRG 4s

Creadan Head   Waterford
                                Harbour

                                    Fl(3)R 10s
                        p28

Dunmore East   ☆
                      Fl WR 8s   W

Tramore Bay

                                Portally
Great   Head   Hook Head
Newtown   *Fl 3s 23M*
Head   Brownstown Head

Note: most marks N of Duncannon omitted for clarity

Lights and Marks

The river channels are marked by port and starboard hand buoys Fl R and Fl G, and by the following principal marks:

Duncannon, Dir Oc WRG 4s, white tower on fort, 13m, W11M R8M G8M, G358°–001·7°, W001·7°–002·2°, R002·2°–006°, provides a leading light for traffic entering from the S. Same tower shows Oc WR 4s R119°–149°, W149°–172°, white over the channel to the N and red over the banks to the W.

Duncannon Rear, beacon Oc 6s 10M vis 000·7°–003·2°. Provides leading line in transit with Duncannon light

Passage Spit, red piled beacon Fl WR 5s 7m W6M R5M, W shore–127°, R127°–180°, W180°–302°, R302°–shore, shows white over the channel to the NW, red over Seedes Bank and close NW and N of the beacon, white over the channel to the SE and red over the banks to the S

Parkswood Point, Fl R 4s 3m 3M

Seedes Perch, pile Fl(2) R 4s 3m 3M

Barron Quay, white post, Fl R 2s 3m

Cheek Point, white pole beacon QWR 6m 5M, W 007°–289°, R 289°–007°, shows white over the channel to the SW and N, red over Carter's Patch bank to the SE

Sheagh, beacon Fl R 3s 3m 3M

Kilmokea, beacon Fl 5s

Kilmokea Point Jetty, 4×2FG vert

River Barrow Railway Bridge, 2FR hor, traffic signals

Snowhill Point, ldg lts 255°, front Fl WR 2.5s 5m 3M, W 222°–020°, R 020°–057°, W 057°–107°, rear, Flour Mill Q 12m 5M. Sectored light shows white over channel to the E, red over channel to the SW and white inshore to the W

Belview Container Terminal, 2FG vert

Queen's Channel ldg lts 098°, front Oc R 6s 8m 5M, black tower, white band, rear Q 15m 5M, white mast

Beacon Quay Fl G 3s 9m

Cove Fl WR 5s 6m W6M R4M, white tower, R 111°–161°, W 161°–234°, R234°–087°, W087°–111°. Shows red over channel to NW, white over channel to NE, red inshore over the S bank to the E

Smelting House Point, QG 8m 3M

Ballycar, Fl 3s 3M

Waterford City Marina, 2FR vert.

Caution

Commercial traffic in the River Suir is fairly heavy, and a sharp lookout is required at all times. Skippers of small vessels are reminded that IRPCS Rule 9 specifies that a vessel under 20m in length or a sailing vessel shall not impede larger vessels confined by a narrow channel. The Rivers Suir and Barrow above Duncannon Bar may be considered a "narrow channel" in terms of this Rule. Waterford Harbour Radio, VHF Ch 14, monitors shipping movements. A car ferry crosses the estuary between Passage East and Ballyhack.

Duncannon

Close N of Duncannon Point there is available

Duncannon from the NW. The fort and lighthouse are on the point, bottom R

anchorage, sheltered from winds between NE and S. Duncannon is a small holiday village with a pier occasionally used by fishing vessels. **From the S,** leave Duncannon Point (with its conspicuous fort and directional light tower) and the end of the pier 0·5 cable to starboard. The pier has 2·5m at LAT at its outer end, and there is a small drying harbour NE of it. Anchor N of the pier in 2 to 3m, sand and mud, holding reported poor. There are tidal eddies in the bay. Duncannon village has a shop, PO and pubs.

Arthurstown

Anchorage is also available off Arthurstown Pier, 1·5M NW of Duncannon Point, in 1·5 to 2m. The pier dries. Pubs at Arthurstown village.

Passage East

Passage East has a small drying harbour and a car ferry slip, but there is no convenient anchorage or alongside berth. The village has pubs, shop and PO.

Ballyhack

There is a boatyard at Ballyhack (Carroll's, Ballyhack Boatyard 051 389164) offering hull (wood, metal, GRP), mechanical, electrical and electronic repairs. Slipway but no travelhoist. Anchorage is available W of the village in 2 to 3m, clear of the car ferry slip. The small harbour dries. Shop and pub at Ballyhack.

River Suir – Ballyhack to Waterford

The main channel NW of Ballyhack runs close to the W shore, with Seedes Bank and Carters Patch in mid-channel. The channel then turns W round Cheek Point and runs N of Little Island, with a training wall extending NE from the island. A mid-channel course here clears all dangers, and the training wall should be left to port.

Catherine's Bay

There is a feasible anchorage NE of Buttermilk Point (1M NNW of Passage East) in 3m, mud. No

Ballyhack (bottom) and Passage East (top), from the N. The ferry has just left Passage East.

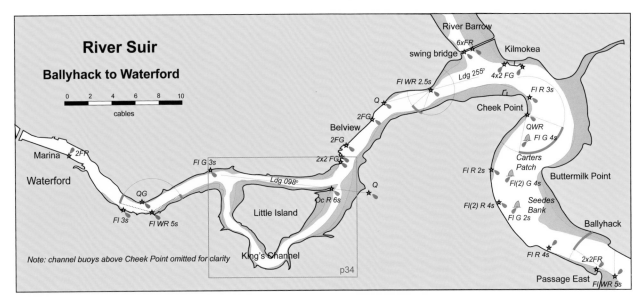

facilities ashore.

Cheek Point

There is a small drying harbour 2 cables W of the Cheek Point light. The bar between the main channel of the Suir and the channel to the harbour has 1·1m at LAT, and the channel and the end of the pier have 2m. The channel is marked by two pairs of lateral buoys QG, QR, Fl(2) G 5s and Fl(2) R 5s. Pubs ashore.

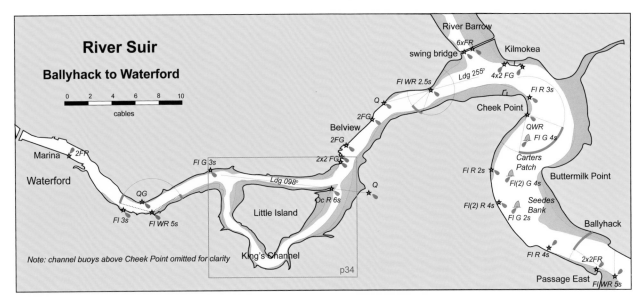

River Suir above Cheek Point; Cheek Point Harbour (centre), Belview container terminal (top centre), Little Island (top L), with King's Channel to its L.

King's Channel

⊕*KC* 52°15'·4N 7°02'·2W

AC2046 and Plan

The channel S of Little Island, 2M E of Waterford city centre, has a least depth of 2m at its E end, and 20m in places, and provides a straightforward passage and a tranquil anchorage out of the strongest tides. Careful use of the echosounder is called for when entering at either end from the main channel of the Suir, since the sand bars doubtless shift, but the channel itself is relatively free of dangers. There are no buoys. From the main channel of the Suir, approach the **E entrance** on a course of 180° from a position 2 cables NE of the training wall beacon, hold this course until 0·5 cable off the SE shore, then steer for the mid-channel to the SW. Approach the **W entrance** steering 135° for the centre of the entrance, and as soon as the points are abeam turn S and head for the W tip of the island; when 1 cable N of it, steer to give it a berth of 1 cable to avoid Golden Rock, 50m off the E shore. The deep channel 1 cable inside this entrance is only 0·5 cable wide, but widens out and deepens further in. A chain ferry crosses the channel; avoid passing ahead of it when it is under way. Maulus Rock (0·3m) lies 50m off the W

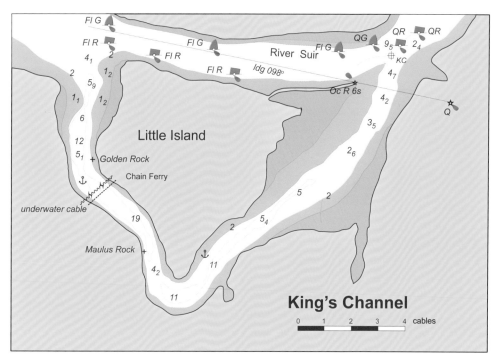

Little Island

Golden Rock

Chain Ferry

underwater cable

Maulus Rock

River Suir

Idg 098°

Oc R 6s

KC

King's Channel

0 1 2 3 4 cables

Facilities

All the facilities of a large seaport town. Supermarkets, shops, restaurants, pubs, PO, doctors, hospital with full A&E. Car rental office opposite the marina. Water and shore power on the pontoons.

River Suir above Waterford

The Rice Bridge is opened periodically for coastal tankers, which discharge at Fiddown, 9M upstream. There are no provisions in place to have it opened for yachts, but for vessels of limited air draft, the River Suir is navigable as far as Carrick-on-Suir, 10M upriver from Waterford.

shore, 3 cables SE of the ferry slip. Anchor either NW of the ferry slip on the W side, or E of the S tip of the island, in 3 to 4m.

Waterford City Marina

On the S side of the river close to the city centre are three marina pontoons, which are available for visitors' use. Marina office 051 309900. The tide runs past the pontoons at 3 kn at springs. Constant +0053 Cobh, MHWS 4·5m, MHWN 3·6m, ML 2·4m.

River Barrow to New Ross

The River Barrow is navigable by masted yachts as far as New Ross, 10M upstream, where it is crossed by a low fixed bridge. The river is tranquil and scenic, and the town has many amenities including a 66-berth marina. It is also a commercial port and accommodates several cargo vessels each week.

At its confluence with the Suir, the Barrow is crossed by an opening railway bridge. Closed

River Barrow railway bridge from the S; Kilmokea power station top R

clearance is 6m. The bridge opens on request by VHF (Ch 14) or phone 086 816 7826 or 051 388137. When transiting the bridge, leave the central pivot point to port. The channel to New Ross is marked by lighted port and starboard-hand buoys and has a least depth of 2m.

New Ross – Three Sisters Marina
The marina is just downstream of the town on the E bank of the river, and has 66 berths, and a breakwater pontoon on its downstream side. Marina manager 086 388 9652. Pumpout station, water and shore power on the pontoons. Showers. Small chandlery. Mechanical repairs – New Ross Outboards 051 421902. The town has shops, pubs, restaurants, PO, filling stations. Constant +0045 Cobh, MHWS 4·5m, MHWN 3·8m, ML 2·6m.

The bridge at New Ross has a clearance of approximately 3m at HW. Above the bridge the Barrow is navigable to St Mullins (11M), and its tributary the Nore to Inistioge (9M) with a least depth of 0·5m at LAT in the channels and two more bridges, also with approximately 3m clearance. There are pools where a deep-drafted yacht might lie afloat at both places up-river.

DUNMORE EAST TO MINE HEAD
The coast between Dunmore East and Mine Head, 24M to the west, is cliffbound and penetrated by two large bays. The popular resort of Tramore stands on the first of these, but Tramore Bay faces southwest and offers no shelter from the prevailing winds. Dungarvan Harbour, facing east, although mostly occupied by drying sandbanks, has a channel leading to the historic town of Dungarvan (7200). To the south of Dungarvan Harbour is a Gaeltacht area, centred on An Rinn (Ring) and the small fishing port of Helvick, where spoken Irish may often be heard. Mine Head lighthouse, built in 1851, has the highest light elevation of any in Ireland.

Tides – Dunmore East to Mine Head
This section has the weakest streams on the coast, with spring rates nowhere exceeding 1 knot. The ENE-going stream begins at HW Cobh –0230 and the WSW-going at HW Cobh +0350. There are at least two-hour periods of slack water.

Dangers – Dunmore East to Mine Head
Robin Redbreast Rock (dries), 0·5 cable offshore 4 cables SW of Dunmore East harbour
Falskirt Rock (dries 3m), 1 to 2 cables offshore 2M WSW of Dunmore East harbour
Swede Rock, 2·7m, 1 cable offshore 7 cables E of

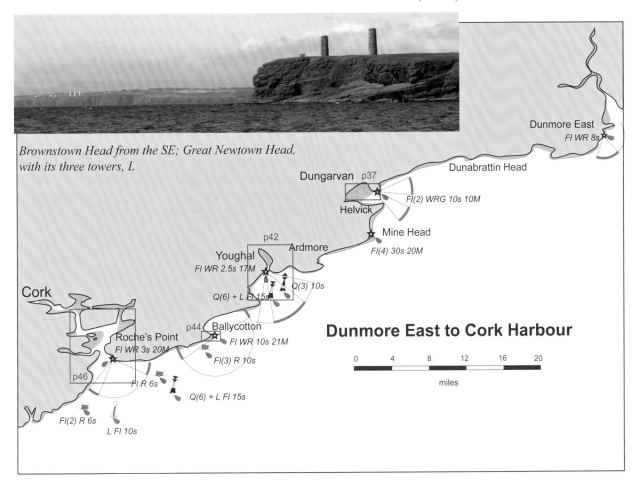

Brownstown Head from the SE; Great Newtown Head, with its three towers, L

Dunmore East
Fl WR 8s

Dunabrattin Head

Dungarvan p37

Fl(2) WRG 10s 10M

Helvick

Mine Head
Fl(4) 30s 20M

p42
Youghal   Ardmore
Fl WR 2.5s 17M
                   Q(3) 10s
Q(6) + L Fl 15s

Cork

p44 Ballycotton
Roche's Point   Fl WR 10s 21M
Fl WR 3s 20M
                   Fl(3) R 10s
p46
        Fl R 6s
                   Q(6) + L Fl 15s

Fl(2) R 6s
        L Fl 10s

Dunmore East to Cork Harbour

0   4   8   12   16   20

miles

Brownstown Head

Carricknamone (1m high), 0·5m E of Ballynacourty Point, with drying reefs including **Carricknagaddy** extending to the shore and 7 cables NNW

Carrickapane (2m high), 8 cables N of Helvick Head

Helvick Rock, 1·4m, 4 cables NNE of Helvick harbour

The Gainers, area of shoals and rocks 2 cables across, drying up to 0·8m, centred 5 cables NNW of Helvick harbour

Whitehouse Bank and **Deadman Sand**, drying sands to the S of the channel to Dungarvan. The sands dry also to the N of the channel and there are rocks drying up to 2·6m

Unnamed stacks 15 and 7m high, 1 to 2 cables E of Helvick Head

The Rogue (2·7m high), 1·5 cables E of Mine Head.

Lights and Marks – Dunmore East to Mine Head

Brownstown Head, 2 conspicuous grey towers on the headland at the SE extremity of Tramore Bay, unlit

Great Newtown Head, 3 conspicuous white towers on the headland at the W extremity of Tramore Bay, unlit. The middle tower is surmounted by the Metal Man, a statue of a sailor in 19th-century uniform, with an outstretched arm pointing out to sea (his twin brother stands in the entrance to the port of Sligo, on the west coast).

Ballynacourty Point, white tower, Fl(2) WRG 10s 16m, W10M R8M G8M, G 245°–274°, W 274°–302°, R 302°–325°, W 325°–117°. Shows green over Carricknamone and Carricknagaddy, white over the channel from the E between Carricknamone and Carrickapane, red over Carrickapane, and white to the S and W over Dungarvan Harbour

Helvick buoy, E Card Q(3) 10s, 4 cables N of Helvick Head and 2 cables W of Helvick Rock

Mine Head, white tower with black band, Fl(4) 30s 87m 20M.

Great Newtown Head from the S, with the Metal Man on the centre tower

Coast – Dunmore East to Dungarvan

Between Dunmore East and Brownstown Head, give the coast a berth of 4 cables to clear Robin Redbreast Rock, Falskirt Rock and Swede Rock. If heading for Cork, a course of 245° from Falskirt Rock passes S of Mine Head (and Ram Head further W). From Brownstown Head, a berth of 3 cables clears all dangers to Ballyvoyle Head, 3M NE of Dungarvan Harbour.

Boatstrand Harbour
52°08'N 7°18'W

Close NE of Dunabrattin Head and not marked on the charts is this harbour, about half a cable each way, just drying in the entrance, which faces E. Further in it is shallower. Pleasant temporary anchorage in settled weather is available off the harbour mouth in 3 to 5m, but beware of the reefs on either hand. The harbour was once used for the import of coal.

Dungarvan
⊕ *DG* 52°04'·3N 7°33'W
AC2049, 2017, Imray C57 and Plan

The channel to Dungarvan has a least depth of 0·7m to the anchorage and 0·1m to the town harbour, so for most yachts the town is only accessible above half tide, and there is a bar with 2·4m, 2 cables W of Ballinacourty Point, which breaks in strong S and SE winds. The channel is, however, well marked by lit port and starboard hand buoys and beacons, and the pilotage is simple. Dungarvan offers a warm welcome to visiting yachts and has excellent facilities within easy reach of its quayside, but depths in the town harbour are restricted. Dungarvan Sailing Club has a 40m-long pontoon on the SW side of the town harbour.

Tides
The streams run at up to 2·5 knots at springs in the channel, and are strongest in the narrows N of Cunnigar Point, where the tide sets NE–SW across the entrance to the harbour. On the S side of the bay the streams are weaker. Constant +0008 Cobh, MHWS 4·1m, MHWN 3·4m, ML 2·3m.

Lights and Marks from seaward
Outfall buoy, yellow, Fl(2) Y 5s, 3 cables SE of Ballynacourty Point
Wyse buoy, PHM Fl R 5s
Ballynacourty buoy, PHM Fl R 10s

The uncharted Boatstrand Harbour is close E of Dunabrattin Head

Glandine buoy, SHM Fl G 10s
Deadman Sand buoy, PHM Fl R 8s
Davy Murray buoy, SHM Fl G 8s
Spit Bank buoy, SHM Fl G 6s
Whitehouse buoy, PHM Fl R 6s
Black Strand buoy, SHM Fl G 5s
Goileen buoy, PHM Fl R 5s
110 beacon, green perch Fl G 4s
Lookout beacon, red perch Fl R 4s
Castle beacon, red perch Fl R 3s
Pond beacon, green perch Fl G 3s.

Directions

From a position midway between the Outfall buoy and Ballynacourty Point, steer 302° for the Wyse port-hand buoy, the first of the channel marks, and then follow the buoys. There is a bar with 2·4m, 2 cables W of Ballynacourty Point, which breaks in gales from the S and SE. The least depth in the channel is 0·7m between the Deadman Sand and Davy Murray buoys, and the channel is 1 to 1·5 cables wide except between the Glandine and Deadman Sand buoys where it narrows to 0·5 cable. Close N of Cunnigar Point is a pool with 10m, and the tide runs strongly NE–SW across the point. The channel to the town harbour has 0·1m.

Anchorage

Anchor close N of Cunnigar Point in 8 to 10m, sand. Swinging room is restricted and mooring to two anchors may be advisable. Anchorage is also available 1 cable S of Ballynacourty Pier.

Dungarvan Town Harbour *(see Plan)*

The channel to the town harbour is marked by two pairs of pole beacons. The harbour largely dries; the one deep spot, with 5m, is occupied by a mooring. The SE end of the pontoon has 0·5m, and the NW end dries 1m. Bilge-keel boats may berth at the pontoon, port side to on the NW end. The best drying spot on the wall is alongside the upstream ladder beyond the pontoon; other places are feasible but should be checked in advance at LW.

There is a slip on the W side of the entrance suitable for trailer sailers.

Facilities

Water on pontoon. Filling station 400m. Supermarkets, shops, PO, laundry, pubs, restaurants, doctors, hospital. Dungarvan Sailing Club, phone 058 45663, www.dungarvansailingclub.com

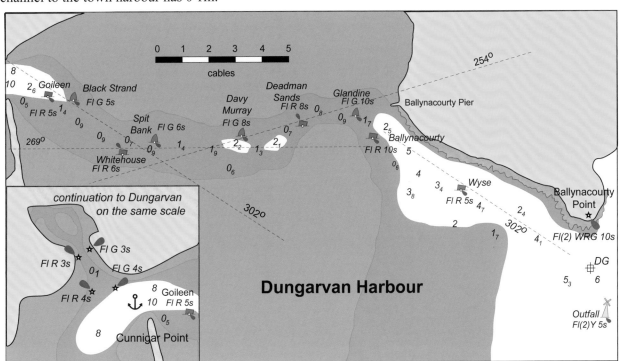

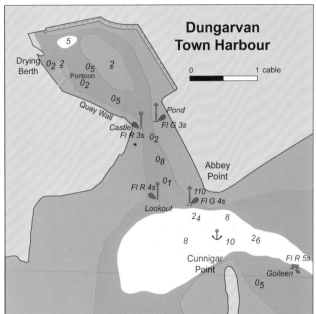

Helvick

The S side of Dungarvan Harbour, E of Helvick Head, is a sheltered anchorage in winds between SE and SW. There are visitors' moorings and a small harbour used by local fishing boats. **From the E**, leave Helvick buoy to starboard and identify the harbour breakwater to the SE. **From the SW**, the above-water rocks E of Helvick Head are clean and steep-to on their E and N sides. **From Dungarvan**, beware of the Gainers, drying rocks 3 to 5 cables NNW of Helvick harbour. The safest approach from Dungarvan is E of the Helvick buoy.

Anchorage

Anchor in 3m, sand, N of the harbour. There are visitors' moorings 2 cables NE of the harbour.

Dungarvan from the SE; Cunnigar Point, bottom centre, Abbey Point, centre R, with the town harbour beyond

Harbour

The harbour, 150m by 50m, has 3m alongside its N wall and 1·5m in the entrance. A temporary berth might be available in emergency, but fishing boat traffic makes it impractical as an overnight stop. The entrance is 20m wide and faces W.

Facilities

Water tap on the harbour N wall. Pub 800m, shop at Helvick village, 1·5km. RNLI inshore lifeboat station in the harbour. Slip suitable for trailer sailers beside the lifeboat station.

Coast – Helvick Head to Mine Head

The coast between Helvick Head and Mine Head is bordered by 75m cliffs and is bold and steep-to. There are several conspicuous stacks close E of Helvick Head, and The Rogue, close E of Mine Head, always shows. The lighthouse tower on Mine Head is conspicuous.

MINE HEAD TO CORK HARBOUR

AC2049, Imray C57

The coast has wide bays between bold headlands, and few dangers offshore. West of Ram Head, the town of Youghal (pronounced "Yawl") (6000) stands on the River Blackwater at the head of Youghal Bay. Sir Walter Raleigh was Mayor of Youghal in 1588, and planted the first potatoes in Europe here. Almost 400 years later the town played the 19th-century whaling port of New Bedford in John Huston's 1956 film of *Moby Dick,* starring Gregory Peck and Orson Welles. Youghal is a minor

Helvick harbour from the W

commercial port, handling about one cargo vessel a week.

Ballycotton, in the next bay to the west, is a quiet holiday and fishing village. The harbour, at the south end of the bay, is small but well-sheltered and is home to small fishing vessels and the lifeboat. Ballycotton's finest hour was the rescue of the crew

Helvick harbour from the NW

Mine Head from the SW; The Rogue, R

of the Daunt Rock lightship in February 1936, still ranking as one of the RNLI's proudest achievements in 180 years of lifesaving.

Tides – Mine Head to Cork Harbour

The coastwise tidal streams are weak, seldom exceeding 1 knot, turning ENE at HW Cobh –0400 and WSW at HW Cobh +0250. HW at Youghal is essentially simultaneous with Cobh. Details of the streams in Youghal Bay and Harbour are given below.

Dangers – Mine Head to Cork Harbour

Longship Rock (dries 4m), 1 cable offshore 1M SW of Mine Head

Blackball Ledge, 3·4m, in Youghal Bay 8 cables S of Blackball Head

Bar Rocks, 0·6m, in Youghal Bay 1·2M SSE of Moll Goggins' Corner

Bog Rock, Clonard Rock, Barrel Rocks and **Black Rocks** (drying 0·6 to 1·8m), on the W side of Youghal Bay, 1·2 to 2·1M N of Knockadoon Head

Small Island (16m high), between Ballycotton Island and the shore to the W

Sound Rock, awash, between Ballycotton Island and Small Island

The Smiths (dries 0·1m), 4 cables offshore 1·5M WSW of Ballycotton Island

Wheat Rock (dries 1m), 4 cables WNW of The Smiths

Pollock Rock, 7·5m, 1.8M ESE of Power Head

Quarry Rock (dries 0·3m), and **Hawk Rock,** 2·7m, 2 cables S of Power Head

Cow Rock (2m high) and the **Calf** (dries 1.4m), extending 1 cable SW of Roche's Point.

Lights and Marks – Mine Head to Cork Harbour

Blackball Ledge buoy, E Card Q(3) 10s

Bar Rocks buoy, S Card, Q(6)+L Fl 15s

Youghal Harbour, W side of entrance, white tower, Fl WR 2·5s 24m W17M R13M, W 183°–273°, R 273°–295°, W 295°–307°, R 307°–351°, W 351°–003°. Shows white over the harbour, red inshore S of Blackball Head, white over the channel N of Blackball Ledge, red over Blackball Ledge and the Bar Rocks, and white over the West Bar

On **Capel Island** and **Knockadoon Head** are conspicuous unlit towers

Ballycotton, black tower, Fl WR 10s 59m W21M, R17M, W 238°–048°, R 048°–238°, Horn (4) 90s. Shows white to seaward of Capel Island to the E and The Smiths to the W, red inshore

The Smiths buoy, PHM Fl(3) R 10s

Power buoy, S Card Q(6)+L Fl 15s

Pollock Rock buoy, PHM Fl R 6s

Roche's Point, white tower, Fl WR 3s 30m, W20M, R16M, R shore –292°, W 292°–016°, R 016°–033°, W(unintens) 033°–159°, R 159°– shore. Shows red to the SE over Pollock Rock, white to seaward between Pollock Rock to the E and Daunt Rock to the W, white over The Sound (entrance channel to Cork Harbour) and red inshore.

Coast – Mine Head to Cork Harbour

The passage of 29M from Mine Head to the entrance to Cork Harbour passes S of Ram Head, Capel Island, Knockadoon Head, Ballycotton Island and Power Head, all bold and steep-to. The coast is cliffbound except in Ballycotton and Youghal Bays, and on the direct course the only significant danger is The Smiths, a dangerous drying reef S of Ballycotton, marked by a port-hand buoy. Pollock Rock, SE of Power Head, has 7·5m and should not trouble a yacht in any but the worst of weather. Youghal Bay has a number of hazards but they are easily avoided, and Ballycotton Bay is clean. There is a conspicuous lattice mast close N of Power Head. Approaching Cork Harbour entrance from the E, give Roche's Point a berth of 2 cables to clear the Calf Rock.

The conspicuous wreck of a crane barge lies under the cliffs close N of Ram Head.

Offshore Installations – Kinsale gas field

Two gas rigs are positioned 28M S of Ballycotton Island in 51°22'N 7°56'W and 8°01'W. The rigs are 2·8M apart and are surrounded by a Prohibited Area extending for 3 cables from each rig and including the area between them. The rigs exhibit R and W lights, Mo(U) 15M.

Ardmore harbour from the W

Ardmore
51°57'·3N 7°42'·5W
AC2049
Entering Ardmore Bay from the E, beware of Black Rocks, a drying reef which extends 2 cables E from the middle of the NW shore of the bay. The two wrecks shown on AC2049 NE and SSW of Ram Head are very old and no longer a danger to navigation. The small Ardmore harbour, in the bay N of Ram Head, has 1·1m alongside its E pier wall;

drying rocks extend E of the W breakwater end to within 30m of the E pier, and also near the shore on the S side of the harbour.

Anchorage
The bay is sheltered from winds between SW and N. Anchor in 2 to 3m, N of the harbour, sand.

Facilities
Shop, PO, pub, filling station.

Ardmore harbour from the NE

Youghal
⊕ *YG* 51°55'·9N 7°48'·7W
AC2049, 2071, Imray C57
The port of Youghal is entered across the East Bar, with a least depth of 2·9m. **From the E**, leave the Blackball Ledge buoy to port and identify the conspicuous light tower on Moll Goggin's Corner. Steer for it, leaving East Point 1 cable to starboard, and when 2 cables short of the light tower turn to starboard

and head for the W extremity of Ferry Point, steering 356°. Leave the town quays 0·5 cable to port. **From the W**, either pass E of the Blackball Ledge buoy as above, or else use the alternative channel across the West Bar, with a least depth of 2·4m; from a position close E of Capel Island, steer 015° for the Bar Rocks buoy, 2M NNE, and leaving the buoy close to starboard steer to leave Moll Goggin's Corner 2 cables to port.

Tidal Streams

About 0·5M S of the West Bar the stream is rotatory clockwise, commencing SSW at –0605 Cobh and turning through W and N to NNE at +0020 Cobh. The stream commences SSE at +0035 Cobh, the maximum rate being 0·5 kn until +0320 Cobh. From +0320 Cobh to +0500 Cobh the rate increases to 1·5 kn. On the East Bar the rates are about the same and the times about 10 minutes later. In the entrance the flood runs from –0505 Cobh to +0130 Cobh. The maximum spring rate is 2·5 kn flood and 3 kn ebb. The ebb runs hard off Ferry Point, forming an eddy in the bight to the S of the point. Constant +0006 Cobh, MHWS 4.1m, MHWN 3.3m, ML 2.3m.

Anchorage

- Off the quays close N of the Town Hall and outside the line of moorings in 6 to 7m. This is close to the town but subject to swell.
- The best anchorage, out of the tide and swell, is close NW of Ferry Point in 5m, sand, with the lighthouse open of Ferry Point and the carpet factory chimney in line with the water tower, 278°.
- N of the moorings in the channel E of Red Bank, NE of Ferry Point, in 2m. Space is restricted.

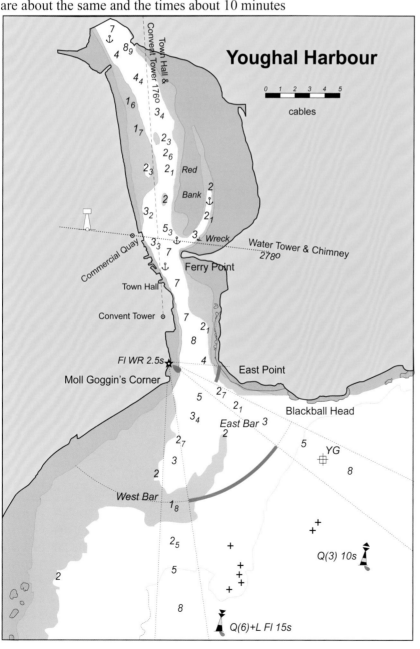

A temporary berth may be available on the Commercial Quay if no ships are expected; call the HM on VHF Ch 16 and 14, Mon–Fri 0900–1700, or phone 087 251 1143. The Commercial Quay has 3m, and all the other quays dry. The area E and NE of the Commercial Quay should be left clear for ships to manoeuvre.

Facilities

Filling station, supermarket, shops, pubs, restaurants, PO, doctors. Youghal Sailing Club. RNLI inshore lifeboat station.

Blackwater Estuary above Youghal

Red Bank, drying up to 0·9m, occupies much of the area N and E of Ferry Point. The channel E of the bank is narrow, and dries at its N end. There is an attractive anchorage S of the road bridge at the head of the estuary, which may be reached by keeping Ferry Point open E of the lighthouse and the conspicuous square Italianate tower of the convent open E of the equally conspicuous Town Hall, until within 5 cables of the NE shore. There are no rocks in the estuary, the sandbanks generally shelve gradually, and the echosounder may be used with

Youghal entrance from the S; Moll Goggins' Corner and the lighthouse, L, East Point, R

confidence. Anchor in 4 to 7m, SE of the bridge.

River Blackwater above Youghal Bridge

The bridge has a clearance of 6·4m, and the river is navigable amid fine scenery as far as Villierstown Quay, 10M upstream The quay is 1M N of the confluence with the River Bride. The river is not buoyed but by keeping towards the outside of bends depths of no less than 3m can be expected.

Coast – Youghal to Roche's Point

At the SW end of Youghal Bay, Capel Island, 29m high and surmounted by an 8m tower, is 3 cables E of Knockadoon Head and clean to within 0·5 cable on its seaward side. The channel between Capel Island and Knockadoon Head has 3·7m with drying reefs on either hand; it is 1 cable wide with the deepest water slightly on the mainland side of mid-channel.

Ballycotton Island is also clean on its seaward side. Stay S of The Smiths port-hand buoy. Power and Pollock Rock buoys can be passed on either hand, and a berth of 4 cables clears all dangers from here to Roche's Point.

Ballycotton

⊕*BC* 51°49'·9N 8°00'·1W
AC2049

The small harbour of Ballycotton faces NE from the tip of the headland W of Ballycotton Island. A stranger is advised against entry at night, since apart from the street lighting the harbour is unlit. The approach is from the N; the entrance is only 25m wide between the piers, and the harbour has many moorings including that of the lifeboat. There is 3·5m at LAT between the pier heads, but the harbour shallows steadily towards its SW side. It

Youghal from the SE; Ferry Point, R

Capel Island from the S

may be possible to raft up against the wall on the E side, but check on fishing boat movements before leaving a yacht for any length of time.

Anchorage

Anchor in the bay N of the harbour entrance in 5 to 7m. There are visitors' moorings NE of the harbour. Constant –0005 Cobh, MHWS 4·1m, MHWN 3·3m, ML 2·3m.

Facilities

Small shops, pubs, restaurants, PO. RNLI all-weather lifeboat station.

Ballycotton Sound

There is a least depth of 2m in the sound between Ballycotton Island and Small Island, but Sound Rock, which dries, lies in mid-channel. The channel is navigable in settled weather, keeping to the Ballycotton Island side, although particular care must be taken to avoid lobster pots.

Ballycotton from the NW

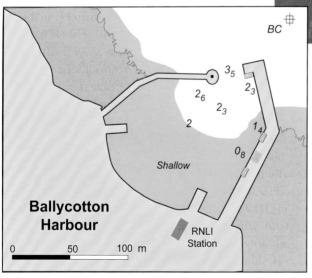

Ballycotton Harbour

0   50   100 m

CORK HARBOUR

⊕ *CO* 51°46'·5N 8°16'W
AC1765, 1777, 1773, Imray C57

Cork shares with Paris and New York the distinction of being founded on an island in the middle of its river. The city's name in the original Irish, *Corcaigh*, means a marsh, and it was amid the marshy islands of the River Lee that the first settlements here were built 1400 years ago. The city survived centuries of power struggles, and played a leading and heroic role in the establishment of the modern Irish state. Cork today is a vibrant and prosperous place and

Ballycotton from the E; Ballycotton Island and lighthouse, L

Ballycotton harbour entrance from the NE

was European Capital of Culture in 2005. The city has a population of 130,000.

Cork owes its growth and development to its fine natural harbour, on the shores of which the Royal Cork Yacht Club, the world's oldest, was founded in 1720. The harbour witnessed the departure of millions of emigrants; it was the last port of call of the *Titanic* and the destination of the *Lusitania*. Today it is a major international port and a premier centre of yachting, with its biennial Cork Week among the world's most prestigious racing events.

Cork Harbour is entered through The Sound, 8 cables wide between Roche's Point on the E and Weaver's Point on the W.

Tides – Harbour Entrance to Crosshaven
The stream sets N–S through The Sound, reaching

1·5 kn at springs, 2 kn off Fort Meagher, and turning at HW and LW Cobh. The ebb tide in the Owenboy River may continue for a short time after LW, especially after heavy rain. Persistent S winds can significantly raise the tidal levels in the harbour, and vice versa.

Dangers – Harbour Entrance to Crosshaven
The Calf (dries 1·5m) is 1 cable SW of Roche's Point, with the **Cow** (2m high) between it and the point. Apart from these, almost the only hazards in Cork Harbour are sandbanks and the ever-present commercial and naval traffic. The buoyage in the entrance reflects the presence of **Harbour Rock**, 5·2m, a broad shoal slightly E of mid-channel off Roche's Point, but yachts may safely disregard this.

Cork Harbour from the NW: Cobh, foreground with a cruise ship at the Deepwater Quay. Haulbowline Island with the naval dock R, Spike Island top centre, Whitegate oil jetty top L, Crosshaven top R and Roche's Point in the distance.

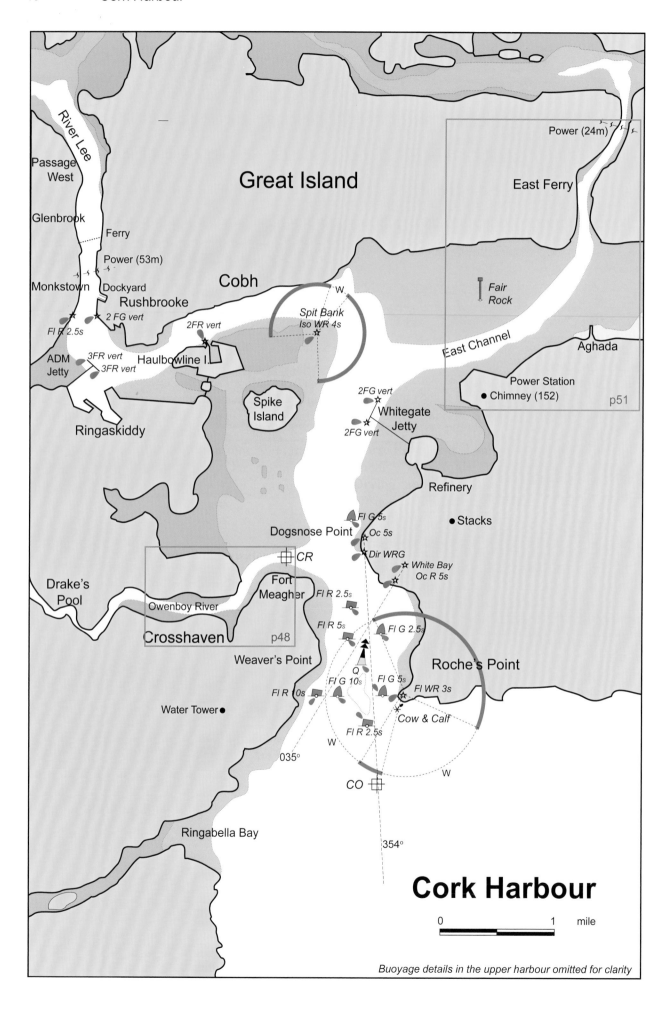

Cork Harbour

Buoyage details in the upper harbour omitted for clarity

River Lee

Passage West

Glenbrook

Ferry

Power (53m)

Monkstown

Dockyard

Rushbrooke

2 FG vert

Fl R 2.5s

ADM Jetty

3FR vert

3FR vert

Ringaskiddy

Great Island

Cobh

2FR vert

Haulbowline I.

Spit Bank
Iso WR 4s

W

Spike Island

Power (24m)

East Ferry

Fair Rock

East Channel

Aghada

Power Station
Chimney (152)

p51

2FG vert

Whitegate Jetty

2FG vert

Refinery

Stacks

Drake's Pool

CR

Fort Meagher

Owenboy River

Crosshaven

p48

Weaver's Point

Fl R 0s

Water Tower

Dogsnose Point

Fl G 5s

Oc 5s

Dir WRG

White Bay
Oc R 5s

Fl R 2.5s

Fl R 5s

Fl G 2.5s

Q

Roche's Point

Fl G 10s

Fl G 5s

Fl WR 3s

Fl R 2.5s

Cow & Calf

W

035°

W

CO

354°

Ringabella Bay

0   1   mile

Lights and Marks – Harbour Entrance to Crosshaven

Cork, safe water buoy, RWVS, L Fl 10s, AIS, Racon (T), 5M S of Roche's Point

Daunt Rock buoy, PHM Fl(2) R 6s, 7 cables offshore 4M SSW of Roche's Point

Roche's Point, white tower, Fl WR 3s 30m, W20M, R16M, R shore–292°, W 292°–016°, R 016°–033°, W (unintens) 033°–159°, R 159°–shore. Shows red over Pollock Rock, white to seaward between Pollock Rock to the E and Daunt Rock to the W, white over The Sound (entrance channel to Cork Harbour) and red inshore

Fort Davis, ldg lts 354°, Oc 5s 10M, front 29m, rear 37m, on Dogsnose Point, 1·2M N of Roche's Point. Front also shows Dir WRG 17M, FW 353°–355°

Outer Harbour Rock buoy, PHM Fl R 2·5s, 2·5 cables WSW of Roche's Point

Chicago Knoll buoy, SHM Fl G 5s, 1.5 cables NW of Roche's Point

W1 buoy, SHM Fl G 10s, 5 cables WNW of Roche's Point

W2 buoy, PHM Fl R 10s, 2 cables W of W1 and 2 cables S of Weaver's Point

The Sound buoy, N Card Q, 4 cables NW of Roche's Point

W4 buoy, PHM Fl R 5s, 3 cables ENE of Weaver's Point

W3 buoy, SHM Fl G 2.5s, 2 cables NE of W4 and 6 cables NNW of Roche's Point

White Bay, ldg lts 035°, Oc R 5s 5M, white huts with black panels, front 11m, rear 21m

W6 buoy, PHM Fl R 2·5s, 3 cables N of W4

Dogsnose Bank buoy, SHM Fl G 5s, 2 cables NW of Dogsnose Point

C1 buoy, SHM Fl G 10s, 3 cables N of Fort Meagher

C2A buoy, PHM Fl R 7.5s, 1 cable SW of C1

C2 buoy, PHM Fl R 5s, 2 cables WSW of C1

C1A buoy, SHM Fl G 5s. 0.5 cable N of C2

C4 buoy, PHM Fl R 10s, 1 cable SW of C2

C3 buoy, SHM Fl G 10s, 3 cables SW of C4

Crosshaven Boatyard Marina, 2×2FR vert

Salve Marina, 2×2FR vert

RCYC Marina, 2×2FR vert.

White Bay leading marks and the W3 buoy in The Sound, from the SW. Whitegate refinery stacks over the hill

Caution

Commercial and naval traffic in Cork Harbour is constant and heavy, and a sharp lookout is required at all times. Skippers of small vessels are reminded that IRPCS Rule 9 specifies that a vessel under 20m in length or a sailing vessel shall not impede larger vessels confined by a narrow channel. The whole of Cork Harbour and approaches may be considered a "narrow channel" in terms of this Rule. Cork Harbour Radio, VHF Ch 12 and 14, monitors shipping movements.

CROSSHAVEN

⊕ *CR* 51°48'·8N 8°16'·8W

AC1765, 1777, Imray C57

Entrance from seaward is straightforward. Giving either side N of Roche's Point a berth of 2 cables, identify the channel buoys. Leave Fort Meagher 1 cable to port and give the shore W of it a berth of 2 cables; leave the C2A, C2 and C4 buoys close to port and head SW into the Owenboy River between Curraghbinny and Scotchman's Point. The bottom shoals rapidly outside the buoyed channel. The C3 starboard-hand buoy appears to be very close to the S side, but stay S of it, as the N side is shoal N of the buoy.

Crosshaven Marinas

Crosshaven Boatyard marina has 100 berths and 20 visitors' berths; call VHF Ch M or phone 021 483 1161.

Salve Marina has 45 berths and 12 visitors' berths;

Roche's Point, at the entrance to Cork harbour, from the W; The Cow, R, and Power Head in the distance

Crosshaven from the NE; buoys C2 (L) and C4 (centre).

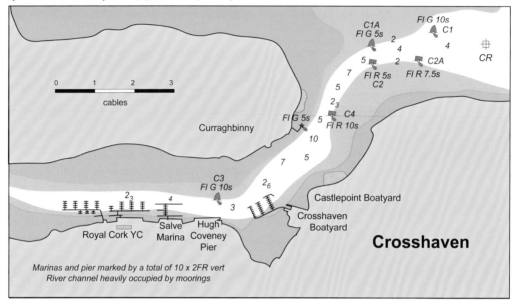

phone 021 483 1145.

The Royal Cork Yacht Club marina has 170 berths and 30 visitors' berths; call VHF Ch M or phone 021 483 1023 or 087 244 9471. Visitors have temporary membership of the club, with the use of showers, bar and restaurant. www.royalcork.com.

Coveney Pier

Coveney Pier (formerly known as the Town Pier) has 3·5m, and has a pontoon for alongside berthing. This is a handy stop for picking up stores, but a yacht should not be left unattended without the permission of the pier manager, 086 310 0095. The pier is used by fishing vessels.

Anchorage

There is no room to anchor in the river. Visitors' moorings are available upstream of the RCYC Marina; contact the RCYC for availability.

Facilities

Water and shore power on all marina pontoons, diesel from the Boatyard Marina and Salve Marina. Shops, small supermarket, pubs, boatyards. Crosshaven Boatyard, hull (wood and GRP) and mechanical repairs. 40 tonne travelhoist, winter storage, www. crosshavenboatyard.com. Castlepoint Boatyard, phone 021 483 2154, travelhoist, winter storage.

Salve and Royal Cork YC Marinas, looking upstream; the C3 buoy, centre, is close to the S side of the river

Crosshaven from the NE; (L to R) Crosshaven Boatyard marina, Coveney Pier, Salve Marina and the RCYC Marina

Salve Marine, phone 021 483 1145, mechanical repairs, www.sailingireland.com/salve1. Riggers, Masts & Rigging (Ireland) 021 483 3878 or 086 389 2614; Matthews, 021 427 7633 or 087 266 7127, www.matthewsofcork.com. Sailmakers, McWilliam, phone 021 483 1505. Covers and canvaswork, R.Marshall 021 481 2078, 086 668 6281. RNLI inshore lifeboat station. Taxis, phone 021 483 1122.

Owenboy River to Drake's Pool

The river is easily navigable for 2M upstream of Crosshaven although very crowded with moorings. The channel is close to the S side at Crosshaven and trends towards the N bank at the first bend up-river. From there on, hold mid-channel.

Two miles above Crosshaven in a wooded bend of the river is one of the most beautiful and sheltered anchorages in Ireland. This is Drake's Pool, and even though there is little if any room now to drop an anchor in it, it is worth the trip just to savour the beauty and tranquillity of the place. The pool is almost fully taken up with moorings; the apparently available space is either shallow or has a hard shale bottom.

The river between Drake's Pool and Carrigaline, 2·5M upstream, is navigable by shallow draft vessels with local knowledge, or by dinghy, near HW.

Anchorage

Anchorage is available in 2m, in mid channel, mud, immediately W of the moorings in Drake's Pool. A tripping line is recommended.

Facilities

See under Crosshaven. Boatyard, filling stations, supermarkets, PO, pubs, restaurants, doctors at Carrigaline, 4 km.

CORK HARBOUR – CROSSHAVEN TO EAST FERRY AND MONKSTOWN
AC1765, 1777, Imray C57

The main channel of the harbour, 4 to 5 cables wide, continues N from Fort Meagher and Dogsnose Point for 2·3M to Cobh (pronounced "Cove"), on the S side of Great Island. On the W side N of

Drake's Pool

"Commercial and naval traffic in Cork Harbour is constant and heavy." LE Emer *heads seaward past Fort Meagher; the tanker* BM Bonanza *unloads at White-gate jetty; the cruise liner* Silver Wind *alongside at Cobh; and the Port Company's barge* Denis Murphy *services a buoy.*

the Owenboy River, the channel is bordered by shallows and drying banks. Spike Island, with its prison and old military buildings, lies close W of the main channel. On the E side, N of Dogsnose Point, is the conspicuous Whitegate Refinery with the jetty of its Marine Terminal projecting NW into the channel. The junction of East Channel is N of the oil jetty. This channel, with a least depth of 4.7m, leads E of Great Island in lovely rural surroundings. East Channel curves to the N and after 2M passes between the wooded slopes of Marloag Point and Gold Point, where it deepens to 18m. East Ferry Marina is located on the W side 0·5M N of Marloag Point. East Passage, as it has become, continues N for a further 1M with 8 to 12m, steep-to between wooded banks, to emerge into a shallow lagoon, 1M long and 2 cables wide, to the N of Great Island. Five cables N of East Ferry it is spanned by a power cable with 24m clearance at HW.

N of Spike Island is the Spit Bank, drying sand 7 cables by 4, with the main channel making a 90° turn to the W around it. W of the bank on the S side of the channel is Haulbowline Island, the principal base of the Irish Naval Service and the site of a now-defunct steelworks. The minor channel S of Haulbowline is spanned by a low bridge and overhead cables. The main channel passes close to the N shore at Cobh and between Haulbowline and Great Island, then turns N and narrows to 2 cables between Passage West and Rushbrooke. To the S, on the outside of this turn, is the cargo, chemical, container and international ferry terminal at Ringaskiddy. Cork Dockyard, on Great Island 1M N of Ringaskiddy, is a large shiprepair facility. Opposite the Dockyard is Monkstown, the principal sailing centre in the upper reaches of the harbour. Monkstown Creek, to the SW, dries.

Tides – Crosshaven to East Ferry and Monkstown
The tides run at 2 kn between Cobh and Haulbowline and up to 3 kn in East Channel, turning more or less at HW and LW by the shore. Heavy rain may increase the duration and strength of the ebb.

Dangers – Crosshaven to East Ferry and Monkstown
N of Dogsnose Point, E of Whitegate Jetty and S of East Channel is a bank with less than 2m, and Whitegate Bay to the SE dries. On the N side of East Channel is a bank with less than 2m in places. **Fair Rock** (drying 0.2m) is 4 cables N of this channel. **Curlane Bank**, S of Spike Island, and **Oyster Bank**, SW of Haulbowline, have less than 1m, and **Spit Bank** dries. Apart from the bridge and overhead cables already mentioned, there are underwater cables and pipelines between Cobh and Haulbowline, and between Haulbowline and Spike Island.

Approaching within 0·5 cable of Whitegate Oil

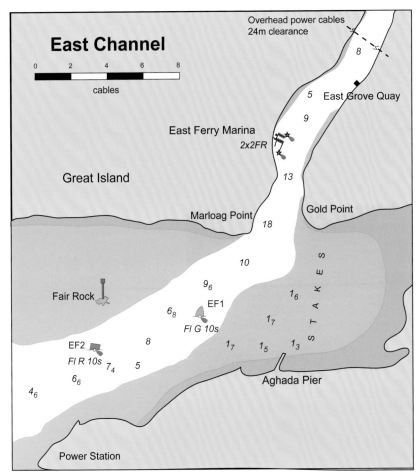

East Channel

Iso WR 4s 10m, W10M R7M, shows red over the channels to S and W and a narrow white sector over the turn
Haulbowline Naval Basin, 2×2FR vert
Ringaskiddy, 2×2FR vert
ADM Jetty (Ringaskiddy), 2×3FR vert
Cork Dockyard, 2FG vert
Monkstown Pier, Fl R 2.5s 4m 4M (occas)

East Channel

East Channel leads to East Passage, E of Great Island, and the marina at East Ferry. The entrance lies E of the No.9 channel buoy, 5 cables NNE of Whitegate Jetty. The conspicuous Aghada power station is on the SE side of the entrance. East Channel has a navigable width of at least 4 cables and a bar with 4·6m, and is marked by two lit buoys.

Directions – East Channel and East Passage

From a position 3 cables N of Whitegate jetty, steer 060° for 1·5M until East Passage, between wooded slopes, can be identified to the NE. Then steer for the mid-channel. East Passage is steep-to on both sides with 5 to 12m in mid-channel, and with its strong tides can be surprisingly subject to swell in winds between S and W.

Marina

East Ferry Marina, with 75 berths, is on the W bank 5 cables N of Marloag Point. Phone 021 481 3390.

Facilities

Water and shore power on pontoons. Diesel. Pub and restaurant.

Jetty is prohibited.

Lights and Marks – Crosshaven to East Ferry and Monkstown

The main channel is marked by port and starboard hand buoys showing Fl R and Fl G lights. Apart from these the principal marks are as follows.

Whitegate Jetty, 2×2FG vert

EF2 buoy, PHM Fl R 10s, 3 cables SSW of Fair Rock

EF1 buoy, SHM Fl G 10s, 6 cables ESE of Fair Rock.

Fair Rock, red perch, unlit

East Ferry Marina, 2×2FR vert

Spit Bank, piled structure on the E end of the bank,

East Channel; Fair Rock perch, L

East Ferry from the N

an anchorage with 1·6m in the approach from the EF1 buoy in East Channel, and 1·3m alongside the pier. There is almost 2m on the direct line from East Ferry to Aghada but do not err E of the line as there are stakes on the bank. Shop and pubs near Aghada pier.

Cobh
There is no facility for yachts to go alongside at Cobh, and no anchorage in the channel. Cobh is the Tidal Standard Port for the south coast; MHWS 4·1m, MHWN 3·3m, ML 2·3m.

Monkstown
Anchor in 2 to 5m, on the W side of the channel opposite the dockyard.

Facilities
Cork Dockyard offers cranage and winter storage for yachts, phone 021 481 1831. Electrical/electronic repairs, Dan O'Connell, phone 021 484 2013.

Anchorage
Anchor 5 cables further N, in 7 to 9m, clear of the moorings off East Grove Quay on the E bank. The quay has a piled extension with 1·7m at LAT, and is available as a temporary berth. Pub and restaurant at the quay. More sheltered anchorage in S to SW winds (but remote from any facilities) is available where the lagoon opens up at the N end of East Passage. The bottom here shelves gradually to the W but suddenly on the E side.

Aghada
Aghada, on the S shore opposite East Passage, has

Cork Harbour – River Lee, Monkstown to Cork City
AC1773
The limit of navigation in the centre of Cork City is 6M upriver from Monkstown. Before proceeding upriver, permission must be obtained from the HM; call Cork Harbour Radio, VHF Ch 12 or phone 021 427 3125. West Passage is the name given to the narrow 1M stretch running N from Monkstown between Great Island and the mainland. At Marino Point, the W tip of Great Island, it turns NW and opens out into the wide but shallow section known as Lough Mahon. The deep channel is here maintained

East Passage from the SW; Marloag Point L, Gold Point R

Spit Bank light from the E. Haulbowline Island, L

by dredging and is less than 1 cable wide, marked by port- and starboard-hand buoys. The river narrows 2M further NW and turns W past the Tivoli container terminal. There are quays on both sides and a maintained depth of 5·2m in the uppermost reach. At the head of navigation the river divides into N and S channels, with Penrose Quay on the N bank and Albert Quay on the S, before it is spanned by the first of the city's many bridges. Yachts are normally advised to berth at Penrose Quay.

Tides

The stream runs at up to 3 kn at springs in the narrows between Rushbrooke and Passage West, less elsewhere, turning more or less at HW and LW. The ebb continues a little longer than the flood, the difference depending on recent rainfall. Constant (Cork city) +0007 Cobh, MHWS 4·5m, MHWN 3·6m, ML 2·5m

Facilities

All the amenities of a major seaport city, including a large regional hospital with full A&E facilities. Chandlery on Penrose Quay (Union Chandlery, phone 021 455 4334, www.unionchandlery.com), in the city centre (Matthews, phone 021 427 7633, www.matthewsofcork.com) and at Frankfield Industrial Estate, Kinsale Road (CH Marine, phone 021 431 5700, www.chmarine.com), electronic supplies and repairs (Dunmast Ltd, phone 021 431 8400). Ferries from Ringaskiddy to Roscoff; Cork International Airport, 5M from city centre. Train connections to Dublin, bus connections to all parts of Ireland.

Cobh

The narrows at Passage West, from the S. Monkstown L and the dockyard at Rushbrooke R

Chapter 2

Cork Harbour to Crookhaven

Kinsale

This beautiful coast has anchorages and harbours in abundance, and many islands large and small. There are no large towns, and no marinas west of Kinsale, but West Cork is well-populated and there is plenty to occupy the visitor ashore. The coast is mostly cliffbound, with beautiful bays and long sheltered inlets. Several of the headlands have the conspicuous ruins of signal towers, which are not as ancient as they look but were built (in the days not long before radio) to pass information and orders by flag signals to passing ships.

Kinsale (4000), magnificently situated on the estuary of the River Bandon, has a fine natural harbour and is a major tourist and sailing centre, renowned for its many restaurants and the picturesque buildings lining its ancient narrow streets. Apart from its marinas full of yachts, Kinsale has a significant fishing fleet, and handles small cargo vessels at its quay. The town is rich in history, and was the scene in 1601 of the final and decisive battle of the Anglo-Irish war of Elizabethan times,

which was to establish English rule in Ireland for the next 300 years. The impressive ruins of Charles Fort, dating from the latter part of the 17th century, dominate the harbour entrance.

The Old Head of Kinsale has been marked by a lighthouse since 1665. The present tower – the third – was built in 1853. The headland has seen many shipwrecks, among them the loss of the *City of Chicago* in 1892, when the ship's master kept his engines running to hold the doomed ship against the cliffs and enable his passengers and crew to scramble ashore safely. Ten miles to the south of the Old Head, in May 1915, the *Lusitania* was torpedoed and sunk with the loss of 1,198 lives. She lies in 88 metres of water and is marked on the charts in 51°25'N 8°32'W.

Seven miles west of the Old Head, Courtmacsherry is a pretty and unspoiled village, a thriving sea angling centre and home to one of the longest-established lifeboat stations in Ireland. Further west, the village of Glandore and the fishing port of

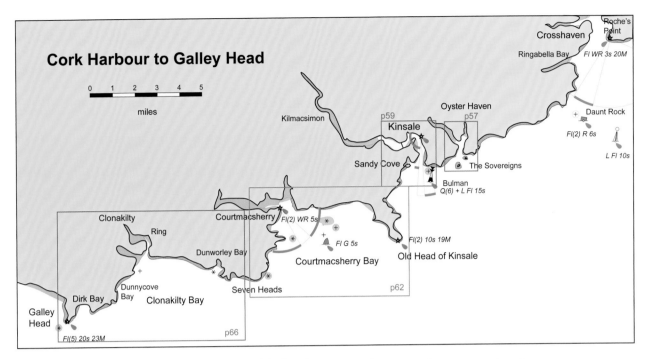

Union Hall face each other across a steep-sided and beautiful inlet. Glandore and its little stone harbour were laid out in the 1830's by the philanthropic landlord James Barry, and here was the setting for an early experiment in communal living by the notably eccentric William Thompson. This rated a mention in Marx's *Das Kapital*, but may be a little hard to imagine when in Glandore today.

Baltimore was the scene in 1631 of a raid by North African pirates, who carried off the population (at that point mostly English settlers) into slavery. The village has links, formal and informal, with its somewhat larger namesake across the Atlantic. Cecil Calvert, Lord Baltimore, founded the colony of Maryland in the early 17th century. Today, the American schooner *Pride of Baltimore II* is a regular visitor to Ireland's most southwesterly harbour.

Between Baltimore and Mizen Head is a fabulous cruising ground of bays and islands, with the fine natural harbours of Schull and Crookhaven and many smaller harbours and anchorages. The labyrinth of channels among the islands offers good sailing (in spectacular surroundings) almost irrespective of wind direction.

Charts

SC5622 and SC5623 cover the area described in this chapter. In terms of individual charts, the general chart AC2424 Kenmare River to Cork Harbour, or Imray's C57 Tuskar Rock to Old Head of Kinsale and C56 Old Head of Kinsale to Dingle Bay, give coverage, The Imray charts have several useful harbour plans, but AC1765, 2092, 2129 and 2184 are all essential nevertheless. AC2053 Kinsale and Oyster Haven, 2081 Courtmacsherry Bay and 3725

Baltimore Harbour are optional.

Note – Tidal Streams

Between Cork and Cape Clear, the tide generally runs parallel to the coast and turns (according to all published sources, including this one) approximately two hours after high and low water at Cobh. More specific details are given below. However the timing appears to vary somewhat, and the tide is frequently observed to turn an hour or more earlier than predicted. The stream close inshore at the headlands (in any case) tends to turn earlier than offshore.

CORK HARBOUR to KINSALE

AC1765, Imray C57, SC5622

The coast between Cork and Kinsale is fringed by 30 to 50m cliffs, and the coastwise passage is straightforward, with the headlands clean and steep-to. Inshore of the Sovereigns, the mile-long inlet of Oyster Haven is peaceful and pretty, but is open to the south and suffers from somewhat poor holding ground. It is a centre for quiet and unobtrusive water sports.

Tides

Tidal streams run parallel to the coast, turning ENE at –0420 Cobh and WSW at +0150 Cobh *(but see Note, above)*. The rate is 1 to 1·5 kn at springs around the headlands and 0·7 kn at the Daunt Rock.

Dangers – Cork Harbour to Kinsale

Carrigabrochel (dries 1·8m), extending 1·8 cables offshore 1M S of Weaver's Point

Wreck 1·5 cables E of Fish Point, the S side of Ringabella Bay

Ringabella Bay from the E

Daunt Rock, 3·5m, 7 cables offshore 4M SSW of Roche's Point

Carrigadda (Long Rock), dries, extending 3·5 cables SE from the centre of Carrigadda Bay

Little Sovereign (16m high), 2 cables offshore between Kinure Point and Blinknure Point

Sovereign Patch, 2·1m, between the Little Sovereign and the shore

Big Sovereign, two islets 22 and 28m high separated by a narrow cleft, 5 cables S of the entrance to Oyster Haven and 6 cables SW of the Little Sovereign

Harbour Rock, 0·9m, in Oyster Haven 3 cables N of Kinure Point

Bulman Rock, 0·9m, 3 cables S of Preghane Point.

Lights and Marks

Daunt Rock buoy, PHM Fl(2) R 6s, close E of the rock

Cork, safe water buoy RWVS L Fl 10s, AIS, 1·7M ESE of the Daunt Rock

Bulman buoy, S Card Q(6)+L Fl 15s, 1 cable SW of the rock.

Coastwise passage

The Daunt Rock, 4M S by W of the entrance to Cork Harbour, is a pinnacle which breaks in bad weather and is marked by a port-hand buoy. The Sovereigns, marking the entrance to Oyster Haven, are bold and steep-to. From Weaver's Point, a berth of 2 cables off the headlands clears all dangers to the Little Sovereign and passes well inside the Daunt Rock.

Stay outside the line between Robert's Head and Reanies Point, to avoid the drying reef Carrigadda in the bay. Passage is possible in moderate weather between the Little Sovereign and the shore, staying either N or S of mid-channel to avoid the Sovereign Patch. The W side of the entrance to Oyster Haven is clean if given a berth of 0·5 cable. Heading for Kinsale, the recommended course is S of the Bulman buoy, but passage N of the Bulman Rock is possible in settled weather by leaving Preghane Point not more than a cable to starboard. The N end of the Big Sovereign in line with Frower Point 082° leads clear N of the Bulman.

Ringabella Bay
51°46'·4N 8°18'W

Ringabella Bay, 1·6m SW of Weaver's Point, offers temporary anchorage in winds between SW and N, in 2 to 3m, sand. The inlet extends 1·2M SW, but beyond Ringabella Point it dries.

Oyster Haven
⊕OH 51°41'N 8°26'·9W
AC1765, 2053, SC5622·15

Oyster Haven offers sheltered anchorage in all but S winds, when it is subject to swell. From the E, give Kinure Point, the E side of the entrance, a berth of a cable and head for Ferry Point on the W side to avoid Harbour Rock. The W arm of the inlet, the Belgooly River, is the more sheltered but is shoal on either side and is somewhat encumbered with

The Sovereigns from the E; the Old Head of Kinsale in the distance, L

The Big Sovereign in line with Frower Point leads inside the Bulman Rock. View from the W; Bulman S Card buoy, R

Oyster Haven from the S; the Big Sovereign, foreground, and the Little Sovereign, R

moorings. The N arm is wider but more exposed and has poorer holding.

Anchorage

Anchor in 2 to 3m, either NNW of Ferry Point in mid-channel, keeping Kinure Point open of Ferry Point, or on the W side of the N arm. The holding ground is poor in weed and gravel, so care must be taken to ensure the anchor is well bedded in. Be prepared to lift it and re-lay. There are no facilities ashore.

Belgooly River above Oyster Haven

It is possible with care towards HW to take a dinghy upriver as far as Belgooly, 3M. Filling station, shop, pubs at Belgooly.

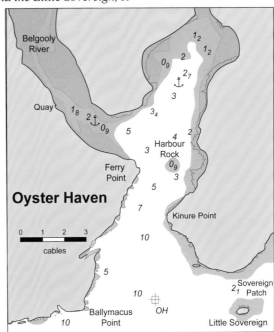

moorings.

Oyster Haven from the SW

Oyster Haven; the Belgooly River from the SE

Kinsale Harbour from the NE; Blockhouse Point, bottom L, with the ruins of James Fort on the summit; Castlepark Marina, L centre, Trident Marina, the Town Pier and the Yacht Club Marina, R. Kinsale bridge, top.

Kinsale entrance, from the SW

KINSALE

⊕*KS* 51°40'·5N 8°30'·2W

AC1765, 2053, SC5622·16, Imray C56, C57

Kinsale Harbour, the estuary of the River Bandon, may be entered by day or night in all weathers. The approach is straightforward and well marked and lit. The Bar, with 3 to 4m, is a broad sandbank in mid-channel 8 cables within the entrance.

Tides

The stream runs fairly into and out of the harbour, reaching 1.5 knots at springs and turning at HW by the shore. Constant –0012 Cobh, MHWS 4.1m, MHWN 3.3m, ML 2.3m.

Dangers

Farmer Rock (dries 0·6m), 0·5 cable offshore 3 cables S of Money Point

Spur Bank, 1 to 2m, SE of Blockhouse Point.

Note that the drying rock Carrignarone, off Middle Cove, shown on older editions of AC2053, has been built over and now forms the foundation of the boatyard's travelhoist pier.

Lights and Marks

Charles Fort, white beacon on the wall of the fort providing a leading light, Fl WRG 5s 18m W8M, R5M, G6M, G 348°–358°, W 358°–004°, R 004°–168°. Shows white over mid-channel.

Spur buoy, PHM Fl(2) R 6s, 2 cables WNW of Charles Fort

Spit buoy, PHM QR, 4 cables N by W of Spur

Crohogue buoy, PHM Fl(3) R 10s, 2 cables WNW of Spit

Kinsale YC Marina, 2FG vert

Town Pier, 2FG vert

Fishermen's pontoon and ferry slip, 2×2FG vert

Castlepark Marina, 2×2FR vert.

Directions

After clearing the Bulman, a berth of 0·5 cable clears all dangers in the entrance. Identify Charles Fort on the E side and pass between it and the Spur buoy, then leave the Spit and Crohogue buoys to port. The area S of Crohogue has many moorings. The reach SW of Crohogue, stretching 5 cables to Lobster Quay to the W and Castlepark Marina to the E, is

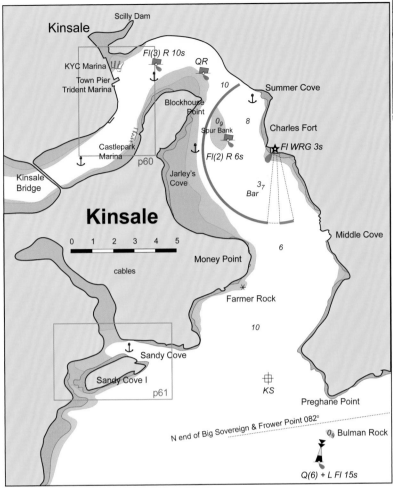

Middle Cove from the NE

clean and free of dangers. The area to the N and NW of the Kinsale YC Marina shoals rapidly and dries at LW. Kinsale Bridge, with 5m clearance, spans the channel 8 cables SW of Crohogue buoy. There is 7m at LAT in the SE half of the channel right up to the bridge.

Marinas
Kinsale Yacht Club Marina, with 170 berths and 50 visitors' berths, N of the Town Pier. Call VHF Ch M, 021 477 2196 or 087 678 7377, or come alongside the long outer pontoon, rafting up as permitted. The outer pontoon has 8m at LAT and with suitable notice the very largest yachts can be accommodated. Visitors have temporary membership of Kinsale YC, with showers, bar and meals. www.kyc.ie.

Middle Cove

Charles Fort

Entering Kinsale; Blockhouse Point, L

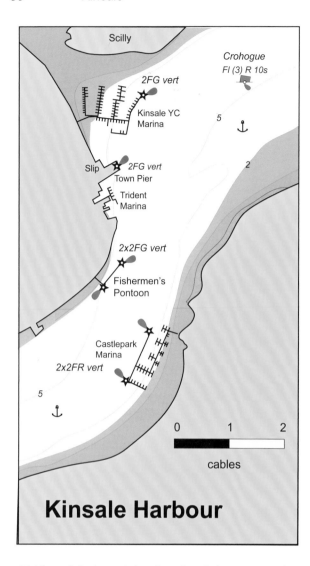

Kinsale Harbour

Trident Marina, 6 berths, S of the Town Pier. Phone 021 477 2927. This is the base for a small charter fleet, www.sailireland.com.

Castlepark Marina, with 70 berths and 20 visitors' berths, on the E side 3 cables SSE of the Town Pier. Call VHF Ch 6, 16 and M or phone 021 477 4959.

Harbour

The Harbour is managed by Kinsale Harbour Commissioners. The Town Pier is normally reserved for commercial, fishing and naval vessels; for a temporary berth contact the HM on VHF or by phone, 021 477 2503. The harbour cruise boat operates from the Town Pier and a jetty S of the Kinsale YC marina. There is a slipway suitable for launching trailered boats. The fishermen's pontoon, 2 cables S of the Town Quay, is strictly reserved for fishing vessels. The harbour office monitors VHF Ch 16, working channel 14. There is a speed limit of 6 knots in the harbour.

Anchorage

Anchorage immediately S and E of the Town Pier is prohibited, to allow room for large vessels to manoeuvre. Anchor in mid-channel SW of Castlepark Marina in 5 to 7m, mud, or S of Crohogue buoy in 2 to 3m, mud and sand. The Harbour Commissioners charge a fee for anchoring; this fee is also incorporated in all marina charges.

Summer Cove

Summer Cove, on the E shore opposite Blockhouse Point, is a delightful spot for a short visit. Anchor in 2 to 3m off the pier. There may be visitors' moorings, provided by the pub for the use of customers. The pier dries.

Middle Cove

Middle Cove, on the E side opposite Money Point, is a rocky bay in which there is a boatyard with a travelhoist dock.

Jarley's Cove

Temporary anchorage is available in 2m, off the beach on the W side S of Blockhouse Point.

Facilities

Water and shore power at all marinas. Diesel at Castlepark and Trident marinas, or by tanker on the Town Pier (Ross Oil, phone 086 258 3544). Showers at Kinsale YC. Filling station, supermarket, shops, pubs, many restaurants, PO, doctors. Car rental. Bus services to Cork, also serving Cork International Airport, 10M NE. Taxis, phone 021 477 2642 or 021 477 4900. RNLI inshore lifeboat station. Middle Cove boatyard, phone 021 477 4774, hull, mechanical, rigging, electrical and electronic repairs, 40 tonne travelhoist, winter storage. O'Mahony Sailmakers, phone 086 326 0018. Divers. There are many tourist attractions in Kinsale and its environs; Charles Fort is particularly worth a visit.

Kinsale harbour; the Yacht Club marina, R, the Town Pier and Trident marina, centre, and Castlepark marina, L

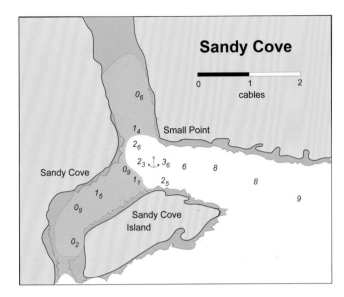

River Bandon above Kinsale Bridge

For vessels which can clear under the bridge (7m), the river is navigable as far as Kilmacsimon, 6M from Kinsale Bridge. Hold the mid channel on the reaches and stay wide on the bends. The lower stretch is marked by several port-hand buoys. There is a boatyard at Kilmacsimon (Kingston Marine, phone 021 477 5134, www.boatsireland.com).

Proposed Developments

At the time of writing (2008) there are outline proposals for marina developments in the NE arm of the drying creek at the head of the harbour (locally known as the Scilly Dam), and also to the SW of Castlepark Marina.

Sandy Cove

Immediately W of the entrance to Kinsale Harbour is the inlet of Sandy Cove, a cable wide and 2 cables in length and sheltered by Sandy Cove Island, 28m high. Sandy Cove offers a delightful anchorage in moderate winds

between S and NE. Anchor in 4m, N of the N point of the island. The drying branch to the N, 5 cables in length, and the channel W of Sandy Cove Island may be explored by dinghy near HW. The W channel is encumbered by rocks at its S end. No facilities ashore.

KINSALE TO COURTMACSHERRY

AC1765, 2092, 2081, SC5623, Imray C56; see Plan of Courtmacsherry Bay

Bullen's Bay, 2.5M N of the Old Head, is foul for 3 cables offshore. Bream Rock, above water, is close inshore 4 cables NNE of the headland, which is steep-to. The bays to the NE and NW of the Old Head are named Holeopen Bay, East and West, and are so called because the peninsula at that point is penetrated by caves, several of which are navigable by dinghy near HW in very calm conditions. The greatest care must be taken, but the passage of the caves is an unforgettable experience. The cliffs all round the Old Head are clean to within 50m, and anchorage may be found in either bay in 9 to 11m while exploring the shore, but the yacht should not be left unattended.

Courtmacsherry Bay has a number of drying

Sandy Cove from the E

Sandy Cove

and sunken rocks, but they are well enough marked to be easily avoided. Courtmacsherry Harbour, in the NW corner of the bay, offers excellent shelter and is accessible in daylight with modest rise of tide. The bar has least depth 1·2m; the channel to the pier is narrow and demands careful pilotage.

The Old Head of Kinsale from the E

Tidal Streams

Off the Old Head of Kinsale and across the mouth of Courtmacsherry Bay the W-going stream makes at +0205 Cobh and the E-going stream at –0420 Cobh *(but see Note on page 55).* The spring rate off the Old Head is 2·5 kn. These streams form a race which extends over 1M from the Old Head, to the SW during the W-going stream and to the SE during the E-going stream. In settled weather and offshore winds, a passage close to the Head avoids the tidal slop; in heavy weather, when the race can be dangerous to smaller craft, give the Head a berth of over 2M. The stream close inshore to the N of the Head, on both sides, always runs S. Further W, the spring rate offshore is 1·5 kn, reaching 2 kn off the Seven Heads. There is little stream in Courtmacsherry Bay.

Dangers

Numerous **drying and below-water rocks** extending up to 3 cables offshore at Bullen's Bay, 2M N of the Old Head of Kinsale on the E side

In Courtmacsherry Bay:

Barrel Rock (dries 2·6m), near the middle of the bay, 1·25M from the N shore and 3.3M WNW of the Old Head of Kinsale

Black Tom, 2·3m, 6 cables W by S of Barrel Rock

Blueboy Rock, 0·2m, 4 cables E of Barrel Rock

A **sunken rock** 2 cables NE of Barrel Rock

The **Inner Barrels,** 5 cables N of Barrel Rock, an extensive patch which dries 0·5m at one point

Horse Rock (dries 3·6m), 4 cables off Barry's Point on the W shore of the bay

Drying and sunken rocks extending 3 cables offshore from Garrettstown Strand in the NE corner of the bay.

There are no dangers on the direct course from the Old Head to Seven Heads.

Lights and Marks

Old Head of Kinsale, black tower with white bands, Fl(2) 10s 72m 19M, Horn (3) 45s.

Black Tom buoy, SHM Fl G 5s, 5 cables SSE of the rock

Barrel Rock perch, derelict but clearly visible pole beacon on Barrel Rock

Wood Point, white pole beacon, Fl (2) WR 5s 15m 5M, W 315°–332°, R to shore to N and W. The white sector leads from the SE between Black Tom and the Horse Rock.

Courtmacsherry bar buoy, SHM Fl G 3s, 1 cable NNE of Wood Point.

The channel to Courtmacsherry pier is marked by three unlit green starboard-hand spar buoys.

Courtmacsherry Harbour · p63 · Fl G 3s · Coolmain Point · Garrettstown · Wood Point · Fl(2) WR 5s · Inner Barrels · A · Broadstrand Bay · Black Tom · Barrel Rock · Blueboy Rock · Blindstrand Bay · Barry's Point · Horse Rock · Fl(2) 10s 19M Old Head of Kinsale · Fl G 5s · Coolim Cliffs · Cotton Rock · Seven Heads · Carrigashoonta

Courtmacsherry Bay

0   1   2   3

miles

A. Coolmain Point and Wood Point in line lead N of the Inner Barrels

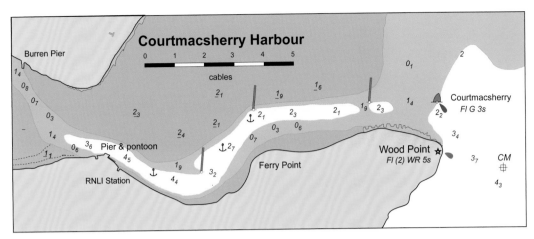

Courtmacsherry Harbour

⊕*CM*   51°38'N 8°40'·5W

See Plan

The harbour is entered between Wood Point and Coolmain Point. The bar at the entrance breaks in strong to gale force S or SE winds. The entrance should not be attempted in these conditions, or at night. If unable to enter Courtmacsherry due to failing light or low tide, safe overnight anchorage, in moderate weather with winds from S through W to NW, is available in Broadstrand Bay, S of Wood Point – see below.

Approach from the Old Head

From a position 1 cable S of the Old Head, a course of 271° leads S of Black Tom buoy and S of all the dangers in the bay. The high ground between Barry's Point and Carrigrour Point (the Coolim Cliffs) will be seen ahead on this course. Leave Black Tom buoy to starboard and steer 317° for Courtmacsherry bar. If the Barrel perch can be clearly identified to the N, it is safe to take the short cut N of Black Tom in most weather conditions, leaving the Barrel perch a cable to starboard.

There is also a passage N of the Inner Barrels, which is straightforward but not recommended to a stranger in bad weather. From a position one cable SW of the Old Head, steer 300° for 3M until 5 cables from the N shore of the bay with the tip of Wood Point in line with Coolmain Point bearing 280°. Alter course on to this transit, which leads N of the Inner Barrels, and clear of all dangers off the N shore of the bay. Approaching Coolmain Point, give it a berth of 2 cables, and continue towards Wood Point and the Courtmacsherry buoy.

Approach from Seven Heads

Give the shore NE of Seven Heads a berth of 3 cables to avoid Carrigashoonta and Cotton Rock; identify Barry's Point and Horse Rock (which almost always shows) and steer to pass in mid-channel between them.

Entrance Directions – Courtmacsherry

The channel inside the bar has 2 to 4m and is marked by three unlit starboard-hand spar buoys.

Barrel Rock, and the entrance to Courtmacsherry, from the SE. Wood Point is L of the Barrel Rock perch

Wood Point from the SE; Courtmacsherry buoy, R

Courtmacsherry entrance, looking W; the first spar buoy W of the bar, L. The second spar buoy is barely visible in the picture but is just R of centre - it appears to be very far over to the N, but the S shore is shoal

Courtmacsherry; the second spar buoy R, the pier L centre

Leaving the bar buoy close to starboard, steer for the first of these. The second spar buoy is a further 4 cables due W. When within 20m of the second spar buoy, turn 60° to port for the third and last one. The channel is narrow, so care is required to stay on the line, and continuous use of the echo sounder is essential. In particular give Ferry Point a berth of a cable, even though the beach appears steep-to – this is deceptive. Once round the last mark, head for the end of the pier, staying close N of the moorings on the village side of the channel. The deep channel is close to the shore, half a cable wide and extends one cable past the pier.

The north channel shown on AC2081 has filled in; in fact the charts, based on a survey of 1907, no longer provide an accurate representation of the harbour W of the bar buoy. Care must be exercised in the use of GPS chartplotters in Courtmacsherry Harbour for this reason.

Anchorage and berthing

Anchor either N of Ferry Point, or N of the moorings and E of the lifeboat station, leaving room for the lifeboat to pass. Good holding in 2 to 3m, stiff mud. Anchored boats will normally lie to the tide. The area in front of the pier should be kept free to allow manoeuvring room.

Beyond the pier is an 18m-long pontoon for the use of visiting yachts and the sea angling boats. It is usually advisable to approach the pier or pontoon stemming the tide. The pontoon has 2·5m at LAT and the pier extension 4·5m. Manoeuvring room off the pier is somewhat restricted, with deep water extending only 50 to 75m N – see the plan. The stone pier E of the extension has 0.9m and can be used as an alongside berth at neaps. The dock inside the pier dries. There is some fishing boat traffic at the pier, and sea angling boats leave daily in summer at 1000 and return at 1800.

Courtmacsherry from the E; the bar buoy, bottom, Wood Point, lower L, and the pier, upper R centre

Courtmacsherry pier from the NE

It is appreciated if space at the E end of the pontoon is left available for their use at these times.

Courtmacsherry provides excellent shelter in winds from S through SW to W, and moorings are in use all winter. Strong NW winds (force 7 or 8) raise a short steep chop at the pier while gale to storm force SE winds produce a swell at high tide. In these conditions it is better to lie to an anchor.

At the time of writing (2008) planning permission for a 192-berth marina is being sought.

Tidal Streams
Tides run at up to 3 kn at springs in the harbour, the flood starting at –0600 Cobh and the ebb at –0010 Cobh. Constant –0018 Cobh; MHWS 3·7m, MHWN 3·0m, ML 2·1m.

Facilities
Pubs, hotel/restaurant, small shop in the village; diesel, water and shore power at the pontoon (for diesel contact Courtmacsherry Sea Angling 023 46427). Mechanical repairs, Marine Parts (Irl), 023 40170. RNLI all-weather lifeboat station. Buses to Cork, taxis (087 795 6055, 087 210 4964).

Argideen River to Timoleague
Burren Pier, on the N side opposite Courtmacsherry, has 0·5m at its head but is short of securing points. Below half tide, when the banks uncover to reveal the river channel, it is possible to take a dinghy up to Timoleague, where the ruins of the 14th-century Franciscan abbey are the finest medieval monastic remains in County Cork.

COURTMACSHERRY TO GLANDORE HARBOUR
AC2092, SC5623, Imray C56

Tidal Streams
At Seven Heads and from there to Toe Head the E-going stream starts at –0420 Cobh and the W-going stream at +0205 Cobh *(but see Note on page 55)*. Spring rate offshore is 1·5 kn, but reaches 2 kn off Seven Heads and 2·5 kn off Galley Head. There are S-going eddies on both sides of Galley Head, from which the stream sets continuously onto the Doolic Rock. There is a race extending 1·5M SSW which can be dangerous in strong SW winds even with a fair tide. There is little stream in Clonakilty or Glandore Bays.

Dangers
Horse Rock, dries 3·6m, 4 cables off Barry's Point **Carrigashoonta** and **Cotton Rock,** close NE of Seven Heads. These rocks dry only 2m, not 3·1 and 3·6m as charted, and Carrigashoonta is slightly further offshore than shown on AC2081. Carrigashoonta is not marked on the smaller-scale charts.
Cow Rock (dries 2·6m), in Dunworley Bay
Horse Rock (dries 0·4m), 1·25 cables N of Cow Rock
Doolic Rock (dries 3·7m), 3 cables SW of Galley Head
Sunk Rock, 0·4m, 1·5 cables SSE of Doolic Rock
Cloghna Rock, 0·9m, 6 cables offshore 1·7M NW of Galley Head

Blindstrand (L) and Broadstrand Bays, from the SE. Quarry Point, centre

Lights and Marks

Wind Rock, green stayed perch SHM, unlit, at the entrance to Clonakilty Harbour

Galley Head, white tower Fl(5) 20s 53m 23M, visible from seaward from 256° to 065°. The light is obscured inside the line of Seven Heads on the E side and inside the line of the Stag Rocks off Toe Head to the W.

For details of dangers and marks in the entrance to Glandore Harbour, see below.

Broadstrand and Blindstrand Bays

51°37'N 8°40'·5W

Anchorage is available in settled weather, with winds between S and NW, in Broadstrand and Blindstrand Bays to the S of Wood Point. These bays, particularly Broadstrand, offer an alternative to Courtmacsherry in suitable weather if caught by failing light or a falling tide. Approaching from the E towards Broadstrand Bay, steer 295° from Black Tom buoy and alter course to the W when off the mouth of the bay, passing clear N of Horse Rock. Anchor in 3m, sand, on the N side of the bay. Blindstrand Bay, to the S of Quarry Point, is narrower; anchor in 3m, sand, keeping Quarry Point W of N.

Seven Heads

There is deep water in mid-channel between Horse Rock and Barry's Point. Give the shore NE of Seven Heads a berth of 3 cables to avoid Cotton Rock and Carrigashoonta. Leganagh Point, the most E of the Seven Heads, is 40m high, and has the ruin of a Lloyd's signal tower on its summit. A berth of 2 cables clears all dangers S of the Seven Heads.

CLONAKILTY BAY

AC2092, SC5623 and Plan

Clonakilty Bay lies between Seven Heads and Galley Head. The bay has no harbours or anchorages which are both safe and easily accessible. Between Dunworley Bay and Ring Head are a number of drying and below-water rocks within 3 cables of the shore, and Anchor Rock, with 2·3m, lies 3 cables NE of Duneen Head.

Dunworley Bay

⊕*DW*   51°34'·5N 8°46'W

This bay immediately W of Seven Heads is exposed to the SW, but offers an attractive temporary anchorage in settled or easterly weather, and has a splendid beach. Cow Rock, in the middle of the bay, normally breaks, but Horse Rock, drying 0·4m, is 1·25 cables N of Cow Rock and may not show. Give Dunworley Head a berth of 2 cables and anchor off the beach in 3 to 4m, sand.

Clonakilty Harbour

⊕*CL*   51°35'·2N 8°51'W

Clonakilty Harbour is used by small fishing vessels based at Ring, NE of Inchydoney Island and 1M N of Ring Head. The bar, close W of Wind Rock (dries 0·5m), has less than 0·5m and is exposed to the S, and the channel is not deep enough for a yacht to lie afloat at LW. Entry should be attempted only in settled conditions on a high and rising tide, with great care and continuous use of the echosounder. Keep the starboard-hand perch on Wind Rock close aboard and stay 0·5

Clonakilty Bay

Clonakilty

Water Tower

Ring

Inchydoney

Ring Head

⊕*CL*

+ Anchor Rock

Duneen Head

Cow Rock

Dunworley Bay

⊕
DW

Seven Heads

⊕ *DC*

Dunnycove Bay

Dirk Bay

⊕ *DB*

Fl(5) 20s
Galley Head

Doolic Rock

0   1   2   3

miles

Clonakilty Harbour entrance from the S; Wind Rock perch, R centre

cable off the E side past South Ring. The "slip" marked close SW of Arundel Mills on AC2092 is Ring Pier, which just dries at LWS. The tide runs strongly in the channel, and there are many small-boat moorings. Restaurant and pubs at Ring; supermarkets, shops, restaurants, pubs, PO, laundry, doctors at Clonakilty, 1.8 km.

Dunnycove Bay

⊕*DC* 51°33'·7N 8°53'·3W

This bay N of Dunnycove Point offers temporary anchorage in moderate weather and winds between SW and N. Anchor in 7m, close NW of the point.

Ring (Clonakilty Harbour) from the SW

Dirk Bay

⊕*DB* 51°32'N 8°56'W

There is anchorage in this bay to the E of Galley Head in settled weather with winds between W and NE, and it has a splendid sandy beach in its NE corner. Enter close to the W shore to avoid Carrickduff (dries 1·5m) on the E side, with sunken rocks extending 1 cable SW from it. Anchor a cable off the beach in 3 to 5m, sand.

Dunnycove Bay from the E

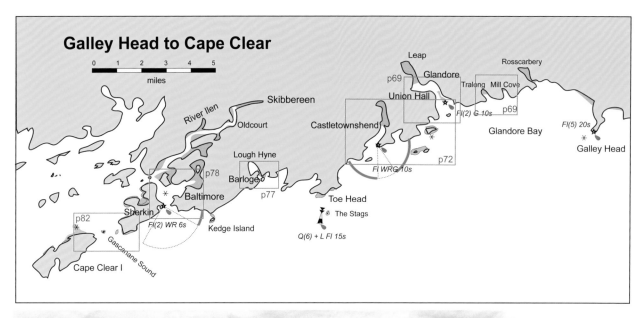

Galley Head from the NW, with Doolic Rock (R centre) and Sunk Rock (breaking, R)

GLANDORE BAY

AC2092, SC5623·15, Imray C56

This bay lies between Galley Head and Toe Head, and has two excellent harbours – Glandore and Castle Haven – and some delightful smaller anchorages.

Galley Head to Glandore Harbour

Rounding Galley Head, give it a berth of at least 7 cables to clear Doolic and Sunk Rocks, or else pass inside the Doolic, keeping closer to the Head than the rock. The Head itself is steep-to. In fresh winds or poor visibility keep well outside the Doolic. A course of 283° from Galley Head leads to the entrance to Glandore Harbour.

Mill Cove and Tralong Bay

These two bays E of Glandore offer temporary anchorage in offshore weather. Mill Cove is very narrow and almost entirely taken up with small-boat moorings. Mill Cove Rock and Black Rocks, forming one cluster, are conspicuous and extend nearly 2 cables offshore to the W of Mill Cove They are shown on the charts as drying but in fact stand 9 to 14m above HW. Tralong Bay lies 6 cables W of Mill Cove and 1M E of Goat's Head at the entrance to Glandore Harbour. The pyramidal Tralong Rock (11m high) at the W side of the entrance has rocks 0·5 cable SE of it, and between it and the shore to the NW. Enter in mid-channel and anchor in 3m in

the middle of the bay. The head of the bay dries out. The remarkable Drombeg Stone Circle stands 1.6 km by road NW of Tralong Bay.

The shore between Tralong and Goat's Head is foul for a distance of 1 cable nearly all the way.

Tralong Bay from the SE

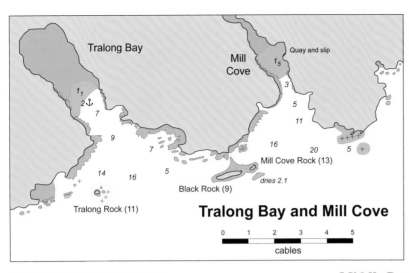

Tralong Bay and Mill Cove

0 1 2 3 4 5

cables

GLANDORE HARBOUR

⊕ *GD* 51°32'·5N 9°05'·4W

AC2092, SC5623·6, Imray C56 and Plan

The entrance lies between Goat's Head and Sheela Point. Goat's Head, on the E side, is a bluff headland, 79m high.

Dangers

Sheela's Rock (dries 1·5m), 1 cable SE of Sheela Point.

Reefs extending 1 cable W and 2 cables N and E from Adam's Island

Unnamed rock with 3m, almost in the middle of the sound between Adam's Island and Sheela Point.

A **sunken rock** between the W side of Eve Island and the shore

Unnamed rocks which partly uncover, extending 1 cable from the NE shore, 1 cable N of Grohoge Point

The Dangers, 3 drying reefs in a line NNW–SSE dividing the entrance to Glandore Harbour, 2 to 5 cables N of Eve Island

Sunk Rock, 1·5m, 1 cable N of the Dangers

Lights and marks

Glandore SW, 5m green column, SHM, Fl(2)G 10s, on the Outer Danger rock

Outer Danger, grey perch, unlit

Middle Danger, green perch SHM, unlit

Inner Danger, green perch SHM, unlit

Sunk Rock buoy, SHM, Fl G 5s.

Entrance directions

From the E, steer to pass midway between Goat's Head and Adam's Island, giving the island a berth of 2 cables, then keep Eve Island close aboard to port – or as the local saying goes, avoid Adam and hug Eve. Leave Glandore SW beacon, all the marks on the Dangers, and the Sunk Rock buoy, to starboard. (The grey perch on the Outer Danger marks the secondary channel to the NE of the Dangers.) A stranger should not attempt to pass between the separate reefs making up the Dangers. If making for Union Hall, give Coosaneigh Point, E of the pier, a berth of 1·5 cables to avoid a shoal patch extending N from the shore. From the W, give Sheela Point a berth of 1·5 cables, hold mid-channel between Sheela Point and Adam's Island and keep Eve Island close aboard to port.

Anchorages

• To the S and SW of the pier at Glandore, nearer to the W side of the bay in 2 to 3m, as permitted by the extensive moorings. The shelter is not good here in S to SE winds. There are visitors' moorings.

• Close to the bluff on the N side opposite Union Hall gives the best all-round shelter as well as being out of the way of fishing boat traffic. In any case a clear channel one cable wide must be left for access to the

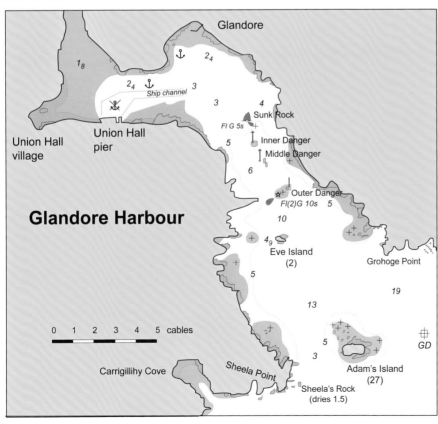

Glandore Harbour

0 1 2 3 4 5 cables

Approaches to Glandore and Union Hall from the S; Adam's Island, lower L, Eve Island centre

pier at Union Hall, and an anchor light should be shown. There is heavy fishing boat traffic around the clock.

The tidal stream in the anchorages is slight.

Facilities
Water on piers at Glandore and Union Hall. Fuel by tanker at Union Hall. Shops, PO, pubs, taxis at Union Hall. Hotel and pubs at Glandore. Buses to Cork and Skibbereen from Leap, 3 km. Filling station at Leap. Glandore Harbour Yacht Club operates from

Glandore Inn, and can advise on all local facilities. HM at Union Hall pier 028 34737, mobile 086 608 1944, VHF Ch 6.

GLANDORE HARBOUR TO BALTIMORE
AC2092, 2129, SC5623 and Plan
The coast continues cliffbound and scenic, penetrated by several excellent natural harbours, with uninhabited small islands close offshore and the spectacular Stag Rocks 8 cables south of Toe Head.

Glandore Harbour from the W; Union Hall bottom R, Glandore top L

Glandore entrance marks, from the S. Glandore SW beacon, L foreground; Middle Danger perch, centre; Inner Danger perch, L centre (R of the church); Sunk Rock buoy, L of the church. The grey perch marking the E side of the Outer Danger, extreme R.

Glandore

Tidal Streams

In Stag Sound, between Toe Head and the Stags, the E-going stream makes at –0435 Cobh and the W-going stream at +0150 Cobh *(but see Note on page 55)*. The stream runs at 2 kn at springs, and there is often a confused sea in Stag Sound, especially in W winds against the ebb tide. The tides also run strongly off Kedge Island.

Dangers

Belly Rock (dries 0·4m), 1·5 cables S of South Rock, S of Rabbit Island

Copper Rock (dries 2·7m), 1·5 cables S of Seal Rocks, W of High and Low Islands

Row Rock, 2m, a cable SSW of Copper Rock.

The **wreck of the *Kowloon Bridge,*** extending 2 cables SW from the Stags

Union Hall Pier

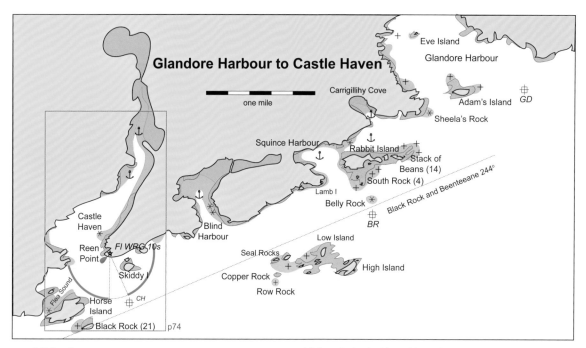

Lights and Marks

Reen Point, white pillar Fl WRG 10s 9m, W5M R3M G3M, G shore –338°, W 338°– 001°, R 001°– shore, shows green over Skiddy Island, white over the approach from the SSE, and red over Horse Island and Black Rock.

Kowloon Bridge buoy, S Card Q(6) + L Fl 15s

Barrack Point, white tower Fl(2) WR 6s 40m W6M R3M. R 168°–294°, W 294°–038°, obscured elsewhere. Shows red over Kedge Island and Whale Rock, white over the approach to Baltimore Harbour between SE and SW.

Lot's Wife, 8m pointed unlit white beacon on Beacon Point (50m), the E side of the entrance to Baltimore Harbour

Loo buoy, SHM Fl G 3s, close NW of Beacon Point.

Glandore Harbour to Castle Haven – inshore passage

Rabbit Island, 17m high with two conspicuous notches in its profile, lies half a mile SW of Sheela Point and is foul on its E and S sides. At its E end the Stack of Beans (14m high), conical in shape, must be given a berth of 1·5 cable on its E side. The reefs S of Rabbit Island end in South Rock, 4m high and steep-to on its S side, but Belly Rock,

(dries 0·4m), lies directly on the inshore course to Castle Haven, and is particularly dangerous. High Island (46m high), with Low Island (10m high), and Seal Rocks further to the W, may be regarded as one cluster which should not be approached too closely as there are rocks off and between them.

To pass S of Belly Rock, keep Black Rock (21m high, S of Castle Haven) in line with Beenteeane, the more N'ly of the twin summits on the Toe Head peninsula, bearing 244°. (Waypoint ⊕ *BR* 51°31'·3N 9°07'·2W is 2 cables S of Belly Rock.) To pass inside Belly Rock sail close up to South Rock with the Big Stag, S of Toe Head, just open N of Seal Rock 228°. In poor visibility, keep Sheela Point open E of the Stack of Beans 008°, altering course to the NW only when High Island is close aboard, to pass N of Low Island and Seal Rocks. When clear S of Belly Rock and N of Seal Rocks steer for Skiddy Island at the entrance to Castle Haven. The beacon on Reen Point is not conspicuous from more than 2M away.

The passage N of Rabbit Island is navigable with great care towards HW. There is a least depth of 1·2m at the narrows, with a reef extending right across from the mainland shore, and a rocky head drying 1·6m in mid-channel. Stay 50 to 75m from the island shore at this point, on a course of 060°– 240°.

Approach to Glandore Harbour from the SW; Rabbit Island, L, Stack of Beans, L centre, Adam's Island, centre

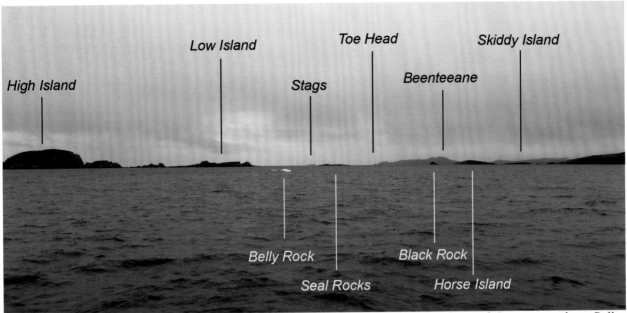

View from the ENE illustrating the landmarks for avoiding Belly Rock. Black Rock in line with Beenteeane clears Belly Rock to the S; the Stags open N (i.e. to the right) of Seal Rocks clears it to the N

Anchorages

The **channel N of Rabbit Island** offers secure anchorage in winds between S and NE, in depths of 2 to 8m, sand. **Carrigillihy Cove,** on the mainland side N of Rabbit Island, is narrow, and its inner part dries out. Drying rocks extend 50m from the shore on the W side of the entrance. Temporary anchorage is available in settled weather in 2 to 3m, no further in than the small coves on the E side of the inlet.

Squince Harbour, W of Rabbit Island, offers sheltered anchorage in offshore winds. Keep mid-channel in the entrance and anchor in 3·5 to 4m, 1·5 cables from the W shore. Squince Harbour is not secure in strong onshore winds. **Blind Harbour** lies 1M W of Squince Harbour and is also insecure in onshore winds. Keep slightly to the W shore when making the narrow entrance and anchor in the middle of the harbour in 1·5m.

Glandore Harbour to Toe Head

On the direct course pass either inside or outside High Island. If going inside, follow the directions (above) for clearing Belly Rock and then steer to pass N of Seal Rock. To pass outside High Island give it a berth of a cable.

Galley Head to Castle Haven and Toe Head

There are no dangers on the direct course between Doolic Rock and Toe Head. If bound for Castle Haven, there is no saving in distance in passing inside High Island, but if doing so, refer to the directions under *Glandore Harbour to Castle Haven – inshore passage* (above) to avoid Belly Rock.

Passing outside High Island, leave it 2 cables to starboard and hold a course S of W until Seal Rock is well abaft the beam, to clear Row Rock, before steering for Skiddy Island.

Passage NW of Rabbit Island, from the E; the mid-channel drying rock, R, with Squince Harbour beyond

Blind Harbour, looking NW

CASTLE HAVEN

⊕*CH* 51°30'·5N 9°10'·2W

AC2129, SC5623·14, Imray C56 and Plan

Castle Haven is an excellent natural harbour, and the inner reaches of the inlet provide nearly perfect shelter. Castletownshend, on the W shore, is a most attractive and historic village. It was named after Richard Townsend, a soldier in Cromwell's service who was granted the estate in the 1640's, but the eponymous castle was a stronghold of the O'Driscolls long before that. Castletownshend (the "h" was apparently added in the 1870's) retained its pronounced Anglo-Irish ambience well into the 1950's (the "Irish RM" stories were written here by the cousins Edith Somerville and Violet Martin). A visit to the beautiful St Barrahane's Church reveals the quite remarkable contribution to Empire made by the "big houses" of Castletownshend.

Directions

Skiddy Island, 9m high and flat-topped, with ledges extending 1 cable all round, lies 2 cables S of Reen Point. There is no passage between Skiddy Island and the shore. Horse Island, 35m high with a tower on its E side, is close to the W shore and is generally foul all round. Black Rock (21m high and conspicuous from most directions) is 2 cables SE of Horse Island and is steep-to on its S side. There is a boat passage inside Horse Island called Flea Sound, but it is very narrow and obstructed by rocks. Enter Castle Haven between Reen Point and The Battery. Keep the Stags (S of Toe Head) and Flea Island, N of Horse Island, in line 208° astern to lead clear up the harbour. Note the position of **Colonel's Rock** (0·5m), 0.5 cable off the E shore 2 cables N of Reen Point. To the N of the village, the harbour is narrowed by a promontory on the W side, on which stands a conspicuous hotel with a castellated roofline, and close to which is Cat Island, which never covers.

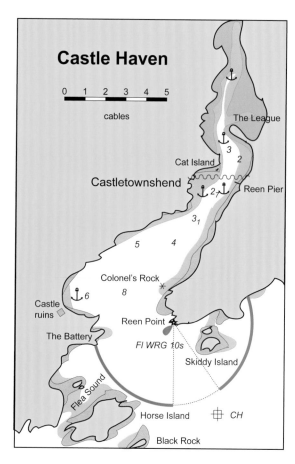

Castle Haven stretches a further 1.3M N between steep wooded slopes, restricted and sheltered by The League, a gravel spit extending 1.5 cables from the E shore, and sandbanks to the N of it. From here the channel, 0.5 cable wide, is close to the W shore; the lagoon at the head of the inlet dries.

Anchorage

Anchor off Castletownshend village nearer either shore, where the holding is best; there is sea-grass with limited holding in mid-channel. In strong S winds there is better shelter above Cat Island, where there is 3 to 4m in mid-channel, but the available space here is mostly occupied by moorings. Further upstream again (where an anchor is marked on the Plan) there is adequate room if a yacht is moored with a kedge; the wooded shores here are very attractive and a dinghy trip to the head of the navigation is well worthwhile. Both quays at the village dry, but are convenient for landing. The pier at Reen on the E side of the harbour is

Castle Haven from the S; Black Rock bottom L with Horse Island and The Battery beyond, Skiddy Island centre R, Reen Point centre and Castletownshend beyond

Castle Haven entrance, from the S. The beacon on Reen Point (centre, above) is small and inconspicuous

Above: Reen Point beacon (centre) from the SW through the gap between Horse Island (L) and Black Rock (R)

a piled concrete structure with 0·4 m at LAT at its outer end.

The bay on the W side, N of The Battery, is also a feasible anchorage.

Caution

A submarine telephone cable runs across the harbour from the village slip to the slip just N of Reen Pier; avoid anchoring near this line. Above Cat Island a tripping line is strongly recommended.

Tidal Stream

The stream is slight off the quay but stronger above Cat Island, though a yacht will be tide-rode at times anywhere in the anchorage. Constant –0028 Cobh; MHWS 3·7m, MHWN 2·9m, ML 2·0m.

Facilities

Shop, pubs, restaurants. Water from tap on the village slip, also on Reen Pier. Petrol but no diesel.

Castle Haven from the SW; Castletownshend L, Reen Pier R with The League beyond

The Stags, from the E

CASTLE HAVEN TO BALTIMORE
AC2129, SC5623·14

Giving Horse Island and Black Rock a berth of a cable, there are no dangers on the direct course to Toe Head. There is a conspicuous ruined tower on the high ground 7 cables NE of Toe Head. Foul ground extends 3 cables from the shore close W of Toe Head, ending in the Belly Rocks, which dry.

The Stags are a group of jagged rocks 20m high, lying 7·5 cables S of Toe Head. Stag Sound, 6 cables wide, is free of danger. The colossal wreck of the ore carrier *Kowloon Bridge* lies 1 to 3 cables SW of the Stags and is marked at its SW extremity by a S Card buoy.

Toehead Bay and Tragumna Bay
51°28'·7N 9°16'·7W
AC2129, SC5623·14

These bays are exposed to the prevailing winds and their shores are foul in places, but either can be a pleasant temporary anchorage in offshore winds and no swell. The best spot is the bay on the W shore of Tragumna Bay.

Barloge Creek
⊕*BC* 51°29'·4N 9°17'·3W
AC2129, SC5623·14, see Plan

This delightful anchorage lies inside Bullock Island

and is sheltered by Carrigathorna to the S. The Stags just closed behind Gokane Point 122° leads to the entrance. Bullock Island has two prominent stands of conifers on its summit. (Tranabo Cove, which lies E of Bullock Island, is exposed to the S and is not recommended.) Enter Barloge midway between Carrigathorna and Bullock Island, and pass W of the above-water rock (2·5m high) to the SW of the island. The SE extension of this rock dries 2·5m. The entrance is deep and steep-to on both sides. Follow a mid-channel course W of the rock; the entrance is very steep-to but the creek shoals quickly once the NW face of the island opens up.

Anchorage
W of Bullock Island in 3 to 4m in good shelter, except in strong S or SE winds. Anchor clear of weed for good holding; the water is normally clear enough to spot the clean patches. The bottom is mud.

Lough Hyne
This lovely lake is connected to Barloge by a narrow channel which becomes a scour at half-tide. The ingoing stream makes at –0320 Cobh and the outgoing at +0115 Cobh, but these times are very susceptible to weather conditions. A visit to the Lough by dinghy is strongly recommended, as the scenery is beautiful, but beware of being unable to

Barloge Creek and Lough Hyne, with Tranabo Cove on the R

*Gokane Point in line
with the Stags leads
to Barloge entrance*

Approach to Barloge, from the SE. The entrance is L of Bullock Island, with its stands of conifers, centre

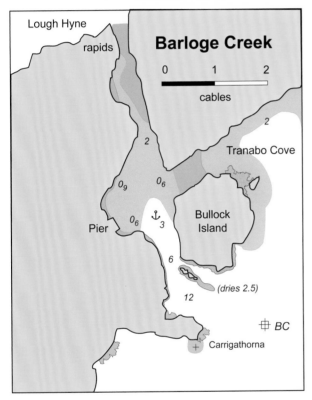

make way against a flood tide on the way back out – it runs at 5 to 6 knots at springs. Because of what is effectively a sill at the entrance, the flow reverses very suddenly at the turn, and in the space of five minutes can change from one knot flood to one knot ebb. Lough Hyne was designated as Ireland's first marine nature reserve in 1981. As a half-tide lake of low salinity and extraordinary depth, it has a unique ecosystem, and attracts intensive study.

Barloge to Baltimore
AC2129, SC5623·14
There are two rocks just S of Carrigathorna, so leave it at least a cable astern before turning for Kedge Island, distant 2·75M. A berth of two cables clears all dangers on the coast to the SW.

Kedge Island should be given a berth of a cable to the S. There is, however, a narrow passage 7·3m deep between the innermost rock, called Carrigatrough, and Spain Point on the mainland. This passage, no more than 50m wide, should only be attempted under power, and in settled conditions. The coast W of Kedge Island is generally steep-to, but beware of Whale Rock, which dries 1·8m and is 0·5 cable offshore and 5 cables E of the entrance to Baltimore. The conspicuous Lot's Wife beacon in line with the SW face of Black Point, 318°, leads just outside Whale Rock. The ruined Telegraph Tower on the hill (142m) NW of Spain Point is conspicuous.

BALTIMORE HARBOUR
⊕*BL* 51°28'·1N 9°23'·3W
AC2129, 3725, SC5623·13, Imray C56 and Plan
Baltimore is a fishing port, a major centre for sailing and diving, and the ferry port for the islands to the south-west. The harbour is 1M across each way, mostly between 2 and 6m deep, somewhat subject to swell in E and SE winds but offering safe anchorage. Its S entrance is straightforward and navigable in any weather, day or night. As the southwesternmost harbour in Ireland, Baltimore is often the first port of call for yachts arriving from the Azores, the Caribbean or the United States.

Tidal Streams
The streams run fairly through both the N and S entrances, meeting near Lousy Rocks. The flood stream runs E and SE on the N side of Sherkin Island and N on its E side commencing at +0545 Cobh. The ebb stream runs W and S, commencing at –0025 Cobh. Constant –0015 Cobh; MHWS 3·6m, MHWN 3·0m, ML 2·1m.

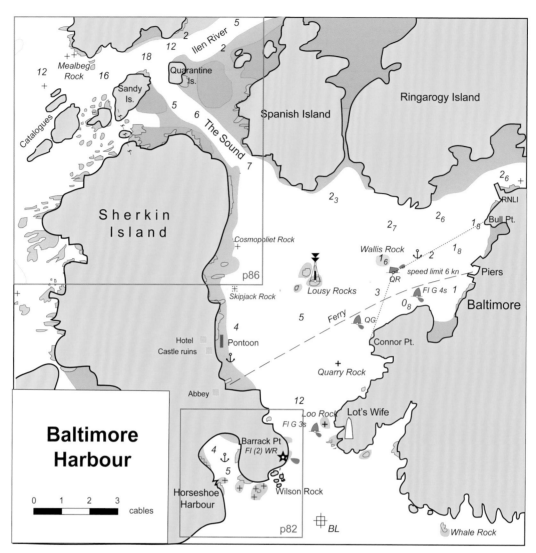

Baltimore Harbour

0   1   2   3
cables

Dangers
Unnamed rock (drying 0.6m), 0·4 cable off Beacon Point
Loo Rock, 0·2m, 1 cable NW of Beacon Point
Rocks with 1.7m and 0.5m, close E of Barrack Point
Quarry Rock, 2·1m, 2 cables NNE of Loo Buoy
Lousy Rocks (dry 0·6 to 2·4m), in the middle of the harbour, extending 0·5 cable N and WSW from the S Card perch.
Wallis Rock, 1.6m, 3 cables W of Baltimore Pier
Ransome Rock, 2·3m, 1 cable WNW of Lousy Rocks perch
Skipjack Rock (awash), **Great Globe Rock** (2m high with ledges drying 2m extending E), **Globe Rocks** (1m high, with a rock drying 2.1m to the E), and **Cosmopoliet Rock** (dries 0·4m), all within 1 cable of the shore of Sherkin Island W of Lousy Rocks
Narrows Ledge, 0.1m, 0.5 cable off the shore of Sherkin Island at the S entrance to The Sound.

Lights and marks
Barrack Point, white tower Fl(2) WR 6s 40m W6M R3M. R 168°–294°, W 294°–038°, obscured elsewhere. Shows red over Kedge Island and Whale Rock, white over the approach between SE and SW.

Baltimore entrance, from the S; Barrack Point, L, and Beacon Point with Lot's Wife, R. Loo buoy and the Lousy Rocks perch are just visible, centre

Baltimore from the NE; the pier and harbour bottom L, with the yacht pontoon and the Cape Clear ferry at the S pier; the S entrance and Lot's Wife, upper L; Sherkin Island, upper R; Gascanane Sound and Cape Clear Island, top R

Directions

Lot's Wife is conspicuous and unmistakable. Approach the entrance with Loo buoy bearing N and leave it close to starboard. To avoid Quarry Rock steer N (towards Lousy Rocks perch) till the N pier at Baltimore comes in sight, then pass N of the two starboard-hand buoys, leaving the Lousy Rocks beacon and the Wallis Rock buoy to port. There is a speed limit of 6 knots in the area between Connor Point, Wallis Rock and Bull Point.

North Passage, the N exit from the harbour, between Sherkin Island and Spanish Island, is described after the directions for Cape Clear, below.

Anchorage

- NW or W of the N pier, in 2 to 3m, leaving room for fishing boats and ferries to manoeuvre. As a guide, stay NW of a line from the Wallis Rock Buoy to Bull Point. An anchor light is recommended.
- Between May and October a pontoon is moored to the end of the S pier. Contact Atlantic Boating Services, 028 20123 / 087 235 1485, VHF Ch. 16 or 9.
- Visitors' moorings are available; contact Atlantic Boating Services as above, or Vincent O'Driscoll, 028 20218 / 087 244 7828. In W

Lot's Wife, 8m pointed unlit white beacon on Beacon Point (50m), the E side of the entrance
Loo buoy, SHM Fl G 3s, close NW of Beacon Point.
Two SHM buoys, the outer QG, the inner Fl G 4s, mark the ferry channel NW of Coney Island.
Lousy Rocks beacon, S Card perch, 12m, unlit
Wallis Rock buoy, PHM QR.

Baltimore Pier from the anchorage NE of the Wallis Rock buoy; the pontoon may be identified by the thicket of masts in front of the S pier, centre

Sherkin Island; the abbey and the ferry pier

Sherkin pontoon

winds there is a good anchorage N of the pier at Abbey Strand on Sherkin Island. A pontoon is also moored here between mid-May and mid-September. Berthing charges are payable at the Islander's Rest Hotel, 028 20116.

Anchoring is not permitted in the fairway between Baltimore and Sherkin piers, N of the green buoys. Note that the W end of the N pier at Baltimore is fouled by rocks. The navigable water in Church Strand Bay, to the E, is entirely taken up by moorings.

Facilities
Water on the pontoon and N pier. Shore power on the pontoon. Shop, hotel (with showers); restaurants and pubs. Diesel (contact Cotter's supermarket) and gas. Limited chandlery. HM 028 20123, mobile 087 235 1485, VHF Ch 16 & 6. Glénans Sailing School. Baltimore SC on the quay is active in July and August and also has showers. Ferries to Sherkin and Cape Clear Island. RNLI all-weather lifeboat station. Taxis. Buses to Skibbereen. Sherkin Island has water and shore power on the pontoon; hotel and pub.

BALTIMORE TO CAPE CLEAR ISLAND AND THE FASTNET
AC 2129, 3725, SC5623·12 and Plan
Cape Clear Island was once home to 1200 people, but the famine of the 1840's and long years of

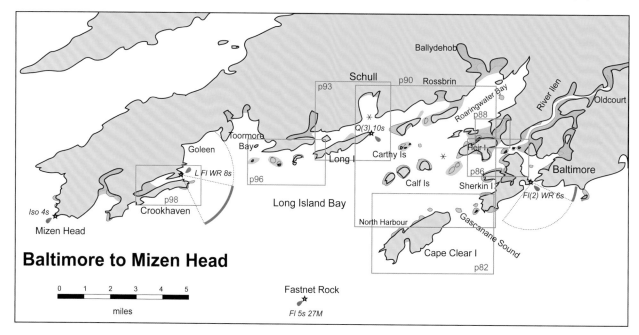

Baltimore to Mizen Head

hardship and emigration took a heavy toll. Today the population of 125 comprises fishermen, artists, writers and many involved one way or another in the hospitality business. Cape Clear is a Gaeltacht area and the southernmost inhabited point of Ireland. It attracts Gaelic scholars, artists and the many birdwatchers who come to observe the passage of tens of thousands of seabirds on their daily flight between the coast of Kerry and their feeding grounds in the Celtic Sea. Ireland's very first saint, Ciaran, was born on Cape Clear about 350AD. The island is locally known as Cape Clear or simply Cape, and not (as it is labelled on the charts) Clear Island.

North Harbour, from where the ferries sail to Baltimore and Schull, is a narrow inlet on the island's northwest coast. The deep part of the harbour is very constricted, but it is a lovely spot and a popular port of call for yachts. The old lighthouse, long disused, standing at a height of 133m near the centre of the SE side of the island, is conspicuous. Carriglure, a group of sunken rocks, lies 0·5 cable off the cliffs under it.

Gascanane Sound provides the simplest route from Baltimore to North Harbour and the islands of Long Island Bay. The S shore of Sherkin Island is steep-to.

Tidal Streams

In Gascanane Sound the streams run at 3 kn springs and cause dangerous eddies, especially near the rocks in the centre. The SE-going stream makes at +0520 Cobh and the NW-going stream at –0055 Cobh.

SW of Cape Clear the streams are are not well documented, but it is probable that they run E and W between Cape Clear and the Fastnet Rock, the E-going stream starting at –0420 Cobh and the W-going stream at +0150 Cobh, spring rate 2 to 2·5 kn. Off Blananarragaun the streams are complex. It is thought that the E-going stream divides at the Bill of Cape Clear, setting NE along the N shore of the island and S to Blananarragaun, forming a large eddy E of Blananarragaun. The W-going stream forms an eddy W of Blananarragaun. The result of this is often a heavy and confused sea between the Bill of Cape Clear and Blananarragaun, off which a race is formed on both streams.

Within 1M N and S of the Fastnet Rock the streams run SSE and NNW, the E-going stream making at –0405 Cobh and the W-going stream at +0200 Cobh, spring rate 2·2 kn. With W winds the E-going stream runs for 7h and increases by 0·5 kn, and the converse with E winds. There can be a tide race with the E-going stream, extending for 1M SE of the rock.

Dangers

Carrigmore (6m high), in the middle of Gascanane Sound, with drying and underwater reefs extending 1·5 cables to the NW

Gascanane Rock (dries 1·8m), 2·5 cables W of Carrigmore

Crab Rock, reef extending 2 cables N from Illaunbrock

North Harbour, Cape Clear. The yacht is at the only deep-water berth. Two ferries at the ferry berth

View to the W from close to Gascanane Rock; Cape Clear Island, L, Avaud Rocks, L centre, Illauneana, R centre

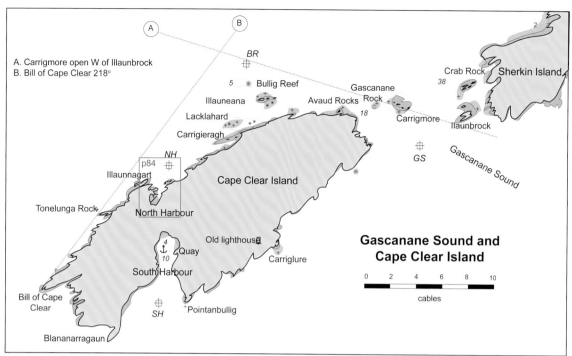

A. Carrigmore open W of Illaunbrock
B. Bill of Cape Clear 218°

**Gascanane Sound and
Cape Clear Island**

0   2   4   6   8   10
cables

Avaud Rocks, drying and above-water rocks extending 0·75 cable off the NE corner of Cape Clear Island. Unnamed on the charts

Drying and underwater rocks extending 1 cable SE and 0·5 cable NW from **Illauneana**

Lacklahard and **Carrigieragh,** drying and underwater reefs between 2 and 5 cables SW of Illauneama

Bullig Reef, two rocks awash at LW, 2 cables NW of Illauneana.

Tonelunga Rock (dries), 1 cable offshore near the ruins of Doonanore Castle, 7·5 cables from the Bill of Cape Clear.

Lights and marks

Fastnet Rock, grey tower, Fl 5s 49m 27M, Horn (4) 60s, Racon (G) 18M.

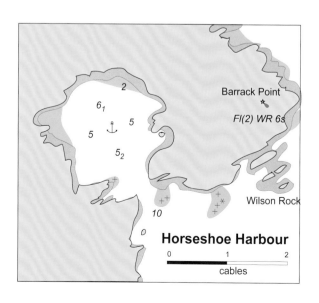

Horseshoe Harbour

0   1   2
cables

Horseshoe Harbour
AC3725, SC5623·12 and Plan

This almost landlocked pool 1.5 cables across, on the S side of Sherkin Island, provides secure anchorage except in S or SE winds, but underwater rocks extend 0.5 cable southwards, W of Wilson Rock, and also from the E point of the entrance. The entrance is only 40m wide between these rocks and the cliffs to the W. From the E, give the shore a berth of 1 cable and enter on a course of 340°, keeping the W point of the entrance close aboard, and turn N when the pool opens up, to avoid a rock on the W side just inside the entrance. Approaching from the W, the shore is steep-to. Anchor in 5m, mud, in the middle of the pool. Pubs and restaurant, 1 km. Do not be caught here in strong winds between SE and SW.

Gascanane Sound
⊕ *GS* 51°26'·9N 9°26'·9W

Gascanane Sound separates Cape Clear Island and Sherkin Island. Carrigmore and the drying Gascanane Rock lie in the middle of the sound. Gascanane Rock is a particular danger as both tidal streams set on to it; the channel E of Carrigmore is wider and safer. Illaunbrock, off Sherkin, is steep-to on its S and W sides, but a ledge called Crab Rocks extends 2 cables N. The W channel is narrower, and the position of Avaud Rocks must be noted. A strong S or SE wind creates a turbulent sea in Gascanane Sound – especially on the S-going tide – which can be dangerous, and the Sound should not be attempted in strong to gale force winds. Local legend maintains that the sailor making a first passage of Gascanane

View from the WNW, nearing the transit line to avoid Bullig Reef; Carrigmore coming W of Illaunbrock 107°, centre. The W channel of Gascanane Sound, R, Sherkin Island, L

Bill of Cape Clear bearing 218° (centre R), clears Bullig Reef. The Fastnet Rock may just be discerned at R

Sound must compose a poem in its honour.

North Coast of Cape Clear Island

Illauneana (13m high), 2 cables off the N shore and 7 cables W of Gascanane Sound, has foul ground all round; to the SW, and within 2 cables of the island shore, are the dangerous Lacklahard and Carrigieragh reefs. There is a narrow deep channel between Illauneana and the shore, which is used by the ferryboat in settled weather, but do not be tempted to follow. Bullig Reef, with two rocks awash at LW, extends 3 cables NW of Illauneana and is a particular danger as it lies across the course from Gascanane Sound to North Harbour and Crookhaven, and from North Harbour to the N entrance to Baltimore. A waypoint of 51°27'·6N 9°29'·2W *(⊕ BR on Gascanane Sound Plan)* provides a berth of a cable to the N of Bullig Reef. The transit marked on AC2129 is no longer of use since the church on Sherkin Island cannot be identified at a distance. Carrigmore (in Gascanane Sound) open W

of Illaunbrock 107° *(see photograph)* leads clear N of Bullig Reef. From Gascanane Sound, steer 295° for the W end of West Calf Island, leaving Illauneana 3 cables to port, and hold this course until the coast W of North Harbour opens up with the Bill of Cape Clear bearing 218° *(see photograph)*. Identify North Harbour, with the cluster of buildings behind it, and do not steer for it until it is well open. From this point a course of 265° leads to Brow Head, and 276° to Crookhaven. From the W, approaching North Harbour, beware of Tonelunga Rock, off the NW shore of the island.

North Harbour

⊕NH 51°26'·7N 9°30'·2W
No large-scale chart published; see Plan

Immediately E of the entrance to North Harbour are several above-water rocks of which Minnaun Rock is the W'most. Leave Minnaun Rock 50m to port and steer for the end of the outer (N) pier. Do not err to the NW as the bight N of the pier is foul. The

Approaching North Harbour, Cape Clear (centre L)

North Harbour, Cape Clear, from the S

with baulks of wood in a heavy swell, such as would be experienced in heavy weather between NW and NE. With a forecast of such conditions, however, a yacht is recommended not to remain in North Harbour but to seek shelter in Baltimore or Schull.

Water on N pier; pubs, restaurant, small shop.

South Harbour

⊕*SH* 51°25'·5N 9°30'·2W
AC2129, 2184, SC5623·12

South Harbour lies just to the E of Blananarragaun, and offers good anchorage in settled weather or in N winds. It is exposed to wind and swell between SE and SW. The anchorage is in the centre of the harbour in 4 to

entrance is 25m wide and the cliffs on the SE side are clean. Most of the area of the harbour to the SW has less than 1m at LAT, and the inner harbour dries. The only spots with 2m at LW are (1) on the round head of the outer pier, just inside the end, and (2) at the steps on the central pier. The latter is also the ferry's berth. In spite of this, North Harbour somehow manages to accommodate large numbers of visiting yachts in summer.

The ferries require most of the available space S of their berth for manoeuvring, which precludes anchorage for shallow draft or bilge-keel yachts which could otherwise take the ground there at LW. The inner harbour dries, with a firm level bottom, and can be closed off

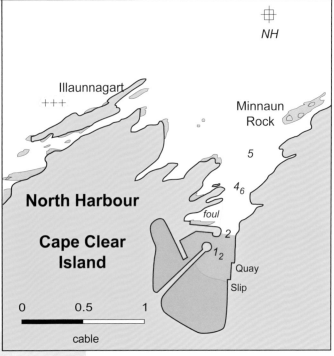

6m, with good holding. Pointanbullig, on the E side of the entrance, has rocks 0·5 cable off it. In settled weather it is possible to lie alongside the quay in the SE corner, but this is not advisable for an overnight stay.

Fastnet Rock

Four miles WSW of Cape Clear is the Fastnet Rock, a lonely pinnacle 28m high. The best-known seamark in Ireland, and the logo of the Irish Cruising Club, the Fastnet lighthouse was built in 1903, replacing an earlier tower of 1847 whose stump is still

Entering North Harbour

visible. The loom of the Fastnet is often the first sight of Ireland for the transatlantic sailor, and the rock is perhaps the most famous racing mark in the world.

There is a rock, with 3·4m over it, 2 cables to the NE of the Fastnet. The tidal streams set strongly around the Rock, so resist the temptation to get too close.

South Harbour, Cape Clear; the quay on the SE side

Traffic Separation Scheme

There is a TSS south of the Fastnet. The W-bound lane is 2 to 4M from the rock and the E-bound 6 to 8M from it. The lanes should be crossed as near to right angles as possible. The inshore traffic zone extends 2M S of the rock.

NORTH PASSAGE FROM BALTIMORE HARBOUR

51°29'·2N 9°23'·6W

AC2129, 3725, SC5623·12 and Plan

The North Passage provides a convenient access direct to Roaringwater Bay, avoiding Gascanane Sound. The pilotage is intricate but not unduly challenging. Hare Island, as it is called on the charts, is properly spelt Heir.

Dangers

Mealbeg, dries, close S of Turk Head

Two Women's Rock (above HW), 3 cables E of Heir Island, with shoals and rocks extending 2 cables N and 1 cable S

Unnamed rock, with 1m, 3 cables S of Two Women's Rock

Mullin Rock, 2·1m, 3 cables NW of Drowlaun Point, Sherkin Island

Bream Rocks (dry 1·8m), and **Greymare Rocks**, with less than 2m, forming a reef extending for 3·5 cables NE–SW, 2 cables S of Heir Island

Toorane Rocks, reef 5 cables by 2, extending NE–SW, 2 cables W of Bream Rocks. The SW part dries 2·8m and the NE part has two heads above HW.

Directions

From Baltimore, pass either side of Lousy Rocks, giving the beacon a berth of a cable. Entering The Sound, between Spanish Island and Sherkin Island, identify the small Quarantine Island ahead and head for the mid-channel between it and Sandy Island to the SW. The channel between Sherkin and Sandy Island appears

The Fastnet Rock

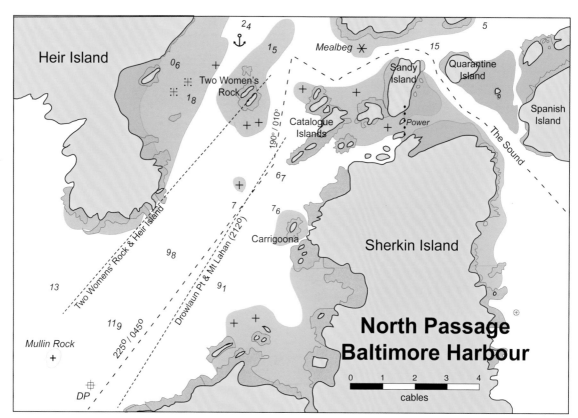

wide at HW but is rock-strewn and spanned by a low overhead power cable. This cable continues NW across the main channel, but underwater.

Skirting the N shore of Sandy Island close to port, identify the N'most of the Catalogue Islands, 3 cables WSW, and steer for it, erring nothing to the N so as to pass clear S of Mealbeg. When 0.5 cable from the Catalogues, turn to starboard and steer 300° towards the low hill (22m) near the E end of Heir Island. When the centre of Two Women's Rock comes in line with the SE tip of Heir Island 225°, turn to port and steer 190°. Hold this course past the SW rocks of the Catalogues and until Drowlaun Point (on Sherkin) bears 212° and comes slightly to the right of Mount Lahan (77m) at the E end of Cape Clear. From this point a course of 225° will clear

both the unnamed 1m rock and Mullin Rock, and pass 1·5 cables NW of Drowlaun Point (waypoint *DP*, 51°28'·7N 9°26'·2W).

Anchorage

There is reasonable anchorage in 1·5 to 2·5m in good shelter N of Two Women's Rock and between Heir Island and the mainland. Fine sandy beaches. There is a substantial pier and slip at the NE point of Heir Island. Ferries run to Cunnamore Pier and (in summer) to Baltimore.

Passage from seaward

For the N entrance to Baltimore from the W, see *Schull and Cape Clear to Baltimore North Passage*, below.

North Passage from Baltimore; view NW through The Sound, between Sandy Island (L) and Quarantine Island (R)

The Catalogue Islands from the ENE. Heir Island, R

Two Women's Rock (centre) in line with the SE tip of Heir Island; Cape Clear Island beyond, and Sherkin Island L

Drowlaun Point slightly to the R of Mount Lahan on Cape Clear Island

Ilen River to Oldcourt
AC2129, SC5623·12

The Ilen River is navigable as far as the boatyards at Oldcourt, 4M upriver from Quarantine Island at the N end of The Sound, and 5M from Baltimore. The river is scenic and tranquil, and the trip is well worth making even if not going to one or other of the yards. AC2129 or SC5623 is essential, and even though the survey of the river dates from 1846 the channel is not much changed. Passage should however only be attempted on a high and rising tide, and only in daylight. There is a minimum depth of 1m at LAT, the shallowest point being close off the N point of Inishbeg. There are no navigational aids in the river.

Leave Quarantine Island close to starboard and head for Inane Point, 5 cables ENE. Give Inishleigh on the N bank a berth of 1.5 cables to clear the shoals off its E side, and stay 0.5 cable off Inane Point while rounding it to open up the next stretch of 1·3M to Inishbeg. As with most winding river channels, the general rule is to stay wide on the bends. Hold mid-channel on the stretch to Inishbeg, then turn wide, staying on the Inishbeg (E) side of the turn to the N. Stay mid-channel at the narrows W of Inishbeg and do not turn to starboard until the slip at Reenadhuna is almost abeam. Keeping the house at Reenadhuna directly astern, head for the point on the N shore opposite the slip at the N end of Inishbeg. When 1 cable from this point, turn to starboard and head for the slip on Inishbeg. Leave it 50m to starboard and head for the jetty 2 cables E on the S bank beyond Inishbeg, leaving it 50m to starboard. From there to Oldcourt, stay in mid-channel.

Coming down-river, Quarantine Island is hard to discern until quite close; the power cable poles on Sandy Island are however prominent on the skyline, and a conspicuous square white warning signboard on the N point of Sandy Island makes a good mark *(see photograph)*. Keep the sign fine on the port bow until The Sound opens up to the S.

Competitive rowing craft use the river frequently, and a good lookout should be kept for them.

Oldcourt
51°32'N 9°19'·3W

There are two boatyards at Oldcourt. O'Donovan's (Oldcourt Boats, 028 21249) has a pontoon for temporary berthing, a slipway for vessels up to 30m and 400t, and a 70-tonne travelhoist, one of the largest in Ireland. Hull (wood, metal and GRP) and mechanical repairs, mobile crane, winter storage. Hegarty's (028 22122) has a slipway for vessels up to 20m and 150t. Mobile crane, hull and mechanical repairs, winter storage.

Ilen River, N of Inishbeg, from the E; Reenadhuna House, R

Sandy Island from the Ilen River, looking downstream; the conspicuous signboard, R centre, and Quarantine Island, L. The Sound, leading to Baltimore, is just visible between the two islands.

Anchorage

Anchorage is possible wherever convenient out of the main channel in the river, and temporary anchorage is possible in mid-channel at Oldcourt. An alongside berth at Oldcourt may be available by permission; phone the yards. There is a pub at Oldcourt.

Skibbereen

Above Oldcourt the river is shallower but it is possible with care to reach Skibbereen, 2·5M upstream, by dinghy near HW. There is a landing in the middle of town at the head of a short tributary channel on the starboard hand, a cable upstream of the iron girder footbridge. Skibbereen has filling stations, supermarkets, shops, PO, doctors and comprehensive chandlery (CH Marine, phone 028 23190). Taxis, phone 028 22296 and 028 21258.

Passage N of Heir Island – Goose Island Channel

⊕ *GI* 51°30'·2N 9°26'W

AC2129, SC5623·12 and Plan

This passage gives direct access above half tide from Baltimore to the Skeam Islands, Roaringwater Bay and Horse Island. The wider channel, to the W of Goose Island, has 1.4m least depth while the channel to the E has 1.3m. There is little trace now of the sandspit marked on the charts to the SE of Goose I. From Baltimore, after passing Mealbeg keep close to the E side in 1 to 2m (LAT); at half tide only one of the Corrignamoe group of rocks,

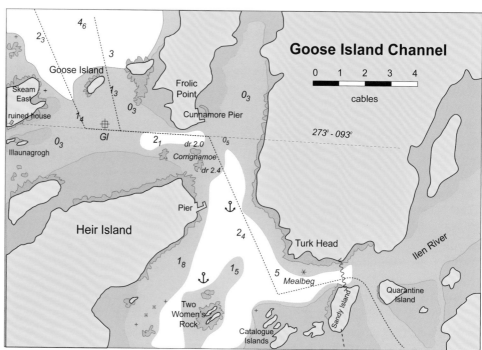

S Approaches to Goose Island channel, seen from Heir Island; Cunnamore Pier, R, Corrignamoe Rocks centre L, Goose Island at extreme L

Heir Island from the E; the pier, bottom R, and Two Women's Rock, lower L. The Calf Islands, top

which are N of the NE point of Heir Island, will be showing. Steer for the head of Cunnamore Pier. When 0·5 cable from it, turn to port and steer 273°, with the ruined house on Skeam East fine on the starboard bow. Pass either one-third of the channel's width to the W of Goose, or stay 50m from the E side of the island. There is a drying outlier one cable W of Frolic Point. The centre of Goose Island touching the NE point of Heir Island clears the rocks off the NE point of Skeam East. There is good anchorage off the beach on Skeam East. The narrow passage S of Skeam East, between it and Illaunagrogh, is clear but needs great care; and there are many half-tide rocks S of Illaunagrogh.

Skeam East from W of Cunnamore Pier; the ruined house landmark, above centre, and R

Goose Island E channel, from the NW; Goose Island, R, with Heir Island pier beyond the leading yacht. Corrignamoe Rocks just visible in front of the pier. Sandy Island and Baltimore in the distance.

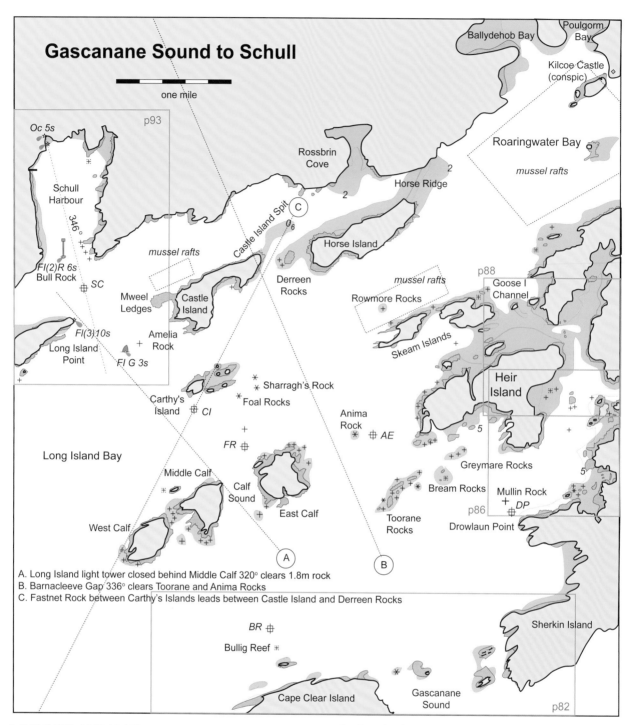

Gascanane Sound to Schull

one mile

Oc 5s

p93

Schull
Harbour

346°

Fl(2)R 6s
Bull Rock   ⊞ SC

Mweel
Ledges

Castle
Island

Fl(3)10s
Long Island
Point

Amelia
Rock

Fl G 3s

Carthy's
Island   ⊞ CI

Sharragh's Rock

Foal Rocks

FR ⊞

Long Island Bay

Middle Calf

Calf
Sound

West Calf

East Calf

Rossbrin
Cove

Castle Island Spit   Ⓒ

0·6

Horse Ridge

Horse Island

Derreen
Rocks

mussel rafts

mussel rafts

Rowmore Rocks

Skeam Islands

Anima
Rock   ⊞ AE

Toorane
Rocks

Bream Rocks

Ballydehob Bay

Poulgorm
Bay

Kilcoe Castle
(conspic)

Roaringwater Bay

mussel rafts

p88

Goose I
Channel

Heir
Island

5

Greymare Rocks

Mullin Rock
DP

p86

Drowlaun Point

A. Long Island light tower closed behind Middle Calf 320° clears 1.8m rock
B. Barnacleeve Gap 336° clears Toorane and Anima Rocks
C. Fastnet Rock between Carthy's Islands leads between Castle Island and Derreen Rocks

Ⓐ

Ⓑ

BR ⊞

Bullig Reef

Sherkin Island

Cape Clear Island

Gascanane
Sound

p82

LONG ISLAND BAY
AC2129, 2184, SC5623·12
Long Island Bay lies between Cape Clear and Castle Point, and extends NE into Roaringwater Bay. The area offers many anchorages, lovely cruising and fascinating pilotage.

Tidal Streams
In the entrance to Long Island Bay, between Crookhaven and the Fastnet, the streams set E and W, the E-going stream making at –0455 Cobh and the W-going at +0115 Cobh. Spring rate is 2·5 kn around the salient points and in the narrow channels between the islands, decreasing in strength towards

the head of the bay. The generally E-going stream sets SE and S through the channels between the outer islands, the W-going stream NW and N.

Dangers
There are many drying and underwater rocks within a cable of the shores in this area. The principal hazards further offshore are:
Bullig Reef, two rocks awash at LW, 4 cables N of Cape Clear Island.
Bream Rocks (dry 1·8m) and **Greymare Rocks**, with less than 2m, forming a reef extending for 3·5 cables NE–SW, 2 cables S of Heir Island
Toorane Rocks, reef 5 cables by 2, extending NE–

SW, 2 cables W of Bream Rocks. The SW part dries 2·8m and the NE part has two heads above HW.

Anima Rock (dries 0·1m), in mid-channel between East Calf and Heir Island

Rock with 2·1m, in mid-channel between East Calf and the Carthy's Islands group

Rock with 1·8m, 2·5 cables SW of East Calf

Rock with 1·8m, 2·5 cables SW of Middle Calf

Foal Rocks (dries 2m), **Sharragh's Rock** (dries 2·8m), and a **rock** 1 cable N of Sharragh's Rock uncovering at LW, all 3 to 5 cables E of Carthy's Island.

Amelia Rock, 2·1m, 4 cables WSW of Castle Island

Rowmore Rocks, with less than 2m, 2 cables NW of West Skeam Island.

Derreen Rocks (dry 3.4m), between Horse and Castle Islands

Mweel Ledges (drying 3.6m), extending 2 cables W of Castle Island

Bull Rock (dries 1.8m), in the middle of the entrance to Schull Harbour

Baker Rock (dries 0·1m), 0·5 cable off the W shore of Schull Harbour, 1·5 cables N of Schull Point.

Lights and Marks

Amelia buoy, SHM Fl G 3s

Long Island Point, white tower Q(3) 10s 16m 8M

Schull leading lights 346°, Oc 5s 11M, front 5m rear 8m, white lattice masts NE of Schull pier. Difficult to distinguish by day.

Bull Rock, stayed perch PHM, Fl(2) R 6s 4m 4M.

Gascanane Sound and Cape Clear to Schull

Making N from Gascanane Sound or Cape Clear Island, course can be set W of West Calf Island or through Calf Sound, between East and Middle Calf Islands. The only danger on the course W of West Calf is the Bullig Reef (described in *North Coast of Cape Clear Island,* above). For Calf Sound, steer first for the highest point of Middle Calf (11m). Long Island Point light tower closed behind the NE point of Middle Calf Island 320° clears the rock (with 1·8m) SW of East Calf. Hold mid-channel through the sound and when clear head for Amelia buoy 313°, distant 1·25M. The buoy and Long Island Point will be almost in line on this course, which passes to the

SW of the Carthy's Island group. Carthy's Island should be given a berth of at least a cable. Give Long Island Point a berth of a cable, and leave Bull Rock perch well to port on entering Schull Harbour. Mweel Ledges extend almost 3 cables W of Castle Island, with mussel rafts N of them.

Carthy's Island group

⊕ *CI* 51°29'·4N 9°30'·5W (3 cables SW)

There are several dangerous rocks to the SE and E of the Carthy's Island group. If Foal and Sharragh's Rocks are not showing, a mid-channel course between the Carthy group and East Calf clears them. Near LW the 2·1m rock S of Foal Rocks may be hazardous; waypoint ⊕ *FR* 51°29'·3N 9°29'·7W clears it to the S.

Anchorage

There is an attractive daytime anchorage inside the Carthy's Island group. Approach through the narrow channel SE of Carthy's Island, which has least depth 3m, or else by the channel between North and South Carthy's Islands, which has 1·2m. If using this entrance, keep the N face of South Carthy's Island open so as to pass well N of Sharragh's Rock and its N outlier. This anchorage is subject to some swell if there is a sea running in the bay. It is also exposed to NW winds when the rocks NE of Carthy's Island cover as the tide rises, and the holding is reported poor due to kelp.

ROARINGWATER BAY

51°31'·5N 9°26'W

The channel E of East Calf Island is wide and deep but the dangerous Toorane and Anima Rocks lie in mid-channel. To clear W of these rocks (and E of Sharragh's Rock), steer 336° for the conspicuous Barnacleeve Gap. The Gap is just E of Mount Gabriel, which is 404m high with two conspicuous white radar domes on its summit – from the S they look like a crab's eyes *(see photograph)*. If bad visibility prevents this line being seen, steer for East Calf Island and approach to 1 cable off its SE point before turning on to a course of 010° to leave the foul ground E of East Calf to port and Anima Rock to starboard. Alternatively, stay close W of longitude 9°28'·4W once well clear N of Gascanane Sound.

Carthy's Islands anchorage from the E

Mount Gabriel (L) and Barnacleeve Gap (R) from the SE

Toorane Rocks are usually marked by breakers but the westernmost heads only show at extreme LW.

Anima Rock dries only 0·1m and frequently does not break. It may be passed on its S side with the S shores of Middle and West Calf Islands just open S of East Calf Island, 250º until the W point of Horse Island bears 335°. To pass E of Anima Rock, take safe bearings on Trabawn Rock (off the SW end of Heir Island) which always shows, or use waypoint ⊕*AE* 51°29'·3N 9°27'·9W, 2·5 cables E of Anima Rock. There is a deep channel N and NE of Toorane and Greymare Rocks but this is not recommended without local knowledge.

Rowmore Rocks, N of West Skeam Island, have less than 2m but are entirely surrounded by mussel rafts which extend the length of West Skeam and halfway across the channel to the N. They are marked at their NW and NE corners by yellow buoys. Do not attempt the passage between the mussel rafts and the shore of West Skeam.

The inner part of Roaringwater Bay, NE of a line from Audley Cove to Illaunranhee, is almost entirely taken up by mussel rafts. However there is a clear passage along the NW shore, and Ballydehob and Poulgorm Bays offer attractive anchorages. Truchare Rock at the entrance to Poulgorm Bay always shows. Ballydehob Bay has a drying quay immediately below the weir at the bridge, accessible by dinghy and a short walk from the village. PO, shops, pubs, restaurants, laundry.

Castle Island and Horse Island
51°30'·5N 9°29'·3W
Derreen Rocks, which dry 3·4m, lie in mid-channel between Castle and Horse Islands. Castle Island Spit, with 0·6m, extends 4 cables NE from the E end of Castle Island. There is a navigable channel

with least depth 2·7m between these dangers. Approaching from Gascanane Sound with Barnacleeve Gap bearing 336° (see above, Roaringwater Bay), when the Fastnet Rock comes in transit between Carthy's Islands alter course to pass 0·5 cable SE of Castle Island. When the E end of Castle Island is abeam, steer 041° until within 2 cables of the N shore of the Sound to clear S of Castle Island Spit.

The N side of Horse Island is shoal, so it is preferable to hold closer to the mainland side of Horse Island Channel once clear of Castle Island Spit. Horse Ridge, drying 0·6m in mid-channel and 0·2m within 50m of the mainland shore, extends between the NE end of Horse Island and the shore to the NE. It may be crossed near HW, keeping close to the mainland side.

Rossbrin
51°31'·3N 9°28'·2W
AC2129, 2184, SC5623·12
This attractive cove with its ruined castle, 2·5M E of Schull, is substantially protected from swell, but is shallow. There is a small drying pier at the head of the bay, and a slipway in the NW corner. Rossbrin Boatyard, VHF Ch 16 or phone 028 37352, hull (wood and GRP), rigging, mechanical and electrical repairs, winter storage; travelhoist capacity 16 tonnes. Advice on visitors' moorings.

Rossbrin

The Fastnet Rock in the gap between the Carthy's Islands leads between Castle and Horse Islands

Leamcon tower in line with Long Island Point beacon leads between Amelia Rock and the rocks to the SW of Castle Island

Passage SW of Castle Island

Leamcon Tower (on the 107m summit, 1·5M N of Goat Island) in line with Long Island Point beacon 281° leads between the rocks W of Castle Island and Amelia Rock, but also leads very close to the rocks SW of the SW point of Castle Island. (Historic buildings enthusiasts may wish to note that the hilltop tower is not the 15th-century Leamcon Castle; this is the ruin on Castle Point, 1·5M to the SW of the Tower.)

SCHULL HARBOUR

⊕*SC*, 51°30'·5N 9°32'W
AC2129, 2184, SC5623·12, Imray C56 and Plan
Schull Harbour affords good shelter except in strong S or SE winds. The entrance lies between Schull Point on the W and Coosheen Point on the E. Foul ground extends 0·75 cable N of the Bull Rock perch; the rock is otherwise steep-to. The rest of

the W shore is clear, but the E shore should not be approached closer than a cable. A hazardous rock is reported to lie approximately 1.5 cables SE of the S leading beacon, near the 3·7m sounding on AC 2129 and 2184 at the head of the harbour; its position is marked by a noticeable gap in the moorings. It is a tempting but inadvisable place to anchor.

Anchorage

One cable E of the pier in 2 to 4m, good holding. An anchor light and tripping line are essential. Stay clear of the fairway to the pier, which is marked by lines of dan buoys. There are visitors' moorings on the NE side of the harbour; contact Schull Watersports for details. Constant –0027 Cobh; MHWS 3·2m, MHWN 2·7m, ML 1·8m.

There is 3m alongside the pier from the ice plant to the head, but the pier is often occupied by fishing

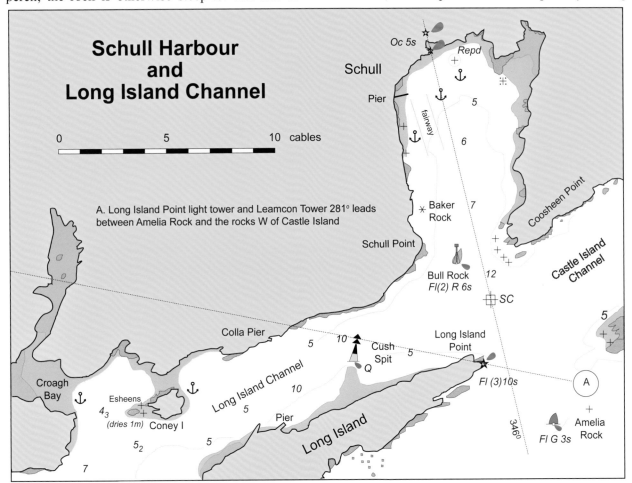

Schull Harbour and Long Island Channel

0   5   10 cables

A. Long Island Point light tower and Leamcon Tower 281° leads between Amelia Rock and the rocks W of Castle Island

Oc 5s

Schull

Repd

Pier

fairway

5

6

Coosheen Point

Baker Rock   7

Schull Point

Bull Rock
Fl(2) R 6s   12

Castle Island Channel

⊞ SC

5

Colla Pier   10   Cush Spit   Long Island Point   5

Croagh Bay   Esheens   Long Island Channel   10

4₃   Q

(dries 1m) Coney I   5   Pier   Long Island

5₂   5

7

Fl (3)10s   A

346°   Amelia Rock
Fl G 3s

Schull Pier from the NW

vessels. The main steps on the N side are used by the ferry to Cape Clear. A pontoon is available for dinghy landing, but may also be crowded in summer. At the time of writing (2008) there are proposals for a 200-berth marina.

Facilities

Water on the pier. Diesel by tanker, phone 028 28116 or 21024. Schull Watersports keeps a range of chandlery, phone 028 28554. Sailmaker, Fastnet Sails, phone Christophe Houdaille 028 28628, mobile 086 176 2377. Shops, pubs, restaurants, bank, PO. Showers at the sailing centre. HM phone 028 28136, mobile 086 103 9105. Schull Harbour Sailing Club. Ferry to Cape Clear Island in summer.

SCHULL AND CAPE CLEAR TO BALTIMORE NORTH PASSAGE
AC2129, SC5623·12

Entering Calf Sound from the N, keep Long Island Point light tower closed behind the NE point of Middle Calf Island 320° to clear the 1·8m rock SW of East Calf Island. When the NW shore of Heir Island opens S of East Calf 052°, steer 090° for Drowlaun Point to clear Toorane Rocks.

Schull is a popular place; the harbour and pier can be crowded at times

Bull Rock and its perch, at the entrance to Schull Harbour, viewed from the SE. Schull pier, R centre

Long Island Channel and Lough Buidhe, looking W from Long Island; Goat Island Little (L, with its beacon), Goat Island (L centre), Dromadda and Duharrig centre. Rock Island lighthouse at the entrance to Crookhaven in the distance

From Cape Clear North Harbour, steer 012° for the middle of East Calf until Carrigmore, in the middle of Gascanane Sound, is open W of Illaunbrock 110° (waypoint ⊕*BR,* 51°27'·6N 9°29'·2W, *Plan on p90*). Then steer 065° to pass 1·5 cables NW of Drowlaun Point (waypoint ⊕*DP,* 51°28'·7N 9°26'·2W, *Plan on p90*). Once past Drowlaun Point, bear to starboard to bring the Point just to the right of Mount Lahan 77m) on Cape Clear Island astern, and stay on this transit until abreast the SW-most of the Catalogues. For the remainder of the passage, with Plan and photographs, see the Directions for the outward passage on p86.

An alternative route from Schull (with sufficient rise of tide) runs N of Heir Island and through Goose Island Channel. Refer to the Directions on p88.

SCHULL TO CROOKHAVEN AND MIZEN HEAD
AC2184, SC5623
Tidal Streams
In Lough Buidhe, Long Island Channel and Castle Island Channel the streams make E and W at a maximum rate of 1·5 kn at springs, but E and W of Goat Island they set N and S. The stream starts S through Man-of-War and Goat Island Sounds and E through Long Island Channel at –0530 Cobh; it starts W through Long Island Channel and N through Goat Island and Man-of-War Sounds at +0030 Cobh. The E-going stream S of Long Island runs towards Sherkin Island and the North Passage to Baltimore.

Long Island pier

Dangers
Esheens, reef drying up to 1m in places, extending a cable W from Coney Island

Sound Rock, dries 1·8m, a cable W of Garillaun off the W end of Long Island

Bulligmore, 0·9m, 6 cables WSW of Illaunricmonia

N and S **Barrel Rocks** (drying 1·4 and 1·8m), 2 cables E of Duharrig

Amsterdam Reef (dries 0·3m), 2 cables SSW of

Amsterdam Rock (0·3m high, not 1·2m as charted), at the W entrance to Toormore Bay

Black Horse Rocks, (drying), extending 0·75 cable N of Alderman Rocks (9m high), on the S side of the entrance to Crookhaven

Lights and Marks
Cush Spit buoy, N Card Q

Goat Island Little, white stone beacon, unlit

Rock Island, white tower, Fl WR 8s 20m W13M R11M, W over Long Island Bay to 281°, R 281°–340°; inside the harbour, R 281°–348°; W to shore. Shows red over safe water offshore to the SE but over Black Horse and Alderman Rocks at the entrance to Crookhaven; white to E and NE, and to the W over the harbour.

Black Horse Rocks, stayed perch N Card, unlit

Mizen Head, white tower, Iso 4s 55m 15M.

Directions
W of the Cush Spit buoy, Long Island Channel is clean on both sides, and the S side of the island is also clean to within a cable of the shore. There are three passages to the W from Long Island Channel: Goat Island Sound, Man-of-War Sound and Barrel Sound.

The S sides of Goat Island Little and Illaunricmonia to the W are also clean, but Bulligmore, WSW of Illaunricmonia, is dangerous, especially in settled conditions when it may not be breaking. Carrigduff (close S of Long Island) open of Goat Island Little 070° leads S of Bulligmore, or stay S of 51°28'·7N.

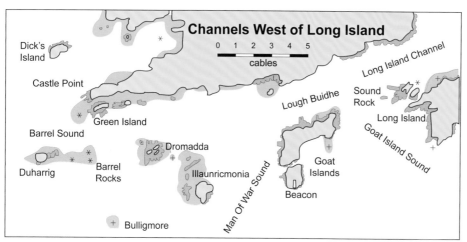

high) is clean on its S and E sides but foul to N and W. Goat and Little Goat Islands, the latter with its white beacon, are clean on their W sides.

Barrel Sound

Barrel Sound lies between Castle Point (on which is the conspicuous Leamcon Castle) and the islets to the NW of Illaunricmonia of which Dromadda (12m high) is the furthest N, and Duharrig (5m high) the furthest W. There is foul ground for 2·5 cables E of Duharrig where the Barrel Rocks dry 1·4 and 1·8m. Green Island, S of Castle Point has foul ground E of it and for 0·25 cable S of it. After passing down Long Island Channel continue a mid-channel course through Lough Buidhe, which lies between Goat Island and the mainland. Then steer to leave Green Island a cable to starboard and pass N of Dromadda, the Barrels and Duharrig. There are no dangers on the course from Duharrig to Crookhaven.

Anchorage

Anchorage is available in 3·5m E of Coney Island, on the N side of the sound, and in Croagh Bay, W of Coney Island, giving the W side of the island a berth of 2 cables.

Anchorage is also available off the small pier on Long Island, W of Cush Spit, in 3m, sand.

Goat Island Sound

Goat Island Sound, between Long Island and Goat Island, is over 2 cables wide at its N end. Sound Rock lies a cable W of Garillaun off the W end of Long Island.

Man of War Sound

Man of War Sound, between Goat Island and Illaunricmonia is free of danger. Illaunricmonia (7m

Toormore Bay

51°30'N 9°39'W
AC2184, SC5623·11
Amsterdam Rock marks the W side of the approach to Toormore Bay; beware the drying Amsterdam

Coney Island (R centre) seen from Long Island; Croagh Bay to the W, with Esheens reef showing

Barrel Sound from the WNW; Leamcon Castle (L), Dromadda in line with the Goat Islands (centre), Illaunricmonia (centre R) and Duharrig (R). Cape Clear Island in the distance

Carrigduff open of Goat Island Little (with the white beacon) clears Bulligmore to the S. View from the WSW

Lough Buidhe and Long Island Channel from the W; Dromadda, bottom, with (bottom to top from lower R) Illaunric-monia, Man of War Sound, the Goat Islands, Goat Island Sound, Long Island, Castle Island and Horse Island. Coney Island centre L and Schull harbour top L

Reef, 2 cables SSW of the rock. Brow Head Tower (111m) well open S of Rock Island lighthouse, 238°, leads clear S of Amsterdam Reef. The E shore of the bay is foul and should be given a berth of 2 cables.

Anchorage

There is a delightful fine-weather anchorage in the bay N of Reenard Point, sheltered from SW to N but untenable in fresh S to SE winds. Anchor off the beach in 3m.

Goleen from the ESE; the church (top L) is conspicuous from seaward.

Goleen from the ESE

Goleen
51°29'·6N 9°41'·5W
AC2184, SC5623·11

One mile N of Crookhaven lighthouse there is a narrow cleft in the rocks, named "Kireal-coegea" on AC2184, which has a quay offering a temporary berth to a small yacht in quiet weather. At the head of the inlet is Goleen village, whose church spire can be seen from some distance off, though the cleft does not become apparent till very close. The high sides provide excellent shelter from offshore breezes but the inlet is open to the SE. There are no dangers in the approach but in the entrance itself there are rocks awash at HW on the N side, so keep over to port. The quay marked on the chart is the old one; the new quay, 30m long, on the S side, is closer to the mouth of the creek. Turning room is very restricted, with only 40m between the quay face and the cliff opposite. There is no room to anchor and the inner part of the inlet dries. Shop, PO, pubs, restaurant at Goleen.

CROOKHAVEN
⊕ *CK* 51°28'·5N 9°42'W
AC2184, SC5623·11, Imray C56 and Plan

The lighthouse on Rock Island at the N side of the entrance is conspicuous. Alderman Rocks (9m high) lie from 2 to 3·5 cables offshore, E of Streek Head at the S side of the entrance. Black Horse Rocks extend 0·75 cable N of them, marked by an unlit N Card beacon which should not be approached closer than 0·5 cable. Alderman Sound, W of Alderman Rocks, should not be attempted as it is narrowed by rocks on both sides. Crookhaven offers all-round shelter although somewhat windswept in heavy weather, and is very easy to enter by day or night. The inlet is 2M long and at its entrance is 2 cables wide, but it narrows to 1·5 cables about 5 cables from the entrance and then opens up again to about 3 cables in width W of Rock Island. Both shores are steep-to. There are several old watch towers on the shores.

Streek Head is 44m high and bold, with several stacks including Gokane, 6m high, close inshore. There is only a slight tidal stream in the harbour. The tide sets strongly through Alderman Sound and care should be taken not to be drawn into it in calm weather. Constant –0045 Cobh; MHWS 3·3m, MHWN 2·7m, ML 1·8m.

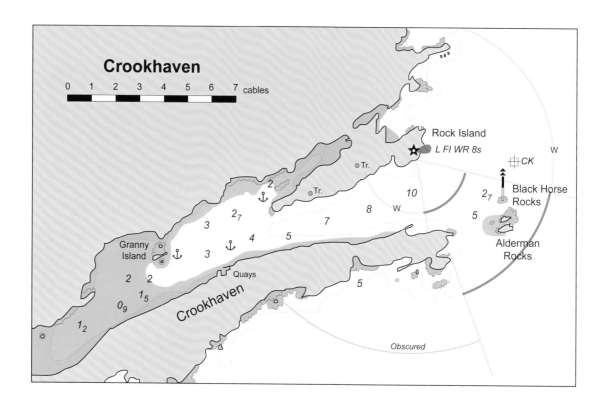

Crookhaven from the E; Alderman Rocks, bottom L, Crookhaven village, L centre. Brow Head top L, with Barley Cove and Mizen Head at top

Rock Island lighthouse from the ESE; Black Horse Rocks and perch, L

Crookhaven from the E

Anchorage

- There are visitors' moorings in mid-channel off the village.
- Anchor off the village and well out in the middle of the bay in 3m, good holding, but weedy in places.
- In E winds, anchor N of the W point of Rock Island.
- In fresh W winds some shelter may be had in the lee of Granny Island on the N shore, NW of the village; beware of Row Rock (dries 0·3m), close S of Granny Island.

Facilities

Shops, pubs, restaurants. Dinghy landing pontoon. Water on the quay. Crookhaven Sailing Club near the quay.

Chapter 3

Dunmanus Bay and Bantry Bay

Approaches to Berehaven from the S; Pipers Sound, centre, Bere Island and Berehaven R, Dunboy Bay L, Castletownbere harbour upper L centre

The south west coast of Ireland is penetrated by four long and deep inlets, geologically rias, or drowned river valleys, rather than fjords. These four – Dunmanus Bay, Bantry Bay, Kenmare River and Dingle Bay – are surrounded by spectacular mountain scenery, and the five peninsulas and their villages are renowned tourist destinations.

Mizen Head, Ireland's most southwesterly point, has a lighthouse which – somewhat surprisingly – was built as recently as 1959. The elegant bridge spanning the chasm between the shore and the lighthouse stack, however, dates from 1907, because it was built to provide access to the fog

signal on the Mizen, which is on the same stack but pre-dates the lighthouse by 52 years. The one-time keepers' houses are now a lighthouse museum, with quite possibly the finest view of any museum in the world.

Dunmanus Bay is one of Ireland's less-well-travelled inlets, but is a beautiful and peaceful place with several fine anchorages.

The wide and deep inlet of Bantry Bay has been a vital commercial and strategic harbour for centuries. It was here, at Dunboy Castle in 1602, that the forces of Donal Cam O'Sullivan Bere made Ireland's last stand against the English in the

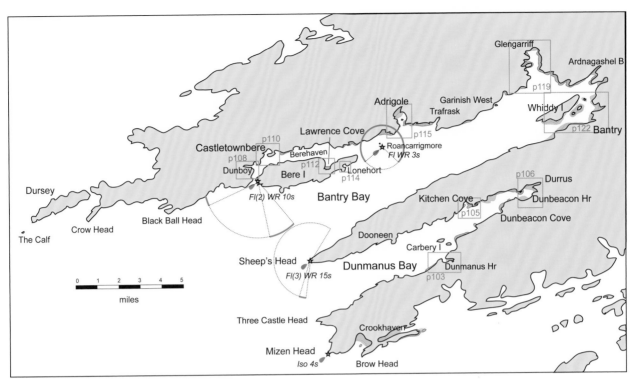

Tudor wars, after the Battle of Kinsale was already lost. An abortive French invasion was aimed here in 1796, and as a result the Bay, and many other strategic places around Ireland, were fortified with Martello towers, their squat circular design and their name copied from the fort at Cape Mortella in Corsica. Bantry Bay was one of the four so-called Treaty Ports, continuing to be used as a base by the Royal Navy after the partition of Ireland in 1921 and only relinquished in 1937. The relics of its military past may be seen in abundance on Bere Island, where some of the old buildings have been maintained as training bases by the Irish defence forces. Castletownbere (Castletown Bearhaven on the charts) has traditionally been the centre of the whitefish fishery in Ireland, but in common with many other fishing ports its economy is facing severe challenges. It is a no-nonsense place with few pretensions, but nonetheless a lovely town with a fascinating history. If you have read the bestselling *McCarthy's Bar* in paperback you may recognise the front cover picture in the main street of Castletownbere.

The busy market town of Bantry (3000) stands at the head of the bay, its broad harbour sheltered by Whiddy Island. At the west end of Whiddy is an oil jetty, with a huge tank farm ashore. The facility was built in the 1970's to accommodate the world's largest ships, but the jetty has been disused since 1979 when the tanker *Betelgeuse* exploded while alongside, killing 51 people, most of them members of the ship's crew. The modernistic statue of Saint Brendan the Navigator in the square at

Bantry, presented to the town by the oil company to celebrate the opening of the terminal, stands as a mute and ironic memorial to the disaster. Whiddy's tanks are used as a storage and transhipment facility for crude oil, and each year about a dozen tankers, of 25,000 to 320,000 deadweight tonnes, load and unload from a mooring buoy 6 cables north of the jetty. Bantry town itself is rich in history; the impressive Bantry House is open to the public and hosts regular concerts.

Facing Whiddy Island in the northeast corner of Bantry Bay is the picture-postcard natural harbour of Glengarriff, a deservedly popular destination by land and sea. The bay is sheltered by tree-clad islands, the largest of which, Illnacullen or Garinish Island, has an extraordinary Italianate garden designed a hundred years ago by the English architect Harold Peto for the island's owner Annan Bryce. With the eccentric energy characteristic of his era and the help of the eminent gardener Murdoch MacKenzie from Inverewe in Scotland, Bryce capitalised on the location's famously mild climate to turn a windswept and rocky islet into a paradise of subtropical plants. The gardens – well worth a visit – are open to the public and there is a ferry to the island from the jetty at Glengarriff.

Charts
The small craft folio SC5623 Bantry Bay to Kinsale covers the whole area of this chapter in detail. In terms of individual charts, on the smaller scale, AC2424 Kenmare River to Cork Harbour or Imray's C56, provide coverage. The Imray chart has several

Mizen Head from the S, with Three Castle Head beyond

useful harbour plans, but AC2552 is essential for Dunmanus Bay and AC1838 and 1840 for Bantry Bay.

Tidal Streams

Between Crookhaven and Mizen Head the streams set E and W. Off Mizen Head and Three Castle Head the streams run S, and NW by N, forming eddies off Three Castle Head. The S-going stream makes at –0505 Cobh and the NW-going at +0120 Cobh. The spring rate off Mizen Head is 4 kn and off Three Castle Head 3 kn, decreasing to 1·5 kn 5M offshore. This results in a race off Mizen Head, which may extend the whole way N across Dunlough Bay to Three Castle Head, and can be dangerous to smaller craft, especially with wind against tide. Tidal streams in Dunmanus Bay are almost imperceptible.

Dangers – Crookhaven to Dunmanus Bay

Black Horse Rocks, (drying), extending 0·75 cable N of Alderman Rocks (9m high), on the S side of the entrance to Crookhaven

Devil's Rock, awash at HW, in the middle of Barley Cove bay

Carrignagower, awash at HW, 1 cable offshore 5 cables ESE of Mizen Head.

South Bullig, 4·6m, 4 cables SW of Three Castle Head

Lights

Mizen Head, white tower, Iso 4s 55m 15M.

Sheep's Head, 7m white tower Fl(3) WR 15s 83m W18M R15M, R 007°–017° W 017°–212°, obscured elsewhere. The narrow red sector leads W of the South Bullig rock, and the light is obscured E of this.

Offshore weather buoy

Weather buoy M3, yellow, Fl(5) Y 20s, 28M WSW of Mizen Head in 51°13' N 10°33' W.

Crookhaven to Dunmanus Bay

Brow Head, 1·75M E of Mizen Head, is 111m high and slopes steeply seaward. There is a ruined signal tower near its summit. Over a hundred years ago, Guglielmo Marconi built a radio station here to receive the news from America and to transmit the European news to passing liners. Between Brow Head and Mizen Head lies Barley Cove, which has the finest beach in West Cork.

Mizen Head

In settled conditions Mizen Head may be approached to within a cable (but beware of Carrignagower, 5 cables ESE); however in heavy weather, especially with wind over tide, it should be given a berth of a mile.

DUNMANUS BAY

AC2552

Dunmanus Bay is 3·5M wide at its entrance between Sheep's Head and Three Castle Head, and extends 13M ENE. The bay has three good anchorages: Dunmanus Harbour, Kitchen Cove and Dunbeacon Harbour; there is also an anchorage at Dunbeacon Cove on the S shore, near the head of the bay.

Generally the outer part of the bay is steep-to and free of dangers, but **South Bullig,** 4·6m, 4 cables SW of Three Castle Head, breaks in heavy weather. Bird Island, 51m high and 3M from Three Castle Head, is close to the shore, and the passage inside it is foul. There are sunken rocks extending 1 cable offshore, 1M SW of Dunmanus Point.

Dunmanus Harbour

⊕*DH* 51°32'·9N 9°40'W

Inset on AC2552, and Plan

There are sunken rocks off the E side just inside the entrance which may extend further than on the Plan or on AC2552, and the W side is also foul, restricting the entrance to 0·5 cable. Enter on a mid-channel course heading for a point 50m W of the ruins of Dunmanus Castle on the S shore. Anchor in the centre of the harbour in 4 to 6m, sand and soft mud. The E side of the harbour dries out. There is sometimes a roll in the harbour if the swell is

Dunmanus Harbour from the E; Sheep's Head. top R

running up the bay outside. Constant –0050 Cobh; MHWS 3·4m, MHWN 2·7m, ML 1·9m.

Dangers – inner part of Dunmanus Bay

Carbery Breaker, 2·3m, extending 3 cables from the W end of Carbery Island

Murphy Rocks, dry 1·5m, 1·5 cables off the

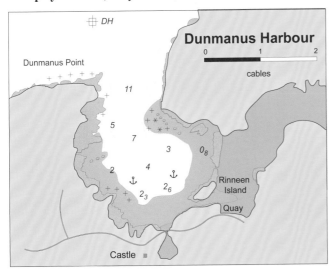

mainland shore E of Carbery Island

Carriglea Rock, dries 3·2m, at the W entrance to Dunbeacon Cove.

Unnamed rock with 1·7m, 3 cables offshore, 5 cables ENE of Reen Point, E of Kitchen Cove

Carrigtuil, dries 0·2m, in the bay W of Rossmore Point at the entrance to Dunbeacon Harbour

Murphy Rock, awash at LW, on the S side of Dunbeacon Harbour

Carrigbroanty, dries 0·5m, 3 cables ENE of Mannion's Island in Dunbeacon Harbour.

Carbery Island

Carbery Island, 15m high and 4 cables long, lies in the middle of the bay, with the smaller Furze and Cold Islands to its E. There is a single house on Carbery, occasionally occupied. Carbery Breaker extends 3 cables from the W end of the island, and the NW and SW shores are foul for 1·5 cables. The gap in Knockaughna Mt. (268m) open N of Carbery Island 080° clears Carbery Breaker to the N *(see photograph on p104)*. There is a clear passage between Furze and Carbery Islands in mid-channel, staying within 1 cable SE of Cold Island to avoid Murphy Rocks. The other channels between the islands and E of Furze Island are foul.

Between Carbery Island and Drishane Point the S shore of the bay should not be approached closer than 2 cables. East of Drishane Point the shore is clean until Carriglea Rock is reached, at the W entrance to Dunbeacon Cove.

North Shore of Dunmanus Bay – Sheep's Head to Kitchen Cove

If approaching from Sheep's Head the N shore is steep-to as far as Kilcrohane, opposite Carbery

Dunmanus Harbour and Castle

Gap in Knockaughna Mountain (L) open N of Carbery Island clears Carbery Breaker

Dooneen Pier from the SE; note the bollard on top of the rock, L centre

Island. Give Pointabulloge a berth of over 1 cable to the S and 2 cables to the W to avoid the reefs off it, and give the coast from there to Kitchen Cove a berth of a cable. Lord Brandon's Tower, 49m, in the bay W of Pointabulloge, is conspicuous. Dooneen Pier, 2 cables N of Dooneen Point, might offer an intriguing temporary berth in settled weather; the pier has projecting bolts on its face, but opposite it is an above-water rock with a substantial bollard on top, and there is 5·6m of water between the pier and the rock. Kilcrohane Pier, 1 cable N of Kilcrohane Point, is small and not recommended for alongside berthing.

Kitchen Cove
⊕*KC* 51°35'·45N 9°38'·1W
Inset on AC2552, and Plan
Kitchen Cove is 1·5M beyond Pointabulloge. The

Kitchen Cove from the SE; Owen's Island at L

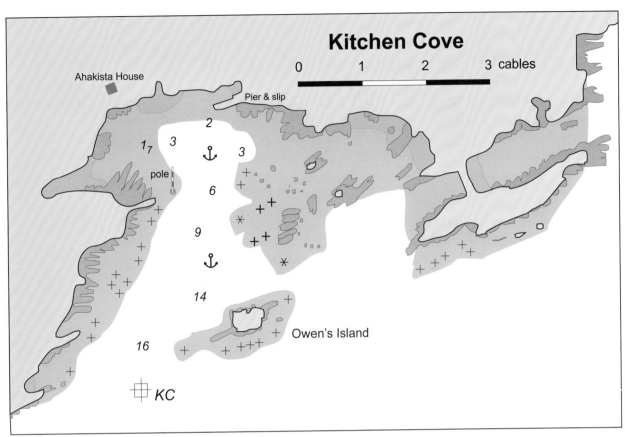

entrance, 2 cables wide, is between Owen's Island and the W shore. Owen's Island is a low grassy islet in front of the cove with rocks awash at HW extending 0·75 cable off its W side and 0·5 cable off its E side. All the E side of the harbour is strewn with rocks, and there is also a dangerous rock, drying 0·2m, 0·5 cable off the inner point on the W side. This rock is marked by a slim red-and-white banded pole. The N shore is wooded.

Anchorage

The best anchorage is NW of Owen's Island, midway between it and the W shore in 9m, mud. The NW corner of the bay, in front of Ahakista House, is taken up by moorings, but anchorage is available in 3 to 4m in the centre of the bay, S of the pier. The holding is variable, good in the centre but poor in the corner SE of the pier. The pier, with 1.5m at its outer end, extends 0.5 cable WSW from the rocky point where "Quay" is marked on AC2552. Water tap on the pier; pubs at Ahakista.

Kitchen Cove to Dunbeacon Harbour

There is a narrow passage N of Owen's Island, but

Kitchen Cove from the NW

The inner part of Kitchen Cove from the SE; the pole beacon and Ahakista House, L, and the pier head, extreme R

Three Castle Head, Bird Island and Carbery Island in line lead between the dangers in the upper Bay

the safe course is S of the island. Beyond Reen Point are several dangers in the middle of the bay; a rock with 1·7m lies 3 cables offshore, 5 cables ENE of Reen Point. **Doona Rock**, 7·5 cables E of Reen Point and off the S shore, with 4·9m, and another rock with 4·1m, 2 cables W of Doona Rock, may break in a heavy swell. Three Castle Head, Bird Island and the N side of Carbery Island in transit 232° lead between Doona Rock and the 1·7m rock. Good visibility is necessary for this clearing line

(see photograph).

When past these dangers, the course for the entrance to Dunbeacon Harbour is clear. Give Twopoint Island, 5 cables W of Dunbeacon Point, a berth of a cable, and avoid **Carrigtuil** (dries 0·2m) in the bay W of Rossmore Point.

Dunbeacon Cove
51°35'·5N 9°35'·3W
Dunbeacon Cove may be identified by the wall of

Four Mile Water and Durrus Pier, at the head of Dunmanus Bay

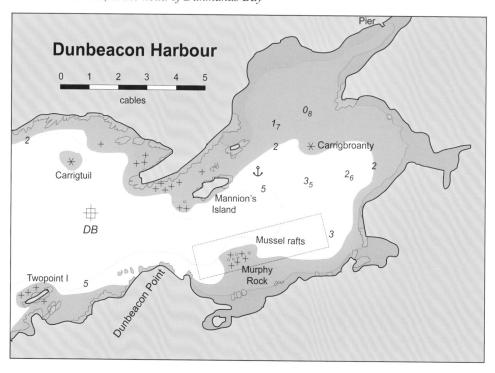

Dunbeacon Harbour and Dunmanus Bay from the E; Mannion's Island, centre, Four Mile Water and Durrus pier and village, bottom. Note the mussel rafts, L

a ruined castle to the NE. The cove is small and its inner portion dries, so it offers limited shelter. Anchor midway between the E shore and Carriglea Rock in 4m, mud. Land at the quay up the cove, which dries at LW. Restaurant 1·5 km on the Durrus road.

Dunbeacon Harbour
⊕ *DB* 51°36'·4N 9°34'W
Inset on AC2552, and Plan
Dunbeacon Harbour is shallow on its N and NE sides, and is obstructed by **Murphy Rock**, awash at LW, on its S side. Halfway between Mannion's Island and the E shore is the drying rock **Carrigbroanty**. The S half of the Harbour is occupied by mussel rafts, and Murphy Rock may be avoided simply by staying N of the rafts.

Anchorage
Anchor close to the E side of Mannion's Island in 2 to 4m, with Twopoint Island in line with the S side of Mannion's Island. The pier marked at Sea Lodge on AC2552 is ruined. There is a pier, with 0·5m at its head, on the N shore at the narrows of Four Mile Water, the channel leading to Durrus village from the NE corner of the bay. Durrus, 1·5 km from this pier, has shops, PO, restaurants and pubs. Constant –0040 Cobh; MHWS 3·3m, MHWN 2·6m, ML 1·9 m.

Sheep's Head
Sheep's Head is 168m high with fine cliffs. The little lighthouse dates only from 1968, and the headland was so inaccessible at the time that all the construction materials had to be carried in by helicopter. The Head is steep-to but **North Bullig Rock** with 6·2m over it lies 1·5 cables to the SW and breaks in severe weather. There is less tidal stream round this head than round any of its neighbours.

Castletownbere from Pipers Sound; the Port Entry Light is on the lower of the two orange leading daymarks, R, marking the channel in Pipers Sound. The harbour entrance, L

BANTRY BAY
AC1838, 1840, Imray C56 and Plan

Note: placename spellings
The charts and Ordnance Survey maps use the forms Bear Island, Bearhaven and Castletown Bearhaven. However the accepted and almost universal forms are Bere Island, Berehaven and Castletownbere.

Tidal Streams
The tidal streams are barely perceptible except in the entrance to Berehaven and Bantry Harbours. With strong S or SW winds a current sets into the bay around Sheep's Head. In the entrances to Berehaven the tidal streams run in from +0550 Cobh and out from –0025 Cobh; spring rate 2 kn (W entrance), 0·5 kn (E entrance). Constant at Castletownbere –0030 Cobh; MHWS 3·5m, MHWN 2·7m, ML 2·0m.

Dangers – Castletownbere and Approaches
Rock with 1·5m, 0·25 cable E of The Pipers, S of Pipers Point
Harbour Rock, 3·7m, in mid-channel 3·5 cables NNE of Pipers Point
Foilnaboe Rocks, a group of three drying 1·8m, 0·5 cable N of Fort Point
Rocks with 2·4m, 1·25 cables NE of Foilnaboe Rocks
Colt Rock, dries 2·1m, on the W side of the channel above Dunboy Point
Little Colt Rock, dries 0·9m, between Colt Rock and the shore to the N
Walter Scott Rock, 2·7m, 2 cables S of Dinish Island
Long Point, rocky ledge, awash at HW, extending 1 cable W of Sheep Island.
Perch Rock, 1m, on the E side of the narrows between Came Point and Dinish Island

Lights and Marks
Ardnakinna Point, white tower Fl(2)WR 10s 62m W17M, R14M, R 319°–348°, W 348°–066°, R 066°– shore. Shows red over the dangers off Sheep's Head and Three Castle Head and white over the safe approach from seaward
Castletownbere Port Entry Light 024°, orange gable, Dir Oc WRG 5s 4m W14M R11M G11M, G 020·5°–024°, W 024°–024·5°, R 024·5°–027·5°. Rear leading daymark, orange gable
Castletownbere No 1 buoy, SHM IQG, close NW of Foilnaboe Rocks
Colt Rock, PHM perch, unlit. The can topmark is surmounted by a profile of a horse.
Castletownbere No 2 buoy, PHM IQR
Walter Scott buoy, S Card Q(6) + L Fl 15s
Sheep Islands, N Card beacon, Q 3m 3M
Cametringane Spit, red col PHM, QR
Leading beacons 010°, white pillars, red stripe, Oc 3s 1M, front 4m, rear 7m.

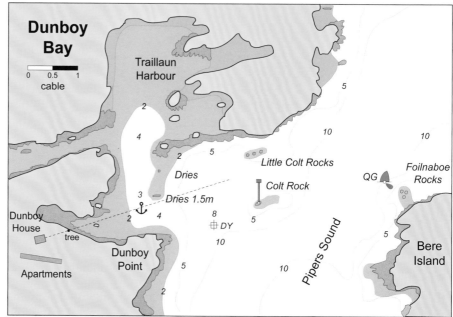

Dunboy anchorage from the NE; the restored Dunboy House, centre, with new apartment buildings behind. The front doorway of the house left of the solitary tree on the shoreline leads clear S of the drying rock, which was marked by the orange buoy, R, when this picture was taken in 2008

Colt Rock perch

Western Entrance to Berehaven

51°37'N 9°55'·4W

AC1840

Pipers Sound lies between Fair Head (45m) on the W and Ardnakinna Point on Bere Island. Inside Ardnakinna Point, the entrance narrows to 1·75 cables between Pipers Point on the W and Naglas Point on the E. **The Pipers**, which lie close to the S extremity of Pipers Point, are high, but give Pipers Point a berth of 1 cable to avoid a rock close E of them. The leading daymarks at Castletownbere may

then be identified. These marks in line 024° lead up the sound E of Harbour Rock and between the No 1 and No 2 buoys. The shore N and S of Fort Point, on the island side 7 cables NNE of Naglas Point, is foul for 0·5 cable off. Sheep Islands, 5 cables NE of Fort Point, are flat and grassy, and have foul ground extending for 1·5 cables W.

Dunboy Bay

⊕*DY* 51°38'N 9°55'·2W

AC1840 and Plan

Dunboy Bay, on the W side of Pipers Sound, provides sheltered anchorage except in E winds. The bay is dominated by Dunboy House, which was built from 1886, burned down in 1921 and is being restored as an hotel; new apartments have been built behind it. The ruins of the historic Dunboy Castle are not now discernible from seaward. A rock drying 1·5m lies one cable N of Dunboy Point. Approach the anchorage midway between Colt Rock perch and Dunboy Point to avoid the drying rock and the foul ground extending 0·3 cable N from the point. The front doorway of Dunboy House left of a conspicuous

Castletownbere from the SW; the quays on Dinish Island (R centre) have been extended NE'wards since this picture was taken. Also visible is the former Perch Rock starboard-hand beacon (centre) which was removed in 2007 and has not so far (2008) been replaced.

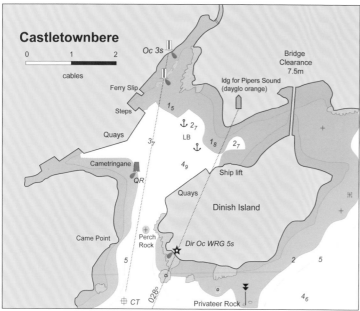

solitary tree on the edge of the grass above the sea wall leads S of the rock *(see photograph)*. Anchor in 2m, NW of the point.

There are oyster beds in Traillaun Harbour to the N of Dunboy Bay and in the SW corner of Dunboy Bay.

CASTLETOWNBERE
⊕*CT* 51°38'·6N 9°54'·5W
AC1840, Imray C56 and Plan

As an important fishing port, Castletownbere offers some of the best marine technical services, and also the best and handiest supermarket, on the south-west coast, but it has a strictly limited capacity to host yachts and the hospitality of the harbour should not be presumed upon.

The leading marks in line 010° lead through the entrance; err nothing to the E, to be sure of avoiding Perch Rock. The channel has a maintained depth of 3·7m and is only 36m wide at the narrows between Came Point and Perch Rock. The harbour area has maintained depths of 2·4 to 4·9m. A car ferry runs from Castletownbere to a slip on Bere Island, inside the Sheep Islands and S of their beacon.

Anchorage and berthing
Priority must be given to fishing vessels, ferries and the lifeboat, but there is room to anchor and good holding in the harbour, and a temporary alongside berth may be available for fuel, water and stores. Yachts should anchor NE of a line between the ferry slip and the ship lift on Dinish Island, in 2·4m. Keep well clear of the quays, and do not anchor in front of the lifeboat, which is moored fore and aft in this area. For an alongside berth contact the HM 027 70220, fax 027 70329, VHF Ch 16 and 14 (after hours 027 70128). The harbour limits extend beyond Castletownbere to include all of Berehaven from W and E entrances.

There are visitors' moorings in the bay to the E of Dinish Island (see below). The island is connected to the shore by a bridge with 7·5m clearance. At the time of writing (2008) works are in progress to extend the quays on Dinish Island NE'wards.

Facilities
Water on the pier, diesel by tanker. Petrol, gas at filling stations. Supermarkets, shops, pubs, restaurants, hotels, PO. Bus to Bantry. Small chandlery, Limar Marine, 027 70830; marine electronics, phone 027 70016. Marine engineers, Joe Tim O'Sullivan 027 70388, John O'Sullivan 027 70129 and Richard Power 027 70298.

Dangers – Berehaven
Privateer Rock, dries 1·5m, 1 cable S of Dinish Island
Volage Rock, 2·4m, 2 cables SE of Minane Island (5m high), 4 cables E of Dinish Island
Hornet Rock, 1·2m, 6 cables E of Minane Island
The **wreck** of the ***Bardini Reefer***, 6 cables E of Hornet Rock
Palmer Rock, 1·8m, 1·5 cables offshore 3 cables NE of Turk Island at the entrance to Lawrence Cove.

Castletownbere entrance; Cametringane Spit beacon, L, and the leading marks (white with red stripe), R

Privateer Rock perch

Lights and marks

Walter Scott buoy, S Card Q(6) + L Fl 15s
Privateer Rock perch, pole beacon with S Card topmark and radar reflector
Hornet Rock buoy, S Card VQ(6) + L Fl 10s
Beal Lough beacon, G pillar SHM, Fl G 3s
Bardini Reefer buoy, N Card Q
George Rock, Isolated Danger Buoy Fl(2) 10s.

If the perch on Privateer Rock can be clearly identified, it is safe to pass in mid-channel between it and the Walter Scott buoy; otherwise stay S of the buoy. The perch is a thin pole and carries a S topmark but is not painted as a cardinal mark. There are no dangers on the S side of Berehaven if the shore is given a berth of 1 cable. Pass N of the *Bardini Reefer* buoy or well to the S nearer the island shore; the wreck, a 4000-ton cargo ship which sank in 1982 after a fire on board, sits listing to starboard with her bows to the N and the remains of her upperworks, funnel and foremast conspicuous above HW. The isolated George Rock has over 7m of water and does not present a hazard to yachts.

There are fish cages off the Bere Island shore S of the Hornet Rock buoy and E of Lawrence Cove, and also NE of the George buoy, N of Carrigavaddra and NW of Roancarrigbeg; and mussel rafts off the mainland shore outside Mill Cove and NW of the George buoy.

Castletownbere visitors' moorings

There are three visitors' moorings close W of Minane Island. These are best approached on 036° with Fort Point and Pipers Point in line astern, to avoid rocks off Dinish and to the SW of the buoys.

Mill Cove
51°39'N 9°51'·9W
AC1840

Mill Cove, on the N side of Berehaven and to the N of Hornet Rock buoy, affords some shelter in N winds. Illaunboudane is a 1·5m high islet close to the E side of the entrance and there are rocks which dry 1·2 and 2·4m, 0·25 cable W and S of this. There is also a rock which dries 0·9m, 1 cable SW of Carrigagannive Point at the W side of the entrance. All the N part of the harbour dries out; anchor immediately inside the line of the E and W points of the entrance. There are oyster beds in the cove. There is a small stone pier at Sea Point E of Mill Cove.

Beal Lough is a small cove E of Sea Point which has a narrow entrance and a depth of 1·2m, soft mud bottom. A car ferry crosses from Pontoon Pier in Beal Lough to Lawrence Cove, and there is no room for a yacht to anchor. There is a sunken rock 0·5 cable SSW of the entrance.

LAWRENCE COVE
⊕ *LC* 51°38'·4N 9°49'·3W
AC1840 and Plan

Lawrence Cove (Lawrence's Cove on the chart), on the S side of Berehaven, is a good anchorage except in winds from a N'ly quarter, and has a small marina which is completely secure in all winds. From the W, the Bere Island shore is clean to within a cable; from the E, give the shore a berth of 2 cables to clear Palmer Rock and another rock N of Turk Island. Both these rocks have 1·8m at LAT. There is a fish farm E of Palmer Rock, marked on its N side by two yellow buoys. Turk Island is shown on the charts as

The wreck of the Bardini Reefer *and its N cardinal buoy, from the NE, near HW. Bere Island Boatyard is on the island shore to the SW, beyond the wreck*

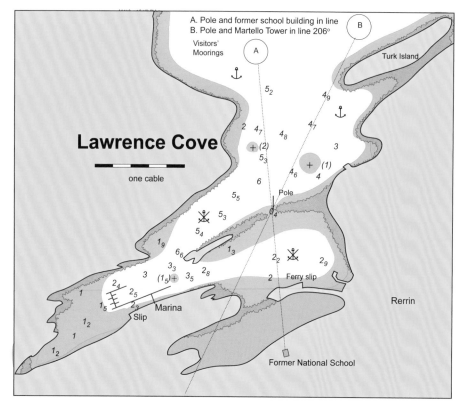

the island and the marina.

Enter the cove in mid-channel between Turk Island and the W shore. If the pole beacon on the reef can be identified, keeping it between the two-storey former school building and the Martello tower on the skyline to the SW clears the dangers in the approach *(see photographs)*.

Lawrence Cove has many signs of its military and naval past, and there is an army training base on its shores.

Marina

Lawrence Cove Marina occupies the SW corner of the cove. The marina has a least depth of 2·3m alongside. A rock with 1·5m, near the NE end of the long pontoon, is marked by a small buoy; there is 2·5m of water between the pontoon and the rock. Water and shore power on the pontoons. Slipway and 14t travelhoist, hardstanding for 20 boats; showers, toilets and laundry. Diesel. VHF Ch 16 & 37. Phone and fax 027 75044, www.lawrencecovemarina.com.

Anchorage

Anchorage in the narrow part of the channel or in

2m high but is actually about 10m.

SW of Turk Island the bay is narrowed by two rocks, one on the W side with 2m and one on the E side with less than 1m. The low island in the centre of the cove to the SW has the remains of a pier on its W end, and is joined to the E shore by a reef which almost entirely dries. The gap in the reef, with 0·4m at LAT, is marked by a slim pole. The ferry uses this passage near HW but at other times passes between

Entering Lawrence Cove, with the pole marking the gap in the reef (centre) midway between the former school (the two-storey grey building, extreme L) and the Martello tower on the hilltop, R

Approaching Lawrence Cove Marina. View from the NE; the yellow buoy and rusty tank are on the old pier at the W end of the low island

Lawrence Cove from the SW; the marina has been extended since this picture was taken

the pool SE of the island is not feasible due to the ferry and marina traffic. Anchor in 4 to 6m in the outer part of the cove (where there are also visitors' moorings) or in the bay S of Turk Island, staying well out of the fairway.

Facilities – Bere Island
Shops, PO and pub at Rerrin. Bere Island Boatyard, 027 75975, is on the Berehaven shore S of the *Bardini Reefer* wreck. Ferries from the NW end of the island (5·5 km by road) to Castletownbere and from Lawrence Cove to Pontoon Pier (4km by road from Castletownbere).

EASTERN ENTRANCE TO BEREHAVEN
51°38'·9N 9°45'·8W
AC1840, Imray C56
Lonehort Point, the E end of Bere Island, is a long low point with a shelf of rock running out for a distance of 0·5 cable. There are the 2·7m-high remains of an old pile lighthouse on the point. The islets of Roancarrigmore and Roancarrigbeg are 1·3M to the ENE.

Dangers – E and S of Bere Island
Carrigavaddra, rocky patch drying 2·7m, extending 5 cables ESE of Lonehort Point
Wrinkle Rock, dries 0·3m, between Lonehort Point and Carrigavaddra

Rock drying 0·6m, 0·5 cable S of Roancarrigmore
Sunken rocks extending 1·5 cables S of Roancarrigbeg
Wreck between Roancarrigmore and Roancarrigbeg
Doucallia Rock, dries 1·2m, 6 cables ENE of Roancarrigmore
Bulliga Ledge, 3·7m, 2·5 cables SE of Bulliga Point
Feagh Rock, 0·9m high, 4 cables S of the centre of Bere Island, with Greenane Rock (12m high) inshore of it.

Lights and marks
Carrigavaddra, S Card perch, unlit
Roancarrigmore, white tower, black band, Fl WR 3s 18m, W18M R14M, W 312°–050°, R 050°–122°, R (unintens) 122°–242°, R 242°–312°. Reserve light W8M, R6M, obsc 140°–220°. Shows white to seaward S of Bere Island, red elsewhere

Directions
Give Carrigavaddra beacon a berth of a cable, and do not attempt to pass between it and Lonehort Point. Roancarrigbeg, 3 cables N of Roancarrigmore, is an irregular patch of rocks, 2 cables long and 1 cable wide. At HW it forms four flat-topped islets 6m high, with the conspicuous remains of a wreck on it. The channel between Roancarrigmore and

Roancarrigbeg is fouled by rocks and a wreck, and is not navigable without local knowledge.

South side of Bere Island

Between Doonbeg Head (84m), the island's S point, and Cloonaghlin Head, 2M E of it and with a Martello tower on its summit, lies **Feagh Rock** (0·9m high), S of **Greenane Rock** (12m high). As it lies 1 cable outside the direct line of the heads it is important to keep well out from and between Doonbeg and Cloonaghlin Heads, especially at night. There is an islet, Carrignanean, close S of Doonbeg Head.

Lonehort

⊕*LH* 51°38'·1N 9°47'·5W
AC1840 and Plan
This cove 7·5 cables SW of Lonehort Point offers splendid shelter in reasonable weather,

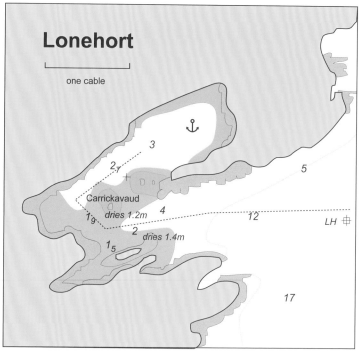

but as there are no marks in the entrance it must be entered with caution. The line on the plan indicates the course to follow. Carrigavaud, the rock in the entrance, is sharp-tipped and dries about 1·2m. Its position when covered is often indicated by weed. The rock on the S side, which never covers, runs out below water at its E and W ends and extends as a half tide reef (drying 1·4m) about 30m N into the channel at its E end. Steer to pass 50m N of this rock to clear its half-tide portion. As the W end of this rock comes abeam and the small creek in the SW corner opens up, close the W shore to clear Carrigavaud before turning NW. Then keep the N shore close aboard. There is a least depth of 1·9m in the entrance.

Anchor in the centre of the pool at the NE end of the cove in about 3m. Swinging room is somewhat limited.

Berehaven to Adrigole

East of Roancarrigmore and Roancarrigbeg the position of Doucallia Rock must be noted as it is in the direct approach to Adrigole, and on the course up Bantry Bay to Glengarriff. Bulliga Ledge, with 3·7m, 7 cables NNE of Doucallia and 3 cables offshore, should not trouble a yacht except in a heavy swell. To pass between Doucallia and Bulliga Ledge, bring Leahern's Point, S of Lonehort Harbour, just open S of Roancarrigmore bearing 238°. The centre of the entrance to Adrigole Harbour bearing due N leads E

Lonehort Harbour from the S

Entering Lonehort. View from the ENE; the above-water rock on the S side, L, with the small creek beyond; Carrigavaud is just visible as the smooth slick on the water below the trees on the skyline, R centre. Tidal height about 1·4m

Doucallia Rock (breaking, L) from the NE; Leahern's Point just open S of Roancarrigmore (centre) leads between the rock and Bulliga Ledge

of Doucallia. In addition, Mehal Head just open S of Shot Head 077° leads between Bulliga Ledge and Doucallia, and a waypoint of 51°39'·15N 9°43'·7W gives Doucallia a berth of 2 cables on its SE side.

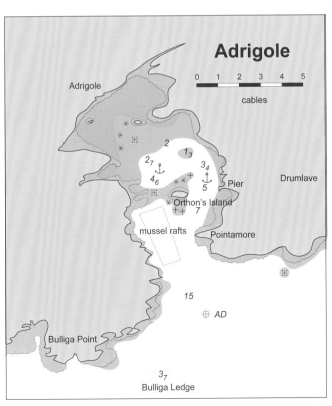

ADRIGOLE
⊕*AD*   51°40'·3N 9°43'·1W
AC1840 and Plan

This is one of the most beautiful anchorages on the coast. The entrance NE of Bulliga Point is 2 cables wide and the harbour then opens out. Orthon's Island shelters the inner part of the harbour. There are mussel rafts on the W side of the entrance, which should be left to port. The passage between Orthon's Island and the W shore is obstructed by rocks. Enter on a mid-channel course and then steer to pass midway between the island and the E shore, giving the S end of the island a berth of 1·5 cables. There are rocks extending 1 cable off the N, W and S sides of the island. The innermost portion of the harbour near the N shore dries out.

Anchorage
Depending on wind direction, anchor in 4 to 5m, 0·5 cable NW of the pier on the E side, or 1·5 cables N of Orthon's Island in 4m, or (in strong W winds) closer to the W shore NW of the island. Holding good in soft mud. There are visitors' moorings NE of Orthon's Island. In gales between W and N very heavy squalls come down from the high hills which surround the harbour. Shop, pub, filling station at Drumlave, 800m from the pier; shop, pubs, restaurants, PO at Adrigole village at the head of the bay. West Cork Sailing Centre (027 60132 and VHF

Adrigole from the S; Orthon's Island R centre

Ch 72), on the pier, offers dinghy and kayak rental and can supply diesel. Water at the pier. Buses to Bantry and Cork (Harringtons, 027 74003). The pier has a slipway on its S side.

ADRIGOLE TO GLENGARRIFF
AC1838, Imray C56
The N shore of the upper bay is fringed by low cliffs,

and the headlands are clean and steep-to. There are several attractive bays, and Glengarriff Harbour is arguably the most beautiful anchorage in Ireland.

Dangers
Drying and below-water rocks extending 2 cables NE and 1 cable S from Sheelane Island
Carrigathowder Rock (dries), 0·5 cable off the

Adrigole from the S; Orthon's Island, R centre

Adrigole

Adrigole

mainland shore NW of Sheelane Island
Rocks drying up to 3m within 2 cables E and NE of Garinish West
Coulagh Rocks (drying 1·4 to 1·7m), S of Coolieragh Harbour
Muccurragh Rock (dries 1·1m), 1 cable offshore, NE of Coolieragh Harbour

Lights and marks
Sheelane South buoy, PHM Fl(2)R 6s, 2 cables S by W of Sheelane Island
Coulagh South buoy, PHM Fl R 3s, 6 cables SSE of Muccurragh Point
Tanker Mooring Buoy, Mo(U) 15s, Horn Mo(U) 30s, between Four Heads Point and Whiddy Island.

Heading E from Adrigole, give the shore a berth of 2 cables to avoid a rock awash at LW, 1·5 cables offshore and nearly 5 cables E of the entrance, and the drying Corrigna Ledge, 3 cables further E. Leahill Jetty, 2·5M E of Shot Head, is a loading facility for stone quarried nearby. There is a clear passage in mid-channel between Sheelane Island and the shore, but beware rocks on either hand and also the outermost of the Coulagh Rocks and Muccurragh Rock to the E. There are fish farms

or mussel rafts at Coolieragh Harbour and on both sides of the entrance to Glengarriff. These are marked by lit yellow buoys, but the lights may not be entirely reliable. Sheelane South and Coulagh South port-hand buoys mark the limit of the deep water for tankers approaching the Whiddy terminal. The large yellow Tanker Mooring Buoy 6 cables N of the oil jetty on Whiddy Island has a restricted area of radius 3 cables round it.

Trafrask Bay
51°40'·3N 9°40'·8W
This bay faces SW but nevertheless offers pleasant anchorage in settled conditions. Anchor in 3 to 6m in mid-channel, SW of the moorings. There is a single visitors' mooring.

Garinish West
51°41'·8N 9°35'·1W
There is good anchorage in the inlet N of Garinish West. The safest approach passes E of the rocks to the E of the island. Enter the cove steering 255° in mid-channel and anchor in 3 to 4m, mud, off the middle of the island. There is a small drying pier at the head of the cove, labelled Derreenacarrin Quay on the chart but locally known as Zetland Pier.

Garinish West (L) and Sheelane (R) from the W

Approach to Garinish West anchorage from the SE; note the drying rocks, centre

Coolieragh Harbour

51°42'·2N 9°34'·7W

This is a feasible anchorage, with the Coulagh Rocks providing a measure of shelter in moderate SW'ly weather. From the SW, do not turn in until Muccurragh Point bears due N (long 9°34'·4W) to avoid the Coulagh Rocks, and stay E of the mussel rafts. The E side of the bay is foul for a distance of 1·5 cables offshore. Anchor in 5m at the head of the bay.

GLENGARRIFF

⊕ *GG*   51°43'·8N 9°32'·4W

AC1838, Imray C56 and Plan

Glengarriff Harbour was the birthplace of the Irish Cruising Club, which was founded by 19 yachtsmen who met there on 13th July, 1929, aboard five cruising yachts. The harbour, sheltered by tree-clad islands, is one of the prettiest in Ireland. **From the SW**, after passing Four Heads Rocks, the entrance to the harbour is clear and course may be shaped to leave Gun Point to starboard. Illnacullen (Garinish) is 41m high with a conspicuous Martello tower on

its summit. **Yellow Rocks**, 2·4m high, with foul ground to E and W, lie a cable S of Illnacullen. Ship Island (5m high), which is close to the E side of Illnacullen, is foul on its E side and should be given a berth of 1 cable. Keep closer to the E shore than to Ship Island, and then alter course for Bark Island (8m high). Do not go between Bark Island and Friar Island (to the NW) as there is a drying rock in mid-channel. Also beware the drying **Pot Rock** (Pot Island on the chart) 0·5 cable WSW of Bark Island. Pot Rock no longer has the post shown on the chart.

Caution – Overhead Cable

There is a high voltage cable from the centre of the N side of Illnacullen to the nearest point of the mainland to the NW, clearance 15m. The channel W of Illnacullen is not navigable.

Anchorage

There is a delightful anchorage in perfect shelter in 3m, NE of Bark Island, or further NW closer to the pier. A tripping line is advised. There are visitors'

Glengarriff from the SW; Illnacullen R foreground with Garvillaun and Ship Island beyond; Bark and Friar Islands, and Glengarriff village, upper L

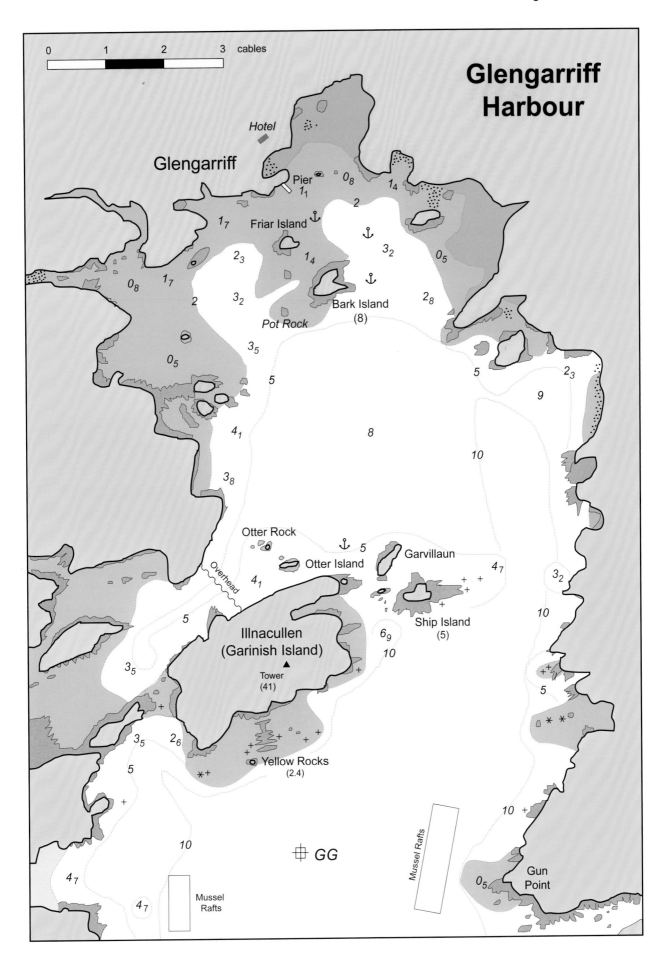

Glengarriff Harbour

0   1   2   3   cables

Hotel

Glengarriff

Pier

0_8

1_4

1_1

2

Friar Island

1_7

3_2

0_5

2_3

1_4

Bark Island
(8)

2_8

0_8

1_7

2

3_2

Pot Rock

0_5

3_5

5

5

2_3

9

4_1

8

10

3_8

Otter Rock

5

Garvillaun

4_7

3_2

Otter Island

4_1

Ship Island
(5)

10

Overhead

5

Illnacullen
(Garinish Island)

6_9

10

3_5

10

Tower
(41)

5

3_5

2_6

Yellow Rocks
(2.4)

5

10

10

GG

4_7

Mussel
Rafts

Mussel
Rafts

0_5

Gun
Point

4_7

Glengarriff from the SSE; Bark Island, L

Glengarriff anchorage; Bark Island, extreme L, and Friar Island, centre R

moorings. Anchorage is also available anywhere S of Bark Island in 7 to 8m. Near Illnacullen, anchor about 0·5 cable N of its NE point, E of Otter Rock, in 4m.

Facilities

Water on the pier; shops, PO, pubs, restaurants, hotels, filling station. Buses to Bantry, Killarney and Cork.

BANTRY

⊕*BY* 51°42'·4N 9°28'W
AC1838, Imray C56 and Plan
Whiddy Island, 2·75M long, lies NE – SW in the SE corner of Bantry Bay, sheltering Bantry Harbour to the SE.

Tidal Streams

The streams are slack in the harbour. Off the NE end of Whiddy Island they do not exceed 0·5 kn but they reach 1·5 kn in the W entrance. Constant –0035 Cobh; MHWS 3·4m, MHWN 2·6m, ML 1·9 m.

Dangers

Morneen Rocks (dry 1·1m), 7 cables SE of Gun Point

Castle Breaker (3·8m), SW of Ardnamanagh Point

Carrignagappul (dries 2m), 1M NE of Ardnamanagh Point

Carrignafeagh, dries, 3 cables S of Whiddy Point East

Seliboon Rock (2·3m), 1 cable W of Bantry Town Pier

Black Rock (dries 0·3m), close inshore below Bantry House

The Beaches, bar with least depth 2m, S of Whiddy Island

Cracker Rock, (1·7m), 2 cables N of Relane Point

East, Middle and West Gerane Rocks, drying and above-water reefs extending 5 cables WSW of

View down Bantry Bay from the NE; Carrigskye, L foreground, and the entrance to Glengarriff, R

Whiddy Point West.

There are mussel rafts in Ardnagashel Bay (the inlet NE of Ardnamanagh Point), N and S of Gurteenroe Point, between Whiddy Point East and Horse Island and all round Chapel Island. These are marked by lit yellow buoys, but the lights may not be entirely reliable. A green starboard-hand buoy marks the E extremity of the rafts SE of Chapel Island.

Lights and marks
Tanker Mooring Buoy, Mo(U) 15s, Horn Mo(U) 30s

Horse Island buoy, SHM Fl G 6s
Gurteenroe buoy, PHM Fl R 3s
Chapel Island buoy, SHM Fl G 2s
Whiddy Island W Clearing Light, white mast Oc 2s 22m 3M, vis 073°–106°
Whiddy Oil Terminal, 2×QY 10m 2M
Whiddy Point West, Y col Fl Y
Gerane West buoy, W Card Q(9) 15s

Directions – Glengarriff to Bantry
After passing Gun Point, steer 140° to clear Carrigskye (1·2m high) by 1 cable and pass 2 cables

Bantry Harbour from the E; Bantry Pier centre, Whiddy Island with its oil jetty and tank farm, top R; the airstrip on South Beach, upper L

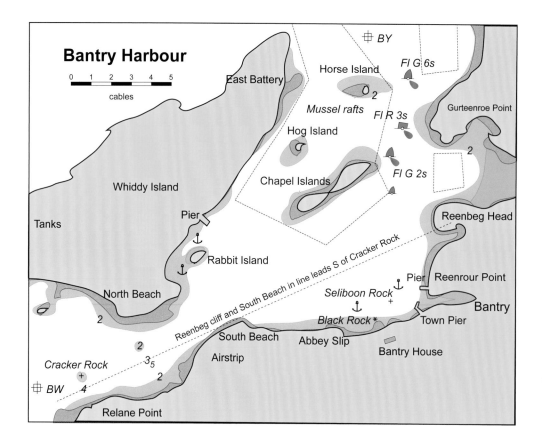

Bantry Harbour

0 1 2 3 4 5
cables

BY

Horse Island

Fl G 6s

East Battery

Gurteenroe Point

Mussel rafts

Fl R 3s

Hog Island

Chapel Islands

Fl G 2s

Whiddy Island

Reenbeg Head

Tanks

Pier

Rabbit Island

Pier

Reenrour Point

Seliboon Rock

Bantry

Reenbeg cliff and South Beach in line leads S of Cracker Rock

Black Rock

Town Pier

North Beach

South Beach

Abbey Slip

Bantry House

Cracker Rock

Airstrip

BW

Relane Point

SW of Morneen Rocks. After passing Carrigskye steer for the East Battery (22m high) near the NE corner of Whiddy Island; this avoids Castle Breaker and Felaun Rocks. The islands in Bantry Harbour are generally foul all round and should be given a berth of a cable (1·5 cables E and W in the case of Horse Island), but the area around them is in any case almost entirely taken up with mussel rafts. The buoys lead in W of Gurteenroe Point.

Ardnagashel Bay
51°43'·5N 9°27'·5W
There is a pleasant anchorage at the head of this bay NE of Ardnamanagh Point. Most of the bay is occupied by mussel rafts but there is a clear passage along both shores, which also leads clear of the drying

rock Carrignagappul. Anchor in 3 to 6m, mud, E or W of the reef at the head of the inlet. Filling station, shop, pub and restaurant at Ballylickey, 1km.

West Entrance to Bantry Harbour
⊕*BW* 51°40'·3N 9°30'·8W
AC1838
The channel S of Whiddy Island is relatively shallow and the bar, with 2m least depth, may break in a heavy swell. The deepest water is between Cracker Rock (1·7m) and the S shore, where there is 4m. From a position 1·5 cables NW of Relane Point, identify the cliff of Reenbeg Point on the far side of Bantry Harbour, and bring it in line 063° with the HW mark of South Beach *(see photograph)*. There is 3·5m least depth on this line, E of Cracker Rock.

Carrigskye, L, and Whiddy Island, R. View from the NW

HW mark of South Beach in line with Reenbeg cliff leads S of Cracker Rock. The red and white striped poles are part of the airstrip and not marine navaids

Bantry Town Pier

Give North Beach a berth of at least 0·75 cable.

Anchorages

- 1·5 cables NNW of the Town Pier, soft mud. Stay more than 1 cable from the pier at Reenrour Point on the N side as it is foul. There is also room to the W of the Town Pier between it and Seliboon Rock. The pier is not recommended for yachts alongside as the outer berth and steps must be kept clear for fishing boats and the Whiddy Island ferry. The inner part of the pier dries; however there is 2m at the second and third berth. The dredged area of the basin is narrow so keep close to the pier. Visitors' moorings by arrangement; contact Bantry Bay SC (Gordon Harwick 027 50081, or the Anchor Bar 027 50012).
- NW of Bantry House outside moorings in 3m, fair holding. Abbey Slip, close by, is suitable for launching trailer sailers.
- SW or NW of Rabbit Island in 1·5 to 4m, mud. This anchorage offers the best shelter in W to NW winds. There is a pier on Whiddy Island N of Rabbit Island.

At the time of writing (2008) works are in progress around the inner quays at Bantry, which effectively precludes their former use as a temporary berth near HW.

Whiddy pier from the SE; Rabbit Island, L

Facilities
Water, diesel from Town Pier, shops, PO, pubs, restaurants, hotels. Bus services to Cork. Bantry Bay Sailing Club. Whiddy Island has a pub, open in summer.

COAST WESTWARD OF BERE ISLAND
AC1840
From Fair Head, at the W entrance to Berehaven, past Black Ball Head to Crow Head, there are no dangers.

Pulleen Harbour
51°36'·8N 9°58'·1W
AC1840
Pulleen Harbour, 1·5M W of Pipers Sound, is a small cove only suitable for exploration by the smallest yachts of moderate draft, and in very settled weather. Beware of lobster pots. The outer anchorage is between the 4·6 and 8·2m soundings on AC1840, bottom weedy. There is a very restricted inner anchorage NE of the 4·6m sounding which can be entered after half flood by a yacht drawing 1m, passing between two grass-topped rocks and anchoring immediately beyond them. This inner pool has about 2m, clean bottom, but there is scarcely room for even a small yacht to swing safely to one anchor. It is sheltered except from due S and normally swell-free except near HW. It would be prudent to reconnoitre the inner anchorage by dinghy.

Black Ball Head
Black Ball Head is a bold, dark headland 81m high with an old watch tower on its summit. Off this head there is sometimes a tidal race with both streams but more particularly with the W-going stream opposed to the wind. There is a small cove on the W side of the head called Black Ball Harbour but the anchorage is unsafe and there is an above-water rock which narrows the entrance.

Crow Head
Crow Head, with Crow Island (62m high) and Leamascoil Rock (18m high) close to it, is bold and cliffbound. Two cables S of Crow Island is **Cat Rock** (dries 3·3m) which almost always shows or breaks. There is a clear passage between Cat Rock and Crow Island *(see photograph)*. **Bull's Forehead** (0·9m) lies 1·5 cables to the W of Crow Island, and is particularly dangerous since it frequently does not break. A berth of 3 cables will clear the dangers off Crow Island. From outside the Cat Rock, a course towards Dursey Tower (250m) leads well clear of the Bull's Forehead.

Pulleen Harbour from the S

Black Ball Head from the W; Bere Island beyond

Cat Rock (breaking, L), the Calf (L centre), Dursey Island (R) and Crow Island (extreme R)

The Calf (21m) and the Heifer (10m), almost a mile SW of Dursey Head. The cast-iron lighthouse on the Calf was built in 1866, strengthened in 1870 and swept away by a gale in 1881. Miraculously, the keepers survived. The light was replaced by a new tower on the Bull, three miles to the NW, in 1882. The stump on the Calf remains.

Chapter 4

Dursey Sound to Cahersiveen

Derrynane

The Kenmare River, like its neighbours to north and south, is a beautiful inlet with magnificent scenery and a character all of its own. It gives the enduring impression of being a great and well-kept secret. Although the shores of the Kenmare River are on well-trodden tourist routes – the Ring of Beara to the south and the Ring of Kerry to the north – and they have some of the finest anchorages in Ireland, the visiting yacht will often have a bay to herself. And as it happens, the two Rings are much better seen from the sea than from the land.

The village of Allihies, overlooking the mouth of the bay south of Cod's Head, was for 150 years the unlikely centre of an important copper-mining industry, which at its peak employed 1300 people and paid for the Puxley family's palatial Dunboy House outside Castletownbere. Whenever the industry hit a recession – as it did frequently – the workers emigrated, which is why in the former copper-mining town of Butte, Montana, two of the commonest surnames are Healey and O'Sullivan.

Derrynane Harbour, NW of Lamb's Head, is a splendid anchorage, and the nearby Derrynane House was the family home of the great 19th-century orator and reformer Daniel O'Connell. The house and its glorious gardens are open to the public.

Towering cliffs are the salient feature of the coast from here all the way to Dingle and Brandon Bay. Seven miles offshore are the Skelligs, not only breathtaking in their scenery but a UNESCO World Heritage site, and treasures in their bird life and antiquities. Valentia Island's coastguard radio station can trace its origins back to the earliest days of the transatlantic telegraph, and the island shelters an excellent natural harbour in which a 200-berth marina is under construction (2008). The picturesque town of Cahersiveen, two miles up-river from Valentia Harbour, also has a fine marina.

Charts

The general chart AC2423 Mizen Head to Valentia, and Imray's C56, cover the area of this chapter. The Imray chart has several useful harbour plans, but AC2495 Kenmare River, with five insets, is

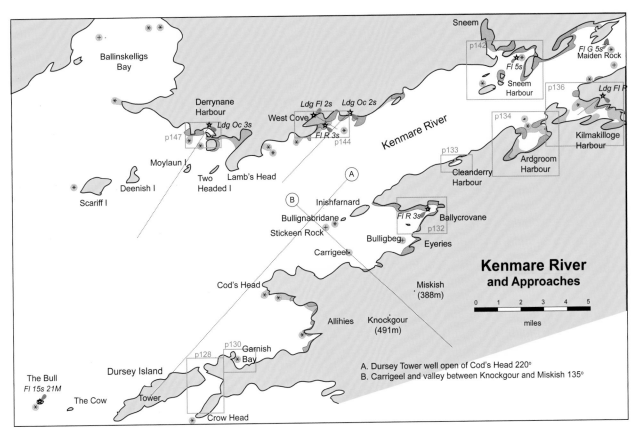

Kenmare River and Approaches

A. Dursey Tower well open of Cod's Head 220°
B. Carrigeel and valley between Knockgour and Miskish 135°

essential. AC2125 is the only Admiralty chart which shows any detail of Valentia Harbour.

KENMARE RIVER
AC2495, Imray C56

The inlet extends 28M ENE of the line of Scariff and Dursey Islands, at which point it is 7·5M wide. There are many unmarked hazards and the shores must, in general, be approached with caution, but there is no danger in a mid-channel course as far as Sneem and Kilmakilloge, the most popular anchorages, 16M from the entrance. The S shore up to Kilmakilloge Harbour is described first, followed by the upper bay and then the N shore.

Tidal Streams
Tidal Streams set fairly into and out of the Kenmare River. The ingoing stream makes at +0505 Cobh and the outgoing at −0120 Cobh. The spring rate is 0·5 to 0·8 kn in the outer bay, increasing to 1·5 kn in the inner bay with turbulence off Dinish and Dunkerron Islands with the ebb and strong W winds. Between Scariff and Dursey Islands the streams run N and S, running N with the ingoing stream. Between Dursey Head and The Bull the S-going stream makes at −0350 Cobh and the N-going at +0235 Cobh, spring rate about 3 kn. The streams run in the directions of the channels between the rocks, causing a turbulent sea and often a race near Gull Rock and S of the Cow.

Dangers – Dursey Sound to Ballycrovane
Tholane Breaker (dries 0·3m), 1·5 cables offshore 5 cables S of Cod's Head
Bulligmore, 2·1m, midway between Carrigeel and Eyeries Island at the entrance to Ballycrovane
Bulligbeg, 0·6m, 3 cables NW of Eyeries Point
Stickeen Rock, 1·5m, 7 cables WSW of Inishfarnard
Bulligabridane (dries 1·2m), 4 cables ENE of Stickeen Rock

Lights and Marks
The Bull, white tower Fl 15s 83m 21M, Racon (N)
Carrigduff, grey concrete beacon, unlit, in Garnish Bay
Illaunnameanla, red square tower Fl R 3s, in Ballycrovane Bay

DURSEY SOUND
⊕*DY* 51°36'N 10°09'W
Inset on AC2495, and Plan

Dursey Sound, between Dursey Island and the mainland, is 1 cable wide at the narrows, which are further constricted by **Flag Rock** (0·3m) in mid-channel. The tide runs at 4 kn at springs, turning N at +0135 Cobh and S at −0450 Cobh, setting across Flag Rock and forming eddies and overfalls there. There are eddies on both sides of the S entrance during the S-going stream. A cable car crosses the sound, with a clearance of 21m under the car itself and 25m under the cables. **From the S,** the narrows

Dursey Island from the E, with the Bull and the Cow beyond ,and the Calf top L

are difficult to discern until well into the bay, when the channel opens up to the NW. Having cleared the Bull's Forehead off Crow Head, steer for Illanebeg on the island shore. Look out for lobster pots SW of the entrance. Keep very close to the island shore going through the narrows, and if marginal in headroom take care not to pass while the cable car is crossing. There is usually a disturbed sea at the N entrance to the Sound, which could become dangerous in strong to gale force winds. The sea rebounds from the cliffs of **Glasfeactula Rock**, 9m high, at the E side of the N entrance. Be prepared for sudden changes in wind direction going through the sound, especially near the N entrance where heavy squalls from the high ground may be met. **From the N**, the approach is clear.

In fine weather it is possible to anchor off the jetty in Dursey Sound.

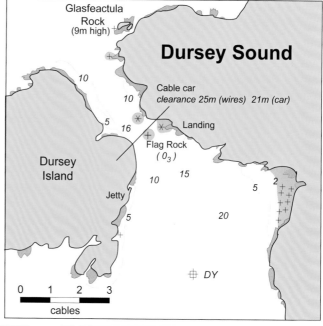

Approaches to Dursey Sound from the S; the jetty, L, and the cable car pylons, L and centre

Dursey Sound from the N; the cable car crossing

Dursey Island

Dursey Island is 3·5M long and its highest point, on which stands an old watch tower, is 250m high. On its N side are the highest cliffs in County Cork. Its shores are clear of danger except off Dursey Head, where **Cuckoo Rock** is close inshore but **Lea Rock**, which dries 3·4m, is 1·5 cables SW of the Head. The N side of the Bull open S of the Cow 300° leads S of Lea Rock; Scariff Island, 9M N, open of Mealbeg Point (2 cables NW of Dursey Head), bearing 003°, leads W of it.

The Bull, the Cow, the Calf and the Heifer

The Bull lies 2·5M WNW of Dursey Head and is 89m high. It is perforated SE–NW by an arched cavern through which breaking seas roll in bad weather. There are two detached rocks W of The Bull, one of which, the **Gull**, is 6m high. There is an increasing colony of gannets on the Bull.

The Cow lies between the Bull and Dursey Head, but slightly closer to the Bull, and is 62m high. It also has arched caverns. The Calf (21m high) and the Heifer (10m high) lie close together 7·5 cables SW of Dursey Head. There is often a considerable rebound of the waves in the channels between Dursey Island and the Cow and Calf.

Dursey Head to Ardgroom

The N side of Dursey Island is steep-to. Ballydonegan Bay, between Dursey Sound and Cod's Head, is entirely exposed and offers only limited shelter in Garnish Bay, *see below.* Beyond Cod's Head is Coulagh Bay, with Ballycrovane Harbour in its NE corner. **Carrigeel** (2·4m high) is 4 cables N of Rahis Point, on the S side of Coulagh Bay. **Bulligmore**, midway between Carrigeel and Eyeries Island at the entrance to Ballycrovane, breaks in a heavy swell. Between Bulligmore and the shore at Eyeries Point

The Bull

to the SE are several shallow patches, including **Bulligbeg** (0·6m). The N side of Coulagh Bay is formed by a series of islands and rocks which extend for 2M W from Kilcatherine Point. **Stickeen Rock**, the W'most of these, has 1·2m and may not break. **Bulligabridane** (dries 1·2m) is 4 cables ENE of Stickeen Rock. Dursey Island tower well open of Cod's Head, 220° leads N of it. Carrigeel, 2·4m high, in line with the bottom of the valley between Miskish and Knockgour Hills and bearing 135° just clears Stickeen to the W. In line with the summit of Knockgour, bearing 146°, it leads between Stickeen and Bulligabridane. In clear weather Miskish and Knockgour are easily recognised but Carrigeel can be hard to pick out against the land. Note that in a heavy sea the breakers extend W and N of Stickeen so give it a berth of at least 2 cables in these conditions.

The Cow, from the E

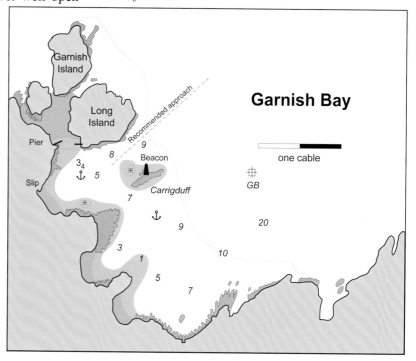

Dursey tower and Cod's Head in line (R). Come a little further N to clear Stickeen Rock. Inishfarnard, L, and the Bull, just visible at extreme R

Garnish Bay from the NE; Garnish and Long Island R, Carrigduff beacon L centre

Garnish Bay from the E; Carrigduff beacon, R

Garnish Bay

⊕*GB* 51°37'N 10°07'·3W
AC2495 and Plan

Garnish Bay is an open roadstead in the SW corner of Ballydonegan Bay. It can be used for anchorage only in settled weather and with the wind between SE and W. **Carrigduff** (dries 2m), marked by a concrete beacon, divides the bay in two. There are two anchorages:

• W of the Carrigduff beacon. It is important to find an area clear of weed and the water is usually clear enough to allow this. There is the least swell in this anchorage and it is convenient for landing. The approach N of Carrigduff beacon is kept clear of pots and nets; stay close to the shore of Long Island to the N when entering.

• 1 cable S of the beacon in 5 to 7m, sand. There is more room in this anchorage and the holding appears to be good.

Ballydonegan Bay

51°37'·8N 10°04'·3W

In swell-free conditions this bay S of Cod's Head offers attractive temporary anchorage. Approach from the WSW and anchor off the beach in 3 to 5m. sand. Bird Rock, on the N side of the bay, does not cover as shown on the chart but stands 1·2m above HW.

Shops, pubs, PO at Allihies, 2km.

Ballydonegan beach and the colourful houses of Allihies village

Ballycrovane from the E; Eyeries Island top, Illaunameanla R centre and the pier in the inlet, bottom

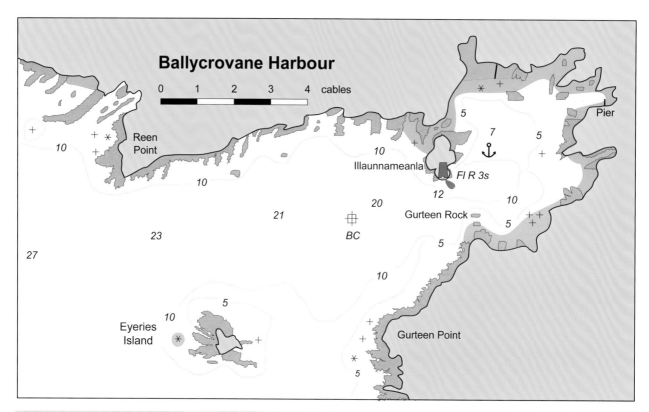

Ballycrovane from the W; Illaunameanla, L, with its port-hand beacon, centre

Ballycrovane pier from the W

Ballycrovane Harbour

⊕*BC* 51°42'·6N 9°58'W

Inset on AC2495, and Plan

From the W and Cod's Head, steer 057° with The Bull just showing astern till the summit of Inishfarnard is abeam, then steer to pass midway between Eyeries Island and the mainland N of it.

From the E, use the passage between Inishfarnard and Kilcatherine Point, which has a least depth of 7·8m in mid-channel. See above for clearing lines for Stickeen Rock. Eyeries Island is 4m high and has

rocks all round it for a distance of 1·5 cables. After passing it, identify Illaunameanla, with its red pillar beacon, at the NW side of Ballycrovane Harbour. **Gurteen Rock** is 0·75 cable off the S shore and dries 3·4m. The N and E shores of the harbour are foul for over a cable. There is a fish farm close S of Inishfarnard.

Anchorage

One cable NE of Illaunameanla in 4 to 5m, stiff mud. Exposed to W winds and subject to swell after bad

Cleanderry Harbour from the E

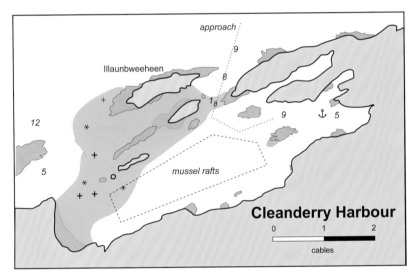

weather from that direction. Constant –0055 Cobh; MHWS 3·5m, MHWN 2·8m, ML 2·0 m.

The inlet leading to the pier, in the NE corner of the bay, is much less obstructed than AC2495 would suggest. There is deep water for a width of 50m as far as the pier, and a depth of 2m at the end of the pier. A temporary alongside berth may be available. Shops and pubs at Eyeries, 3 km.

Cleanderry Harbour

51°45'N 9°56'*W*
AC2495 and Plan

Cleanderry Harbour is 3M NE from Kilcatherine Point. Its entrance is concealed behind the low-lying Illaunbweeheen, which is long and grass-covered. It can be identified by Shamrock Hill to the W and a big patch of scrubby trees on the hillside above it. The entrance is only 7m wide at LW with low rocks on either side, and has a least depth of 2m. The pool inside has depths up to 13m, but it is heavily obstructed by mussel rafts and their associated plant and hardware. The W end of the harbour is exposed at HW when the rocks cover, and the best shelter is at the E end where there is space to anchor clear of a few moorings, but not much room to swing. Smooth water and a very careful, slow approach are essential. There are two

Ardgroom from the E; Dog's Point, top R, Cus Island, centre, Bird Island, lower L. Note the mussel rafts, L

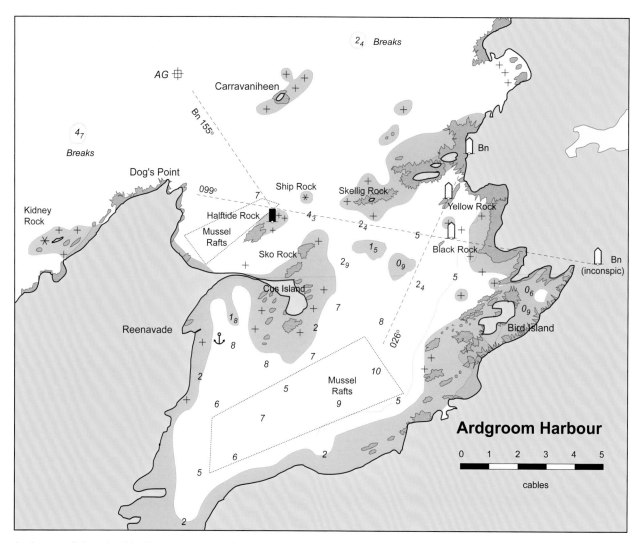

drying reefs just inside the entrance and to port, and the course to the E end lies between them.

ARDGROOM HARBOUR

⊕*AG*   51°46'·2N 9°53'·1W
Insets on AC2495 and Imray C56, and Plan
Ardgroom Harbour, on the S side opposite Sneem, offers excellent shelter but the entrance is narrow and intricate. **Kidney Rock** (0·5m high) is a cable offshore, 4 cables SW of Dog's Point. **Carravaniheen** (1m high), with submerged rocks extending NE and SW, lies N of the entrance, and 3 cables NE of Carravaniheen is a rock with 2·4m, which sometimes breaks. Across the mouth

of the bay and protecting the harbour is a ridge of rocks and islets; the entrance channel lies in the centre of this ridge and has a rocky bar with least depth 2·4m. Unlit beacons, including two pairs of leading beacons, mark the channel. The rocks are too numerous to list individually but the principal dangers are as follows:

Ship Rock (dries less than 0·5m), 4 cables E of Dog's Point and a cable NW of the bar
Halftide Rock (dries) 1·5 cables SW of Ship Rock, with a beacon on it
Skellig Rock, 1m high, 2·5 cables E of Ship Rock, with drying and sunken rocks extending a cable W

Halftide Rock beacon from the ESE; Dog's Point, L

Ardgroom beacons from the SE; Black Rock, L, and Yellow Rock, upper centre

Ardgroom beacons from seaward; Black Rock, L, and the rear beacon of the second pair (NE of Yellow Rock), above

Mussel rafts surround the beacon and extend a short distance to the NE. Skirt the rafts and identify the white pillar on Black Rock. A bearing of 099° on Black Rock, with the Halftide Rock beacon almost directly astern, leads across the bar and clear N of the 1·5m and 0·9m rocks. The rear beacon of this leading pair is difficult to distinguish among the trees, and should not be depended upon. Once across the bar, identify the second pair of leading marks to the NE. The front mark is the pillar on Yellow Rock and the rear mark is on the shore 1·5 cables beyond it. As soon as these marks come in line, turn to starboard and steer 206° keeping the beacons in line astern. Skirt the mussel rafts on the S side of the bay and steer for the pier at Reenavade when it bears NW.

and marking the NE side of the bar
Sko Rock (dries), 2 cables SW of Skellig Rock, marking the SW side of the bar
Unnamed rocks with 1·5 and 0·9m, 1·5 to 2·5 cables SE of the bar
Black Rock (dries 2·1m), 3·5 cables ESE of the bar
Yellow Rock (awash at HW), 2·5 cables E of Skellig Rock
There are mussel rafts between Dog's Point and Halftide Rock, and in the SW arm of the bay, S of Cus Island.

Directions
Enter between Carravaniheen and Dog's Point, steering 155° for the beacon on Halftide Rock.

Anchorage
Anchor 0·5 cable E of the pier at Reenavade in 4m, fair holding. Shop/PO/cafe and Internet access at Ardgroom village, 3 km by road, but the head of the inlet to the SW is accessible by dinghy and is only 500m from the village.

KILMAKILLOGE HARBOUR
⊕ *KM* 51°47'N 9°50'·3W
Insets on AC2495 and Imray C56, and Plan
Kilmakilloge, including also Bunaw and Collorus Harbours, is one of the most attractive inlets on

Reenavade Pier

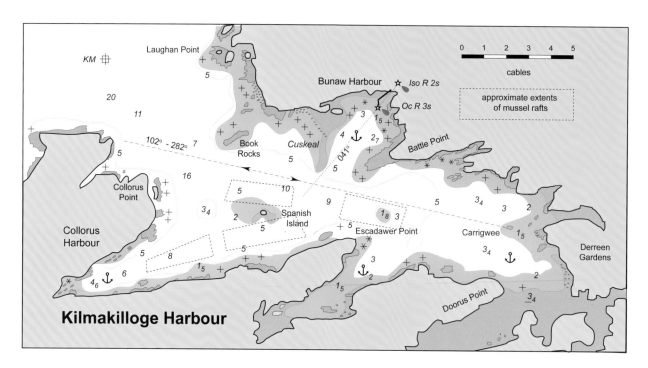

Kilmakilloge Harbour

the coast, and offers access in all weathers, and excellent shelter. The entrance, between Collorus Point and Laughaun Point, is 1·5M NE of Ardgroom and 7·5M from Kilcatherine Point.

Dangers

Most of the shore of the Harbour is foul to a distance of a cable off. The principal dangers are:

Book Rocks (dry 0·3m), extending 2·5 cables offshore, 4 cables S of Laughaun Point

Cuskeal (dries 0·3m), a rocky spit extending 3 cables offshore and forming the W side of Bunaw Harbour

Drying and below-water rocks extending 2 cables SW from Battle Point, S of Bunaw

Unnamed rock with 1·8m, 2·5 cables S of Battle Point

Carrigwee (dries 3·4m), 3 cables N of Doorus Point at the E end of the Harbour

Lights

Bunaw, ldg lts, yellow poles, black bands, front Oc R 3s 9m, rear Iso R 2s 11m

Collorus Harbour

From the NW, Collorus Point should be given a berth of 1·5 cables. From the NE, give Laughaun Point a berth of 2 cables. Steer to pass midway

Kilmakilloge Harbour. from the SE; Escadawer Point centre with Doorus Point lower L and Collorus Point upper R. Note the mussel rafts

between Collorus Point and Spanish Island (4·3m high). This leads clear W of Book Rocks, whose position may be identified by the 52m grassy cliff behind them to the NE.

Bunaw

From the mid-channel between Collorus Point and Book Rocks, steer 102° for the woods near Dereen House at the E end of Kilmakilloge Harbour, and leave Spanish Island 2 cables to starboard. Identify Bunaw pier and when it bears 037°, turn to port and steer for it.

Kilmakilloge

Follow the directions for Bunaw as above but hold the course of 102° towards Derreen Woods to pass clear N of the 1·8m rock 1.7 cables off Escadawer Point. There are fish farms in the bay and a platform moored S of Escadawer Point. Nearly 1 cable SE of Escadawer Point there is the very thin stump of a perch which covers and which marks the extremity of a reef off the point.

Bunaw Harbour and pier; note the fish cages off Battle Point, lower L.

Kilmakilloge: Spanish Island from the SW, with mussel rafts on three sides. Bunaw pier on the far side of the bay, L

Bunaw pier

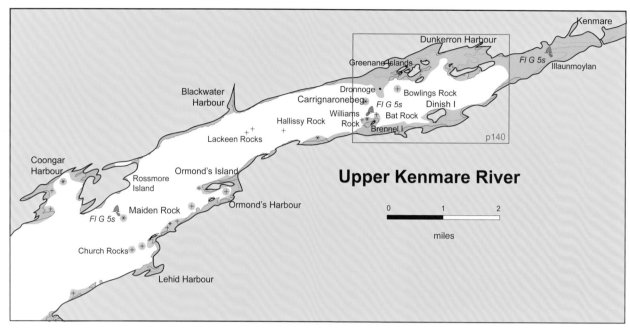

Upper Kenmare River

0   1   2

miles

Anchorage

- In the middle of Collorus Harbour in 5m, abreast a small disused boat slip on the S shore. The holding is rather soft and unreliable, with weed.
- In Bunaw Harbour, on the leading line between the pier and Cuskeal in 3 to 4m. An anchor light is recommended. There is 0·4m alongside the pier, on the village side, and 0·8m N of the steps, with a clean gravel bottom.
- 1 cable SW of Carrigwee in 3 to 4m.
- S of Escadawer Point in 1·5 to 3m, avoiding the stump perch mentioned above.

There is a convenient landing above half tide near a road bridge SE of Dereen. No facilities at Collorus Harbour; pub (with showers) and limited stores at Bunaw; filling station, pub/restaurant and PO at Lauragh village, E of Dereen. Dereen gardens are open to the public.

UPPER KENMARE RIVER
AC2495

Dangers

The N shore of the River is clean for 5M above Coongar Harbour, opposite and N of Kilmakilloge, but the S side is foul up to 2 cables offshore, and there are several hazards in mid channel. The following are the principal dangers in the fairway.

Church Rocks, 1·4m, 5 cables NW of Lehid Harbour

Blackwater Harbour

Dinish Island from the SW

Maiden Rock (dries 0·5m), in mid-channel S of the summit of Rossmore Island
Unnamed rock with 1·4m, 4 cables WSW of Ormond's Island
Lackeen Rocks, 2·4m, and **Hallissy Rock**, 3·4m, in mid-channel NE of Ormond's Island
Carrignaronebeg (dries 2·6m), in mid-channel 3M ENE of Ormond's Island, with foul ground extending ENE to the Greenane Islands, and including the above-water heads of **Carrignaronemore** and **Dronnoge**
Bowlings Rock, 0·8m, 3 cables E of Dronnoge
Brennel Island (3m high), 6 cables S of Dronnoge, with drying and submerged rocks extending 2 cables to the NE, NW and SW.

Lights and Marks

Maiden Rock buoy, SHM Fl G 5s, 3 cables NW of the rock
Carrignaronebeg, tripod beacon, unlit
The jagged remains of a perch on **Williams Rock**, E of Brennel Island, are visible below HW.
Bat Rock buoy, SHM Fl G 5s, N of Brennel Island
Illaunmoylan buoy, SHM Fl G 5s, in the approaches to Kenmare Quay

Directions

A course of 066° from Maiden Rock buoy leads clear of all dangers to the mouth of Dunkerron Harbour. The narrows N of Brennel Island is 3 cables wide, marked by Carrignaronebeg beacon to the N and Bat Rock buoy to the S.

Coongar Harbour

51°48'·7N 9°49'W
Coongar Harbour, on the N shore, provides sheltered anchorage in winds between W and SE. Its shores are foul all round and there is no convenient landing. Give the shore of Rossmore Island, to the E, a berth of 2 cables on entering, and anchor in 3·5 to 9m towards the head of the bay.

Lehid Harbour

51°48'·2N 9°47'·2W
Lehid Harbour, on the S side opposite Rossmore Island, should be approached from the W, leaving Church Rocks to port. It has an extremely narrow entrance between rocky ledges on either side, and is only accessible by the smallest yachts in settled weather. There is anchorage in the centre of the harbour in 3m.

Ormond's Harbour

51°49'·3N 9°45'·8W
Ormond's Harbour is sheltered by Ormond's Island (10m) on its N side and by Hog Island (3·3m) on its SW side. Ormond's Island has rocks extending 1·5 cables W and 0·5 cable N and S. The bar between it and the E shore dries 2·8m. There is foul ground between Hog Island and the shore. The entrance is 1 cable wide, and has a least depth of 2·3m over a rock in mid-channel. There is a rock awash at LW just NE of the centre of the harbour. Enter in mid-channel and anchor E of Hog Island in 5m, mud. No facilities.

Blackwater Harbour

51°50'·7N 9°44'·6W
Blackwater Harbour is a very pretty river mouth on the N shore 2·6M NE of the Maiden Rock buoy. There is a stone pier on the W side with 1·2m at the end, sand bottom. In the channel there is 3·5m just beyond the pier but no room to swing and many small boat moorings. Entering, keep 10m off the head of the pier to clear a sandbank in mid-channel. Anchor just outside the point S of the pier in 3·5 to 7m, where there is good shelter in W winds.

Dinish Island

⊕ *DI* 51°51'N 9°39'·8W
Anchorage is available E or SW of Dinish Island, as appropriate for shelter. Beware of rocks on either side of the approach to the SW anchorage. The E anchorage is in 2m, midway between the quay on the E of the island and Dawros Point to the E. The spit on the E end of the island is marked by a black-and-white banded pole. There is a new pier in this bay which is the base of a watersports centre, but the pier is not available as an alongside berth and the depth is limited. Pub/restaurant om the mainland.

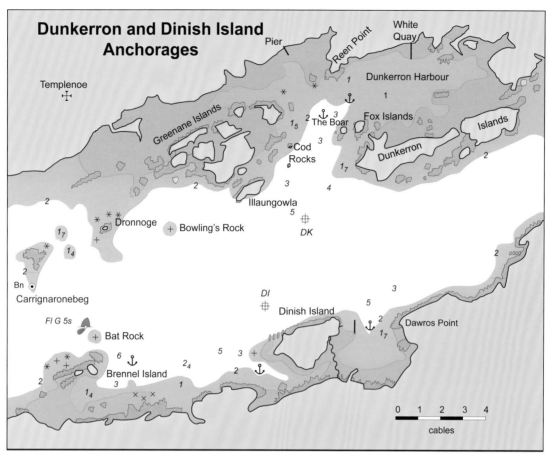

Dunkerron and Dinish Island Anchorages

Dunkerron Harbour

⊕ *DK* 51°51'·4N 9°39'·4W

Dunkerron Harbour, 2M from Kenmare on the N side of the bay, is a very pretty harbour and offers good shelter. The entrance is between Illaungowla on the W and Dunkerron Island on the E. **Cod Rocks** (2·4m and 3m high) on the W side have foul ground on their NW sides. The Fox Islands (4·9m high) on the E side have a reef extending 1 cable W terminating in the **Boar**. Enter close E of the Cod Rocks or leave Dunkerron Island West and the Boar 1·5 cables to starboard. There is a dredged channel leading S into deep water from the pier (known as the White Quay) 4 cables E of Reen Point; the channel follows the projection of the E side of the pier. This channel is narrow and should only be attempted above half tide.

Anchorages

- Between Cod Rock and the Boar in 2·5 to 3·5m.
- Midway between Reen Point on the N shore and the Fox Islands in 1·8m.
- An alongside berth in 1·8m is available on the W side of a pontoon moored E of the pier and at the end of the dredged channel. The pier is in the grounds of Dromquinna Manor Hotel.

Constant –0052 Cobh; MHWS 3·9m, MHWN 3·0m, ML 2·2m.

Facilities

Water on the pier, hotel facilities including showers. Pub and PO at Templenoe village, 1·5 km W.

Kenmare Quay

51°52'·3N 9°35'·3W

Kenmare Quay, 1 km from the town, may be reached at HW but it is not recommended for drying out. The bottom is mud. Anchorage is possible SE of the quay although depths are restricted. Dunkerron Harbour, although further from the town, may be a more attractive base from which to visit Kenmare. Shops, PO, pubs, restaurants, hotels, filling station in Kenmare.

KENMARE RIVER, NORTH SHORE – COONGAR HARBOUR TO DERRYNANE

AC2495

The SE sides of Rossmore, Rossdohan and Sherky Islands are clean and steep-to, and a berth of 3 cables clears all dangers on the direct course of 250° from S of Sherky Island to Lamb's Head. W of Lamb's Head are Two Headed Island, Moylaun, Deenish and Scariff, with deep channels between each one. The beautiful and secure natural harbour of Derrynane lies 3M N of Two Headed Island.

Dunkerron Harbour from the SE; White Quay, R

(above and R) Kenmare Quay

Dangers

Cottoner Rock (dries 0·6m), off Sherky Island

Carrigheela (dries 2·9m), 5 cables SW of Daniel's Island and 4M ENE of Lamb Head

Beara Rocks (3m high), 3 cables offshore SW of a sharp peak (Knocknasullig) 116m high, at the W side of West Cove

Brigbeg (dries 0·3m), 3 cables E of Illaunaweelaun and 1M E of Lamb's Head

Blackhead Rock (6m high) and **Carrigatemple** (dries 3·4m), close S of Lamb's Island, on the SE side of Lamb's Head

Scariff Hedges, drying rocks extending 2 cables W from Scariff Island

Bulligmore (dries 0·3m) and **Muckiv Rocks** (dry 3·6m), respectively SE and NW of the entrance to Derrynane.

Sneem Harbour; Oysterbed Pier centre, Illaunsleagh R, Garinish anchorage L and Sneem village top R

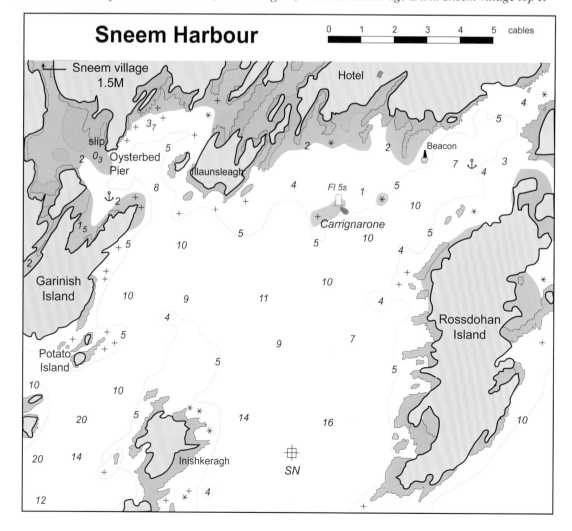

Sneem village from the S; the Quay, centre

Lights and marks

Carrignarone beacon, Fl 5s 2m 2M, in Sneem Harbour

West Cove and approaches:

West Cove outer leading beacons, square white pillars Oc 2s, front on Burnt Island

Limpet Rock beacon, grey metal post on concrete base PHM Fl R 3s

West Cove inner leading beacons Fl 2s, (outer) grey metal post on concrete base, (inner) white stone pillar

Derrynane:

Derrynane, ldg lts 034°, Oc 3s 4M, front 10m rear 16m

Derrynane entrance beacons, SHM green concrete pillar, PHM red concrete pillar, unlit.

Sneem Harbour

⊕*SN* 51°47'·8N 9°52'·8W

Insets on AC2495 and Imray C56, and Plan

Sneem Harbour is entered between Sherky Island to the SW and Rossdohan Island to the NE. There are drying and sunken rocks up to 2 cables SW of Rossdohan, but the W side of the entrance is clean. **From the S**, steer due N midway between the islands until the channel NW of Inishkeragh opens up to the SW, and identify the channel ahead to the NW between Garinish on the port hand and Illaunslea on the starboard. Rocks extend 1·5 cables SW of Illaunslea. To avoid them stay 0·5 cable off the NE point of Garinish while steering NW. As the inlet on the N side of Garinish opens up, identify Oysterbed Pier in the NW corner of the anchorage. **From the W**, identify Inishkeelaghmore, 4 cables NW of Sherky, and shape a course one-quarter of the channel's width SE of Inishkeelaghmore to avoid the Cottoner Rock. A mid-channel course from there between the little Potato Island and Inishkeragh leads NE to the anchorages.

Anchorage

Anchor in the mouth of the N bay on Garinish, 3m, or to the SE of Oysterbed Pier, 5m. Good holding in mud. The N bay on Garinish is well occupied with moorings, and is a thriving seal colony. Visitors' moorings.

Anchorage is also available N of Rossdohan Island in 7m. Give the shore of the island a berth of 2 cables all the way round. Carrignarone (dries 3m) is marked by a lighted beacon, and there is a rock awash at LW, 1·5 cables E of it.

Approaching Sneem Harbour from the W; Sherky, R, and Inishkeelaghmore L

Sneem Quay, 1·5M up-river from the anchorage

Pier

Oysterbed Pier has 3m at LAT on its front face. Approach at a sharp angle to clear the shore on either side. There is a slip suitable for trailer sailers on the W side of the same promontory.

River channel to Sneem

The river is navigable with care by dinghy four hours either side of HW as far as Sneem Quay, 1·5M from Oysterbed Pier. Submerged rocks in the river are usually indicated by patches of weed. The village of Sneem is 500m from the quay.

Facilities

Water on Oysterbed Pier. Hotel on N shore. Shops, pubs, restaurants, PO at Sneem village.

Illaundrane

51°46'·4N 9°59'·5W

Illaundrane anchorage is well sheltered from all winds, but entry requires great care since the rocks are unmarked. The entrance is 3M W of Sherky Island. Enter between Leaghcarrig and Illaunsillagh, and giving each a good berth, pass N or S of a patch which is awash at LW about 1 cable N of Leaghcarrig, then head for the NW shore of Illaundrane, which is clean, and anchor half way along the island in 4m.

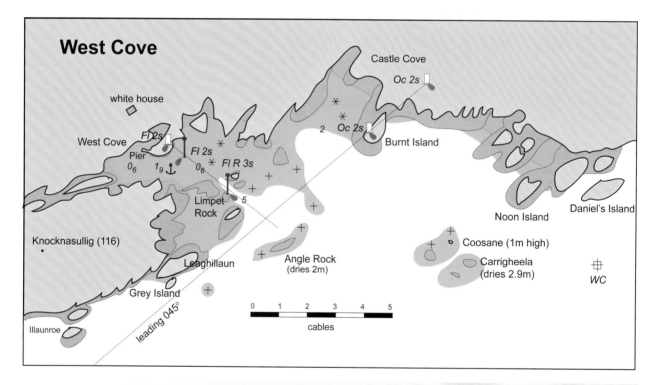

West Cove, from the E; Knocknasullig, L, and Burnt Island, R. Note the conspicuous white house among the trees, R

West Cove; the outer leading beacons from the SW. The front one (lower) is on Burnt Island

West Cove from the E; Leaghillaun and Grey Island L, Angle Rock breaking lower L, Limpet Rock beacon centre and the rear leading beacon upper R.

West Cove

⊕ *WC* 51°45'·7N 10°00'·9W

See Plan

West Cove is a very well sheltered but shallow harbour in the NW corner of the bight behind Carrigheela, 6M SW of Sneem. The approach is marked by lighted beacons but strewn with rocks, and a stranger should not attempt entry after dark. The entrance is narrow and has a least depth of 0·6m, sand bottom.

Directions

From the E, leave Daniel's Island and Noon Island (2 cables W) a cable to starboard, passing between Noon Island and Coosane Rock (which never covers) to the SW. There is a sunken rock 0.5 cable N of Coosane Rock. Steer to pass a cable SW of Burnt Island, and when the lower leading beacon (a white square pillar) comes into view from behind the island, turn to port bringing the two beacons in line 045° astern. A large white house among the trees above West Cove is conspicuous in this approach.

Identify Limpet Rock beacon and the inner leading beacons and turn on to their line *(see photograph)*. Leave Limpet Rock beacon close to port. When 20m from the outer leading beacon, turn to port for the anchorage.

From the W, identify the sharp peak of Knocknasullig (116m), 3M ENE of Lamb's Head, and approach the shore just E of its summit between Illaunroe and Leaghillaun. Identify the two white leading beacons, about 1M to the NE bearing 045°. The front leading beacon is on Burnt Island and the rear beacon on the mainland just NE of it *(see photograph)*. Enter on this line, which is close to Leaghillaun and Grey Island and inshore of the breaker 1·5 cables E of them. Identify the inner beacons, and proceed as above.

Note that Angle Rock ("Carriganglee" on the chart) dries only 2m, and Carrigheela dries 2·9m, not 3·3m for both, as charted.

Limpet Rock beacon (R) and the inner leading beacons (centre) at West Cove. The cottage E of the quay, L

Scariff (L) and Deenish Islands, from the SE. Hog's Head is just closed behind Deenish

Anchorage

The only place with more than 1·5m at LAT is abreast the grey cottage E of the quay; the deep area here is narrow. Further up is mostly 0·4 to 0·7m, sand in the middle or mud NW of the quay, and there are small-craft moorings. Shop and filling station at Castlecove, 1·5 km. Constant –0053 Cobh; MHWS 3·5m, MHWN 2·8m, ML 2·0m.

Lamb's Head – channels between the islands

There is deep water in mid-channel between all the islands outside Leaghcarrig, W of Lamb's Head. The shortest cut, the channel between Leaghcarrig and Two Headed Island, is 1·5 cables wide and 14m deep, and is navigable in the absence of a heavy swell. The bay on the E side of Deenish Island offers a pleasant temporary anchorage in settled weather.

Tidal Streams

Between Scariff and Lamb's Head the stream turns S at –0110 Cobh and N at +0500 Cobh. The spring rate is 1·5 kn.

Derrynane Bay

51°44'·7N 10°09'W

Derrynane Bay (Darrynane on the chart), N of Lamb's Head, is exposed to the prevailing wind and swell, but with settled offshore winds and no swell there is very pleasant anchorage in 9m, E of the abbey ruins on Abbey Island. The N and SE sides of the bay are foul for 2 cables, and the E side, which is sandy, dries out. The sandy beaches are conspicuous from seaward.

Derrynane Harbour from the NW, with Middle Rock in the entrance, bottom. Derrynane Bay beyond the sandspit

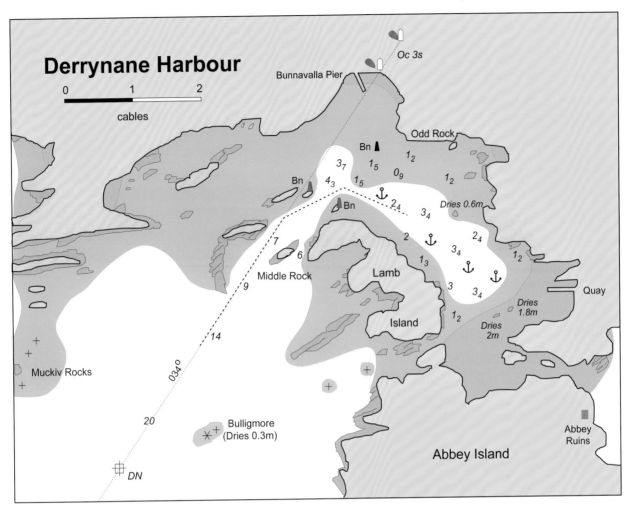

Derrynane Harbour

⊕*DN*   51°45'·3N 10°09'·8W

AC 2495 and Plan

This spectacular anchorage is sheltered in all winds, but the entrance, although well marked, is close between rocks and should not be attempted in a heavy swell from the W or SW. The leading beacons are lit, but a stranger is cautioned against attempting the entrance at night. **From the S**, from a position close W of Two Headed Island, steer 350° and identify the entrance NW of Abbey Island. Muckiv Rocks to the NW almost always break, and in any swell Bulligmore to the SE also breaks. **From the NW**, stay 5 cables SW of Kid's Island (10m high) and Carrigsheehan (9m high), 2·5M ESE of Hog's Head, and keep Leaghcarrick Island closed with Lamb's Head to the SE.

Identify the leading beacons bearing 034°, and steer in on the leading line, leaving Muckiv Rocks to port and Bulligmore to starboard. Bulligmore is particularly dangerous since it may not be breaking, so do not err to the SE of the leading line. The line leads between Middle Rock (0·5m high) to the SE and drying and above-water rocks to the NW. Approaching the entrance, identify the red beacon on the rocks just inside and almost on the leading line.

Leave this beacon close to port and Middle Rock to starboard. The corresponding green starboard-hand beacon is on the rocks close N of Lamb's Island. Turning to leave this beacon close to starboard opens up the anchorage. A third beacon to the NE marks a drying rock, and a further drying rock lies 2 cables to the SE. These are marked on AC2495.

Derrynane leading beacons, seen from Bunnavalla Pier

Derrynane entrance, from the NE; Bulligmore breaking, L centre, and Muckiv Rocks breaking, top R. Bunnavalla pier, foreground, and Moylaun Island, top L

When leaving Derrynane, Middle Rock appears to be much more obviously in mid-channel, and it is easy to be struck by an attack of last-moment confusion. Leave the rock to port when heading out, and keep the leading beacons in line astern. There is a narrow deep channel E of Middle Rock, but it should only be attempted with great care in settled weather, staying close to the rock.

Anchorage

Anchor in the SE half of the harbour, anywhere clear of moorings, in 2 to 3m, sand. Visitors' moorings are available. There is a drying pier and small slip in the SE corner of the harbour, and the new Bunavalla Pier and slip in the N corner below the leading beacons. The latter pier is 75m in length and has 0.5m at its head and 0.1m on each side, and is used by small fishing vessels and the tourist boats to the Skelligs. The harbour is much used by waterskiers.

Facilities

Pub at Derrynane. Shop, pubs, restaurant at Caherdaniel, 3 km. Derrynane House and gardens are open to the public.

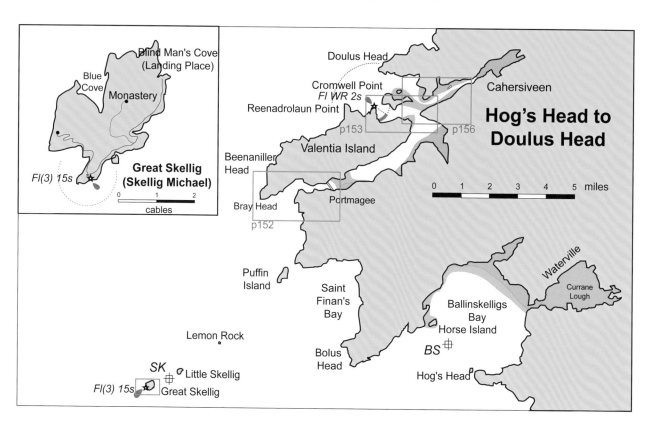

DERRYNANE TO VALENTIA AND CAHERSIVEEN
AC 2423, 2495, 2125

Leaving Derrynane with the leading beacons in line astern, do not alter course to the W until the gap closes between Leaghcarrig Island and Lamb's Head, to the SE. This leads clear SW of the Muckiv Rocks. The cliffs from here to Valentia are 150 to 240m in height and very spectacular, and in moderate to good visibility the craggy pyramids of the Skelligs are conspicuous to the W. Bolus Head, 6·5M WNW of Derrynane, is steep-to, and a berth of 2 cables clears a drying rock off Ducalla Head further NNW. Canduff, the SW point of Puffin Island, is also clean. In fresh onshore winds and swell there can be a very disturbed sea between Bolus Head and Bray Head on Valentia Island.

The W part of Portmagee Sound, S of Valentia Island, offers sheltered anchorage but the bridge across the Sound no longer opens. Bearhaboy Rocks, SW of Bray Head, always show; **Gallaunaniller Rock,** which dries, lies 1·5 cables N of Beenaniller Head. The NW coast of Valentia is clean to within 2 cables of the shore. Rounding Reenadrolaun Point, the NW tip of Valentia, identify Cromwell (Fort) Point, and leave it close to starboard. **By night**, the Skelligs light is obscured N of Bolus Head, and Inishtearaght light is obscured E of Beenaniller Head on the NW side of Valentia, while Cromwell Point light is not visible until clear NE of Reenadrolaun Point; this leaves a 3M gap along the NW coast of Valentia Island where no lights are visible at all.

Tidal Streams
Between the Skelligs and the shore the N-going stream makes at +0500 Cobh and the S-going stream at –0110 Cobh, spring rate 1·5 kn. W of the rocks the tides are complex but do not exceed 1 kn.

Lights
Skelligs Rock, white tower on the SW side of Great Skellig, Fl(3) 15s 53m 19M. Visible from 262° through N to 115°, partially obscured within 6M between 110° and 115°

Inishtearaght, Fl(2) 20s 84m 27M, on the Blasket Islands to the NW

Cromwell (Fort) Point, white tower Fl WR 2s 16m, W17M R15M, W 102°–304° R 304°–351°. Shows red over Harbour Rock and the SW corner of Valentia harbour, white elsewhere.

Ballinskelligs Bay
⊕ *BS* 51°48'N 10°15'W

Ballinskelligs Bay is open to the prevailing wind and swell from the SW, but offers the possibility of a visit in settled conditions with an offshore wind. Hog's Head to the SE has spectacular 160m cliffs; Pig's Rocks (4·6m high), 1·5 cables NW, have a drying reef extending 1 cable W. There are rocks on the NE side of the bay, and **Bay Rock**, with 1·2m, lies 7 cables NE of Horse Island, on the W side.

Anchorage
In settled weather there is temporary anchorage in 4m just N of Horse Island.

Horse Island anchorage, Ballinskelligs Bay, from the SE. The pier is used by boats taking sightseers to the Skelligs

Skellig Michael from the SW; Washerwoman Rock, lower L, and Bray Head (Valentia Island) in the distance. Note the flotilla of small boats standing off while their passengers explore the island

The Skelligs

⊕ *SK* 51°46'·5N 10°31'W

The Great Skellig, or Skellig Michael, 214m high, is a remarkable rocky island 7·5M W by S of Bolus Head. It appears conical from NE and SW but its two summits with a saddle between are visible from SE and NW. The Little Skellig, 130m high and 1·4M to the ENE, is similar in profile to its larger neighbour. Lemon Rock, 20m high and 2·3M ENE of the Little Skellig, is an isolated stack, while the Washerwoman Rock, 1·8m high, is 3 cables SW of the Great Skellig, and has two sunken rocks 0·5 cable off its N end. The Little Skellig is a nature reserve, and home to puffins, fulmars, razorbills, guillemots and 20,000 pairs of gannets; landing on it is prohibited, and in any case very difficult. The ancient monastic remains on the Great Skellig attract a steady stream of visitors, mostly in small passenger boats from Valentia, Ballinskelligs and Derrynane. There is no anchorage, but there is a jetty in a rocky gut on the NE side, which, although naturally subject to swell, gives straightforward dinghy access. There is a

resident maintenance team in summer, who also act as guides, and in order to allow them to exercise their duty to protect the island's antiquities it is requested that visitors land only between the hours of 0900 and 1600. When securing a dinghy at the landing be sure to leave ample room for the ferryboats to berth and manoeuvre.

The five 1400-year-old monastic beehive huts and two oratories, in an astonishing state of preservation, are 150m above sea level and are reached by a flight of 600 steps cut into the rock. The climb demands care and stamina but is not unduly vertiginous. At the very summit of the island is an extraordinary hermit's cell, to which it is presumed a monk could retire when the pace of life on metropolitan Skellig Michael grew too hectic.

The lighthouse 50m above sea level at the S end of the island was built in 1966, replacing a tower built in the 1830's. This was originally one of two, the other being 65m higher on the rock. The upper light was discontinued in 1866.

The landing place, Skellig Michael

Little Skellig from the E

Puffin Sound

51°50'·4N 10°23'·8W

AC2495, 2125

Puffin Sound, between Puffin Island and the shore, is obstructed by rocks but has a narrow passage, 0·25 cable wide, through which the tides run rapidly. It is a very imposing place and the passage is possible, under power only, in calm conditions with no swell. Keep a quarter of the width of the sound from the W side. In bad weather it breaks right across, a most formidable sight.

Portmagee Sound

⊕ *PM* 51°52'·5N 10°25'W

AC2125, Imray C56 and Plan

Portmagee Sound, S of Valentia Island, provides excellent shelter, but access to Valentia Harbour is restricted by a low bridge which used to open but is now permanently closed. The shores at the entrance are high cliffs and there is often a steep and confused sea here. The rocks and islets on the S side of the entrance all show above HW. Reencaheragh Point (21m) on the mainland is foul for a distance of 0·25 cable, and there are above-water rocks off

Portmagee bridge and pier

Valentia Island and Portmagee Sound from W; Bray Head, foreground

Portmagee from the bridge

Scughaphort Reef on the N side. There is the ruin of a fort on this point.

Enter midway between Reencaheragh and Scughaphort Reef and steer 110°. **Anchor Rock**, which dries, lies 0·25 cable off Quay Brack, 4 cables beyond Skuagh Point. When Quay Brack is abeam, alter course to 065°; this leads up parallel to the island shore about 0·5 cable off and to the N of a shallow rocky patch 1·25 cables ESE of Quay Brack. Identify Loughan Islet (4m high) to starboard, and when it comes abeam alter course for the pier at Portmagee on the S shore. There is foul ground around Loughan Islet.

Garracinagh Sound, between Short Island, S of Long Island, and Black Rock to the S, is used by small local fishing vessels but is not recommended for a stranger.

Anchorage

There is good anchorage off Portmagee pier in 5m, although the tide runs strongly. There are visitors' moorings. The pier is used by fishing vessels. The N and E facing walls of the pierhead have deep water at all states of the tide, but yachts should not be left unattended. Diesel, water, showers, mechanical repairs, shop, restaurant, pubs.

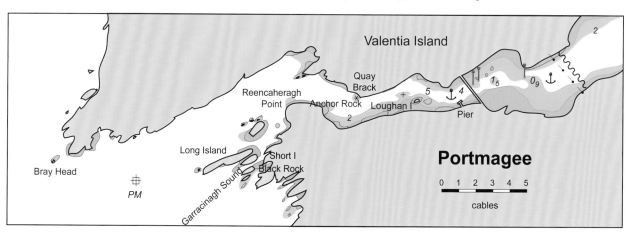

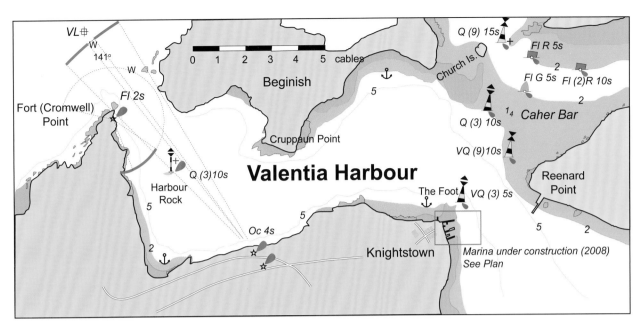

Valentia Harbour
⊕ *VL*   51°56′·3N 10°19′·5W
AC2125, Imray C56 and Plan

The main entrance lies between Cromwell (Fort) Point on the W side and Beginish Island on the E. Steer a mid-channel course along the line of the leading marks on Valentia. Cromwell Point is low and has sunken rocks extending 0·5 cable NNE of it, and there are rocks which show and a sunken rock extending 0·75 cable off the Beginish Island shore. There is often a confused sea at the entrance, which can be dangerous in NW gales. The dangers within the harbour are generally well marked and lit. At the time of writing a 200-berth marina is under construction at Knightstown (2008).

Tidal Streams
In Valentia Harbour the tides set fairly through both the N and S entrances to the harbour, meeting about 2·5M SW of Reenard Point. The ingoing stream makes at +0450 Cobh and the outgoing at –0135 Cobh. The spring rate is 2 kn off Cromwell Point and 1·5 kn off Knightstown. The same times apply to the Fertha River, where the tides run strongly in the channel and off the marina entrance at Cahersiveen. Constant –0058 Cobh; MHWS 3·8m, MHWN 3·0m, ML 2·1m.

Dangers
Harbour Rock, dries 2·6m, 3 cables SE of Cromwell Point

Ledges and sunken rocks up to 2 cables W of Cruppaun Point on Beginish Island

The Foot, gravel spit drying 1·2 to 0·6m in places, extending 1·5 cables ENE from the N pier at Knightstown.

Valentia Harbour from the SE; Knightstown, centre, with Beginish beyond. Reenard Point, R, and Cromwell Point, upper L. Doulus Head in the middle distance and the Blasket Islands on the horizon, L. This picture and the one on p154 were taken not long before the marina pontoons were installed in 2008

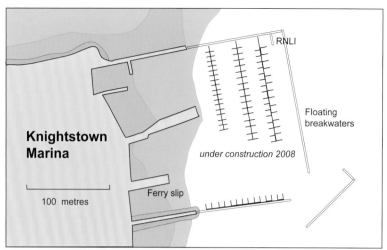

Knightstown Marina

100 metres

Ferry slip

RNLI

Floating breakwaters

under construction 2008

Lights and Marks

Cromwell (Fort) Point, white tower Fl WR 2s 16m, W17M R15M, W 102°–304° R 304°–351°. Shows red over Harbour Rock and the SW corner of the harbour, white elsewhere.

Harbour Rock, perch E Card Q(3) 10s 4m 5M

Valentia ldg lts 141°, front white tower, red stripe 25m, rear 43m, Oc WRG 4s W11M R8M G8M, G 134°–140°, W 140°–142°, R 142°–148° . Shows green close NE of Cromwell Point, white in mid-channel and red close SW of Beginish

The Foot buoy, E Card VQ(3) 5s.

For the dangers and marks in the N entrance from Doulus Bay and in the Fertha River, see the directions for Cahersiveen, below.

Marina *(see Plan)*

The marina is to have floating breakwaters, with an isolated section protecting the entrance from the SE.

It is proposed to build a new car-ferry slip to the S but in the meantime the ferry will continue to use its slip within the marina. A good lookout must be kept for it. 200 berths; water and shore power on the pontoons. Check www.irishcruisingclub. com for updates.

Anchorage

• Anchorage is available S of the marina entrance, staying well clear of the ferry's track

• Just W of the Foot, good holding in 2·5m. Well sheltered in winds from SE to SW. Land on the pebble beach at the back of the harbour pier.

• In strong NW winds better shelter can be obtained in the sandy bay at the SE end of Beginish Island.

• In winds from SE to W, in Glanleam Bay S of Harbour Rock. Anchor in 4m, 1 cable from the head of the bay opposite Glanleam House. The bay is reported subject to downdraughts in gales from S and SW, and the bottom at the NW end is reported weedy.

• The pier at Reenard Point is used by the car ferry, which has a slip on the NW side. A temporary alongside berth may be available on the SE side. The pierhead has 5m at LAT.

Facilities

Shops, pubs, PO, filling station at Knightstown. Water on S pier. Ferry to Reenard Point. RNLI all-

Knightstown piers from the E; the car ferry slip, second from L (before installation of marina pontoons). Note the shallow water over The Foot, R

weather lifeboat station. Slipway travelhoist, hull and mechanical repairs at Murphy Marine Services 066 9476883 or 087 280 9861. HM 066 9476124.

E part of Portmagee Channel

The channel is clean to within 0·5 cable of both shores for 3·5M SW of Reenard Point. An underwater cable and pipeline cross 6 cables E of the bridge, and there are fish farms in the channel. Anchorage in 3m, with easy access to Portmagee village, is available in mid-channel, well clear W of the pipeline and cable, with Reenarea Point bearing 300°.

FERTHA RIVER AND CAHERSIVEEN

AC2125 and Plan

Properly called the Fertha River, the waterway between Valentia and Cahersiveen is labelled "Valentia River" on the charts and is also referred to as the Caher River. Cahersiveen is 2M up the Fertha River from Valentia Harbour and can be approached over Doulus Bar in 2·4m or across the sheltered Caher Bar in 1·4m. The buoyed channel above Caher Bar has least depth 3m.The town has comprehensive facilities and an 80-berth marina.

Dangers

Kay Rock (0·9m), 3 cables ENE of Lamb Island
Doulus Bar (2·4m), between Beginish and the mainland 2 cables ESE of Kay Rock
Passage Rock (dries 1·5m), 1 cable E of Church Island.

Lights and marks

Kay Rock beacon, BRB Isolated Danger, Fl(2) 6s 4M
Passage Rock buoy, W Card Q(9) 15s
Canganniv Spit West buoy, W Card VQ(9) 10s
Canganniv Spit East buoy, E Card Q(3) 10s
The river channel to Cahersiveen is marked by 7 starboard- and 6 port-hand buoys, Fl G and Fl R respectively. Fourteen leading beacons, poles with black and yellow horizontal bands, ten Oc G, two Iso G and two (nos. 11 and 12) Oc R, also mark the channel. The buoys were laid in 2005 and are adequate marks by themselves, but the leading beacons are also to be maintained for the foreseeable future. Some of these beacons are difficult to discern by day.
Cahersiveen Marina entrance, 2FG vert and 2FR vert
Note that the former Ballycarbery Spit beacon is no longer lit or maintained.

Directions

From Valentia Harbour (Knightstown pier), with sufficient height of tide to cross Caher Bar (1·4m

The Fertha River, looking downstream; Cahersiveen Marina, foreground, Foughil Island centre, Caher Bar and Valentia top L

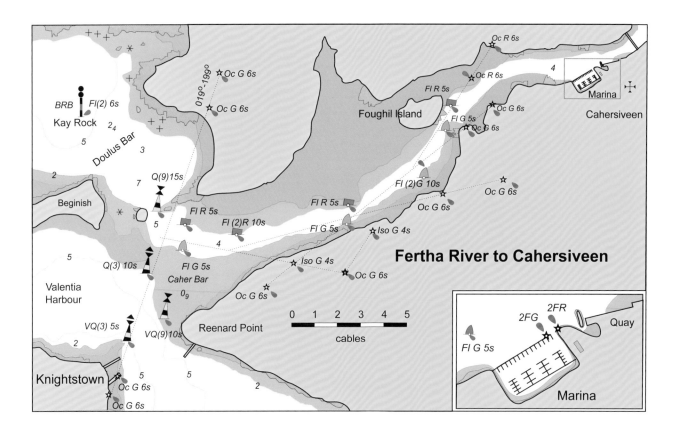

at LAT), leave Canganniv Spit W Card buoy close to starboard, heading 019°. Identify the Canganniv Spit E Card buoy and the first pair of lateral marks to the N, and steer to pass between Canganniv Spit E Card buoy and the starboard-hand buoy ENE of it. Then turn on to a heading of 101° and follow the buoyed channel to Cahersiveen. **From Doulus Bay,** the entrance is straightforward except in heavy weather from the W or NW or in a high swell, when there may be breakers on Doulus Bar. Enter in mid-channel between Black Rocks (N of Lamb Island) and the shore to the N, and identify the beacon on Kay Rock. Giving it a berth of 0·5 cable on either side, head for Passage Rock W Card buoy, leave it to port and follow the buoyed channel round to port and up-river. The tide runs at 2 kn at springs in the river.

Marina

The marina is on the S side 3 cables downstream of the bridge. Diesel (cans), water, shore power, showers, some chandlery. Marina office 06694 72777, manned Mon-Fri 0900-1700, info@ cahersiveenmarina.ie

Anchorage

Anchorage is possible just S of midstream abreast the quay. The projecting breakwater gives some shelter in W winds to the most W'ly berth at the quay, which has 5m. There is a small drying reef on the N shore opposite this breakwater.

Facilities

Shops, PO, pubs, restaurants, filling stations in Cahersiveen, 1 km. Marine engineer J. Kelly 066 9472502. Buses to Tralee & Killarney. Taxis.

Cahersiveen from the W

Chapter 5

Valentia to the Shannon

The ridge of Great Blasket Island falls 280m to the sea on its NW side

North of Valentia Harbour, the eastern part of the wide inlet of Dingle Bay has little to offer in the way of shelter, but the almost landlocked harbour of Dingle on its north shore is an important fishing port and a magnet for yachts. Dingle (1500) is justifiably famous on two counts: its restaurants are renowned for their seafood, and its harbour has been – since 1984 – home to a stage-struck bottlenose dolphin by the name of Fungie.

The Dingle peninsula ends at Dunmore Head, at 10°29'W the westernmost point of the mainland of Ireland, but a mile across a tideswept sound to the west lie the fabulous Blasket Islands. Exploring these islands to the full demands seamanship, vigilance and not a little athletic ability, but they reward the effort tenfold. Everything about the Blaskets is stupendous: the wildlife, the dazzling beach, the towering cliffs, the breathtaking views. The last of the islanders left Great Blasket in 1953, taking with them a rich literature, in Irish and English, recording the lifestyle that died on that day. But one person

– a weaver from Wales called Sue Redican – lives alone on Great Blasket, and has returned there every summer since 1985. If you are from Scotland, this is Ireland's St Kilda; if you are Faroese, you will find the landscape familiar.

In September 1588, Blasket Sound was the scene of a gathering of fugitive ships of the Spanish Armada, seeking shelter from the equinoctial gales. *Santa Maria de la Rosa,* the flagship of Admiral Villafranca, dragged her anchor and foundered on Stromboli Rock, leaving a single survivor out of 500 on board. *San Juan Battisa* had her guns and 500 men transferred to *San Juan de Portugal* and other ships by Admiral Recalde, and was then scuttled. One of the galleons, running before an equinoctial northwesterly gale, made the passage between Beginish and Great Blasket, and it is customary to comment on the outstanding seamanship involved. Be that as it may, given the quality of his charts, there can be no question about the Spanish captain's luck.

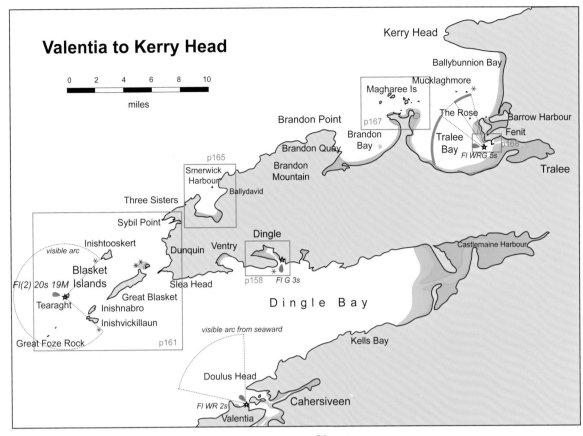

Valentia to Kerry Head

The port of Fenit, in Tralee Bay, has a marina and some specialised cargo traffic. The long estuary of the Shannon, Ireland's greatest river, is the major port on the west coast, with the bulk of its traffic handled at Foynes on the south shore. At Limerick the river gives access (subject to draft and headroom restrictions) to the Shannon Navigation, Ireland's most extensive inland waterway network.

Charts

On the smaller scale, AC2254 Valentia to the Shannon covers the area described in this chapter. The Imray chart C55 Dingle Bay to Galway Bay has plans of Dingle, Fenit and several of the Shannon harbours. AC2789 Dingle Bay and Smerwick Harbour is essential, and gives adequate detail for a passage of the Blasket Islands, but for exploration of the islands AC2790 is preferable. Fenit is

Blasket Sound in an autumn gale; view NW from Dunquin (photo Barbara St Aubyn)

accessible with AC2254, but AC2739 Brandon and Tralee Bays is better, and essential for exploring the Magharees. The passage anchorages of Kilbaha Bay and Carrigaholt, in the Shannon estuary, are likewise accessible with AC2254, but AC1819 Approaches to the River Shannon is preferable. For the Shannon above Carrigaholt, the large-scale charts AC1547, 1548 and 1549 are essential, with 1540 needed only if going to Limerick itself.

Valentia to Dingle and the Blaskets
AC2125, 2789

From Valentia, the simplest route N is through the main entrance at Cromwell Point, but from Cahersiveen the channel N of Beginish offers a shorter passage and obviates the crossing of Caher Bar. See the previous chapter for detailed directions.

Tidal Stream

Across the entrance to Dingle Bay the streams run N and S. There is little stream in the bay. The streams are strong in the entrance to Dingle Harbour.

Dangers

The shores of Dingle Bay are generally clean. **Breaker Rock**, awash at LW, lies 3·5 cables NE of Canglass Point; Reenadrolaun Point on Valentia Island open NW of Doulus Head 223° clears the rock. The dangers in the approaches to Dingle are listed below.

Kells Bay
52°02'N 10°05'W
AC2789

Kells Bay, on the S shore 6M E of Canglass Point, offers shelter in winds between SE and W. There are visitors' moorings in the bay and a small drying pier.

Castlemaine Harbour

This extensive and mostly drying inlet at the head of Dingle Bay lies E of Rossbehy and Inch Points. Extensive drying sandbanks extend W from both points for about 2M. The tidal streams run at 3 to 4 kn through the entrance at springs. The ingoing stream makes at +0605 Galway and the outgoing at +0005 Galway. The bar is subject to movement of the sandbanks, and no reliable directions can be given for entry.

DINGLE
⊕ *DL* 52°06'·7N 10°15'·5W
AC2789, 2790, Imray C56 and Plan

The town of Dingle, at the head of its almost landlocked harbour, is an important fishing port as well as a major tourist centre. Dingle Marina, W of the main pier, has 80 berths.

Dangers

Crow Rock (dries 3·7m), 5 cables SW of Reenbeg Point, W of Dingle Harbour
Colleen Og Rock, 1·8m, halfway between Crow Rock and the shore.

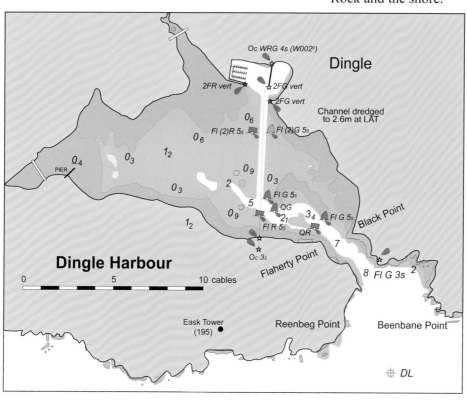

Lights
Dingle, NE side of entrance, white tower Fl G 3s 20m 6M
Black Point buoy, SHM Fl(3) G 5s
Flaherty Point buoy, PHM QR
The channel to the pier and marina is marked by 4 more SH and 2 more PH buoys
Dingle pier channel ldg lts astern 182° Oc 3s
East Pier Heads, 2×2FG vert 5m 2M
Marina Breakwater, 2FR vert
Dingle Pier, Port Entry Light Dir Oc WRG 4s, white 002° over channel, green to E, red to W.

Dingle Harbour from the S; the pier and marina upper L centre.

The entrance to Dingle Harbour lies between Reenbeg Point to the W and Beenbane Point to the E, and is clean, free of dangers, well marked and straightforward by day or night. The entrance is 7·5 cables E of the conspicuous Eask Tower, 195m. The light tower open E of Reenbeg Point 024° clears Crow Rock to the SE. The channel, 40m wide, is dredged to 2·6m at LAT and is marked by five starboard- and three port-hand buoys, all lit. The channel runs NW from the entrance buoys and then N. Leading beacons on the S shore and a directional light at the pier root lead through the dredged channel. The pier itself has heavy fishing vessel traffic and is only available to yachts in emergency. The harbour and marina are managed by the Department of Agriculture, Fisheries and Food.

Anchorage is possible 5 cables S of the marina and 1 cable W of the dredged channel, but care should be taken to avoid a drying patch in this area about 2 cables NNW of the lower leading beacon. There is also an underwater pipeline, and storage pots for lobsters. Contact HM for advice. Anchoring is not permitted in or near the dredged channel. HM phone 066 9151629, e-mail bmfdingle@eircom.net, VHF Ch 16 and 14 (not continuously manned).

Constant –0056 Cobh; MHWS 3·8m, MHWN 2·9m, ML 2·1m.

Facilities

Water, shore power, showers, small chandlery at the marina. Diesel by tanker. Supermarket, shops, pubs, restaurants, PO, laundry, filling station, car rental in town, all within 800m. Radio and electronic repairs, Tom Hand Electronics; mechanical repairs at Griffin's garage. Dingle Sailing Club is based at the marina.

Dingle Pier and Marina

Ventry Harbour from the SE; Ventry Pier, upper R

VENTRY HARBOUR
52°06'·5N 10°20'W
AC2789, 2790

This delightful broad bay has an entrance nearly a mile wide facing SE. It gives good shelter in SW to N winds though there can sometimes be a swell. It is also subject to heavy squalls from the high ground to the W in strong winds. Ventry Strand, on its W shore, is a superb sandy beach.

Directions
The entrance is easily recognised 2M W of the prominent Eask Tower. Parkmore Point on the W side of the entrance is at the E end of a long line of diminishing cliffs. Valentia lighthouse (Cromwell Point) open of Doulus Head leads to it. The only danger in the entrance is the 2·9m ridge extending SW from the shore 2·5 cables S of Ballymore Point. This ridge will break heavily in a big swell. It can be avoided by keeping S of the line joining Paddock Point, the E side of the entrance, and the conspicuous church W of the centre of Ventry Strand.

Anchorages
* Off the NE end of the beach in 4·5m, sand.

Ventry Pier, in the NE corner of the bay

There are visitors' moorings here, and a pier and slip offer a convenient landing and access to the village.
* On the S side of the bay about 1 cable N of the pier at Cuan (Coon on the chart) in 3m, sand.

Facilities
Restaurant, shop, pub and PO in the village. Shop and pub 1·5 km from the S anchorage.

BLASKET ISLANDS
AC2790
Dangers
Wild Bank, 5·2m, 2·5M SW of Slea Head, and **Barrack Rock**, 8·2m, 3·5M SW of Wild Bank, break in gales.

W and NW of Beginish in the Blaskets is an area of **stacks, drying and underwater rocks** too complex to describe in words; the **Connor Rocks**, above HW, and a **rock** (drying 0·3m) 2 cables to the W of them, mark the N limit of the shoals. Overfalls occur up to 1.5M N to NW of them

Scollage Rock (dries 3·7m), 0·5 cable W of Lure, the 44m stack off Dunmore Head

Stromboli Rock, 1·8m, 3 cables W of Lure, with another 1·8m rock 1 cable ENE of it

Fohish Rocks (dry 2·7m), 5 cables SSE of Inishvickillane

Unnamed rock (dries 0·3m), 3 cables W of Inishvickillane

Sound Rocks (dry 0·8m), 2 cables E of the N end of Inishnabro

Unnamed rock (drying 0·3m), 2 cables SW of Inishtooskert

Unnamed rocks (drying 2m and 0·8m), 3 cables WSW of Tearaght

Great Foze Rock (27m high), 2.8M WSW of Inishvickillane, **Little Foze**

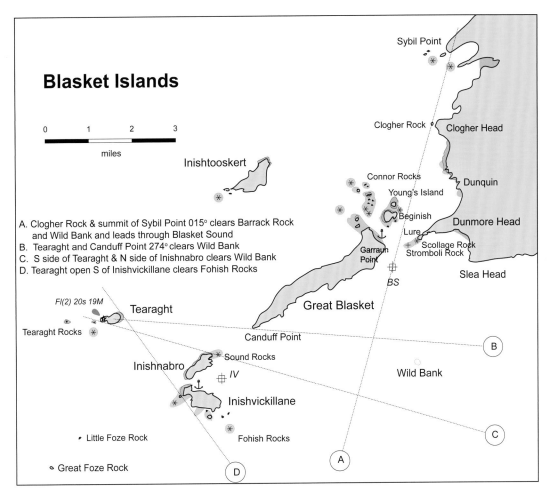

Blasket Islands

A. Clogher Rock & summit of Sybil Point 015° clears Barrack Rock
   and Wild Bank and leads through Blasket Sound
B. Tearaght and Canduff Point 274° clears Wild Bank
C. S side of Tearaght & N side of Inishnabro clears Wild Bank
D. Tearaght open S of Inishvickillane clears Fohish Rocks

Rock (7m high), 2.1M W by S of Inishvickillane, and **Tearaght Rocks** (13m high), 5 cables W of Tearaght, are all conspicuous by day but are unmarked, and dangerous at night.

Lights and Marks
Inishtearaght, Fl(2) 20s 84m 19M, Racon (O), on Tearaght Island. Visible from 318° through N to 221°; obscured from NE through E to SE.

Tidal Stream
In Blasket Sound the N-going stream makes at +0445 Galway and the S-going stream at –0140 Galway. The spring rate is from 2 to 3 kn. The duration of these streams can be much affected by the wind. There are overfalls on Wild Bank and on the uneven bottom among the islands, and a pronounced S-going eddy off the strand at Great Blasket during the N-going tide. The tidal stream is always to the W at up to 2 kn in the sound between Inishvickillane and Inishnabro.

The Blasket Islands from the NE. Young's Island and Beginish, L foreground; Great Blasket, L, with Inishvickillane (and Inishnabro (behind Great Blasket) beyond; Tearaght, top, and Inishtooskert, extreme R

Inishvickillane and Inishnabro from the NE. The Great Foze Rock, in the distance, is the westernmost land in Ireland

Magnetic Abnormality

A local magnetic abnormality is reported near the Blasket Islands.

Approach from the S and E

Clogher Rock, the stack off Clogher Head N of Blasket Sound, in line with the summit of Sybil Point 015° leads 2 cables E of Barrack Rock, 1·5M W of Wild Bank and mid-channel through Blasket Sound. Tearaght over Canduff Point (the SW extreme of Great Blasket) 274° leads 0·5M N of Wild Bank. The S end of Tearaght touching the NE end of Inishnabro 287° leads 1M S of Wild Bank.

Inishvickillane

⊕*IV* 52°03'N 10°36'W

Inishvickillane, 134m high, in the shape of a long ridge when viewed from the SE, and Inishnabro, 174m high, rising towards its N end, are the southernmost of the islands. The SW and SE sides of Inishvickillane are foul with stacks, rocks and breakers for 4·5 cables. From the SE, Tearaght open S of Inishvickillane clears Fohish Rocks to the S, while keeping the channel between Inishvickillane and Inishnabro open clears all dangers E and S of Inishvickillane.

Anchorage

Anchorage is available in 10 to 12m in the bay on the NE side of Inishvickillane. Give the N shore of the island a berth of 2 cables in the approach from the E, and anchor at least a cable offshore, as the bottom is foul with weed and rocks inside the 10m line. The bay is sheltered from winds between SE and N, and with relatively weak tidal streams it is the best anchorage in the Blaskets, but it has little competition for the title and is (naturally) subject to swell. In fine weather landing is easy on the small shingle beach but the steep path which winds up the cliffs is in a dangerous state and should not be attempted. An outcrop of rock at the N end of the bay, known locally as An Leirigh, provides an alternative landing place but even in fine weather a surge or swell can make landing difficult, and in fresh easterlies, impossible.

Traditionally, the island is regarded as home of the fairies and today it is also home to a more visible herd of red deer. There are a number of important archaeological features including the remains of an early Christian monastic settlement. The island is privately owned and has a single house which is occasionally occupied.

In settled weather the passage in mid-channel between Inishvickillane and Inishnabro presents no difficulty.

Inishnabro

The only possible landing place on Inishnabro (in very settled weather) is through a cave in the middle of the SE side of the island, N of the 14·3m sounding on AC2790. The entrance to this cave runs N–S and is close S of a larger cave entrance which runs in E–W. The cave is about 2m wide and 5m high. It leads into a tiny rocky pool open to the sky, with enough flat rock to land and pull up a dinghy. It is possible to scramble up a gulley above the pool and reach the flat middle neck of the island by a dry stone wall. Even on a very calm day there is a surge and scend in the cave.

The N tip of the island is formed by

Inishvickillane anchorage from the NW

Tearaght seen from Inishvickillane (L); Inishnabro on the R

superb cliffs and arches. There is a strong tide rip on its NE side.

Tearaght

Tearaght is pierced by a tunnel running N–S. In appearance it is a pinnacle from E or W. There are steps both E and W of the S entrance to the tunnel, seldom usable because of the nearly continuous swell. Cables and hoists stretch across this area for landing supplies for the lighthouse. The island has large puffin and storm petrel colonies.

Inishtooskert

Inishtooskert lies 4M N of Inishnabro and is 171m high, with steep cliffs on its NW side and a conspicuous cockscomb pinnacle on its N end. There is no anchorage or landing place. In calm weather it is possible to jump from a dinghy on to rocks on the SE side, but the ever-present swell and surge make this difficult. It is a steep climb to the top of the island, on which there is the ruin of an oratory.

Great Blasket
52°06'·5N 10°30'·4W

Great Blasket is separated from the mainland by Blasket Sound, 1M wide. The W side of the island has stupendous cliffs rising to 280m at Slievedonagh. At the NE end of the island is the old village, above a sandy bay which offers reasonable shelter and easy landing. In summer, and subject to weather conditions, tourist boats visit daily and a visitor centre and tearoom are opened.

Both sides of Great Blasket are clean as far as the N point of the island, and all dangers show above HW. There is a rock with 3·7m close inshore at Garraun Point, the E point of the island.

Anchorage

Anchor in 5m, sand, off the bay at the NE end. There is a strong tide and a pronounced S-going eddy into the bay on the N-going tide. Land at the slip at the S end of the beach.

Blasket Sound
⊕ *BS* 52°05'·8N 10°30'·3W
AC 2790, 2789

The passage of Blasket Sound is straightforward in daylight. From the S, transits to avoid Wild Bank are

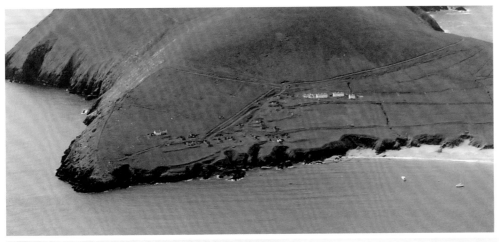

Great Blasket; the anchorage and the old village from the NE

Blasket Sound from the SE; Great Blasket and Inishtooskert, L, Beginish, centre, Lure and Dunmore Head R

given above. The Sound, with its exposed position, uneven bottom and strong tides, can be rough. Beginish (13m) and Young's Island (11m) form the W side of the sound and appear as one island from N or S. **Theogh Rocks** extend SE of Beginish, and there is a rock awash at LW 1·75 cables NE of Young's Island. Clogher Rock, the stack off Clogher Head to the N, in line with the

Blasket Sound from the SW; Clogher Head and Sybil Point, top L, Lure R

summit of Sybil Point, 015°, leads between Garraun Point and Stromboli Rock, and 2 cables E of Theogh Rocks and the rock NE of Young's Island. On the mainland side, there is a slip near Dunquin, which is used by the Blasket ferries. The landing place with its winding path down the cliff is a striking sight from seaward, but it is not suitable for berthing a yacht, and the approach is fringed with rocks.

The passage W of Beginish, obstructed by the drying Ballyclogher and Stookeen Rocks, is not recommended.

NORTH COAST OF THE DINGLE PENINSULA
Blasket Sound to Tralee Bay
AC2789, 2739, Imray C55

The mainland coast N and E of Blasket Sound is spectacularly scenic, with towering cliffs, offshore stacks and the remarkable cones of the Three Sisters, to the W of Smerwick Harbour. Smerwick offers good shelter and is an ideal point of departure for the Aran Islands or Connemara. Further E, between Ballydavid Head and Brandon Point, is one of the most impressive stretches of coast in the whole of Ireland, rising in 400m cliffs – the highest in Kerry – to Brandon Mountain. In fine weather, with its wonderful scenery and abundant bird life, it makes as fine a point of departure or landfall as anyone could desire; while a dawn landfall on Brandon Mountain will never be forgotten.

On the W shore of Smerwick Harbour is the site of Dún an Oir, the Golden Fort. In 1578 one of Frobisher's ships, returning from Baffin Island, was run ashore here. Her cargo, of what was believed to be gold ore, was unloaded before she broke up. The "ore" was seized by the Earl of Desmond, then in rebellion, and (found to be worthless) it was built into the walls of the fort. Within two years the rebellion was put down, Dún an Oir was destroyed and 700 men of the garrison were massacred here.

East of Brandon Point lies the wide sweep of Brandon Bay, with the Magharee Islands (The

The landing place at Dunquin in heavy weather. Note the traditional curraghs drawn up

Seven Hogs on the chart) off its E point and Tralee Bay beyond. Fenit, at the E end of Tralee Bay, has one of the few marinas on the west coast.

Dangers
Between Clogher Head and the Magharees a berth of 3 cables clears all dangers. In Tralee Bay are the following dangers:
Breaker, with 9m, 2M N by E of Rough Point
Breaker, with 4·3m, 1·8M NNE of Rough Point
Rock drying 0·9m, 2 cables N of Mucklaghmore
Breaker, with 3·3m, 4 cables S of Mucklaghmore
Boat Rock, dries 4·3m, 4 cables ENE of Illaunabarnagh
Wheel Rock, dries 3·5m, 1 cable W of Fenit pier head.

Lights
Ballynagall Pier, Fl R 3s 4m 3M
Brandon Pier, 2FG vert 5m 4M
Little Samphire Island, Fl WRG 5s 17m W16M R13M G13M, R 262°–275° and 280°–090°, G 090°–140°, W 140°–152°, R 152°–172°. Shows white over the approach from the NW between the Magharees and Mucklaghmore, green over the Magharees and the peninsula S of them, red over

Mucklaghmore and Illaunnabarnagh to the NNW and red also over the S part of Tralee Bay.
Great Samphire Island, QR 15m 3M
Fenit pier head, 2FR vert 12m 3M.

Smerwick Harbour

⊕*SK* 52°13'N 10°24'W
AC2789 and Plan

Smerwick Harbour is an open bay between the East Sister and Dunacapple Island, 1M to the NE. The entrance faces NW. There are rocks and breakers between Dunacapple Island and the shore to the E. The harbour is exposed to considerable ground swell and – while not an ideal refuge in bad weather – provides shelter from winds between NE and W. **Carrignakeedu** (awash at LW) is a cable offshore off Bull Creek on the E side of the bay.

Anchorages

- On the W side N of the slip marked "Boat Harbour" on AC2789, about 1·5 cables off the cliffs in 10m, good holding in stiff mud.
- In N winds the bay at the NE corner of the harbour offers shelter, off the mouth of the stream there. The end of Carrigduff reef in the SE corner of this bay is reported to be 0·75 cable further W than charted.
- In SE to SW winds, just W of Carrigveen on the S side of the harbour in 2·5m, sand.

There are visitors' moorings in the bay on the SE side of the harbour, E of Carrigveen.

Ballydavid Pier (at Ballynagall on the chart) has 0·5m LWS near the head and may offer a temporary alongside berth, but it is subject to swell, and was reported in 2006 fouled by a large fisherman anchor and rope 1m away from the side of the pier and 4m from its seaward end.. Constant –0047 Cobh; MHWS 3·8m, MHWN 2·9m, ML 2·1m.

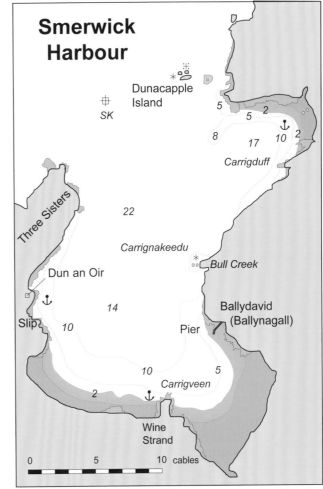

Ballydavid Pier

Smerwick Harbour from the SE; Carrigveen and Wine Strand, centre L; Ballynagall (Ballydavid) centre R. The Three Sisters, top L

Brandon Quay

Facilities

There are roads to the beach at Wine Strand, E of Carrigveen, and 1M further W. Shop, pubs, restaurants, PO at Ballyferriter, 1·5 km SW; filling station 1·5 km from Wine Strand. Shop and pub at Ballydavid (Ballynagall).

Brandon Bay

52°17'·5N 10°07'W
AC2739

The bay is exposed to the N and a heavy sea can set into it; it is well sheltered from SW to W. At Brandon village, 1·5M S of Brandon Point, there is a drying quay. Anchor in 6m, mud and sand, just NE of the quay; there is a patch of rock just S of the line of the quay. The anchorage is not safe with the wind N of NW or with a heavy swell. Shop, pubs, PO.

Magharee Sound

52°19'N 10°05'W
AC2739 and Plan

The sound provides a simple short cut to Fenit from the W and is easily navigable in moderate weather. It should be avoided in bad weather or heavy swell, which breaks on the banks N of the islands as well as in the sound, especially on the ebb. The W entrance is free of danger if the visible rocks are given a good berth. Steer a middle course between the islands until abreast of **Mucklaghbeg**, 6m high, to avoid **Illaundonnell** and **Illaunlea** on the S side which cover at half tide. Between these, the S side of The Rose Islet, Fenit Castle and Church Hill E of Tralee Bay, all in line 106° gives the best water. This transit can sometimes be difficult to see, and an easier mark is the N side of Gurrig Island just open S of Illauntannig astern, 280°, having given the latter a reasonable berth. Once through, course can be set for Little Samphire Island. If approaching Fenit from the W and passing N of the Magharee Islands, Illaunbarnagh, 9m high and flat in shape, open twice its own length N of Mucklaghmore, 30m high and pudding shaped, 110°, leads clear N of the banks. Kerry Head and Loop Head in line, 002°, leads clear E of them and W of Mucklaghmore.

Tidal Stream

The E-going flood through the sound starts at +0505 Galway and the W-going ebb at –0120 Galway, rate 2 to 3 kn.

Anchorages

In settled weather, temporary anchorage is available E of Illauntannig, on which there are beehive huts and a stone cross. The anchorage is a pool with 2m, off the house on the island; the marks for it are the W point of Scraggane Bay in line with the E point of Illauntannig, and the S side of Illaunturlogh on the middle of Thurran Rock, which dries 2·5m and is steep-to. The point of Loop Head on the E point of Reenafardarrig leads W of the rock in 1·2m.

Scraggane Bay from the E; Doonagaun, R, Brandon Point, top. Scraggane Point pier, centre R

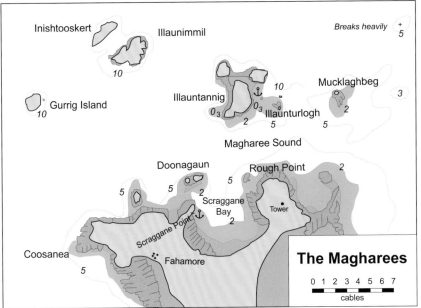

Scraggane Pier

Scraggane Bay, on the mainland side of the sound, provides safe anchorage and good holding in winds between E and SW. Some swell may enter at high water when the rocks inside Doonagaun are covered. There is a pier on the W side. Anchor as close ENE of the pier as draft permits. There is 2m with the pierhead 287° and the E end of Illauntannig 023°. A shoal runs out from the head of the bay nearly to its centre where it is awash at LAT. Pub and restaurant at Fahamore, 1 km.

TRALEE BAY
AC2739

Entry by day in clear weather is straightforward either N of the Magharees or through the Sound. From the W at night, set course to pass 3M N of the Magharee Islands and hold this until the white sector of Little Samphire light is entered. From the N, get into the white sector of Little Samphire light as soon as it is picked up, and head straight for the light. As soon as the 10m sounding is reached alter course to 180° and hold this until the red sector is reached bearing 090°, then stand in towards the QR light on Great Samphire Island. Give Little Samphire Island a berth of 2 cables and Great Samphire Island a berth of 1 cable. As Great Samphire Island (the S end of Fenit breakwater) comes abeam, identify the 2 FR vert lights on the pierhead. Be on the lookout for any traffic coming out.

In strong W winds there is good anchorage with very little swell on the W side of Tralee Bay. The best place about 3 cables offshore in 3m is with Little Samphire lighthouse bearing 103°; this is just N of a rocky outcrop 2·5M S of Rough Point.

Fenit Harbour
⊕*FT* 52°16'N 9°53'W
AC2739, Imray C55 and Plan
Fenit Harbour is formed by breakwaters running N

Fenit Harbour and marina from the SE

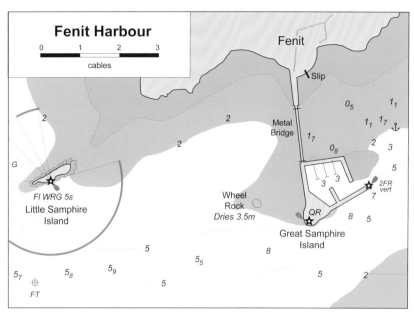

Fenit Harbour

0   1   2   3
cables

Fenit

Slip

Metal
Bridge

Wheel
Rock
Dries 3.5m

Fl WRG 5s
Little Samphire
Island

Great Samphire
Island

QR

2FR
vert

FT

shops, pubs, restaurants, PO. Repairs – O'Sullivan Marine, Tralee. Tralee Bay Sailing Club is based at Fenit. Constant –0037 Cobh; MHWS 4·6m, MHWN 3·5m, ML 2·6m.

Barrow Harbour
52°18'·5N 9°52'·4W
AC 2739
This narrow inlet lies NE of Fenit Island and is accessible only in settled swell-free weather. The entrance lies between Illaunnacusha (6m high) and Crow Rock (13m high). Steer for the centre of the gap between the Martello tower and the islet 1 cable off it. Just before bringing the islet abeam turn to starboard to pass close to it, and then follow the slight curve in the channel along the beach on Fenit Island towards Fenit Castle, a square tower. Anchor opposite the castle in 3·5m. The channel is 0·5 cable wide and the tide runs strongly. The inner bay dries out.

and E from Great Samphire Island and connected to the N shore by a bridge. Great Samphire Island has a conspicuous statue of St Brendan the Navigator on its summit, its stance and site clearly owing their inspiration to the Metal Men of Sligo and Tramore. The harbour, managed by Tralee & Fenit Harbour Commissioners, has some cargo and fishing vessel traffic and an RNLI all-weather lifeboat. Its N half is occupied by a 140-berth marina.

Marina
VHF Ch. 37 & 80, 066 713 6231. Diesel, water, showers, laundry. Fenit village has

(above) Little Samphire Island, seen from Great Samphire; (left) Fenit Harbour entrance; (below) Barrow harbour from the NW, with Illaunnacusha and Crow Rock bottom L; and (above right) St Brendan in Metal Man pose on Great Samphire. Note QR below his left elbow; no doubt the saintly Navigator would have approved

THE SHANNON ESTUARY

The Shannon estuary, 50M in length from Loop Head to Limerick, is little travelled by yachts but offers a wide variety of anchorages and scenery, and amply rewards the visitor. There is a marina at Kilrush on the N side 16M from Loop Head. Tides in the estuary are strong, up to 4 kn. The outer part of the estuary, below Kilrush, is home to a large pod of bottlenose dolphins.

Charts

A yacht caught out by bad weather on passage from Kerry to Galway can make Kilbaha or Carrigaholt with AC2254 (Valentia to the Shannon) or 2173 (Loop Head to Slyne Head) but for safe pilotage of the estuary AC1819 (Approaches to the Shannon) is to be preferred. For exploration of the upper reaches of the estuary, the largest-scale charts are essential.

Tidal Streams

Between Foynes and the sea the flood starts at –0500

Galway, and the ebb at +0100 Galway. The main ebb stream runs SW from Kilcredaun Head, forming a race with heavy overfalls in winds between S and NW.

Dangers – Loop Head to Kilrush and Scattery Roads

Beal Bar (dries 0·1m), 8 cables WNW of Beal Point
Baurnahard Spit (dries 2·5m), 1·2M W of Kilrush
Carrigillaun (dries), 2 cables W of Kilrush
Wolf Rock, 1m, 1 cable off the mainland shore opposite Hog Island, 5 cables SE of Kilrush
Carrig Donaun (dries 0·3m), stony patch 1·5 cables E of Scattery Island.

Lights and Buoys

Loop Head, Fl(4) 20s 84m 28M
Ballybunion buoy, N Card Q, Racon (M) 6M
Kilstiffin buoy, PHM Fl R 3s
Kilcredaun Head, white tower, Fl 6s 41m 15M
Kilcredaun buoy, PHM Fl(2+1) 10s
Tail of Beal buoy, W Card Q(9) 15s
Carrigaholt buoy, PHM Fl(2) R 6s
Beal Bar buoy, N Card Q
Doonaha buoy, PHM Q(3) R 5s
Letter Point buoy, PHM Fl R 7s
Asdee buoy, PHM Fl R 5s
Scattery Island, white tower, Fl(2) 8s 15m 10M
Kilrush Fairway buoy, L Fl 10s
Kilrush Marina entrance channel, outer leading lights Oc 3s 355°
Kilrush Lock S side, beacon SHM Fl G 6s
Kilrush Marina entrance channel, inner leading lights Oc 6s 070°
Rineanna buoy, PHM QR
North Carraig buoy, N Card Q.

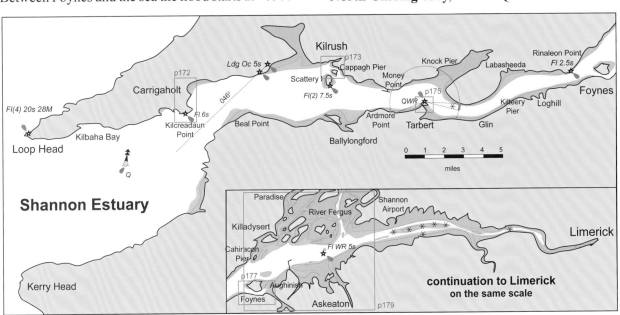

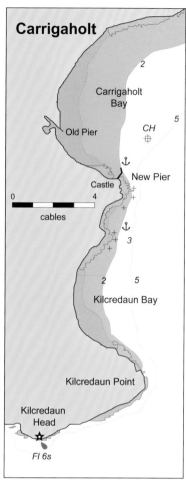

Carrigaholt New Quay

Caution

The Shannon estuary is a major port, and very large ships use the channel. The whole estuary should be regarded as a "narrow channel" within the meaning of IRPCS Rule 9, and small craft and yachts should not impede commercial shipping.

Directions – main channel

As noted above, the area between Loop Head, Kerry Head and the Tail of Beal Bar is subject to heavy overfalls and a tide race. To avoid these, stay 0·5 to 1M off the N shore E of Loop Head, which is free of off-lying dangers. Kilstiffin Bank, which has 7m, breaks in bad weather or a big swell. Kilbaha cliff in line with Kilcloher Head, 260°–080°, leads through the Seven Fathoms Channel N of the bank. Keep 1 cable off Kilcredaun Head to avoid the race on the ebb. Off Kilcredaun Point, 0·5M beyond the head, the ebb runs SW up to 4 to 5 kn, but the tide off Carrigaholt Road is weaker and at Carrigaholt Castle is negligible. In poor visibility Kilcredaun Head can be distinguished by a white stain on the rocks beneath the lighthouse and immediately above the HW mark.

Heading seawards with a fresh W wind, or with a W swell, it is best to pass Kilcredaun Head at slack water. A yacht leaving with the ebb in these conditions must be prepared to meet very steep short seas in the race. As above, stay within 1M of the N shore to find the calmest water.

Kilbaha Bay

52°34'N 9°51'W
AC1819

This is a useful passage anchorage 3M inside Loop Head, sheltered in winds from W to NE but with indifferent holding, exposed to swell and tidal eddies: a pleasant spot in fine weather, but if unsettled, Carrigaholt is much preferable. There are submerged rocky ledges on both sides of Kilbaha Bay, so keep to the middle approaching the anchorage. Coming in along the line of the local mooring buoys is a good approach. Anchor in 4m in the centre of the bay with the pierhead bearing 250°. SE winds send in a nasty short sea. Constant –0015 Galway; MHWS 4·3m, MHWN 3·3m, ML 2·4m.

Pier

The pier is good with a clean sandy bottom. Abreast of the second bollard from the steps it dries 1·4m. In SE winds, when the bay is exposed, the pier offers shelter.

Water on the pier. Shop, pub, PO, filling station.

Carrigaholt

⊕*CH* 52°36'·2N 9°41'·7W
AC1547, Imray C55 and Plan

This bay, 1·5M N of Kilcredaun Point, gives good protection from all W winds. The most convenient anchorage is 0·5 cable N of the New Quay at the castle, in 3m, excellent holding and no tidal stream to speak of. There are visitors' moorings. Better shelter in W or NW wind may be found off the small bay S of Carrigaholt Castle and N of Kilcredaun Bay, good holding in 3m, sand. Constant –0015 Galway; MHWS 4·9m, MHWN 3·7m, ML 2·8m.

New Quay (Carrigaholt Castle)

The New Quay has 3m at the pierhead berth and 1 to 2m just S of the steps, but is unsafe in NW winds. An overnight berth may be available but the fishing boats must be accorded priority. Water on the quay.

The Old Quay, 4 cables NW, dries. Shop and pubs at Carrigaholt.

KILRUSH

⊕*KR* 52°37'·6N 9°30'·2W
AC1547, Imray C55 and Plan

Kilrush Channel, between Scattery Island and the shore, is the direct approach from the W to Kilrush Marina and Cappagh Pier (Cappa Pier on the chart). Approaching from the SW on a course of 055° and giving Scattery Island a berth of 2·5 cables, identify the fairway buoy W of Cappagh pier in position 52°37'·6N 9°30'·2W. From there, a line of port- and starboard-hand buoys leads 355° up the channel. The water level in the basin is maintained by a barrage and lock NE of Watch House Point. The lock is manned during working hours but can be opened at any time by prior arrangement, phone 065 905 2072. Constant +0010 Galway; MHWS 5·0m, MHWN 3·7m, ML 2·7m.

Approach from the SE

Wolf Rock, with 1m, is dangerous near LW and lies 1 cable offshore on the E side of the channel between Hog Island and the shore. Keep well over towards Hog Island; when Scattery Lighthouse is in line with the E part of Hog Island, the rock is abreast.

Marina

Inside the barrage, the inner leading marks lead 070° to the marina, which has 120 berths and 3m at LAT. The channel is dredged to 2·5m. Outside working hours the outer lock gate is left open so that yachts can berth in the lock. Marina VHF Ch. 80, phone 065 9052072, fax 065 9051692, mobile 086 2313870. www.kilrushcreekmarina.ie.

Facilities

Diesel, water, shore power, showers, laundry, chandlery, 45 tonne travelhoist. Supermarkets, shops, pubs, restaurants, filling station, PO, doctors in Kilrush. Hull, mechanical, electrical and electronic repairs by approved contractors; contact the marina office. Western Yacht Club operates from the marina. RNLI inshore lifeboat station.

Cappagh Pier

Cappagh Pier, 2 cables SE of the entrance to Kilrush, is the pilot station for the Shannon estuary, and the outermost berth at the pier is reserved for the pilot boat. The inner berths dry about 0·6m and may be used at suitable rise in reasonable weather. It would not be safe to dry out there.

Water on the pier. Small shop, pub.

Kilrush

Kilrush Lock and Marina from the W

Anchorage

- There is temporary or fair-weather anchorage 50m SE of Cappagh pier in 1·5m, fairly good holding. In SW or W gales this anchorage is smooth during the ebb, but with the flood there is a heavy tidal sea caused by an eddy which runs out from the anchorage against the wind. If remaining overnight an anchor light is essential.

- A better anchorage is in the bay on the NE of Hog Island with good shelter from SE to SW; the tide here runs SE on both flood and ebb. Anchor outside yachts on moorings. The anchor should be buoyed. A large yellow buoy lies in the anchorage to NE of Hog Island. This is used by the pilot boat in SE gales.

- Scattery Roads. There is good shelter from SW to N winds in the bay on the SE side of Scattery Island. Give the S end of the island a berth of 2 cables and anchor in 2 to 3m between 1 and 2 cables NE of the slip near the lighthouse, sand. Note that it shoals quite suddenly from 4 to 1m. Just outside this anchorage there is an eddy on the flood which causes a sea in strong S wind.

- Off the jetty on the E side of Scattery is convenient for visiting the island, but due to the tide is less comfortable than Scattery Roads. Good holding in 2 or 3m, 1·5 to 2 cables from the jetty. S of the line of this jetty a shoal extends 2·5 cables

from the island shore. About 150m NE of the jetty there is a patch of stones which, like Carrig Donaun further NE, is awash at LWS.

Tidal Streams

In the channel S of Scattery Island, between the Rineanna and Carrig Shoals, there are heavy overfalls on the ebb with strong W winds; these are worst near the Rineanna buoy. Avoid most of this by keeping between the buoy and Scattery Island. Avoid the windward edge of Rineanna Shoal. Both shoals have least depth 4m.

RIVER SHANNON – KILRUSH TO FOYNES
AC1547, 1548

This 15M stretch of the river has several major landmarks on its banks including the power stations at Money Point and Tarbert, but also delightful and quiet anchorages. A car ferry crosses the river from Tarbert to Killimer. Foynes, behind Foynes Island on the S shore, is the principal commercial port on the Shannon.

Dangers

The Bridge, 17m, in mid-channel S of Money Point

Boland's Rock (dries 1·4m), 1·5M E of Tarbert Island

Dillisk Rocks (dry 0·3m), 6 cables E of Labasheeda

Point
Long Rock (dries 2·8m), 1M WSW of Garraunbaun
Point on the S shore
Carrigeen Rocks (dry 0·3m), 1M ENE of
Garraunbaun Point
Elbow Rock (dries 1·4m), in mid-channel between
Foynes Island and Durnish Point
Long Rock (dries), 1 cable NE of Elbow Rock.

Lights and marks
Money Point jetty, 3×2 FR vert
Tarbert tanker jetty, 2×2 FG vert
Tarbert Island, N Point, white tower Iso WR 4s
18m, W14M R10M, W 069°–277°, R 277°–287°,
W 287°–339°. Red sector shows over Boland's
Rock to the E, white elsewhere.
Ballyhoolahan Point, Ldg lts 128°, front white
tower Iso 3s 13m 3M, rear white beacon, green
stripe, Iso 5s 18m 3M
Kilkerin buoy, PHM Fl(2) R 6s
Gorgon buoy, SHM Fl(2) G 6s
Bolands buoy, PHM Fl(2) R 6s
Bolands perch, PHM, red, unlit
Carraig Fada buoy, SHM Fl G 5s
Garraunbaun Point, white beacon, Fl(3) WR 10s
16m W8M R5M, R shore–072°, W 072°–242°, R
242°– shore; red sectors cover Long and Carrigeen
Rocks.
Loghill buoy, SHM Fl G 3s
Rinealon Point, black column, white bands, Fl 2·5s
4m 7M.

Entrance to Foynes:
The main entrance, to the SW of Foynes Island, is
marked by four pairs of green and red pile beacons,
QR, IQR, QG and IQG, including **Hunts (Weir)
Point**, red beacon QR 2m 2M and **Colleen Point**,
green beacon QG 2m 2M, and by
Barneen Point, red pole beacon L Fl R 5s
Leading lights 108°, grey pole beacons Oc 4s
10M, front 34m, rear 39m
In the channel to the E of Foynes Island
are:
Elbow Rock buoy, PHM, unlit
Long Rock buoy, SHM, unlit

**Ballylongford Creek and Saleen
Quay**
52°34'·5N 9°28'·4W
AC1547
Ballylongford Creek is situated on the
S side of the estuary opposite Scattery
Island. The entrance, SE of Carrig
Island, is marked by an unlit starboard-
hand buoy a cable N of Reenturk Point.

The channel to Saleen Quay, 8 cables up-river, has
about 1m and is marked by locally-maintained
buoys and perches. It is advisable to enter on a rising
tide. There is 0·6m alongside the quay, with a good
drying berth beyond the first set of steps by the shed.
There is also 1m along the S end of the quay but this
is usually taken up by local boats. There are oyster
beds on the shores beside the channel entrance.

Shops, pubs, PO, filling station at Ballylongford
village, 1·5 km.

The Bridge
52°35'·7N 9°25'·8W
AC1547
This rocky ridge about 3M E of Scattery Island and
opposite Ardmore Point on the S shore, extends
over halfway across the estuary from the N shore.
Although its least depth is 16m there are heavy
overfalls with both flood and ebb in strong W
winds. It can be avoided by keeping within 0·5M of
Ardmore Point.

Anchorage E of Ardmore Point
52°35'N 9°25'2W
AC1548
This gives shelter from SE to SW and is useful if
forced to leave Tarbert in SE wind and ebb tide.
There is a solitary white house on the shore W of
Glencloosagh valley. Anchor in 2m, somewhat
nearer to Ardmore Point than to this house with
Scattery Lighthouse just open of Ardmore Point.

Tarbert
⊕ *TT* 52°35'N 9°21'·3W
AC1548 and Plan
The vicinity of the tanker jetty NW of the island is
a prohibited area. At springs the ebb tide runs at 4
kn from the piers out past the lighthouse, causing
heavy overfalls in strong NW and W winds. Off the
pier the tide always runs NW, as there is an eddy on

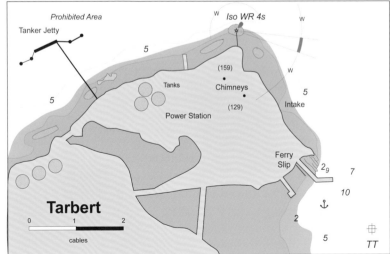

the flood, and the tide also sweeps through a tunnel in the pier. The S side of the pier must be left clear for the ferry. A berth may be available on the N side of the pier between the steps and the tunnel, or to the E of the steps. There is at least 1·8m at LW and good shelter in all conditions except near slack water in strong NW to NE winds. Constant +0035 Galway; MHWS 5·0m, MHWN 3·8m, ML 2·7m.

Anchorage
Either S of the elbow of the outer pier and E of the inner quay in 2m or further S with the inner quay in line and with Knock village on the Clare side in line with the end of the outer pier in about 3m, sheltered water in winds between SW and NW, excellent holding; exposed however to W and NW winds, Tarbert Island being low-lying. Do not obstruct the ferries.

Facilities
Pub 400m from the pier. Shops, pubs, PO, filling station at Tarbert village, 1·5 km and accessible by dinghy towards HW.

Knock Pier
52°36'·5N 9°21'W
AC1548
Clonderalaw Bay, on the N side opposite Tarbert, is a long inlet most of which dries. Knock Pier is 1M within the bay on its NW side and is approached across drying mudflats. When the rock at the base of Tarbert Lighthouse covers, which corresponds to HW neaps, there is 1·8m at the pier. Stay close to the pier when going alongside its E side to avoid the ruins of the E pier. Pubs and PO.

Caution
The flood sets SSE across Boland's Rock, so do not pass N of it with the flood, unless with ample wind or power, to avoid being swept onto the rock.

Glin
52°34'·6N 9°17'W
AC1548
Glin Pier is on the S shore 3M upstream of Tarbert lighthouse and 0.25M N of Glin village. The ruined pier extension on iron piles is conspicuous, but the original stone pier has a clean muddy bottom on its E side and offers shelter in winds between SE and WSW. In summer a pontoon, which dries at LW, is moored to the pier. Be careful not to be set onto the ruined staging by the tide.

Anchorage
Anywhere ENE of the pier in 4m good holding, well sheltered in S winds, exposed from W to NE. At night Rinealon Point light just open of Garraunbaun Point light is a good anchoring mark. The first half of the ebb runs W but at half tide a strong eddy runs E until LW, when the flood commences and continues running E until HW.

Facilities
Shops, pubs, restaurants, PO and filling station at Glin village.

Kilteery Pier
52°35'·7N 9°13'·5W
AC1548
Kilteery Pier is on the S side of the estuary opposite Labasheeda. The pier dries about 1.2m but can provide an attractive temporary berth. Loghill village, 1·5 km E, has a shop and pubs.

Labasheeda Roads
52°36'·5N 9°15'W
AC1548
This anchorage on the N shore gives good shelter in W and NW winds with good holding. The best place is NE of Redgap Point as close as possible to the mudbank to avoid the SW-going ebb. Labasheeda village has PO and pub and can be reached by dinghy with sufficient rise of tide. There are visitors' moorings in the bay.

Anchorage
The bay west of Rinealon Point is well sheltered in N and NE winds and is out of the strength of the ebb tide. It lies off Aillroe Hill which is conspicuous on the shoreline 6·5 cables W of Rinealon Point with the road along its S slope. Anchor abreast the hill about 0·75 cables from the shore in 4m.

FOYNES
⊕*FY* 52°37'·1N 9°07'·8W
AC1549, Imray C55 and Plan
The channel between Foynes Island and the S shore is the best natural harbour in the Shannon with shelter from all winds, easy access and good facilities. However, there is a 3 kn ebb stream through the channel, and Foynes is a busy commercial port, managed by Shannon Foynes Port Company. The port office monitors VHF Ch 16 and 11, 24 hours. HM phone 069 73103.

Directions
Approaching from the W, there is shoal water extending 1 cable off the S shore as far as Poultallin Point at the entrance. From the W end of Foynes Island a shoal runs out for 2 cables with a rock on its

Foynes Harbour from the E; Foynes Island upper R, East Pier, R

S edge. Otherwise the channel is clear, and is well marked.

Approaching from the NE, the channel lies between mudbanks with some rocks and a least depth of 2·1m, and requires more care than the W entrance. Approach with St Senan's Hospital bearing 215°; the hospital is a very conspicuous, flat-roofed building S of the railway station. Long Rock lies in mid-channel with a green buoy on its W side; leave this buoy to port entering. Two cables further on a red buoy marks **Elbow Rock.** From the Elbow Rock buoy steer for the East Pier and the anchorage. Above half-tide a yacht drawing 1·8m may approach the Long Rock buoy direct from the N, keeping both buoys in line bearing 192°. To clear the rock on the end of the spit E of Sturamus Island, keep Foynes church open its own width of Gammarel Point which gives 0·6m at LWS. To clear the mud spit S of this rock and E of Foynes Island, keep St Senan's Hospital open half its length of Gammarel Point, which gives 1·2m at LWS; or open its full length gives 3m.

Anchorage

Anchor E or SE of Gammarel Point. Foynes YC has a marina pontoon 250m long off the clubhouse at Colleen Point, W of the port area. The clubhouse has the usual facilities during the summer. There are visitors' moorings. Landing is practicable only at the YC pontoon, since the commercial port area, with its associated security constraints, occupies the entire waterfront at the village. Constant +0050 Galway; MHWS 5·2m, MHWN 4·0m, ML 2·8m.

Facilities

Filling station, shops, pubs, PO, doctors.

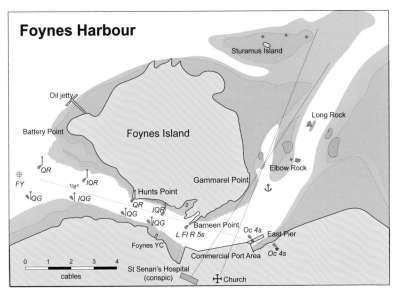

Foynes Harbour

Sturamus Island

Oil jetty

Battery Point

Foynes Island

Long Rock

FY

QR

108°   IQR

QG   IQG

Gammarel Point

Elbow Rock

Hunts Point

QR   IQR

QG   IQG

Barneen Point

L Fl R 5s

Foynes YC

Oc 4s   East Pier

Commercial Port Area

Oc 4s

0   1   2   3   4
cables

St Senan's Hospital
(conspic)

Church

RIVER SHANNON, FOYNES TO LIMERICK
AC1549, 1540

Above Foynes the character of the river changes and there are many drying and submerged rocks, some in mid-channel, and many around the islands in the mouth of the River Fergus. Proceeding up-river to Limerick it is advisable to stay in the buoyed channel.

Dangers

The dangers are too numerous to list in exhaustive detail, but the principal ones are as follows:

Colonel Rock (dries 0·3m) 1M NE of Inishmurry
Herring Rock (dries 2·7m), 1M E by N of Aughinish Point
Beeves Rock (dries 1·4m), **Cork Rock** (dries 5·2m) and **Wide Rock** (dries 4m), in mid-channel 1·5M ENE of Aughinish Point
The Needles, extensive drying reef 2M NE of Aughinish Point
Horse Rock (dries 2·8m), 1·4M SW of Rineanna Point
Moylaun's Children (dry 0·3m), at the end of the reef extending 1M SW from Rineanna Point
Roadway Rock (dries 2·4m), in mid-channel of the River Fergus between Coney and Feenish Islands
Carrigkeal (dries 2·1m), **Middle Ground** (dries up to 5·5m at **Bridge Rock**) and **Bird Rock** (dries 2·1m), together extending 3M in mid-channel E of Dernish Island
Logheen Rock (dries 1·3m), 7 cables N of Carrigclogher Point
Carrigdirty Rock (dries 2·7m), 6 cables NE of Carrigclogher Point
The Scarlets and **The Whelps**, (dry up to 1·6m), in mid-channel N of Newtown Point
Ardbane Rock (0·2m) and **Horril's Rocks** (dry 0·8m), E of Newtown Point.

Lights and marks

The main channel is well marked by lit port- and starboard-hand buoys, and by the following principal fixed marks:

Beeves Rock, stone tower Fl WR 5s 12m W12M R9m, W 064°–091°, R 091°–238°, W 238°–265°, W(unintens) 265°–064°. Shows white over channels to WSW and ENE, red over dangers to the N and unintensified white to S and SE.
Dernish Island Pier Head, 2×2FR vert 2m 2M
Conor Rock, white tower, Fl R 4s 6m 6M
North Channel ldg lts 093°, front white tower on Tradree Rock, Fl R 2s 6m 5M, rear white tower, red bands Iso 6s 14m 5M
Bird Rock, white tower QG 6m 5M
Grass Island, Fl G 2s 6m 4M

Logheen Rock, QR 4m 5M
Spilling Rock, Fl G 5s 5m 5M
N Side ldg lts 061°, front on Crawford Rock Fl R 3s 6m 5M, rear Crawford No 2, Iso 6s 10m 5M; ldg lts 302°, front on Flagstaff Rock Fl R 7s 7m 5M, rear Crawford No 2 as above
The Whelps, Fl G 3s 5m 5M
Leading Lights 106°, front on Meelick Rock Iso 4s 6m 3M, rear Iso 6s 9m 5M
Braemar Point, Iso 4s 5m 5M
Clonmacken Point, Fl R 3s 7m 4M
Spillane's Tower, Fl 3s 11m 6M.

Directions

Aughinish Island, with its conspicuous aluminium works and its jetty projecting 5 cables N from Aughinish Point, lies 2M upstream from Foynes. The confluence of the Shannon with the Fergus is on the N side 3M above Aughinish. The main channel runs N of Aughinish jetty and S of Beeves Rock beacon. Under sail in light winds, beware of being swept into the jetty by strong tides. A tail of rock extends 2 cables N from Herring Rock, which is particularly dangerous coming downstream as the strong ebb from Beeves Rock sets directly on to it. Note also the reef extending 4 cables S from Horse Rock. Aughinish N Card buoy marks Aughinish Shoal, which has more than 5m and need not trouble a yacht.

Deel River
52°38'·7N 9°00'·5W
AC1549

The Deel, which joins the Shannon 2M E of Auginish Point, has 0·6m at its mouth and somewhat more inside. A port hand beacon, red with white band, marks the entrance. When the Sheehan, the E point of Beeves Rock, is covered, there is a depth of 2m on the Deel bar NW of the beacon. The channel is marked by port-hand buoys up to Massy's Quay, which dries. Moorings may be available. Deel Boat Club maintains a private pontoon at Massy's Quay.

Facilities

Askeaton village, 2 km from Massy's Quay, has supermarket, pubs, PO and filling station. Boatyard at Massy's Quay (Ryan & Roberts Marine Services, 061 392198, fax 061 392344, mobile 087 417 9128), hull and mechanical repairs, mobile crane, winter storage, chandlery.

Beagh Castle Quay

Beagh Castle Quay, on the S shore 2·75M E of Beeves Rock, has old iron fastenings projecting from its face, and is not recommended.

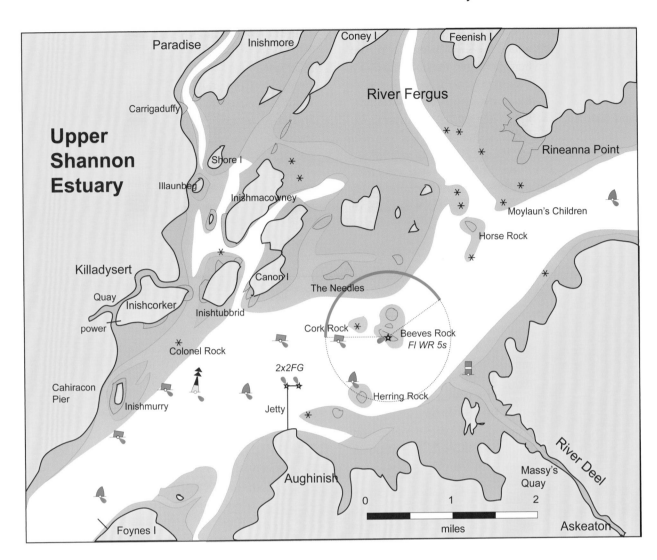

Upper Shannon Estuary

Paradise · Inishmore · Coney I · Feenish I

River Fergus

Carrigaduffy

Shore I

Illaunbeg

Rineanna Point

Inishmacowney

Moylaun's Children

Horse Rock

Killadysert

Quay · Inishcorker

Canon I

The Needles

Inishtubbrid

Cork Rock

Beeves Rock
Fl WR 5s

power

Colonel Rock

2x2FG

Cahiracon Pier

Inishmurry

Jetty

Herring Rock

River Deel

Massy's Quay

Aughinish

0   1   2

miles

Foynes I

Askeaton

RIVER FERGUS

The mouth of the Fergus is a sandy estuary 5M long by 3M wide, with narrow channels winding among islands and drying banks. Several of these channels are navigable but the limit of safe navigation must be taken as Coney Island, 3M from the main channel of the Shannon, since the river is not charted beyond that. The accessible stretch, however, includes several delightful anchorages. The greatest care is required in pilotage and AC1549 must be closely studied.

Cahiracon Pier

52°38'·7N 9°06'·5W
AC1549

This pier, behind Inishmurry on the Clare side N of Foynes, is unsuitable for yachts due to strong tides, and rocks in the approach and around the pier. A derelict freighter is moored to the back of the pier, and several other derelicts are beached in the vicinity.

Anchorage

Anchorage is possible 1·5 cables NE of the pier

abreast the end of the reef running out from Inishmurry, good holding in 2·7 to 5m, with good shelter from WSW to N. No facilities.

Killadysert

52°40'·1N 9°06'W
AC1549

Killadysert lies at the head of a narrow and muddy creek NW of Inishcorker. The entrance is N of the Colonel's Point, the E end of Inishcorker. The tidal streams among the islands are strong and there are many unmarked hazards demanding the greatest care in pilotage. The narrows between the Colonel's Point and Inishtubbrid have a 5-knot tide and boulder banks on each side, and this approach cannot be recommended to a stranger. The channel W of Inishcorker is crossed by a ford and overhead cables, and is accessible only to small boats.

The safer approach to the entrance is the passage between Inishtubbrid and Canon Island, then N of Inishtubbrid, keeping to the N side here until past the rock (drying 0·3m) N of Inishtubbrid. Steer W until 1 cable from the mainland shore, then head for the Colonel's Point. There are a couple of large boulders NW of the point which must be given a fair berth when coming round for Killadysert Creek, but more particularly when leaving as the ebb sets down on them. However, do not go too far from this side. The entrance is marked with port- and starboard-hand beacons. The creek has a least depth of 0·7m and is marked by poles, the quay (N of the W point of Inishcorker) has 0·9m, and there is a pontoon with 1·1m. There is very little room and the creek and quay are liable to silting, but the bottom is very soft mud. Beware of a concrete ledge at the foot of the quay.

Facilities

Water on the quay. Filling station, shops, PO, pubs, doctor at Killadysert village.

Paradise

52°42'·5N 9°03'·5W
AC1549

Paradise House, now a ruin, was the family home of Lieutenant William Henn RN, whose cutter *Galatea* raced against *Mayflower* for the America's Cup in 1886. The *Galatea,* which drew 13 feet 6 inches and displaced 158 tons, was subsequently sailed up to Paradise. The anchorage is in the channel between Inishmore and the mainland, and the approach requires the utmost care in pilotage. The tricky part is between Illaunbeg and Shore Island, where there is the least depth (0·6m at LAT), and drying rocks project from each side. A bearing of 356° on the end of the quay on Shore Island leads between the rocks. **Carrigaduffy (Paradise Rock),** which dries 1·8m, protrudes a little more into the channel than the chart shows. When approaching Inishmore keep to the island side of mid-channel.

Anchorage

Anchor in 2m, sheltered from SW to NW, 1·5 cables E of the ruined landing stage at the boathouse. SE of the landing stage is the N edge of a mussel bank which dries, and immediately upstream of the landing stage is an underwater pipeline across the channel.

Shelter from NW or SE may be found 4 cables NE of the Paradise landing stage, off a slip where the road from Ballynacally meets the shore. Anchor not more than a cable from the island, between the two island quays.

Facilities

Shop, PO, pub at Ballynacally, 1·5 km.

Channel W of Canon Island

52°39'·5N 9°04'W
AC1549

Entering from the Shannon E of Inishtubbrid there is a clear channel between Canon Island and Inishmacowney. E of Inishmacowney are rocks, including **Carriganinneen** (dries 4·9m). This passage leads to the channel N of Inishloe which runs SE to rejoin the main channel of the River Fergus. It is very narrow between steep, drying banks and has least depth about 1m.

Anchorage

Anchorage is available in 4m, N of Canon Island.

RIVER FERGUS, Main Channel

AC1549

Considerable care is needed at the entrance because of the unmarked rocks. The optimum time for entry is within 2 hours of LW so that Horse Rock is uncovered and can be used as a reference point.

Directions

Approach on a course of due N, steering to pass 1 cable E of Horse Rock, and hold this course until Blackthorn Island is abeam to port. Then steer 349° until within 4 cables of Coney Island, and Feenish Island is abeam to starboard. Then steer to pass 1 cable off Curragh Point, the E end of Coney Island, to avoid Roadway Rock.

Anchorage

Anchor E of the island in 2·5 to 5m, sheltered from W to NE. The current here always runs to the S and is not strong.

RIVER SHANNON – RINNEANNA POINT TO LIMERICK

AC1540

This passage is straightforward with an up-to-date chart showing the latest buoyage. Follow the buoyed channel. The drying harbour E of Dernish Island is part of the precincts of Shannon Airport and is prohibited to yachts.

The limit of navigation for masted yachts is the Shannon Bridge at Limerick. It has a clearance of 3·3m at MHWS.

Limerick – Ted Russell Dock

The wet dock at Limerick, with an area of 2 cables by 0.5 cables, is entered through a Lock Gate which opens from 1 hour before HW up to HW. The entrance is on the S bank of the river, 4 cables from the Shannon Bridge. The maximum length of stay is three days. All owners must sign an indemnity form which can be obtained from the Dock Gateman upon entry to the Dock. Yachts should not be left unattended as there is a frequent requirement to shift around the dock to accommodate the movement of commercial coastal traffic. There is no slipway. A crane is available; contact Limerick Cargo Handling, 061- 312733. For vessels which can pass under the Shannon Bridge, alternative berths are available upstream of the bridge at the Custom House Marina. Ted Russell Dock is managed by Shannon Foynes Port Company, HM phone 069 73103.

Constant +0130 Galway; MHWS 5·9m, MHWN 4·5m, ML 2·9m.

Facilities

Limerick has all the facilities of a city, including rail connections to Dublin and Cork and easy access to Shannon Airport.

RIVER SHANNON ABOVE LIMERICK

Access from Limerick to the Shannon Navigation and the extensive inland waterway network connected to it is available via a canal system comprising Sarsfield Lock (immediately upstream of the Shannon Bridge), the Abbey River, the tailrace and headrace of Ardnacrusha Power Station, and the locks at Ardnacrusha. The passage is interesting and worthwhile, but also challenging, and is not for the inexperienced. The lock chambers at Ardnacrusha are 32m by 5·9m – Sarsfield Lock is wider. The weir beside Sarsfield Lock maintains a least depth of 1·7m in the canal system; the weir covers towards HW. The headroom limit is imposed by Baal's Bridge on the Abbey River, where there is 3m headroom for a width of 6m when the tide is below the level of the weir; i.e. the bridge arch is 4·7m above the river bed.

Vessels drawing more than 1·5m must obtain permission from Waterways Ireland (090 649 4232) before making the passage, and all vessels must give 24 hours' notice of intended passage to the lock-keeper at Ardnacrusha. The passage can only be made when the power station is shut down or running one turbine out of four.

Directions for pilotage of the canal and lock system at Limerick are contained in the booklet "City Cruising" by Edgar Heenan, available free of charge from Waterways Ireland, Carrick-on-Shannon, Co.Leitrim, 071 965 0898.

Chapter 6

Loop Head to Slyne Head

Roundstone

This section of the coast falls naturally into three parts. The long NW-facing coast of County Clare has no good harbours but is spectacularly scenic from seaward, its most notable feature being the sheer 200m Cliffs of Moher, while the Aran Islands have an international reputation as a cultural treasure. Their barren stony landscape and sheer cliffs are awe-inspiring, and their antiquities, including the ancient fortress of Dun Aengus, are unparalleled. Galway Bay, to the east, is low-lying with many shallow inlets. Galway is a beautiful and historic city and a vibrant and important commercial and academic centre. The coast of Connemara is rock-studded, challenging and unforgiving in pilotage but rewarding in the security of its anchorages and the splendour of its scenery. This is a Gaeltacht area where spoken Irish may often be heard.

Charts

On the smaller scale, AC2173 Loop Head to Slyne Head covers the area described in this chapter. Imray's C55 Dingle Bay to Galway Bay and C54 Galway Bay to Donegal Bay may be useful for planning, but for exploring the coast the largest-

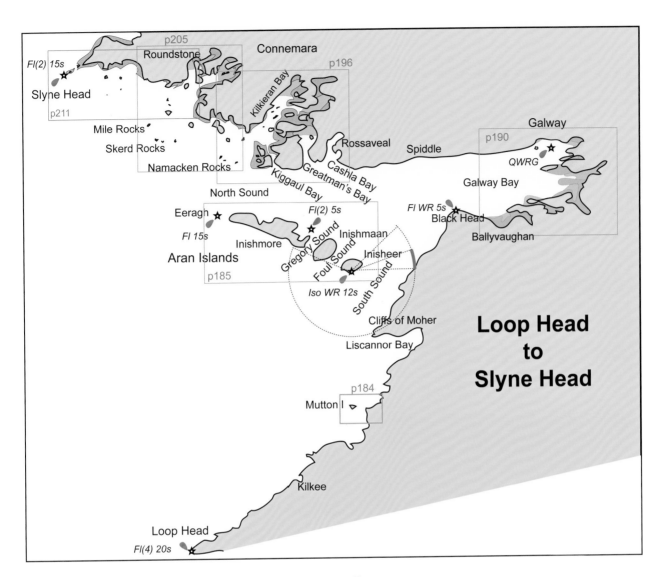

scale charts, with the exception of AC1904 Galway Harbour, are essential. If making the offshore passage from Kerry or the Shannon to Galway or Connemara, AC3338 is optional if 2173 is carried. For Joyce's Pass, inside Slyne Head, AC2708 is indispensible.

Tides
HW all along this coast occurs at about the same time as at Galway. Tidal streams are, in general, slight; where they are significant they are described in the text.

COAST OF COUNTY CLARE – LOOP HEAD TO BLACK HEAD
AC3338, 2173
There are three feasible anchorages, in settled weather, on this stretch; apart from that, the coast is best admired from a safe distance. The Cliffs of Moher, N of Liscannor Bay, are among Ireland's most famous coastal features although far short of being its highest cliffs – that honour belongs to Croaghaun on Achill Island.

Dangers
Grundel Rock (dries 0·3m), 1·2M WSW of Mutton Island
Muirbeg, 0·3m, and **Drumdeirg Rock** (dries 3m), S of Liscannor Bay
Kilstiffin Rocks, 1·5m, 1·5M SSW of Cancregga at the W end of Liscannor Bay.

Lights and marks
Loop Head, white tower Fl(4) 20s 84m 23M
Black Head, white tower Fl WR 20s 20m W11M R8M, W 045°–268°, R 268°–276°. Shows red to the E over Illaunloo and Finavarra Point, white elsewhere.

Kilkee
52°41'·5N 9°40'W
AC3338
Moore Bay, with the town of Kilkee at its head, lies 13M NE of Loop Head and offers possible shelter in offshore winds. **Black Rocks** (dry 2·1m) are in the centre of the entrance 3 cables N of **Duggerna Rock** (0·6m high), and there are drying rocks also 1 cable

Moore Bay from the S; Kilkee, bottom, George's Head, top L

S of George's Head, on the N side. Leim Chaite (Leaconnor) Cliffs, 75m high, are conspicuous 3M N of Kilkee. Mal Bay, 6 to 10M NE of Kilkee, offers no secure shelter though there is a fine-weather anchorage inside Mutton Island.

MUTTON ISLAND

⊕*MI* 52°48'·1N 9°33'W
AC3338 and Plan

Mutton Island, 1M long and 30m high, extends 2M offshore 21M NE of Loop Head. The area is rock-strewn, offers no shelter in a heavy onshore swell and is a lee shore in winds between NW and SW; but despite that the island protects the only worthwhile anchorages on the coast.

Directions

From the SW, identify Mattle Island (10m high) and steer to pass 2 cables W of it. Give the SE side of Mutton Island a berth of 2 cables to clear Mal Rock, which almost always breaks. **From the N**, give the SW corner of Mutton Island a berth of 1·5 to 2 cables to pass between it and Curragh Shoal, 2·1m, then steer E towards Mal Rock until the anchorage opens up. Anchor 1 to 1·5 cables off the ruined cottages at the SE end of the island in 3 to 4m, rock and sand. This anchorage is completely exposed to S and SW.

There is also an anchorage N of the rocky spit connecting the island with the shore, N of the pier at Seafield Point and E of the drying rocks N of the point. **From the N**, 7 cables E of Carrickaneelwar, steer 196° for the end of the pier. Anchor on this line in 4 to 5m sand, when about 2 cables from the pier with the

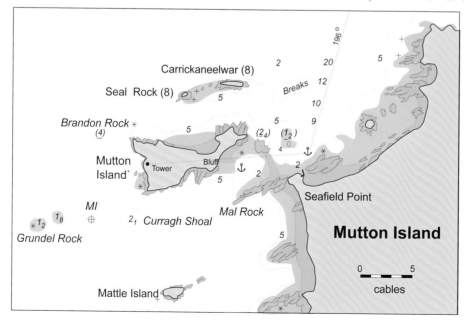

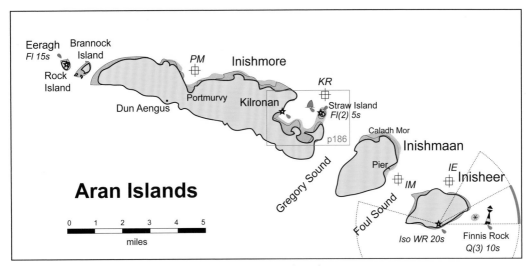

tower and bluff on Mutton Island in line. There is a swell with winds N of W. A narrow channel with 1·8m between drying rocks runs from seaward to the E side of the pier.

THE ARAN ISLANDS
AC3339, Imray C55

The Aran Islands of Inishmore, Inishmaan and Inisheer, with their outliers, make up a group extending 15M NW–SE and sheltering Galway Bay. Inishmore has a good anchorage at Kilronan, and a delightful sheltered bay at Portmurvy, but the other two islands have only open roadsteads; there are major harbour improvement works in progress at Inishmaan and Kilronan. Two major lights – Eeragh and Inisheer – mark the NW and SE extremities, respectively, of the island chain.

Dangers
Finnis Rock (dries 0·4m), 4 cables SE of Trawkeera Point, Inisheer

Pipe Rock (dries), 2 cables NW of Inisheer

The Bar of Aran, 3·4m, at the entrance to Killeany Bay, Inishmore

Bar Rock (dries 0·4m), 2 cables SE of Carrickadda Point and 2 cables NW of the Bar of Aran

Carrickadda (dries 1·2m) and **Carrickymonaghan** (dries 0·4m), NW of Killeany Bay

Cowrugh Shoal, 2·7m, 5 cables offshore E of Portmurvy

Craghalmon (dries 0·6m), 1M NNW of Portmurvy

Brocklinmore and **Brocklinbeg Banks**, N of Inishmore, may break in gale conditions or a high swell.

Lights and marks
Finnis Rock buoy, E Card Q(3) 10s

Inisheer, black tower, white bands Iso WR 12s 34m, W20M R16M, W 231°–245°, R 245°–269°, W 269°–115°. Shows red over Finnis Rock, white elsewhere.

Killeany buoy, SHM Fl G 3s

Straw Island, white tower Fl(2) 5s 11m 15M

Killeany ldg lts 192° Oc 5s 3M, front white col 6m, rear white col 8m

Kilronan Pier, white col Fl WG 1·5s 5m 3M, G 240°–326° W 326°–000°. Shows white towards Killeany Harbour to the SSE, green over the approach from the E.

Eeragh, white tower, two black bands, Fl 15s 35m 23M.

Tidal Streams
The streams run at 1 kn springs in South Sound and 1·5 kn in Foul Sound and Gregory Sound, the NE-going stream commencing at –0520 Galway and the SW-going stream at +0105 Galway.

Southern Approaches to the Aran Islands
Inishmore presents a wall of rock to the S. Its sheer cliffs, rising from 30m at the E end to 80m at the W, are geological cousins of the mighty Cliffs of Moher. The prehistoric fortress of Dun Aengus, one-third of the way along the coast from the W point, and the old lighthouse on the E summit of the island, are conspicuous. A valley running SW–NE at the narrow neck of land between Blind Sound and Portmurvy may make Inishmore appear as two islands when it is first sighted from the S. Inishmaan, also cliffbound, has three large wind turbines near its SW point; these are the tallest features on the islands and provide an excellent landmark. The coast of Inisheer slopes more gradually. The channels between the islands and between Inisheer and the mainland are generally clean and deep; Finnis Rock, E of Inisheer, is marked by a buoy, and a berth of 5 cables clears Pipe Rock, NW of Inisheer. In heavy weather the swell reflected from the cliffs can raise a confused sea in Gregory Sound, while Foul Sound tends to be calmer.

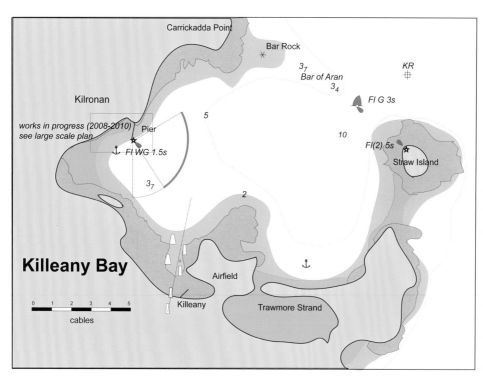

Kilronan

⊕*KR* 53°07'·4N 9°37'·8W

AC3339, Imray C55 and Plan

The village of Kilronan, on Killeany Bay, is the main township and ferry port on the islands. The bay offers all-round shelter in moderate weather, but becomes untenable in strong winds between N and E, while heavy NW weather sends in a considerable swell. At the time of writing (2008) major harbour works are in progress in the bay. The new harbour is expected to be completed by 2010, with four ferry berths, a car ferry slip, a pontoon berth for the lifeboat and a basin and approach channel dredged to 3·5m.

Directions

From the E and Gregory Sound, give Straw Island a berth of 3 cables and leave Killeany buoy to starboard, then steer for the end of Kilronan pier. From the W, it is usually safe to pass halfway between Carrickadda Point and Killeany buoy, crossing the Bar of Aran in 3 to 4m. In a swell, leave the buoy to starboard.

Killeany Bay from the S; Killeany pier and beacons R foreground, Kilronan Pier upper L, Carrickadda Point top R

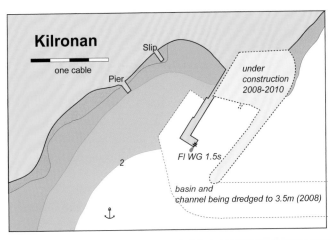

visitors' moorings.

In SE winds better shelter can be found off Trawmore Strand, 1M SE, in 5m, sand, but this is an isolated spot.

Killeany pier, on the S side of the bay, is used by local boats as an emergency shelter in heavy weather. See below for directions.

Piers

There is heavy ferry and fishing vessel traffic (and until 2010 major construction work) at the main pier, which makes it unavailable as an overnight berth for a yacht. The old W pier has 2m alongside after

Anchorage

Anchor SW of Kilronan pier in 3 to 4m, sand. Allow plenty of room for the ferries to manoeuvre, and take due account of the harbour works expected to continue until 2010. Yellow Special Mark buoys moored near the pierheads indicate a Prohibited Area. There are

Kilronan Pier from the SW, prior to its 2008 - 10 redevelopment

Inishmore – Dun Aengus (foreground) and Portmurvy (top L)

half-tide, with a clean bottom, and may provide a temporary berth.

Facilities
Diesel from the fishermen's co-op, water on the pier (tap halfway along). Shops, pubs, restaurants, bicycle hire. Ferries to Rossaveal and Galway, air service to Galway. RNLI all-weather lifeboat station. The ancient fortress of Dun Aengus, with its huge semi-circular walls right on the cliff edge and the *chevaux-de-frise* surrounding them, is not to be missed. Together with the island's other antiquities such as Dún Ducathair (The Black Fort), it places Inishmore on a par with Skellig Michael as one of the world's magical places. The views from the clifftops are superb.

Killeany
AC3339 and Plan
There is a drying harbour formed by a pier projecting NE from the shore on the S side of the bay. A vessel of 1·5 to 1·8m draught can enter and berth alongside at HW−0200. Local boats take shelter here in winter. It is approached by a narrow channel, which also dries. Two white 4m-high beacons in line 192° lead through. The channel is also marked by two haystack-shaped beacons to starboard and two beacons to port. A ruined beacon on the port hand covers at half tide and is inside the line joining the other two port-hand beacons *(it can be seen in the photograph on p186)*. Enter on the leading line till the innermost port-hand beacon is abeam, then head for the end of the pier. The lights on the leading beacons should not be depended upon. A preliminary reconnaissance by dinghy is strongly recommended.

Portmurvy
⊕ *PM* 53°08'·7N 9°44'·4W
AC3339 and Plan of Aran Islands
This bay on the N side of Inishmore offers reasonable shelter in fine weather and offshore winds and is a convenient anchorage for a visit to Dun Aengus. **From Kilronan**, keep 5 cables offshore to avoid Carrickadda and Carrickymonaghan. **From the W**, keep well clear of Scalraun Point on the W side of the bay to avoid Craghalmon Rock (Cragillaun) which appears surprisingly far offshore.

To pass between Murvy Shoal (7m) and Cowrugh Shoal (2·7m) bring the prominent white Kilmurvy House in line with Dun Aengus bearing 224°. (If either of these shoals is throwing up dangerous seas, the conditions are such that a yacht should not be going into Portmurvy anyway). Anchor in 5 to 7m, sand, off the beach and abreast the small pier on the E side. The bottom alongside the pier is reported foul, but the pier may offer a temporary alongside berth above half tide to allow a visit to Dun Aengus. Small shop 400m from the pier.

Channels W of Inishmore
53°08'N 9°51'W
AC3339
Brannock East and West Sounds, between Inishmore, Brannock Island and Rock Island, are navigable with care in moderate weather, although they may break right across in a heavy swell. Stay mid-channel in Brannock West Sound. In Brannock East Sound, hold towards the Brannock Island side to avoid rocks extending 2·5 cables W from Inishmore.

Inishmaan
⊕ *IM* 53°04'·6N 9°33'·7W
AC3339 and Plan of Aran Islands
There is no safe anchorage. The island's main pier is at Cora Point on the E side, off which temporary anchorage may be had in fine weather and offshore winds. A yacht should not be left unattended off Inishmaan. At the time of writing (2008) a new harbour and breakwater are under construction at Caladh Mór (Calamore on the chart) on the N side of the island. There is a very fine ring fort on the summit of Inishmaan.

Inishmaan (E) Pier from the S; Sandhead top L

Inisheer

⊕*IE* 53°04'·5N 9°31'·0W

AC3339 and Plan of Aran Islands

The North Strand provides the best landing, in fine weather only. A yacht should not be left unattended at anchor here.

Inisheer has a 15th-century castle and religious buildings dating from the 8th to the 10th centuries, but a more recent claim to fame is as "Craggy Island" in the popular television series *Father Ted*.

GALWAY BAY

AC1984, 1904, Imray C55

Galway Bay, 6M wide and 10M long, is sheltered from the ocean swell by the Aran Islands. The S shore of the bay, E of Black Head, is fronted by rocks and shallows within which there are a number of creeks offering excellent shelter, but clearing marks are poor and it is not advisable to close this coast in poor visibility or strong onshore winds. The N shore of the bay is exposed and there are no good harbours in the 20M between Galway and Cashla Bay. The head of Galway Bay has several excellent harbours and anchorages among low-lying islands and headlands, and Galway itself is a significant commercial port with a small marina in its wet dock. The principal sailing centre in the bay, and home of Galway Bay SC, is New Harbour (Rinville), entered 2M ESE of Mutton Island.

Tidal Streams

The streams in the bay are generally weak. Apart from the upper reaches of the Shannon estuary, Galway Bay has the largest tidal range on the coast. MHWS (Galway) 5·1m, MHWN 3·9m, ML 2·9m.

Dangers

The dangers in the creeks on the S and E sides of the bay are described in the text. The principal dangers in the approaches to Galway and New Harbour are as follows:

Black Rock (dries 1·6m), 2M WSW of Mutton Island

Margaretta Shoal, 2·9m, 2M SW of Mutton Island

Foudra Rock (dries), 1M W of Mutton Island

Trout Rock (dries 1·2m), 5 cables ESE of the Leverets light

St Brendan's Island, a drying reef extending 1M to the W, N of Ardfry Point on the S side of New Harbour, and culminating in **Cockle Rock** (dries 2·3m), 9 cables WNW of Ardfry Point

Dillisk Rock (dries) and **Rinville Spit**, 1·7m, a reef extending 3 cables WSW from Rinville Point.

Lights and marks

Black Head, white tower, Fl WR 5s 20m W11M R8M, W 045°–268°, R 268°–276°. Shows red inshore to the E, white elsewhere

Spiddle Pier Head, Y col Fl WRG 3·5s 11m W6M R4M G4M, G 102°–282°, W 282°–024°, R 024°–066°. Shows white over the approach, green inshore to the E and red inshore to the W.

Barna Pier Head, Fl(2) WRG 5s 6m W8M R5M G5M, G 250°–344°, W 344°–355°, R 355°–090°. Shows a narrow white sector over the approach from the SSE, green to the E and red to the W.

Black Rock buoy, PHM Fl R 3s

Margaretta Shoal buoy, SHM Fl G 3s

Tawin Shoals buoy, SHM Fl(3) G 10s

Foudra Rock buoy, S Card Q(6)+L Fl 15s

Trout Rock buoy, S Card Q(6)+L Fl

Cockle Rock buoy, N Card Q

Leverets, black tower, white bands, Q WRG 9m 10M, G 015°–058° W 058°–065° R 065°–103° G 103°–143·5° W 143·5°–146·5° R 146·5°–015°. Shows white over the approach from the WSW, red over Mutton Island, green over the causeway and Claddagh, white up the channel to Galway Harbour, red to the N, E and S, and green over Tawin and Margaretta Shoals to the SW.

Rinmore, white tower, Iso WRG 4s 7m 5M, G 359°–008° W 008°–018° R 018°–027°. Shows white over the approach from the SSW, green to the E, red to the W

Nimmo's Pier Head, Fl Y 2s 7m 7M

Galway Approach Channel, Port Entry Light Dir WRG 7m 3M, FG 322·25°–323·75°, AltGW 323·75°–324·75°, FW 324·75°–325·25°, AltWR 325·25°–326·25°, FR 326·25°–331·25°, Fl R 331·25°–332·25°

Outer approach to Galway Harbour

From the SW, Black Head, steep and bold below the bare rocky Doughbranneen Hill (312m), has a small lighthouse on its shore. The red sector of the light covers **Illaunloo Rock** in Ballyvaghan Bay. Knockavorneen Hill (73m) and the Martello towers at Finavarra and Aughinish are conspicuous. Steering NE, identify the Black Rock and Margaretta Shoals buoys and pass between them, then leave Tawin Shoals buoy to starboard and Foudra Rock buoy to port. The black-and-white banded Leverets beacon is conspicuous, and at night its W sector leads between the buoys. **From the W,** steer due E from a point 0·5M S of Spiddle to leave the Black Rock buoy to port, then as above.

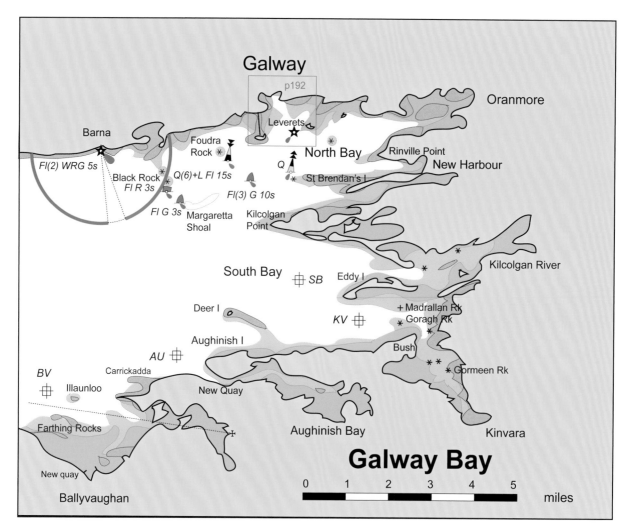

INLETS ON THE SOUTH SIDE OF GALWAY BAY
AC1984

Ballyvaughan Bay
⊕*BV* 53°09'N 9°10'·5W

Ballyvaughan Bay (Ballyvaghan on the charts) lies 3M E of Black Head. In the centre of the bay. **Illaunloo** (0·6m high) is difficult to identify against the land. It is foul for up to 1 cable all round. At the S entrance to the bay the **Farthing Rocks** are an extensive patch, some of which dry 1·7m, and lie up to 4 cables offshore. The inner part of the bay is shallow with extensive drying banks, but a yacht of modest draft may cross these safely with sufficient rise of tide. Shanmuckinish Castle ruin in line with St Patrick's church, 096°, leads between Illaunloo and Farthing Rocks. At HW it is possible to go up to the old quay by the village and lie alongside its SE side, bottom shingle and small stones. It is also possible to go alongside the new quay on its SE side where the shelter is a little better. Both quays dry. There is also a pool with about 3m LWS off the end of the NE pier near the 3·4m sounding on AC1984. It is about 140m long by 90m wide, its long axis lying NE–SW in continuation of the line of the inner face

of the end of the pier. Sound into it and preferably moor with two anchors to reduce swinging. It is very well sheltered at low tide and the NW–SE edges are clean sand. At the E end of the bay Muckinish Strait gives access to a long creek. It is shallow and not recommended.

Shops, pubs, restaurants at Ballyvaughan.

Carrickadda dries 3·7m and extends 7·5 cables W from the shore NE of Finavarra Point. Gleninagh Castle in line with the N side of Illaunloo, 244°, leads just clear of Carrickadda. This line also clears the 2·1m patch NW of Aughinish Point.

Aughinish Bay
⊕*AU* 53°10'N 9°06'W

The entrance to this bay, S of Aughinish Island, is straightforward with the use of AC1984. Give the S shore a berth of 1 cable and anchor at or above New Quay. There is a strong tide in this anchorage, which may be uncomfortable in NW winds as there are overfalls on the ebb and a yacht will be tide-rode. Under these circumstances go further up the bay, with continuous use of the echosounder, as the channel is unmarked. The pier at New Quay offers an alongside berth around HW. Pub at the pier.

Deer Island (2m high) lies 1M N of Aughinish Point. It is foul all round for 1 cable, and a long, shallow spit, which partially uncovers, runs SE from it to the land. This island is also hard to identify against the shore. Once identified it can be used as a reference point in the entrance to South Bay.

South Bay
⊕*SB* 53°12'N 9°02'W
South Bay is divided by Eddy Island which can be identified when Deer Island comes abeam. The S part of this bay leads to Kinvara Bay and the N part to the Kilcolgan River. There is a prominent line of trees just to the E of Newtown House, 1·75M W of Doorus Point at the entrance to Kinvara Bay.

Kinvara Bay
⊕*KV* 53°11'·0N 9°00'W
There are no marks for the deep water entrance between **Madrallan Rock**, with 0·5m, and **Goragh Rock**, dries 1·8m, and it is reported that these rocks are more extensive than charted. This passage should therefore be made with great care and continuous use of the echosounder. It is simpler – with sufficient rise of tide – to keep well N of Madrallan Rock, steering to pass 1 cable S of Fiddoun Island. When Fiddoun Island is abeam and Doorus Point bears about 205° it is safe to stand into Kinvara Bay, giving Doorus Head a berth of 0·5 cables and less than 2 cables to avoid **Comb Rock** which dries 2·9m. There is good anchorage abreast the pier at Bush, in 4m.

To proceed further, first keep Bush pierhead 290° astern which leads N of both **Madden's Island** and **Long Rock**. Tarrea pier will be seen ahead. It is at the end of the road leading W by N from Tarrea village – it must not be confused with the less conspicuous Poltagh quay NNW of it. When Poltagh quay bears N and Tarrea pier is about 1·5 cables distant, steer to pass W of **Gormeen Rock** which covers at half-tide and has a small perch which can be seen at HW. After this keep in mid-channel. At neaps there is anchorage 2·5 cables from Kinvara, with 2m at LWN. Alternatively, berth at the S or W side in the small harbour. The bottom of shingle and small stones is suitable for drying out; it is the only spot in the inlet free of mud at LW.

Facilities
Shops, pubs, PO, restaurants at Kinvara.

Kilcolgan River
53°12'·2N 9°00'W
Enter through Mweenish Strait between Mweenish Island and Eddy Island. This passage is fairly straightforward, with regular shorelines of steep, shelving shingle. Favouring the Eddy Island side of the channel, alter to port to pass within 1 cable of Mweenish Point, which is steep-to, thus avoiding **Meelan Rock**, a group of boulders which dries.

Anchorage
There is good safe shelter NNE of Mweenish Point in Ship Pool. No facilities. Alternatively, if proceeding further and awaiting sufficient rise, anchor in Tyrone Pool, 1M ENE from Mweenish Point; **Yellow Slate Rock**, which dries 0·6m, lies on the edge of the shallows on the N side of the pool opposite Bird Island. After half-flood keep 0·5 cable off the S shore and enter the Kilcolgan River S of Corraun Point. Due to scour there is deeper water in the river than charted. Continue in mid-stream and anchor in 0·5m LWS or 2m LWN 150m short of the quay wall on the N bank of the river at Weir village. The river shallows rapidly abreast the quay.

Facilities
Restaurant at the quay. Shops at Kilcolgan, 1·5 km.

Kilcolgan Point
Kilcolgan Point is deceptive and extends a long way into the bay. It is foul all round and must be given a wide berth. The charted transits are now difficult to discern, but longitude 9°04'·2 clears the point by 5 cables.

NORTH BAY – NEW HARBOUR AND GALWAY
AC1984, 1904, Imray C55
North Bay is the approach to Galway, and also Oranmore Bay, New Harbour and Mweeloon Bay. Oranmore Bay is open to the W and its head is encumbered with rocks. Mweeloon Bay is also open to the W and dries at its head. There is anchorage 7·5 cables inside the entrance. Keep close to Ardfry Point until the tower on it is passed to avoid the **Creggaun Rocks** (dry 1·5m) in the middle of the entrance. It is not recommended.

New Harbour (Rinville)
53°14'·5N 9°00'W
AC1984, 1904
New Harbour is entered between Cockle Rock buoy and Rinville Spit. The inlet offers better shelter than its position would suggest, and yachts have remained on moorings here throughout the year. The dome of Galway Cathedral in line with the W side of Hare Island, 312°, leads clear of Rinville Spit, which extends SW from Rinville Point. The white bungalow used as a mark on the charts no longer

New Harbour (Rinville) from the NW; Galway Bay SC, foreground

exists, but there is a prominent group of white buildings in the same location. A bearing **of** 090° clears **Black Rock** (dries 4·1m) on the S shore. Below half tide it is important to stay close to the N shore, which is clean and can be approached to within 0·5 cable.

Anchorage

Anchor SW of the pier in 2m, mud, or outside the moorings where available. It is safe to dry out at the pier where there is 2m at HWN. A wide slip and breakwater extends SE from the pier; the end of the slip is marked with an unlit perch. Galway Bay SC (091 794527) at the pier. There are visitors' moorings; contact the club for availability.

Facilities

Water and shore power on the quay. Showers, meals and bar at GBSC clubhouse (Wednesdays and weekends). Shops, pubs and restaurants at Oranmore, 3 km.

Galway Harbour

⊕ *GW* 53°15'·5N 9°02'·1W
AC1984, 1904, Imray C55 and Plan
Galway Harbour lies behind dock gates which are opened 2 hours before HW and closed at HW, day and night, 7 days a week. The dock on the SW side has a small marina; intending visitors are advised to check berth availability in adavnce by contacting the Harbour office 091 562329 or VHF Ch 12.

A dredged channel 80m wide with a maintained depth of 3·4m runs for 6 cables SE from the outer pierhead,

W of Rinmore Point. Steer to pass 2 cables W of the Leverets tower, and head 325° for the high intensity directional light, which is easily visible by day. For a short stay or while waiting for the tide to enter the dock, make fast alongside the E side of the pier extending from the dock gates in a narrow dredged cut with 3·4m, known locally as the layby. There is not room to round up in this cut. The berth is exposed in S or SE winds; in gales from these points it is dangerous. A yacht should not be left unattended in the 'layby'; it is also used by the fishing fleet and becomes crowded. On the ebb or after prolonged rain, there is a strong E set out of the River Corrib across the mouth of the harbour. Maintain a listening watch on VHF Ch 12 when entering.

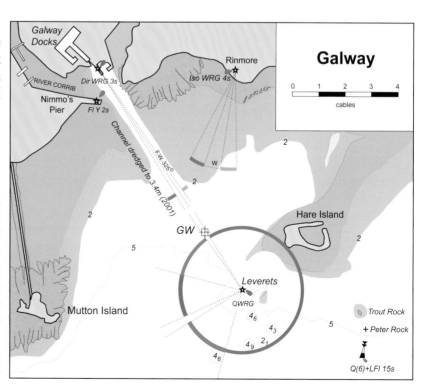

Galway Harbour from the NE; the dock gates, bottom L, and the marina, centre.

Marina
The marina has 20 berths and 5 visitors' berths. Water and shore power on the pontoons; security gate and CCTV cameras.

Facilities
All the facilities of a port city; supermarkets, shops, pubs, restaurants and PO, train and bus connections. Airport. HiWay Oil (091 566406) will deliver diesel if the quantity is sufficient; smaller quantities may be obtained at the nearby oil depot. Boat repairs, but no slipway. Dockside crane, 12t capacity. It is also safe to dry out at Nimmo's Pier, but contact HM beforehand, 091 562329.

Galway is the Tidal Standard Port for the west coast; MHWS 5·1m, MHWN 3·9m, ML 2·9m.

NORTH SIDE OF GALWAY BAY – GALWAY TO CASHLA BAY
AC1984, 3339 and 2096
The N shore of Galway Bay for 20M W of Mutton Island is exposed and apart from the drying harbours at Barna and Spiddle has no safe shelter, but between Black Rock and Cashla Point there are no dangers more than 5 cables offshore. Cashla Bay may be entered by day or night in almost any weather, and has the easiest access of any of the Connemara bays. The fishing and ferry port of Rossaveal (Rossaveel on the charts) lies on its E side.

Dangers
Black Rock (dries 1·6m), 2M WSW of Mutton Island

North Channel Rock (dries 0·6m), 3 cables NW of Black Rock

Carrickanoge (dries) 4 cables off Barna village

Coddu Rock (above water), 2 cables SW of Cashla Point

Rock (dries 1·7m), 5 cables W of Cashla Point

Carrickmarian (dries 3·7m), 2·5 cables S of Killeen Point

Narien Spit, 1·5m, 2 cables S of Carrickmarian.

Carrickadda (dries 1·5m), 5 cables NNW of Cashla Point, with drying and above-water rocks E and SE of it

Coastguard Rock (dries 1·5m), 2 cables ENE of Carrickadda

Unnamed rock, 0·2m, 2 cables W of Tonacrick Point on the E side of the outer bay

Lion Rock (dries), 1 cable W of Lion Point at the narrows

Ship Rock (dries), 0·5 cable E of Curraglass Point at the narrows

Unnamed rock (dries 0·9m), 3 cables N by W of Curraglass Point, with a series of submerged rocks between it and the shore to the SW.

Haberline Rock (dries), 2 cables NNW of Rossaveal pierhead

The head of Cashla Bay is heavily obstructed with drying rocks.

Lights and marks
Tawin Shoals buoy, SHM Fl(3) G 10s
Margaretta Shoal buoy, SHM Fl G 3s
Black Rock buoy, PHM Fl R 3s

Barna Pier Head, Fl(2) WRG 5s 6m W8M R5M G5M, G 250°–344°, W 344°–355°, R 355°–090°. Shows a narrow white sector over the approach from the SSE, green to the E and red to the W.

Spiddle Pier Head, Y col Fl WRG 3·5s 11m W6M R4M G4M, G 102°–282°, W 282°–024°, R 024°–066°. Shows white over the approach, green inshore to the E and red inshore to the W.

Cashla Bay Entrance (Killeen Point), W side, white col Fl(3) WR 10s 8m W6M R3M, W 216°–000°, R 000°–069°. Shows red to SW, white over the entrance

Cannon Rock buoy, SHM Fl G 5s

There is also a perch on Cannon Rock

Cashla Bay (Lion Point), white tower with red high-visibility stripe, dir WRG Iso 5s 6m W8M R6M G6M, G 357·5°–008·5°, W 008·5°–011·5°, R 011·5°–017·5°. White sector leads close W of Cannon Rock buoy, green to E, red to W

Lion Rock buoy, SHM Fl G 3s

Ship Rock buoy, PHM Fl R 3s

A further pair of buoys QR and QG lie to the N of the narrows, and an unlit green spar buoy N of Rossaveal Harbour. See Plans and AC2096.

Ard Rí beacon, red col Fl(3) R 6s

Rossaveal Harbour ldg lts 116° Oc 3s 3M, front white col 7m, rear 8m

Coast – Mutton Island to Cashla Bay

A course close S of Mutton Island and Black Rock buoys and then due W clears all dangers as far as Spiddle, 7M W of Black Rock. There is a small drying harbour at Barna, which receives a little protection from Carrickanoge. It has a good sandy bottom. Shops, PO, pubs and restaurants. Between Spiddle and Cashla Point, at the E side of the entrance to Cashla Bay, a berth of 7 cables clears all dangers.

Spiddle

53°14'N 9°18'W

AC1984, 3339

There is a drying harbour at Spiddle with a clean sandy bottom. The face of the quay is rough and it is subject to scend in winds from E through S to SW. Shops, PO and pubs.

CASHLA BAY

⊕ *CB* 53°13'·8N 9°34'·5W

AC2096, Imray C55 and Plan

From the E, identify Coddu Rock, which never covers, SW of Cashla Point. There is a clear channel between this rock and Cannon Rock. At the head of the bay two small round hills, Mount Ballagh and Round Hill, stand out clearly; Round Hill and Curraglass Point in line 346° lead between Cannon

Head of Cashla Bay from the SE; Rossaveal Harbour, foreground, with Ard Rí beacon and Illaunawehichy beyond. Costelloe village, upper R

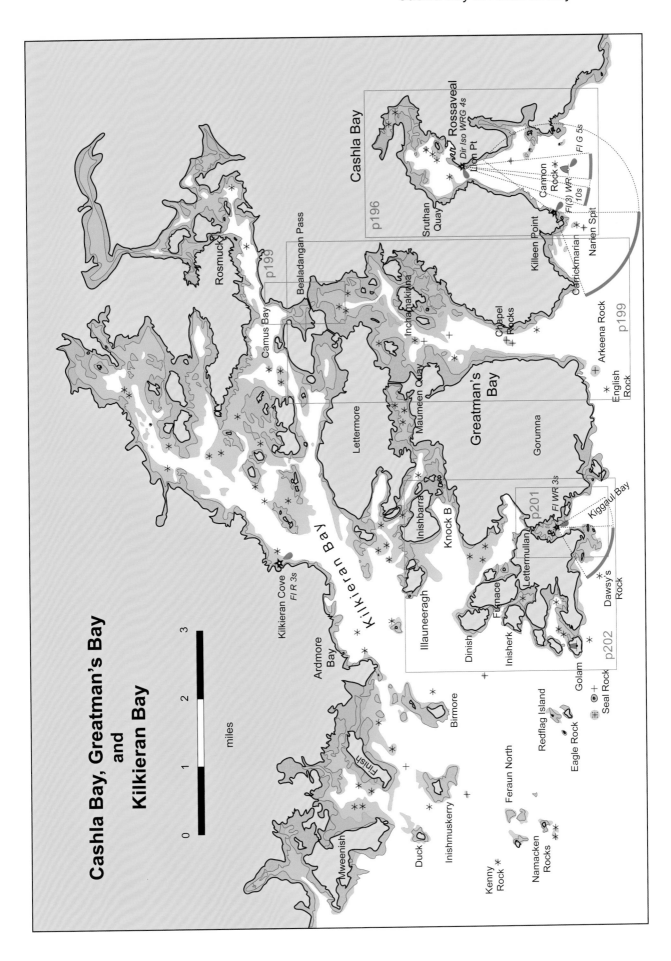

Cashla Bay, Greatman's Bay
and
Kilkieran Bay

miles

0   1   2   3

Cashla Bay

p196

Rossaveal
Dir Iso WRG 4s
Lion Pt
Sruthan Quay
Cannon Rock
Fl G 5s
Killeen Point
Fl(3) WR 10s
Carrickmarian
Narien Spit
Arkeena Rock
p199
English Rock

Rosmuck

Bealadangan Pass

p199

Camus Bay

Inchamakinna

Chapel Rocks

Maumeen Quay

Lettermore

Greatman's Bay

Gorumna

p201
Fl WR 3s
Kiggaul Bay

Inishbarra

Knock B

Lettermullan
Dawsy's Rock
p202

Kilkieran Cove
Fl R 3s

Ardmore Bay

Kilkieran Bay

Illauneeragh

Dinish

Furnace

Inisherk

Golam

Seal Rock

Birmore

Redflag Island

Eagle Rock

Finish

Duck

Inishmuskerry

Feraun North

Mweenish

Kenny Rock

Namacken Rocks

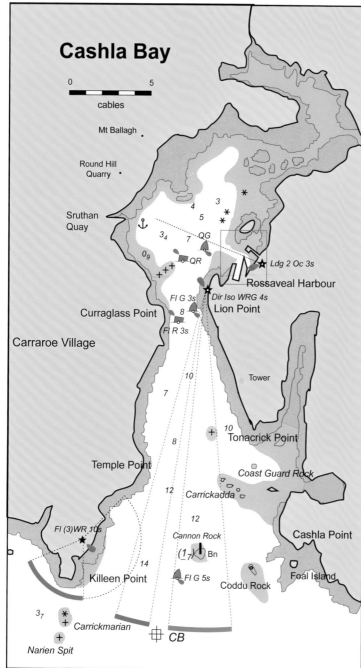

Cashla Bay

0 ___ 5
cables

Mt Ballagh

Round Hill
Quarry

Sruthan
Quay

Curraglass Point

Carraroe Village

Temple Point

Killeen Point

Narien Spit

Carrickmarian

QG
QR
Fl G 3s   *Dir Iso WRG 4s*
Fl R 3s   Lion Point
Ldg 2 Oc 3s
Rossaveal Harbour

Tower

Tonacrick Point

Coast Guard Rock
Carrickadda

Cannon Rock
Bn
Fl G 5s
Coddu Rock

Cashla Point

Foal Island

Fl (3)WR 10s

CB

Sruthan Quay

This pier is named on AC2096 and is the quay at Glashnacally shown on AC3339. Many years ago it was used by Galway hookers to ship turf for fuel to the Aran Islands, and the remains of the little stone pillars which supported their outer bilges when they dried out may still present a hazard when coming alongside. The end of the quay just dries at LAT.

Anchorage

There is good anchorage midway between the QR port-hand buoy and Sruthan Quay, in 2 to 3m, mud, safe in all weathers though it can be very rough in a S or SE gale. There are visitors' moorings. Do not anchor near the line of a sewer indicated by two posts with triangular topmarks, one ashore near the pier and the other on the sewer off the pier; the outer one is reported missing.

Facilities

Water close to the quay. Shop and hotel at Carraroe, 1·5 km; pub, PO and garage (091 572169) at Costelloe, 2 km.

Rossaveal

53°16'·2N 9°33'·9W
AC2096

A dredged channel with 3·7m leads into the busy fishing harbour of Rossaveal (Rossaveel on the charts), from where ferries run to the Aran Islands. A temporary alongside berth may be available – contact the HM (VHF Ch 16, 14, 12, phone 091 572108) for permission.

Facilities

Diesel, water, shore power and mechanical repairs at Rossaveal. Shop (800m) will deliver, 091 572292; pub 1·5 km. Buses to Galway.

and Coddu Rocks, and also clear all dangers on the E side of the outer bay. Alternatively, leave Cannon Rock buoy to starboard. At night, the W sector of Lion Point light leads W of Cannon Rock buoy. **From the W,** the summit of Illaunnanownim just open S of Aillewore Point astern 265°, clears Narien Spit. The old coastguard buildings on the E side of the bay, which are roofless and just above a pier, open their own length N of Knockduff Hill, 150m, bearing 054°, also leads S of the spit. Cruckdough Hill, just to the N of Knockduff, is a very noticeable pimple. At night, the light on Aillecluggish Point on the W side of the entrance shows R over Carrickmarian and Narien Spit.

Once past Carrickadda head for the middle of the narrows and follow the buoyed channel.

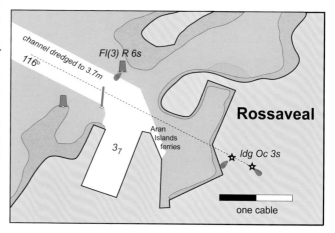

channel dredged to 3·7m
116°
Fl(3) R 6s
Aran Islands ferries
3₇
Rossaveal
ldg Oc 3s
one cable

APPROACHES TO THE CONNEMARA COAST FROM SEAWARD

Landmarks

(positions given for location purposes only)

On the south Connemara shore, Golam Tower, 24m, 53°13'·8N 9°46'·1W, at the entrance to Kilkieran Bay, is the key to most of the inshore passages, while Knockmorden, 350m, 53°23'N 9°42'W, a long hill on the W side at the head of the bay, is unmistakable. Above Mweenish and Ard Bays, Cuileen Hill stands out, 96m, 53°19'·8N 9°51'W. Further W Cashel Hill, 308m, at the head of Bertraghboy Bay, 53°26'N 9°48'W is a prominent conical hill which stands out from the higher Benna Beola (or Twelve Pins) behind it. Errisbeg Hill, 296m 53°24'N 9°57'W, above Roundstone, is easily identified. Nearer Slyne Head, Doon Hill, 61m 53°24'·8N 10°06'·8W, with its Tower, is conspicuous. Offshore, Skerdmore, 18m high, 53°15'·2N 10°00'·5W is the largest of the Skerd Rocks and quite unmistakable. Croaghnakeela (Deer Island), 60m and St Macdara's Island to its E are both readily identifiable.

Caution

It is particularly necessary on this coast to be conscious of the difference between the horizontal chart datum and WGS84, which is the datum used by the GPS system. This offset is documented on up-to-date copies of the charts, and on recently issued editions it is zero, but in the absence of such data an extra allowance of one cable should be made to clear known dangers.

CASHLA BAY to KIGGAUL BAY

AC2096

West of Cashla Bay, the coast of Connemara is entered in earnest. Here are so many unmarked rocks that the only sensible advice to a stranger is to keep a copy of the largest-scale chart close at hand at all times, and to be constantly aware of his position. However the Admiralty surveyors in the 1840's did an outstanding job, and the existence and position of the hazards are, for the most part, extremely well documented. It is a fascinating cruising ground for the adventurous sailor. Greatman's Bay and Kiggaul Bay provide secure and delightful anchorage.

Dangers

In the recesses of the inlets of Greatman's Bay and Kiggaul Bay the rocks are too numerous to list. The principal offshore dangers are as follows:

Keeraun Shoal, 5·5m, 7 cables SW of Keeraun Point

Trabaan Rock, 2·1m, 4 cables ESE of Trabaan Point

Arkeena Rock, 1·8m, 4 cables S of Trabaan Point

Rin Rocks (dry 1·8m), 2 cables WSW of Rin Point in the entrance to Greatman's Bay

Chapel Rocks, 0·6m, in mid-channel 2 cables NW of Dooleen Point

English Rock (dries 1·2m), 8 cables SW of Trabaan Point

Griffin's Rock (dries 3m), 4 cables S of Lettermullan Island

Dawsy's Rock (dries 2·4m), 5 cables W of Griffin's Rock. There is a third rock, awash at LAT, midway between them.

Lights and marks

Kiggaul Bay, Fl WR 3s 5m W5M R3M, W 329°–359°, R359°–059°. Shows white over the approach, red over the dangers to the SW.

Golam Tower, unlit, conspicuous on the summit of Golam Island, 2M W of Kiggaul Bay

GREATMAN'S BAY

⊕*GM* 53°14'N 9°38'W

AC2096 and Plan

This bay can be entered in any summer weather but there are more dangers in the entrance than in Cashla Bay, and the shelter is not so good. The entrance is wide and easily identified from seaward.

Directions

From the E, a berth of 2 cables clears all dangers from Keeraun Point to Carrow Point. Keeraun Shoal breaks in a heavy swell, but can generally be ignored by a yacht in summer conditions. Keeraun Point just open SW of Carrow Point 128° leads SW of Rin Rock, and the conspicuous two-storey white building on Inchamakinna open of Dooleen Point 014° leads W of it. From the W, beware of English Rock, which frequently does not break. It lies in the red sector of Killeen Point light. Golam Tower, which is unmistakable, open S of Loughcarrick Island 282° leads S of the rock. Golam Tower over the NE point of Illaunnanownim 277° leads N of the rock, and also S of Arkeena Rock. Dooleen beaches, which stand out well on the E side of the bay, open E of Trabaan Point 028° lead clear E of English Rock but dangerously close to Arkinna Rock. Inchamakinna building in line with Dooleen Point 014° clears English, Trabaan and Arkeena Rocks. Lettermore Hill open W of Gorumna Chapel ruin (which does not stand out very well) 344° leads E of Trabaan Rock.

Once N of Dooleen Point, stay E or W of mid-channel to avoid Chapel Rocks. Lettermore Church, just NE of Carrickalegaun bridge, is conspicuous from seaward.

Greatman's Bay from N; Lettermore (bottom R) Maumeen Quay (centre R) Inishlay (centre L) Carraveg Bay (top R)

Anchorages

Temporary anchorage in settled weather is available off Dooleen beaches. The quay at Natawny, on the E side of the bay, encloses a small-boat harbour which is not suitable for yachts. N of the quay is a broken-off concrete beacon which is dangerous as it covers before HW. It should be left to starboard entering the boat harbour, not to port as would appear correct. There is indifferent anchorage off the quay with a 3km walk uphill to Carraroe.

The best anchorage, which is sheltered in all winds but is approached between unmarked rocks, is off Maumeen Quay, N of Curnaclea Point on Gorumna Island. The reef E of Curnaclea Point ends in a big, square rock which dries about 1·8m. If this rock is showing leave it well to port and steer for the W side of Inishlay. At half-tide and over, when the square rock is covered, approach close to Eragh Island as there is then no danger from the sunken rocks S of Eragh Spit and the two 1·5m patches NW of Eragh Island. **Corra Rock** (dries 2m) is a square pinnacle, bare of weed and with an outlier to the N of it. It is easily avoided approaching the anchorage either by keeping Lettermore Hill bearing 318° or the prominent church 313°. When the quay is well abeam alter course towards it and

anchor 2 to 3 cables off it in 2 to 3m, mud. There are visitors' moorings. Maumeen Quay is not suitable for alongside berthing.

Facilities

Shop and pub at Lettermore village. Filling station 1·5 km.

Bealadangan

53°18'·7N 9°37'·5W
See Plan

The tidal channel of Bealadangan Pass, at the head of the bay, once offered access direct from the head of Greatman's Bay to Camus Bay and Kilkieran Bay, and it still has its stone beacons, but it has for many years been restricted by the low bridge connecting Annaghvaan and Lettermore Islands to the mainland. However there is a suitable anchorage close to the bridge; this is well worth visiting as it makes an attractive sail up into the heart of Connemara. This passage can be made at or after half-flood. To avoid Corra Rock keep Dooleen Point well open W of Eragh Island 179° or Natawny Pier closed behind the S point of the island 166°. Between Inishlay and Inchamakinna keep well over towards the latter. Then steer to pass E of the small beacon off Nunra

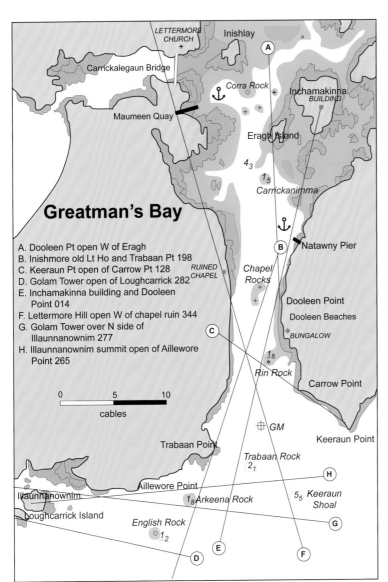

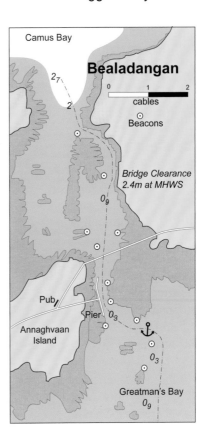

Point on Lettermore Island and continue N towards the beacons at the head of the bay. Leaving the first and second beacons to port, anchor in 2m between the second and third with the next beacon (close S of the quay) in line 289° with a low building with six small windows. The quay S of the bridge has a rough face and the bottom is foul, so it is unsuitable for drying out, but after half-tide it may be used for berthing. Shop and pub.

Bealadangan Pass

For vessels of limited air draft, Bealadangan Pass is navigable. It is best to make the passage near HW (+0010 Galway) as the flow reaches 4 to 5 kn at half tide, the flood running N. The depth at half tide is 1·8m; the clearance under the bridge should be 2·4m at MHWS, 4m at MHWN and 4·9m at half tide. The beacons are large and the Plan shows the way through them. The passage between the rocks is very narrow in places. Keep close to the mainland side when abreast the rock with the two N-most beacons.

KIGGAUL BAY

⊕*KG* 53°13'·5N 9°42'·7W
AC2096 and Plan

This bay is situated between Gorumna and Lettermullan Islands. It is easily identified from seaward by Illaunnanownim to the E and Golam Head 2M to the W. There is no difficulty in reaching the outer anchorage by day, but there are fish cages in the entrance which may be difficult to avoid at night. From the E, give Loughcarrick Island a berth of 3 cables. From the W, keep Carricknamackan Rock open S of Eagle Island 290° to clear Dawsy's Rock and Griffin Spit. Griffin Spit, with 3m, breaks only in a heavy swell.

Anchorage

Anchor close W or NW of the light beacon in 3 to 4m, mud with weed. Good shelter from W and N but untenable in fresh winds between SE and S. There are visitors' moorings. A pier with 0·5m alongside stands on the shore of Lettermullan Island W of the light beacon. Water at the pier; shop and PO at Lettermullan village, 800m.

Inner anchorage

The N part of the bay is accessible to very small yachts for 2 hours either side of HW, with least depth of 2·4m in the approach but very little room for error. Identify the conspicuous pub building (with two chimneys and an extension on its left side) close E of Kiggaul Bridge, and the two stone beacons marking the channel. Leave the light beacon 0·25 cables to starboard and line up the centre of the pub building between the two stone beacons 003°. There are rocks drying 2m, very close W of this leading line. Once past the beacons turn to port round the 12m-high rock N of the west beacon until heading SW towards a grass-topped islet. Anchor in 3m, mud, with the west beacon bearing 132° and the pub 014°, which is very close to the rocks; or in 2m a little NW of this, west beacon bearing 135° and pub 019°. There is a slip 2 cables S of the pub.

KILKIERAN BAY AND APPROACHES
AC2096, see Plan on p193
Kilkieran Bay lies N of Golam Head and extends inland for 14M. It can be entered in any conditions and gives excellent shelter. It is easily identified from seaward by Golam Tower, which dominates all this stretch of coast.

Kiggaul Bay from the S; Leacarrick (bottom L), Kiggaul light beacon (centre). Beyond the bridge is Coonawilleen Bay. Inishbarra (top R) and Illauneeragh (top L)

Tidal Streams
The stream at Golam Head is stronger than elsewhere in North Sound, and may raise overfalls. No accurate information is available, however, on directions and rates at Golam Head. Maximum rates in the bay are 2 kn at the narrows by Kilkieran Point and 1·5 kn near the entrance and off Ardmore Point. The ingoing stream commences at –0520 Galway and the outgoing at +0105 Galway. Constant +0005 Galway, MHWS 4·8m, MHWN 3·7m, ML 2·7m.

Dangers
A comprehensive list of the dangers around Kilkieran Bay would be very long indeed. The most significant are the following:
Ullan Rock, (dries), 1 cable S of Golam
Fairservice Rock, 0·9m, 2 cables E of Seal Rock
and 6 cables WSW of Golam
Seal Breaker (awash), 2 cables W of Seal Rock
Namackan Rocks, drying and above-water rocks 2·5M WNW of Golam
Kenny Rock (dries 1·8m), 5 cables NW of Namackan Rocks
Inishmuskerry Shoal, 0·9m, 5 cables S of Inishmuskerry
Dinish Shoals, 1·5m, 1·7M NNW of Golam
Outer Hard Rock (dries 1·8m), 5 cables NE of Ardmore Point
Fork Rocks and **Carrickanella Rocks** (drying), 6 cables N of Illaneeragh
Lettercallow Spit, 1·2m, 1M N of Illaneeragh

Lights and Marks
Kilkieran Pier, Fl R 3s
There are no lights in the approaches. **Golam tower** is conspicuous. Many of the above-water rocks in the approach, such as **Eagle Rock, Seal Rock** and

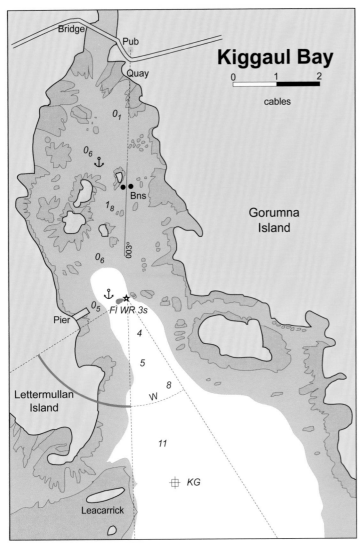

Kiggaul Bay

Golam Harbour
53°14'N 9°46'·5W
Immediately N of Golam Head is the entrance to Golam Harbour, which is obstructed by **Binock Rock** (dries about 2·7m), with a further drying rock close S of it. The best water is about one third of the width of the channel N of Golam Island. Note that there are rocks with less than 2m LAT in this fairway, and a close watch should be kept for lobster pots. As soon as the E side of Golam Island opens up turn sharp to port and keep 0·75 cable off the HW shore of Freaghillaunmore until 2 cables from Crappagh when it is safe to turn E. Anchor anywhere inside. If going right up to the head of the harbour (where shelter is best) take care to avoid the sunken rock SW of the 2·4m sounding. It is usually marked by long streamers of weed. The shelter is good under all conditions. There is no pier, but land near HW in the creek inside Crappagh Island, which gives access to the Lettermullan road. Shop at Lettermullan. There is a fish farm in the bay.

Bollegouh Creek, 53°15'·3N 9°45'·3W, E of Inisherk, affords complete shelter but it is choked with rocks, and local knowledge is necessary to find a safe berth. The entrance to the S of Inisherk is clearer but not to be attempted without reconnaissance by dinghy.

Fish Rock, are easy to identify in clear weather and make good landmarks. **Carricknamackan Little,** square shaped, dries 4·6m and only covers at HWS.

Directions
From the E, Golam Head is steep-to but beware of Ullan Rock, S of the island. Redflag Island well open of Golam Head 305° leads just S of Ullan Rock. Fairservice Rock is frequently not marked by a breaker even when Seal Breaker is showing. There is a fish farm NE of Eagle Rock. Lettercallow Hill and Dinish Point in line 047° lead between the two shallow heads of Dinish Shoals. Illaunmaan in line with Kilkieran Point 033° leads W of the shoals. The S extremity of Illauneeragh in line with Lettermore Hill 066° leads NW of the shoals. There are some ruined cottages and coral sand beaches at the S end of Illauneeragh. **From the W**, Golam Head well open of Redflag Island 126° leads clear S of Inishmuskerry Shoal, and the S extremity of Illauneeragh in line with Lettermore Hill 066° leads in between Dinish Shoals and Birmore.

Bruiser Rock (marked as "existence doubtful") lies 1 cable W of Dinish Island. Lettercallow Hill and Dinish Point in line 047°, as above, clear it. E of Birmore Island there are drying rocks; give the island a berth of at least 4 cables, and stay 4 cables off Ardmore Point (where there are sandy beaches) to clear the Inner and Outer Hard Rocks.

Fork Rocks, N of Illauneeragh, are dangerous as the SW rocks cover first. The W summit of Green Island, W of Illauneeragh, in line with Lettermullan Chapel 168° clears the rocks. The chapel is a grey, slated building. Birmore Island well open to the W of Illaunmaan, 230°, just clears Fork Rocks but leads over the end of Lettercallow Spit.

Anchorages
Anchorages in the bay can be picked from the chart to suit any weather conditions. The following are some of the more useful ones (latitudes and longitudes are given for ease of location and are not waypoints or recommended anchoring positions).
- **E of Illauneeragh**, 53°16'·4N 9°43'·6W. This lovely fine-weather anchorage is off glorious

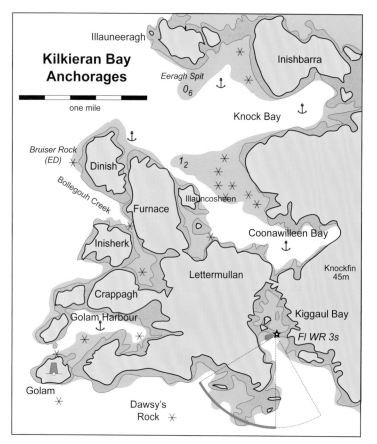

Kilkieran Bay Anchorages

one mile

Illauneeragh

Eeragh Spit
0·6

Inishbarra

Knock Bay

Bruiser Rock
(ED)

Dinish

1·2

Bollegouh Creek

Furnace

Illauncosheen

Inisherk

Coonawilleen Bay

Lettermullan

Knockfin
45m

Crappagh

Golam Harbour

Kiggaul Bay

Fl WR 3s

Golam

Dawsy's
Rock

9°45'·8W. Approach with a wide sweep to avoid the Inner and Outer Hard Rocks. Anchor off the drying pier at the head of the bay. Shop and pub 3 km. A delightful fine-weather anchorage, but in S winds there is a roll. Fish farming reported.

• **Kilkieran Cove,** 53°19'·2N 9°43'·7W. Anchor 0·5 cable off the pier with its head bearing 310°, in 2 to 3m, mud, holding suspect. Good shelter from SE through W to NE, and normally tide-rode. There are visitors' moorings. The pier, with a clean bottom, just dries at the head. Shop and pub.

North Kilkieran Bay

The upper portion of the bay, to the N of Kilkieran Cove, while ideal for dinghy sailing, has so many isolated rocks that it is impossible to give directions to a stranger.

Camus Bay

53°19'·6N 9°38'W
AC2096

This is reached from Kilkieran Bay by Gurraig Sound. The deep water channel through this sound is very narrow with patches of 1m and 1·2m very close to it, and the passage should only be attempted on a high and rising tide. There are three concrete beacons, one on **Bird Rock** and another N of Illaungurraig, which should be left to starboard going E and one on **Yellow Rock** to be left to port. After passing Yellow Rock a house among trees will be seen at Garrivinagh on the N side of the bay. Anchor a cable SSE of the small quay in 2·1m. Shop at Garrivinagh.

sandy beaches, and the island is uninhabited. Approach S of the 0·6m sounding on Eeragh Spit and keep well clear of the small spit SE of the island. Anchor in 2m, shells, N of this spit with the narrow cleft in the island to the N just closed in. Exposed from SE to SW. There is reported to be less than 1·8m at MLWS on the bar S of the anchorage.

• **Inside Dinish Point,** 53°16'N 9°44'·7W, in 2 to 3m, sand, off the beach between Dinish and Furnace Islands. Exposed from NE to NW. A lovely anchorage in good weather, with beautiful views up the bay with the Connemara Mountains as a backdrop.

• **Knock Bay,** 53°16'·2N 9°42'·6W, in the bay S of Inishbarra in 6m, halfway between the island and the reef to the SE.

• **Coonawilleen Bay,** 53°14'·9N 9°42'·9W. Leave Illauncosheen close to starboard on entering and anchor at the head of the bay in 4 to 5m, with the high bluff of Knockfin to the SE. There are fish cages in the bay.

• **Ardmore Bay,** 53°18'N

Kilkieran Cove from the N

Kilkieran Bay from the W. Duck Island R foreground, Mulroa Point with Finish Island and Ardmore Point beyond, L;
Inishmuskerry and Carrigalusk with Birmore and Birbeg beyond, R; Illauneeragh, Inishbarra and Lettermullan Island,
top.

Beyond Leighon Island the entrance to
Bealadangan Pass opens up, leading to Greatman's
Bay, but with very limited headroom under
the bridge. The channel to the ENE is fairly
straightforward though both shores are foul and
there is a rock awash in mid-channel N of Dangan
Hill (29m). There is anchorage off Rosmuck quay
in 4m, mud, at the entrance to the narrow channel
W of Clynagh Island. Shop and PO at Turloughbeg,
1 km. Do not attempt to go beyond this as the tides
begin to run very strongly, forming rapids in places,
and despite a number of beacons, local knowledge
is essential.

KILKIERAN BAY TO ROUNDSTONE
AC2096, 2709
The coast from Kilkieran Bay to Slyne Head is
fronted by a maze of rocks, islands and breakers, and
navigation marks are few and far between. It provides
a challenging and rewarding cruising ground for
the adventurous. The village of Roundstone, N of
Bertraghboy Bay, with its harbour dating from the
early 1800's, is a popular weekenders' retreat.

Caution
It is particularly necessary on this coast to be
conscious of the difference between the horizontal
chart datum and WGS84, which is the datum used
by the GPS system. This offset is documented on

up-to-date editions of the charts, but in the absence of such data an extra allowance of one cable should be made to clear known dangers when navigating by GPS.

Tidal Streams

The tidal stream in the Inner Passage is insignificant. The general stream runs NW and SE, and turns in and out of the bays and sounds. Off the Skerd Rocks the NW-going stream begins at –0320 Galway and the SE-going stream at +0305 Galway. In the narrows at the entrance to Bertraghboy Bay, the tide runs at 2 kn, and possibly a little more at springs; the ingoing stream starts at –0520 Galway and the outgoing at +0105 Galway. Constant (Roundstone Bay) +0003 Galway; MHWS 4·4m, MHWN 3·4M, ML 2·5M.

Dangers

An exhaustive list would be very long indeed. The most significant hazards on the coastal passage are as follows:

Inishmuskerry Shoal, 0·9m, 5 cables S of Inishmuskerry

Namackan Rocks, drying and above-water rocks 2·5M WNW of Golam

Kenny Rock (dries 1·8m), 5 cables NW of Namackan Rocks

Carrickaview (dries 1·8m) and **View Rock** (0·9m), 6 cables S of Mason Island

Fraghan Rock (dries), 4 cables E of Saint Macdara's Island

Tonyeal Rocks (1·5m and drying 0·6m), 1M SW of Saint Macdara's Island

Lebros Rocks (dry 0·6m), 5 cables SW of Mace Head

Rourke's Slate (dries 0·5m), on the S side of Ard Bay

Floor Rock, 1·2m, 6 cables NE of Illauncroaghmore

Smith Rock, 3m, 4 cables NW of Freaghillaun

Oghly Shoal, 1·2m, 3 cables S of Oghly Island in Bertraghboy Bay.

The dangers on the offshore passage to Slyne Head are listed below under ***Roundstone to Slyne Head***.

Lights and Marks

Croaghnakeela, white beacon Fl 3·7s 7m 5M, vis 218°–286°, 311°–325°, 034°–045°. Shows narrow sectors between Skerd and Mile Rocks to the SW and between Tonyeal Rocks and St Macdara's Island to the SE, and a broader sector to the E and NE, obscured elsewhere.

Inishnee, white pillar Fl(2) WRG 10s 9m W5M R3M G3M, G 314°–017° W 017°–030° R 030°–

080° W 080°–194°. Shows white over the approach from the SSW, green over Smith Rock and E of it, red over the islands and rocks to the SW and white over Roundstone Bay to the W and N.

The **church** on Saint Macdara's Island is conspicuous from the S.

As on the coast further E, the above-water rocks and islets offshore provide good reference points in clear weather. **Eagle Rock** (8m high), **Carricknamackan** (6m high) **Skerdmore** (18m high), **Doonguddle** (12m high) and **Mile Rock** (4·4m high) are relatively easy to identify.

Inner Passage

53°15'N 9°48'W

AC2096 and Plans on pp194 and 203

This channel, inside Eagle, Namackan and Tonyeal Rocks, is the shortest route into Roundstone from the E, offers a small degree of extra shelter to a yacht heading for Slyne Head and presents no difficulty in reasonable visibility. The following description of the islands on the N side is added to help in the navigation of this passage: **Birmore Island** is long, low and green with grey-white shingle patches on its SW side. **Inishmuskerry** has ruined houses, and a very obvious patch of sand on its S side. **Mason Island** has many ruined houses. **Saint Macdara's Island** is a low green hump with a boulder looking rather like a house on its summit. Its ancient church, at the S end of the island, has a very steeply pitched stone roof.

Directions

Golam Head well open N of Redflag Island 125° leads all the way through the Inner Passage. Alternatively bring the summit of Croaghnakeela over the S point of St Macdara's Island, 308°. Feraun North Rock (dries 4·9m) always shows except at highest springs when it would probably be marked by a breaker. Kenny Rock is usually marked by a breaker, as is Inishmuskerry Shoal on the N side of the channel. The shallowest parts of the Tonyeal Rocks usually break, but these are very dangerous rocks which cover a wide area and are liable to break anywhere in a high swell. The channel between them and Saint Macdara's Island is only 5 cables wide. The S point of Inishmuskerry and Carrickaview Breaker in line 114° leads through. The white sector of Croaghnakeela light, 311°–325°, also leads through.

There is a clear channel into the Inner Passage between the Namackan Rocks and the Eagle Rock group. Give Seal Rock (2·4m high), W of Golam, a berth of 3 cables on its W side; there is deep water close W of Fish Rock (4m high), 7 cables to the NW. From the W, Golam Tower open S of Eagle Rock 094° clears the breakers to the S of the Namackan Rocks. It is also possible to enter W of the Namackan Rocks, avoiding Kenny Rock by keeping Carrickadoolagh (2·1m high), close to starboard.

Mweenish Bay
53°16'·2N 9°50'·5W
AC2096, 2709
This bay opens to the N of the inner channel and can be entered either N or W of Inishmuskerry but there are so many isolated and unmarked rocks that it is not recommended for strangers. It is however possible in fine weather and daylight to anchor off the NE side of Inishmuskerry and land on the beach

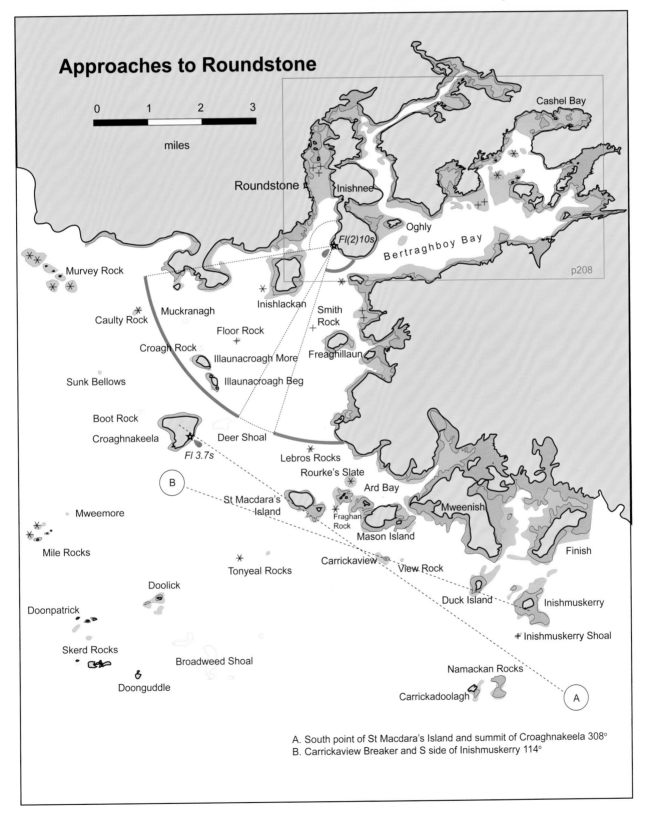

Approaches to Roundstone

0 1 2 3
miles

Roundstone
Inishnee
Cashel Bay
Oghly
Fl(2)10s
Bertraghboy Bay
p208
Murvey Rock
Inishlackan
Smith Rock
Caulty Rock
Muckranagh
Floor Rock
Croagh Rock
Illaunacroagh More
Freaghillaun
Sunk Bellows
Illaunacroagh Beg
Boot Rock
Croaghnakeela
Deer Shoal
Lebros Rocks
Fl 3.7s
Rourke's Slate
B
Ard Bay
Mweemore
St Macdara's Island
Fraghan Rock
Mweenish
Mile Rocks
Mason Island
Finish
Tonyeal Rocks
Carrickaview
View Rock
Doolick
Duck Island
Inishmuskerry
Doonpatrick
Inishmuskerry Shoal
Skerd Rocks
Broadweed Shoal
Namackan Rocks
Doonguddle
Carrickadoolagh
A

A. South point of St Macdara's Island and summit of Croaghnakeela 308°
B. Carrickaview Breaker and S side of Inishmuskerry 114°

of this delightful little island.

Macdara Sound
53°18'N 9°54'·4W
AC2709
This sound is navigable in calm weather, staying 1·5 to 2 cables off the summit of the 2·7m-high islet S of Saint Macdara's Island in order to clear Fraghan Rock. Once the church comes abeam, keep the island shore close aboard to port, to avoid Carrickaher (dries 3m). There is a steep sea on the ebb in Macdara Sound in fresh S winds or with any swell running outside. Straddle Pass, which leads E of Mason Island, is not recommended to strangers.

Saint Macdara's Island
This is a lovely island with wonderful views of the Connemara Mountains and the coast. The restored church dates from the 6th century and is one of the oldest in the country. Anchor in the little bay off the beach in the Sound, but not too close in as there are isolated boulders near the beach.

Ard Bay
53°18'·6N 9°53'·4W
AC2709
Ard Bay affords shelter in all except NW winds, and its continuation, Little Ard Bay, affords shelter in all winds. Golam Tower in line with the SW point of Mason Island 131° leads S of Lebros Rocks;

Inishnee light, a small, white column, in line with the SW point of Freaghillaun 003° leads E of them; and Treh Point on Inishtreh (in the entrance to Bertraghboy Bay) just opening W of Freaghillaun 018° leads W of them. Carrickaher and Rourke's Slate on the S side of the bay can be avoided by keeping over to the mainland shore, which is clean to within 1 cable.

Anchorages
Anchor off the N shore of Mason Island or in mid-channel in the lower part of Little Ard Bay, sand. In the latter anchorage a yacht will usually be tide-rode. If proceeding further up Little Ard Bay to get better shelter, the deep water is on the W side and there are half-tide rocks on the E side and in the centre as shown on AC2096. In N winds there is good anchorage off the quay in the unnamed bay NE of Rourke's Slate. Mason Island is uninhabited and has lovely beaches on the NE corner. Near its NW end there is a tiny harbour which is suitable only for small boats. The island is well worth a visit.

Skerdmore
53°15'·2N 10°03'W
AC2709
There is a small bay between Skerdmore and Skerdbeg, entered from the S, in which it is possible to land a dinghy at any state of the tide in very settled weather. The islands are a seal colony.

Roundstone from the S; Mace Head, foreground, Freaghillaun centre, Inishtreh, Inishnee and Roundstone Bay beyond. Inishlackan top L and Bertraghboy Bay top R

Bertraghboy Bay from the SW; Inishtreh centre, Inishnee L with Oghly Island beyond, Illaungorm top R. Note the fish farms.

ROUNDSTONE AND BERTRAGHBOY BAYS
AC2709 and Plan

These bays offer complete shelter and can be approached and entered in almost any weather. They are easily identified from seaward by Cashel Hill (307m) and Mount Errisbeg (296m) and Croaghnakeela Island and the Skerd and Mile Rocks offshore.

Directions

From the E, leave Saint Macdara's Island 2 cables to starboard and head for the E end of Inishlackan. Longitude 9°55'·5W leads 5 cables W of Lebros and Smith Rocks. **From the S**, identify Skerdmore (18m high) and Mile Rock (4·4m high) and steer to pass 5 cables W of Skerdmore. Once clear N of Doonpatrick (2m high) alter course to pass close E of Croaghnakeela. Deer Shoal can be ignored in normal summer weather. Illaunacroaghmore and Illaunacroaghbeg are steep-to on their E sides, where landing can be made in fine weather. **From the W,** the major hazards apart from Floor Rock are **Wild Bellows, Sunk Bellows, Caulty Rock** and **Murvey Rock** *(see the next section **Roundstone to Slyne Head** for detailed directions for avoiding these).*

Mile Rock in view between Illaunacroaghmore and Illaunacroaghbeg 222° leads **over** Floor Rock:

Cashel Hill and Treh Point on Inishtreh in line 043° lead E of Floor Rock and also W of Smith Rock. Treh Point is a boulder beach. It should be given a berth of 2 cables to clear the Small Breakers, on its SW side. There is a fish farm SW of Inishtreh, marked by yellow buoys Fl(2) Y 10s. The SE and SW points of Inishlackan are foul for 2 cables offshore.

Bertraghboy Bay
53°22'·4N 9°54'W
AC2709 and Plan

This bay, also known as Birterbuy, Traghboy or Cashel Bay, offers a choice of anchorages and shelter against all winds and sea, with lovely views of the Connemara Mountains. The W part of the bay is relatively free of dangers, except for Oghly Shoal which can be ignored above half tide. The charted transit on the water tank on Inishlackan is no longer visible. Steer 084° from mid-channel between Inishnee and Inishtreh until the E tip of Oghly Island bears 330°. There is a fish farm S of Salt Point.

Anchorages
- Off a bold bluff on the S shore halfway between the entrance and Rusheen Point, in 2 to 3m.
- E of Croghnut (28m high) at the E end of the bay, in 3 to 6m. Beware of the drying rock S

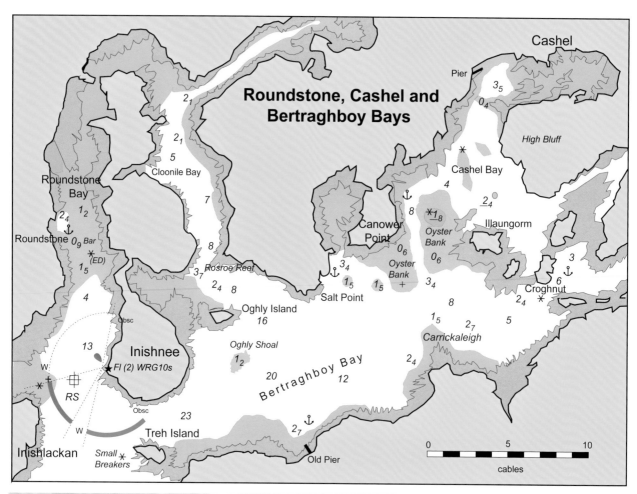

Roundstone, Cashel and Bertraghboy Bays

Roundstone Bay from the S

of Croghnut and leave it to starboard when entering.

- NE of Salt Point in 3 to 4m, with good shelter in W winds. Note the rock 1 cable offshore at this anchorage.
- NE of Canower in 3 to 5m. To reach this anchorage, head for Croghnut until Carrickleagh is abeam, then steer for the channel between the E and W Oyster Banks, course 350° with Carrickleagh astern.
- In Cloonile Bay; note that Rosroe Reef extends 2 cables SW from Rosroe Point. The holding is reported poor and the tidal stream in the channel is strong.

There is a delightful anchorage off the pier at the head of Cashel Bay, but up to date directions are lacking.

Roundstone Bay and Harbour

⊕*RS* 53°22'·7N 9°54'·6W
AC2709, Imray C54 and Plan

The W side of Roundstone Bay, N of Inishlackan, is fringed with half-tide rocks, and there is a bar with least depth 0·9m close S of the harbour. Leave Inishnee Point 1 cable to starboard then steer 353° over the bar. The drying rock charted close to mid-channel in 53°23'·6N is reported not to exist, and the bar has the same depth all the way across from E to W.

Anchorage

Anchor off the harbour a little to the S of the N quay as there is reported to be foul ground off the N quay. There are visitors' moorings S of the bar, but these are a long and exposed dinghy trip from the harbour.

Harbour

The N quay dries 0·5m at its outer end, but the bottom both here and at the S quay is clean.

Facilities

Water on the S pier. Shops, PO, pubs, restaurants. Buses to Galway.

ROUNDSTONE TO SLYNE HEAD

AC2709, 2708

The key to pilotage of this section is again to identify the above-water rocks offshore and use them as reference points. There are beautiful and accessible anchorages at Gorteen Bay and Bunowen Bay. Slyne Head is actually on an island – Illaunamid (23m high), at the end of a string of islets and rocks extending 2M WSW from the mainland. Its black

Roundstone Harbour from the NE; Gorteen Bay and Dog's Bay, top R, Inishlackan and Croaghnakeela, top L

lighthouse tower and the disused tower close SE of it are unmistakable. The two towers were built at the same time in 1836, the installation being designed to provide clear identification and a position line. The S tower was disestablished in 1898. There is one navigable channel through the reefs, known as Joyce's Pass or Joyce's Sound, which is not for the faint-hearted.

Tidal Streams

The N-going stream commences at −0320 Galway and the S-going at +0305 Galway. The rate is 3 to 4 kn at springs off the head and in the channels between the islets inside the head. The streams become weak 2 to 3M offshore. The streams are considerably affected by the strength and direction of the wind. There is a race off the head which can become dangerous in heavy weather or a high swell.

Caution

It is particularly necessary on this coast to be conscious of the difference between the horizontal chart datum and WGS84, which is the datum used by the GPS system. This offset is documented on up-to-date editions of the charts, but in the absence of such data an extra allowance of one cable should be made to clear known dangers when navigating by GPS.

Dangers

An exhaustive list would be very long indeed. The most significant hazards on the coastal passage are as follows:

Floor Rock, 1·2m, 6 cables NE of Illaunacroagh More

Muckranagh, 6·4m, 6 cables NNW of Illaunacroagh More, may break unexpectedly on the ebb tide.

Caulty Rock (dries 4·3m), 1·2M NW of Illaunacroagh More

Sunk Bellows, 1·8m, 1·5M W of Illaunacroagh More

Above-water, drying and sunken rocks extending in a wide arc of 3M from **Murvey SE Rock** (awash at HW), 1M S of Murvey Point, to **Duke's Rock**, 1M SE of Illaunurra

Wild Bellows (dries 3m), 2·1M SW of Murvey Point

Toole Rocks, 8·2m, 1·4M S by E of Wild Bellows, break in gales

Cromwell Shoal, 2·4m, 6 cables WSW of Duke's Rock

Mweel Rock (dries 4m), 7 cables SSW of Carrickfia, in Ballinaleama Bay

Mweel Breaker, 3·7m, 5 cables SW of Mweel Rock.

Lights and marks

Slyne Head, black tower Fl(2) 15s 35m 19M
The following above-water rocks provide useful points of reference:
Skerdmore (18m high), **Doonguddle** (12m high) and **Mile Rock** (4·4m high), S of Croaghnakeela, and **Murvey Rock** (6m high), 8 cables SW of Murvey Point. **Mullauncarrickscoltia** (1·1m high), 1·1M S of Illaunurra, is the key to the coast.

Directions

Heading W from Roundstone, give Inishlackan a berth of 3 cables. The SE points of Inishlackan and Inishnee in line 064° lead S of Muckranagh (which is rarely a hazard in summer weather) but dangerously close to Sunk Bellows; once Illaunacroagh More is abeam, alter course to the W to pass S of Caulty Rock, which almost always shows, and identify Murvey Rock to the NW. Wild Bellows, to the SW, is always marked by a breaker, but Sunk Bellows may only break intermittently. The NE sides of Saint Macdara's Island and Croaghnakeela in line 130° lead N of Sunk Bellows, while the whole of St Macdara's Island open S of Croaghnakeela, 110°, leads S of Sunk Bellows, Wild Bellows and all the dangers to Slyne Head. A confused sea can be met N of Illaunacroaghmore in fresh W winds, especially on the ebb.

Channels between the islands

Inishlackan Sound is navigable with care. Coming from Roundstone, keep well out in the middle of the main channel to avoid the drying rocks on the W side. Bring the light beacon on Inishnee in line 083° with the gap between the right-hand pair of three small humps on the skyline near the summit of the island. This line leads clear through the sound. Coming E from Gorteen Bay, keep well out from Inishlackan until the marks come in line so as to avoid **Gun Rock** (dries 2·7m) and the breakers around it.

Deer Pass is free of danger but the sound between Illaunacroaghmore and Illaunacroaghbeg is very narrow, and lobster pots are often set in it. It can break right across in bad weather.

Gorteen Bay

53°22'·4N 9°56'·5W
This is a delightful anchorage in crystal clear water with a magnificent sandy beach, and is sheltered from most summer winds. Anchor in 3m off the beach. Somewhat subject to swell.

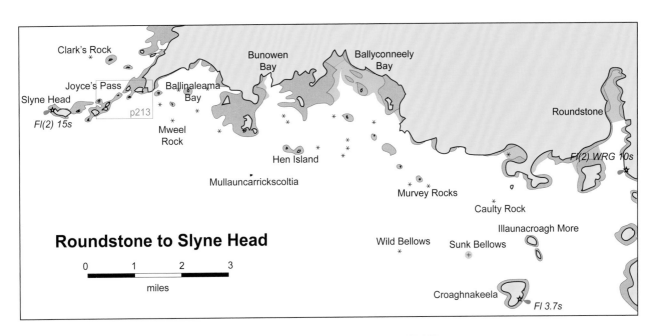

Roundstone to Slyne Head

0   1   2   3
miles

Ballyconneely Bay

53°22'·6N 10°04'W

This large bay lies to the W of Dolan Point. There is no safe anchorage in it which can be reached without local knowledge, and the bay is not recommended.

Bunowen Bay

53°24'N 10°06'·6W

This bay offers good shelter in winds from W through N to NE but becomes untenable in a S gale. Doon Hill, at the head of the bay is a steep, conical hill 61m high with a ruined tower on its summit, and is unmistakable. Giving Hen Island a berth of 4 cables, identify Mullauncarrickscoltia (1·1m high) and when Bunowen House (a prominent, square and roofless building to the E of Doon Hill) bears due N and is over a small strand to the S of it, steer into the bay on this course. It should be possible to see right through the building by most of its windows while on this course, which leads clear of Cromwell Shoal, Carrickcummer and Fortune Rock (dries 0·6m) to the W and the above-water rocks to the E. Anchor N of the pier in the SW corner in 3 to 4m, sand. It is possible to lie alongside the N side of the outer pier, which dries, or alongside the outer, NE end, where a yacht might remain afloat in 1·8m at LWN. Weed off this pier may foul intakes or propellers. Cafe 1·5 km, shop 5 km.

Ballinaleama Bay

53°23'·8N 10°09'·5W

This bay has long sandy beaches but offers no shelter except in its E corner, NE of Horse Island, where there is a drying quay. The approach is intricate, and no adequate directions can be given to a stranger.

SLYNE HEAD

AC2708

With its strong tides, and long projection from the shore, this is a formidable headland and should be given a wide berth in bad weather.

Directions

From the SE, from a position close S of Mullauncarrickscoltia, steer 282° to give the Head a berth of 1M. **From the N,** from a position 1M SW of the lighthouse and if bound E or SE, identify Croaghnakeela Island, 11M ESE and set course accordingly. A course of 102° passes S of Mullauncarrickscoltia, Murvey Rocks and Caulty Rock and so into the approaches to Roundstone. Alternatively, steer 130° to pass S of Skerdmore (18m high). This course also leads N of Eeragh light, W of the Aran Islands.

Joyce's Pass

53°24'·2N 10°11'·7W

AC2708 essential

Joyce's Pass, or Joyce's Sound, SW of Doonnawaul, is the only navigable channel inside Slyne Head. It is short and very narrow, and in bad weather and wind against tide it frequently breaks right across. Even on a calm day the sea is confused. The tide runs at 3 to 4 knots, turning N at –0320 Galway and S at +0305 Galway. In general the Pass should not be attempted in winds above force 4, though the tide, sea state and swell must be taken into account and may make the channel impassable even in light winds. It is advisable to transit near slack water and certainly never with significant wind over tide. There must be little or no swell. However a passage against the direction of wind and sea is easiest, since the conditions in the Pass can be more clearly seen from leeward.

Directions from the SE
First identify Mweel Rock (which almost always shows) and Carrickmweelrough, 0·4m high. Mweel Breaker to the SW of Mweel Rock may not be showing if the sea is smooth. Illaunaleama (18m high) and Doonnawaul (15 m high) can then be recognised and from them the line of rocks terminating in Carrickcluma More (4·7m high) with a breaker 1 cable S of it.

From Mullauncarrickscoltia, steer to pass close SW of Mweel Rock (waypoint 53°23'·65N 10°10'·1W), then steer 292° to pass 1·5 cables S of Carrickcluma More. Giving Carrickcluma More a berth of 1 cable on its W side, turn NE and steer towards Doonnawaul, leaving Carrickcluma Beg also to starboard. The waypoint for this turn is ⊕*JS* 53°24'·15N 10°11'·85W. At this point, observe the sea state through Blind Sound, SW of Joyce's Pass, and make the decision to proceed or not. Note that there is a pronounced tidal set through Blind Sound. As Carrickcluma Beg comes abeam the Pass will open, looking extremely narrow. Turn hard to port and keep in mid-channel steering 303° with plenty of way on. Once through, Carrickarone West (5m high) will be seen 1M away bearing 338° with Clark's Rock (dries 1m) 2 cables NW of it and bearing 324°. Clark's Rock may not show near HW with a smooth sea. Both of these rocks should be left to starboard.

Directions from the NW
Identification from the NW is not so easy, and this may be a lee shore with a long string of similar-looking islets fronted by breakers and half-tide rocks. Wind, tide and sea state are even more critical when heading SE. If in doubt, stay outside Slyne Head.

Doonnawaul and Illaunaleama are considerably higher than the rocks immediately to the SW near Blind Sound. However, Duck Island and Chapel Island may be confused. Approach on a course which will allow identification of Keerhaunmore Hill, 36m high, and possibly the sand cliffs at Toonacurra, which will then allow Carrickarone to be picked up as the land comes closer. With a firm fix on Carrickarone there should be little difficulty in identifying Joyce's Pass. From a position 5 cables SW of Carrickarone (waypoint 53°24'·8N 10°12'·7W), and in good visibility, Croaghnakeela Island (9M distant) will be seen over Carrickcluma Beg bearing 123°; this line leads to the Pass. Waypoint ⊕*JN* 53°24'·5N 10°12'·10W is close NW of the entrance to the Pass. Once through, turn hard to starboard, leave Carrickcluma More a cable to port and head SE into clear water.

OFFSHORE PASSAGE – NORTH SOUND TO SLYNE HEAD
On the direct passage from Cashla Bay, Kilronan or Galway, give the Connemara coast E of Golam Tower a berth of 1M to clear all dangers. Identify Seal Rock (2·4m high), 1M W of Golam, and leave it well to starboard. A course from here to Skerdmore (18m high) with Skerdmore and Doonguddle (12m high) in line 286° clears all the dangers except for Wild Shoals (16·2m), which are not hazardous except in gale conditions. There are no dangers on the direct course from Skerdmore to Slyne Head.

Offshore Weather Buoy M1, yellow, Fl(5) Y 20s, is moored 40M W by S of Slyne Head in position 53°07'·6N 11°12'W.

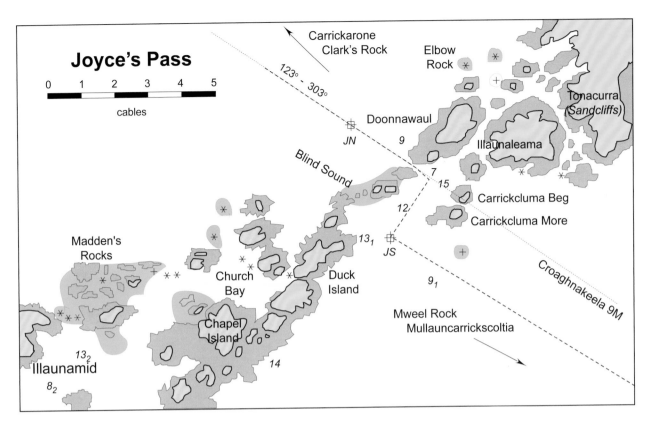

Joyce's Pass from the S; Doonnawaul is the large islet, centre R, with the Pass between it and the two small rocks at centre. The wider channel at lower L centre is Blind Sound, which is not navigable. The N tip of Duck Island shows at bottom L; the outliers of Carrickcluma More at bottom R, Barracarrick beyond Doonnawaul, with the Carrickarone group top L

Chapter 7

Slyne Head to Erris Head

Inishbofin from the SW; Inishturk and Clare island, top R, Achill Head, top L

The coast from Slyne Head to Erris Head is deeply indented, with many bays offering excellent shelter, and magnificent scenery. Long stretches are fronted by islands and rocks which give protection from the Atlantic swell to the channels and bays behind them. The populated islands include Inishbofin (199), Inishturk (58) and Clare (136). On the mainland Diamond Mountain (441m), and Tully Hill (353m) dominate the coast by Ballynakill Bay, while the square massif of Mweelrea (815m) rises north of Killary Harbour, and is the most imposing feature of the whole coast. The superb cone of Croaghpatrick (761m) overlooks the south side of Clew Bay. To the north, Achill Island rises to 664m and slopes west in a ridge to Achill Head. Its terrific cliffs, the highest in the British Isles, form the south side of the entrance to Blacksod Bay. To the west of the bay the low and sandy Mullet Peninsula extends with its offshore islands to Erris Head.

Charts

The general chart AC2420 Aran Islands to Broad Haven Bay spans the whole area of this chapter. For an offshore passage, this chart, together with 1820 Aran Islands to Roonah Head and 2704 Blacksod Bay and Approaches, is adequate, but for detailed exploration of the coast the largest scale charts are all essential.

Tides

The streams offshore are weak, running S from about +0400 Galway to –0330 Galway and N at other times. Near the coast and around salient points, particularly Achill Head and Erris Head, they may attain 1·5 kn. In Achill Sound the tides run at 4 to 5 knots, reaching 8 knots at springs at Bull's Mouth. Tidal constants vary from +0005 Galway at Clifden to +0100 Galway at Bull's Mouth, and MHWS from 3·6m at Bull's Mouth to 4·5m at Westport.

SLYNE HEAD TO INISHBOFIN
AC1820, 2708, 2707
Tidal Streams
The N-going stream at Slyne Head commences at –0320 Galway and the S-going at +0305 Galway. The spring rate is 3 to 4 kn off the head but less 2 to 3M offshore. The streams are considerably affected by the strength and direction of the wind. There is a race off the head which can become dangerous in heavy weather or a high swell. Precise information on the timing and strength of the streams among the small islands to the NE is lacking, but for all

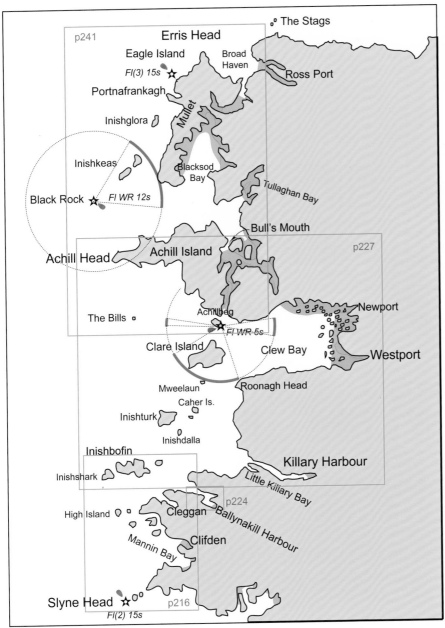

practical purposes the tide may be assumed to turn at the same time as at Slyne Head.

For details of tidal streams around Inishbofin, see below.

Dangers *(above-water rocks are not included)*
Barret Shoals, 22m, 3M NNW of Slyne Head
Clark's Rock (dries 1m), 4 cables W of Carrickarone and 1·5M NNE of Slyne Head
Cloherty Breaker, 2·1m, midway between Carrickarone and Barrnacarrick
Carricknaguroge (dries 4m), 7 cables NE of Carrickarone
Lyalmore Breaker (dries 0·3m), 1·5M NE of Carrickarone and 3 cables W of Lyalmore
Carrigeenboy (dries), 5 cables NW of Lyalmore
Pollticaur (dries 1·8m), 9 cables N of Lyalmore
Mullaunacrick (dries 2·7m), **Carrickawollawaun** (dries 3·7m), **Crowneen Rock** (dries 1·5m), **Testy**

Breaker, 1·8m, and **Young John's Rock** (dries 0·4m), extending 1M NW of Knock Point
Mweem Cruagh, 3·4m. 1·2M W of Eeshal Island
Sharaghmore (dries 0·5m) and **Sharaghbeg** (dries) 4 cables SW and S of Omey, respectively
Glinsk Rock (dries 2·4m), 5 cables W of Omey
Doolickcruagh (dries 2m), 3 cables N of Cruagh
Mweelauntrogh (dries 1·8m), 4 cables E of Friar Island
Carrickaphuill (dries 4·4m), 6 cables NE of Friar Island
Carrickaun, less than 2m, 4 cables NE of Friar Island
Cowrakee (dries 2·7m), N of High Island
Carrickmahoy (dries 1·9m), 8 cables S of Lyon Head

Lights and marks
Carrickrana beacon, white tower, unlit
Fishing Point, beacon, white tower, unlit
Cleggan Point, white col on white hut Fl(3) WRG 15s 20m W6M R3M G3M, W shore–091°, R 091°–124°, G 124°–221°. Shows white over the dangers to the W of Cleggan Bay, red over the approach from the WNW and a wide green sector to the N.
Lyon Head, white col Fl WR 7·5s 13m W7M R4M, W 036°–058°, R 058°–184°, W 184°–325°, R 325°–036°. Shows white over the approach from the SW, red over Cleggan Bay and the dangers to the W of it, white over Ballynakill Harbour, Lecky Rocks and Davillaun, and red inshore to the N and NW.
Gun Rock, white col Fl(2) 6s 8m 4M
Bofin Harbour, leading marks 032°, white towers; the front tower carries a Port Entry Light Dir Oc WRG 6s 22m 11M. Shows a narrow W sector on the leading line and 5° sectors either side, R to W, G to E
Inishbofin Outer Pier, Fl(2) R 8s
Inishbofin Inner Pier leading beacons, triangles on poles, L Fl 6s
Inishbofin Inner Pier, Fl R 5s

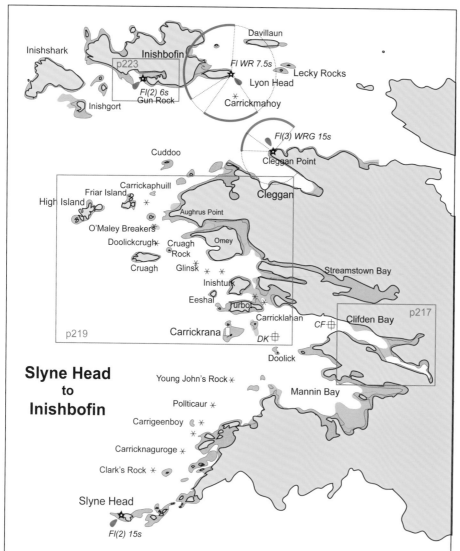

**Slyne Head
to
Inishbofin**

p223
p217
p219

Inishshark
Inishbofin
Davillaun
Fl WR 7.5s
Lecky Rocks
Lyon Head
Fl(2) 6s
Gun Rock
Inishgort
Carrickmahoy
Fl(3) WRG 15s
Cleggan Point
Cuddoo
Cleggan
Carrickaphuill
Friar Island
High Island
Aughrus Point
O'Maley Breakers
Doolickcrugh
Cruagh Rock
Omey
Cruagh
Glinsk
Streamstown Bay
Inishturk
Eeshal
Turbot
Carricklahan
Clifden Bay
CF
Carrickrana
DK
Doolick
Young John's Rock
Pollticaur
Mannin Bay
Carrigeenboy
Carricknaguroge
Clark's Rock
Slyne Head
Fl(2) 15s

Coast NE of Slyne Head
AC2708

Between Slyne Head and Clifden Bay the coast is fronted by a maze of rocks and islets, and must be given a berth of at least 1·5M. Clark's Rock, Carrigeenboy, Pollticaur and Young John's Rock are the outermost of these dangers. Further offshore, Barret Shoals, despite a least depth of 22m, raise overfalls and a heavy and confused sea.

The key to the pilotage of Mannin and Clifden Bays is the prominent 11m-high white beacon on Carrickrana (Seal Rocks), 53°29'·2N 10°09'·5W. From a position 2M W of Slyne Head a course of 043° leads to the beacon. The direct course from Slyne Head to Inishbofin passes 3M W of Carrickrana and through High Island Sound.

Approaches to Clifden, from the W; Carrickrana foreground, with its white beacon, Waverymore and Waverybeg L foreground, and the rocks Mweelaunawaddra, Carricklahan and Mweelaunmore behind Carrickrana. Doolick with a breaking outlier, upper R. Turbot Island, L, Clifden Bay upper R centre and the Twelve Pins of Connemara on the skyline

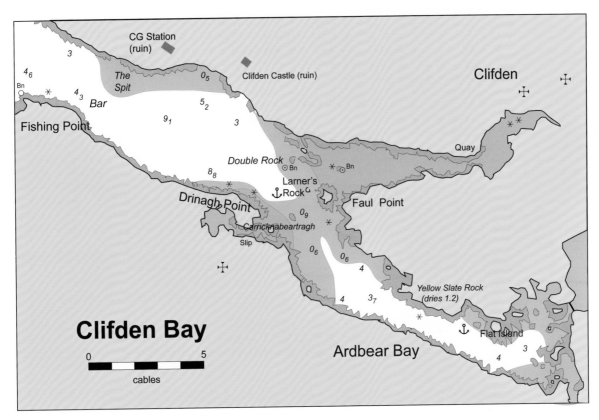

Mannin Bay

53°27'·5N 10°06'W

AC2708

Mannin Bay is exposed to the prevailing swell and offers only indifferent shelter, but is a lovely bay with superb sandy beaches. From a position 5 cables S of Carrickrana, head for Doolick until the peak of Cruagh Island (3M NW of Carrickrana beacon) comes in line with Waverymore 315°, and keep this transit in line astern. From Clifden, hold mid-channel between Doolick and Illaunrush, the islet off Errislannan Point to the E. The best anchorage for a short stay is inside Knock Point in 3 to 4m, a beautiful spot. More secure anchorage can be found in Mannin Creek, crossing the bar at a suitable rise of tide and keeping towards the N shore. Anchor in 4 to 6m in the middle of the creek. There are fish farms in the bay.

Clifden Bay

⊕ *CF* 53°29'·5N 10°05'·2W

AC2708, Imray C54

The transit of Fishing Point beacon with Clifden Castle, marked on AC2708, is of little use now since the castle is difficult to distinguish amongst newer buildings. From a position 3 cables S of Carrickrana beacon, a waypoint of 53°29'·2N 10°07'·5W (⊕ *DK, see plan on facing page)* provides a berth of 2 cables from the reefs N of Doolick. Fishing Point is clean and may be given a berth of 0·5 cable. The best depth on the bar is found by keeping Shindilla

(the SE point of Ardmore islet) just visible outside Fahy Point, 289°. The sandbank on the N shore off the old CG Station has silted considerably and can break in heavy weather with ebb spring tides. The channel to Clifden town dries at LW and there are drying and above-water rocks across the entrance, NW of Faul Point. The outermost of these, Double Rock (dries 2·1m) has an unlit white beacon. There are fish farms in the bay.

Ardbear Bay

There is a bar with least depth 0·9m at the entrance to Ardbear Bay. From a position midway between Double Rock beacon and Drinagh Point, steer 142° for 2 cables to clear Carricknabeartragh (dries 1·4m). When Larner's Rock (1·5m high) bears due N, turn to starboard and steer 160°, with Double Rock beacon directly astern, to cross the bar. Where the bay narrows 5 cables SE of Faul Point, keep the SW side close aboard to avoid Yellow Slate Rock (dries 1·2m). There are fish farms in the bay.

Anchorages

- NW of Double Rock beacon in 3 to 5m, good holding in mud and sand. There are visitors' moorings.
- Between Larner Rock and Drinagh Point in 5m. This anchorage is reported to have poor holding ground with the ebb overfall from Ardbear Bay, particularly in NW winds, but is the most

Clifden from the W; Drinagh Point R foreground, Larner's Rock, Islandagar and Faul Point, R

Ardbear Bay (lower R) and Clifden Bay from the SE

convenient for access to Clifden.

- In the upper part of Ardbear Bay, W or SE of Flat Island and about 1·5 cables off the island, in 3m.

Constant +0005 Galway; MHWS 4·4m, MHWN 3·4m, ML 2·5m. Clifden town is accessible by dinghy above half tide.

Facilities

Diesel, water, shops, pubs, restaurants, PO, laundry, doctors, hospital at Clifden. RNLI inshore lifeboat station.

Passage Northward from Clifden
AC1820, 2707

High Island Sound is the normal fair-weather route for a yacht heading N from Slyne Head or Clifden. A course of 011° from a position 2M W of Slyne Head leads to the sound, and also W of Barret Shoals. High Island breaker, with 8·2m, is very close to this line; in a high swell it can be avoided by keeping the E hill of Inishshark in line with the E side of High Island 347°. This also just clears Gur a Mweem breaker, 7·9m, SW of Cruagh Island. From Clifden, the safest course is to leave Carrickrana beacon to starboard and then steer to leave Cruagh Island and

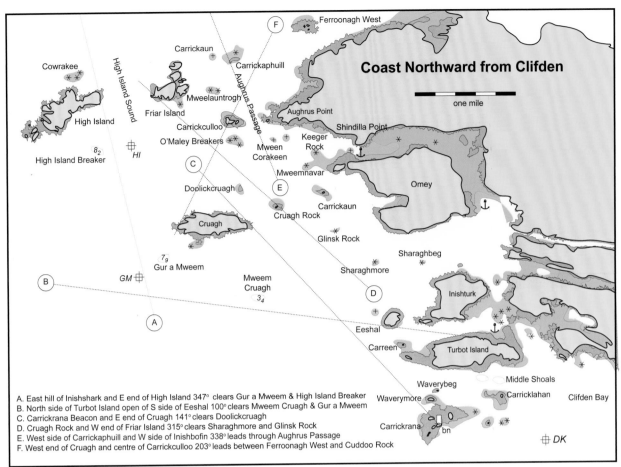

Coast Northward from Clifden

one mile

A. East hill of Inishshark and E end of High Island 347° clears Gur a Mweem & High Island Breaker
B. North side of Turbot Island open of S side of Eeshal 100° clears Mweem Cruagh & Gur a Mweem
C. Carrickrana Beacon and E end of Cruagh 141° clears Doolickcruagh
D. Cruagh Rock and W end of Friar Island 315° clears Sharaghmore and Glinsk Rock
E. West side of Carrickaphuill and W side of Inishbofin 338° leads through Aughrus Passage
F. West end of Cruagh and centre of Carrickculloo 203° leads between Ferroonagh West and Cuddoo Rock

Gur a Mweem to starboard and so to the sound. Waypoints ⊕ *GM* 53°31'·0N 10°14'·1W, 5 cables SW of Cruagh, and ⊕ *HI* 53°32'·4N 10°14'·3W, 5 cables SW of Friar Island, may be useful *(see Plan, above)*. The N side of Turbot Island open S of Eeshal Island 100° leads S of Mweem Cruagh breaker (3·4m). AC2707 gives clearing marks to pass NE or W of it.

In moderate weather the channel N of Carrickrana is straightforward, leaving Carrickalahan (0·8m high) and Waverybeg (1·6m high) one cable to port. In heavy weather or a high swell, Middle Shoals, 2·4m, in mid-channel, are dangerous, and a yacht should stay S of Carrickrana.

If passing N of Cruagh Island note that Cruagh Rock (1·4 m high) and Carrickaun (2·2m high) will always show, and the drying rocks Sharaghmore, Glinsk Rock and Doolickcruagh must be avoided. Glinsk Rock and Doolickcruagh are usually marked by breakers. Pass 1 cable off Cruagh Island and bring Carrickrana beacon in line with the E end of Cruagh Island astern 141° to pass W of Doolickcruagh, and also W of **O'Maley Breakers,** SW of Aughrus Point. High Island Sound itself is clear but the sea can run high in it with formidable breakers on both shores.

Caution

Do not confuse O'Maley Breakers (SW of Aughrus Point) with O'Mallybreaker (off Crump Island, 10M to the NE), or the above-water rock Carrickaun (W of Omey) with the dangerous submerged rock Carrickaun (NE of Friar Island).

Coast from Turbot Island to Aughrus Point

In settled weather this stretch of coast, with its beautiful sandy beaches, is delightful and provides some good temporary anchorages. It should however be avoided in fresh onshore winds or a heavy swell.

Turbot Island

53°30'·2N 10°10'·5W

AC2708, 2707

The channel between Turbot Island and Inishturk, entered between Eeshal Island and Carreen, is clean for almost 1M to the E. **Middle Ship Rock**, which usually shows, marks the W side of the reefs at the head of the channel. The rocks SE of the quay on Inishturk extend further than charted, and a submarine power cable crosses the channel 1·5 cables W of Middle Ship Rock. There is anchorage off Turbot Island in 3m with Middle Ship Rock bearing N.

There is also a pleasant fine-weather anchorage

Coast N of Clifden, from the W; Inishturk centre L, Eeshal, foreground, and Turbot Island, R, with Carreen and Doughty in front. Clifden Bay, top R

off the SE point of Omey Island. From the S, give Eeshal Island a berth of 2 cables and steer to pass 1 cable off the N shore of Inishturk. This leaves Sharaghmore and Sharaghbeg to port.

Kingstown Bay and Streamstown Bay
53°31'·3N 10°09'·7W

These inlets are not recommended. The channels are narrow, shallow and with fast tidal streams, and there is an overhead power cable with a clearance of 15m across Streamstown Bay 4 cables inside the entrance. Heading W and N from here, stay 1 cable off the S shore of Omey and steer 252° to pass between Sharaghmore and Glinsk Rock. The W point of Friar Island in line with Cruagh Rock 315° clears both rocks to the W.

Omey Island
53°31'·3N 10°09'·7W
AC2707
Omey is joined to the mainland by a fine strand which

dries up to 2m. There is fine-weather anchorage E of the SE tip of the island in 2 to 3m, sand. There are fish farms in this area. AC2707 also shows an anchorage NW of Omey Island. It is a very pleasant spot in fine weather only. There is a pier on the E side of Shindilla Point on the mainland side to the N. In the approach, O'Maley Breakers and Mween Corakeen to the N and Keeger Rock and Mweemnavar to the S must be avoided.

Aughrus Passage and Friar Island Sound
Aughrus Passage lies between Aughrus Point to the E and Carrickculloo (5m high) and O'Maley Breakers to the W. Friar Island Sound lies between Carrickculloo and Mweelauntrogh to the E and Friar Island to the W. O'Maley Breakers always show. The tides run fast, especially through Friar Island Sound, and set across the rocks. With the uneven bottom and their exposed position, the passages can be recommended only in fine weather, moderate winds and little or no swell. A fresh SW wind against

Omey from the W, with (L to R foreground) the rocks Mweemnavar, Carrickaun and Glinsk. Shindilla Point and pier, L

Aughrus Passage from the S; Aughrus Point, centre, with Carrickculloo L centre. Cruagh Island, Doolickcruagh (breaking), L, Cruagh Rock lower centre, and Carrickaun and Mweemnavar, R. Friar Island, upper L; Carrickaphuill and Cuddoo Rock beyond the Passage. Inishbofin in the distance

a spring ebb would be dangerous.

Aughrus Passage

53°32'·2N 10°12'·1W *(4 cables S)*

AC2707 essential

This channel is obstructed on its E side by Mween Corakeen with about 1m at LAT, and by a 3·7m patch 2·5 cables W of Aughrus Point. Drying rocks extend 2 cables W of the point, and the channel between the 3·7m patch and Carrickculloo is only 1·25 cables wide. The W side of Inishbofin in line with the W side of Carrickaphuill, 338°, leads through. Carrickaphuill only covers at high springs and would then usually be marked by a breaker. Once through, bring the W end of Cruagh Island in line with the centre of Carrickculloo astern, 203°, and this line will lead between Ferroonagh West and Cuddoo Rock. A waypoint of 53°33'·9N 10°11'·8W, in mid-channel between Feroonagh West and Cuddoo, may be useful.

Friar Island Sound

53°32'·5N 10°13'·4W *(5 cables S)*

AC2707 essential

Friar Island Sound is straightforward if course is set to keep close to the island shore. Watch out for the tide which sets across Mweelauntrogh and runs fast through the sound. In settled weather, temporary anchorage is available in 3m in a tiny cove on the E side of Friar Island.

Friar Island from the E with High Island beyond. Aughrus Passage and Carrickculloo L, and Carrickaphuill R with Carrickaun breaking beyond it. Mweelauntrogh is just showing, centre. The cove on Friar Island can be clearly seen

Approaches to Cleggan

The S side of High Island in line with the N side of Friar Island 236°, or a waypoint of 53°34'·6N 10°09'·7W, leads clear N of the rocks to the W of Cleggan Bay. At night, the red sector of Cleggan Point light shows over safe water, and the white sector shows over the rocks and also up the bay.

Cleggan Point is clean, and the approach from the NE is straightforward.

Cleggan Bay

53°34'·4N 10°08'·6W
AC2707, Imray C54

This bay is open to the NW but offers reasonable shelter in summer and is easy of access. Anchor off the boat harbour, which dries out. In bad weather the inner harbour can be closed by timber baulks placed across the entrance by a crane. An alongside berth at the pier is not recommended due to the ever-present swell and the ferry traffic to Inishbofin and Inishturk. Water near the head of the pier, diesel by tanker (Sweeney Oil, 095 21777). Shops, pubs, PO.

INISHBOFIN

⊕*IB* 53°36'·3N 10°13'·5W
AC1820, 2707, Imray C54 and Plan

Inishbofin is a favourite port of call for yachts cruising the area or on passage N or S. The island lies at the centre of a group of rocks, islets and breakers extending 8M from W to E. The shores and sounds are all foul, and any approach to the group from seaward in poor visibility or a high swell must be made with great caution. Bofin Harbour, on the S side of Inishbofin, is one of the best natural harbours on the west coast, although entry and exit can be tricky in heavy weather from the SW or a high swell.

Bofin Harbour *(see Plan)*

From High Island Sound, a course of 011° leads to the entrance. **From the N**, beware of the drying reef Carrickmahoy (*see below*). Two conspicuous white towers on the N side of the harbour in line 032° lead in close E of a 1·2m patch and then very close to Gun Island with its 12m-high light beacon. It is possible to borrow to the E of the line outside Gun Rock, and to the W of it when abreast the rock. Near HW and with no swell, the 1·2m patch to the W of the line might be ignored, but Bishop Rock (dries 1·4m) must be avoided. Continue on the leading line until the ruins of Cromwell's Fort are well abeam, then turn in to the harbour. Anchor SW of the outer pier in 2 to 4m, clear of the moorings and allowing room for the ferries to manoeuvre.

A channel 30m wide (dredged in 2007 and

Bofin Harbour from the SW; Gun Island and its beacon, bottom L, and the leading beacons on the island shore beyond. The dredged channel to the inner quay is clearly visible, upper R

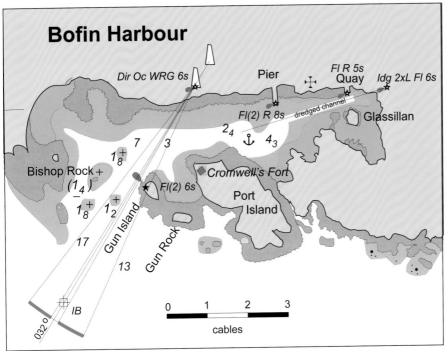

Bofin Harbour

Dir Oc WRG 6s
Pier
Fl R 5s
Quay
Idg 2xL Fl 6s
Fl(2) R 8s   dredged channel
Glassillan
2₄   ⚓   4₃
7   3
1⅛
Bishop Rock ┼
(1₄)
─
1⅛   1½
17
Gun Island
Fl(2) 6s
Cromwell's Fort
Port Island
Gun Rock
13
IB
032°

0   1   2   3
cables

clearly visible in the aerial photograph) leads to the refurbished inner quay, N of Glassillan, and there are leading marks (triangles on poles) on the shore to the E. Yachts should avoid obstructing this channel, which is used by the ferries. There is limited room to anchor in the inner pool, NE of Glassillan (and the soundings have not been checked recently) but there is adequate depth on the S face of the inner quay for a yacht to lie alongside if the ferries do not require the berth. A fenderboard is recommended if going alongside the sheet piling of the outer pier.

Constant +0010 Galway; MHWS 4·1m, MHWN 3·1m, ML 2·3m.

Facilities
Water on both piers. Shop, pub, hotel, cycle hire. Showers at the Community Centre. Ferry to Cleggan. Mechanical and electrical repairs, 095 45807.

Rusheen Bay (Inishbofin)
53°37'·3N 10°10'·3W
Rusheen Bay, on the E side of the island, offers sheltered anchorage in offshore winds. There is a fine sandy beach in delightful surroundings. The quay dries. Black Rocks, on the NE side of the bay, always show, and New Anchor Shoal (1·5m) on the S side can be avoided by keeping Lyon Head beacon bearing due S until off the centre of the bay. There is a restaurant above the bay.

Inishshark
This island, 95m high, has no good anchorage or landing place. There are breakers and rocks off its NW, SW and SE corners. **Kimmeen Rocks** extend

6 cables W of the island with a channel between them and the island through which the tide runs at 2·5 kn. **Inishgort**, S of Inishshark, has foul ground all round, and the channel between these two islands is rock-strewn. **Mweemore**, 7·5m, and **Paddy Lenane's Shoal**, 7m, break in heavy weather. The **Stags of Bofin** extend 6 cables from the NW corner of Inishbofin; the **North Stag Rock** (20m high) in line with **Colleen Rock** (12m high) 055°, leads NW of all the dangers W of Inishshark.

Ship Sound, between Inishshark and the islets SW of Inishbofin, is navigable with care, but the 2·5 kn tide and uneven bottom with patches of 3m and 3·4m make the passage possible only in moderate winds and little sea. Beware of the isolated, drying **Tide Rock**, 2·5 cables E of Inishshark and defining the E side of the channel. In bad weather Ship Sound breaks right across.

Carrickmahoy, 8 cables S of Lyon Head and drying 1.9m, breaks heavily over an extensive area and is particularly dangerous since it lies in the middle of the main channel SE of Inishbofin. Inishshark well open of Inishbofin 290° leads S of Carrickmahoy, and Black Rock open of Lyon Head 331° leads E of it. Approaching from the N, note that the sound between Inishshark and Inishgort (which is very similar in profile but much smaller than Inishshark) opens first while still in the danger area. A waypoint of 53°35'·7N 10°09'·1W, 3 cables SE of Carrickmahoy, may be useful. In a heavy swell there are breakers between Carrickmahoy and Inishlyon.

Tidal Streams
In the channel between Inishbofin and the mainland and in Ship Sound the tidal streams run in the direction of the channels. The spring rate in Ship Sound is 2·5 kn and in the main sound 1·5 kn, stronger around Lyon Head. The ebb, running SW, sets more strongly across Carrickmahoy than the NE-going flood. The tide turns NE at –0350 Galway and SW at –0120 Galway, running NE for only two and a half hours, or sometimes less. It is frequently rough in this channel due to the long duration of the SW-going ebb against the prevailing wind and swell.

Davillaun

Davillaun (24m high) lies 1.3M E of Inishbofin. There are rocks 2 cables W of it of which the outermost, **Mweeldyon,** dries 1·8m. **Couraghy,** which dries, lies 2 cables E of Davillaun with **Davillaun East Breaker,** 2·1m, a further 2·5 cables to the E. Landing from a dinghy can be made in fine weather in the Port Cove on the S side of the island. **Lecky Rocks,** 5·5 cables SE of Davillaun, consist of two groups with a narrow and shallow channel between them. The N rock is 7m high and the S rock 3·4m. They are foul E and W for about 1·5 cables.

There are deep channels between Black Rock and Davillaun and between Davillaun and Lecky Rocks.

Coast – Cleggan to Ballynakill Harbour

Both sides of Cleggan Point and the coast E to Ballynakill consist of cliffs between 15 and 45m high, backed by steep grass slopes with bare rock in places and with occasional guts known as 'ooeys', some with beaches at their heads.

BALLYNAKILL HARBOUR

⊕*BK* 53°34'·6N 10°03'·6W (in approach from W)
AC2706 and Plan

This fine bay is easily entered by day and is a good refuge with excellent shelter, as well as providing scope for day sailing inside in pretty surroundings.

Tully Mountain on the N, much higher than any other hill so near the coast S of Killary, is easily identifiable.

Dangers

There are several above-water rocks in the approach which make useful landmarks, including **Carrigeen South** (0·7m high), **Carricklaghan** (0·7m high), **Glassillaun** (12m high) and the small islet S of it (locally known as the Cow and Calf), a rock at Barracladdy (3·7m high), and (a little confusingly) the **Carrigeen Rocks** (2·2 and 2·8m high). All except Carrigeen South and Carricklaghan have grassy tops. The dangers to be avoided are **Mullaghadrina** (dries 3·4m), 1·5 cables SW of Carricklaghan, a **rock** 0·5 cable S of the "Calf", a **drying rock** 1 cable NE of the 3·7m rock at Barracladdy, **Ship Rock** (dries 1·5m), 2 cables S of Tonabinnia, and **Ardagh Rocks** (dry 3·4m), with an orange beacon, 3·5 cables E of the E Carrigeen Rock. There is a mussel farm E of Freaghillaun South and fish farms E of Ross Point and elsewhere in the bay.

Directions

From the W and Cleggan Point, pass N of Glassillaun and then head for the Carrigeen Rocks, leaving them 0·5 cable to port. When the E Carrigeen Rock comes in line with Braadillaun 357°, keep these marks in transit astern to clear the shallows N

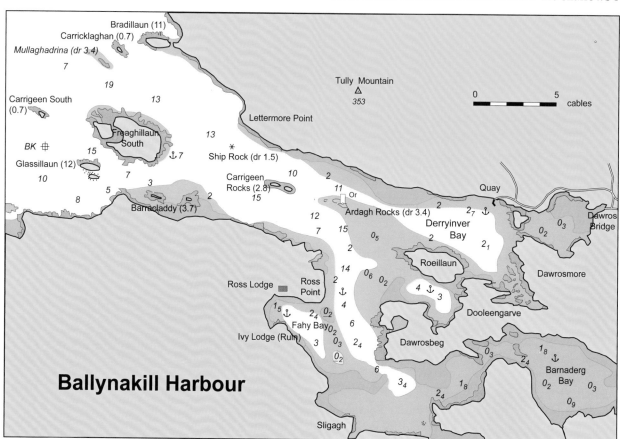

Ballynakill Harbour

Ballynakill Harbour from the S; Tully Mountain, top, Toneillaun foreground, Barnaderg Bay centre R with Roeillaun beyond, Ross Point top L with Braadillaun and Inishbroon beyond and Freaghillaun South just visible, top L. Inishturk behind and L of Tully Mountain, and Clare Island on the horizon, top R. Note the fish farm E of Ross Point.

of Ross Point. **From the N**, Mullaghadrina usually shows, but if it does not, keep Glassillaun open of Freaghillaun South until 1 cable from the latter, then staying 1 cable off the N side of Freaghillaun South, head for the Carrigeen Rocks. Inishbroon open of Braadillaun 325° leads 1 cable SW of Ship Rock. If heading to Derryinver Bay keep Glassillaun just open S of Freaghillaun 273° to pass between Ship Rock and Carrigeen Rocks.

Anchorages
- **Derryinver Bay** (53°34'·2N 9°59'·2W), at the NE end of Ballynakill Harbour. To pass N of Ardagh Rocks and between the banks, keep the W head of Carrigeen Rocks on Glassillaun 276° until Ardagh Rocks are abeam, then steer for Dawrosmore Hill with the N side of Freaghillaun astern 287°. Anchor off the two streams about 100m SW of Derryinver quay, good holding, but buoy the anchor as there are old mooring chains on the bottom. The quay dries.
- Off **Ross Point** (53°33'·8N 10°00'·4W), always accessible, tide-rode but sheltered from the W.
- **Fahy Bay** (locally known as Ross, 53°33'·5N 10°00'·8W), approached over a bar with 0·2m at

LWS, is one of the best anchorages on the whole coast, with good holding in 2 to 3m, mud, and pretty, pastoral surroundings. The only bad wind is SE, when it can become surprisingly rough; in these conditions choose a berth on the S side, close to the trees. The bar is quite sheltered and at neaps a yacht drawing 1·5m could enter at LW. It is about the same depth across most of the entrance of the bay, a little deeper towards the S side.
- The **pool S of Roeillaun** (53°33'·7N 9°59'·5W) is accessible at half-tide and offers better shelter than Ross Point or Fahy Bay in strong SE winds.
- **Barnaderg Bay**, in the SE corner (53°33'·3N 9°58'W), offers perfect shelter with enough depth to lie afloat at neap tides, and can be reached on a rising tide with AC2706 and continuous use of the echosounder. Keelkyle Quay dries 0·9m at the head.

Facilities
PO and shop with petrol pump at Moyard; shop, pub and filling station at Letterfrack, 800m E of Keelkyle Quay.

Fahy Bay from the SW; Ross Point, Roeillaun and Derryinver Bay beyond

INISHBOFIN TO CLEW BAY
AC1820, 2707, 2706, 2667

This section of the coast includes the magnificent fjord of Killary Harbour and the fascinating islands of Inishturk and Clare Island, the latter with its stupendous 460m cliffs and its historical associations with the warrior-queen Granuaile. Clew Bay has a myriad of low grassy islands and a maze of channels, and the picturesque, historic and busy town of Westport at its head.

Tidal Streams
Between Inishturk and the mainland the tides are rotatory and run at less than 0·5 kn at springs. N of Clare Island the W-going stream reaches 1·5 kn, and further E the tides run fairly into and out of Clew Bay, also reaching 1·5 kn at springs. Offshore tidal streams are slight.

Dangers
The dangers inshore and in the approaches to the anchorages are described in the individual directions. The major dangers offshore are as follows:
Pollock Shoal, 3·7m, 3·3M N of Rinvyle Point
Blood Slate Rocks (dry 0·5m), 7 cables W of Frehill Island
Middle Ground, 7 to 21m, extensive area S and E of Caher Island which breaks in heavy weather
Meemore (awash), 1·5M W of Roonah Head

Dillisk Rocks (dry 1·2m), 1·8M SW of Inishgort
Two Fathom Rock (3·4m), 8 cables NNW of the lookout tower on the W end of Clare Island

Lights and marks
Inishbarna, white beacon, unlit
Doonee beacon, unlit
Ardagh Rocks, beacon, orange, unlit
Roonagh Quay ldg lts 144° Iso 10s, front 9m, rear 15m
Inishturk Pier, Fl G 3s 3M
Clare Island Pier, Fl R 3s 5m 3M
Clare Island Jetty, 2FR vert 2M
Dillisk Rocks buoy, SHM Fl G 5s
Dillisk Rocks perch (derelict)
Inishgort, white tower L Fl 10s 11m 10M
Dorinish buoy, SHM Fl G 3s
Cloghcormick buoy, W Card Q(9) 15s
Achillbeg Island, white tower Fl WR 5s 56m 18M, R 262°–281° W 281°–342°, R 342°–060°, W 060°–092°, R(unintens) 092°–099°, W 099°–118°.
Shows red over the shoals in the outer approaches to Newport, white over the deep water NE of Clare Island, red over Clare Island and white to the W, with a narrow unintensified red sector over the Bills Rocks.

The lights and marks in the approaches to Westport and Newport are described in the relevant Directions, below.

KILLARY HARBOUR AND APPROACHES
AC2706, and Plan on p228

Killary Harbour and Little Killary Bay may be entered in daylight in almost any weather conditions, but note that in heavy weather the whole of Middle Ground, E and S of Caher Island, becomes a mass of breakers and must be avoided.

Approaching from High Island Sound, Cleggan or Ballynakill, the outermost danger is **Mweelaunatrua** (dries 1·9m), 3 cables W of Inishbroon. (Inishbroon has yellowish cliffs on its S side and grass sloping to the sea on the N side.) From Cleggan Point, steer to pass 5 cables NW of Inishbroon, and Illaunananima, 1M to the NE. **From Inishbofin**, and passing either side of Lecky Rocks, leave Illaunananima 5 cables to starboard. Identify Corweelaun West (1·9m high) and Corweelaun (0·7m high), NW of Crump Island, and leave them 2 cables to starboard. The summit of Illaunananima

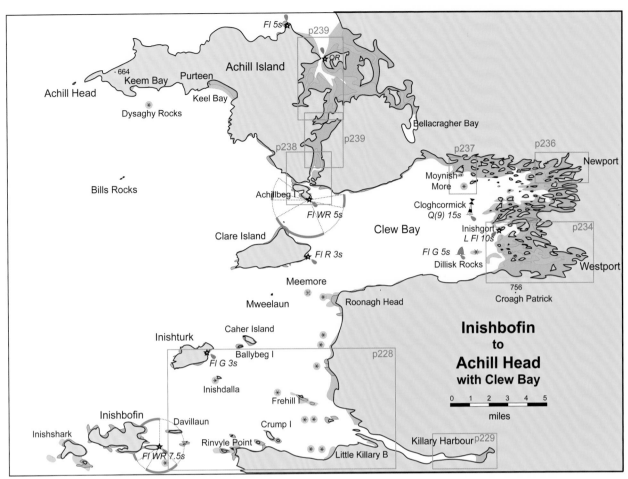

in line with Corweelaun West 258° astern leads S of **O'Mallybreaker** (dries 0·5m) but across a bar with least depth 6m. In heavy weather, steer to pass 5 cables N of Corweelaun West and hold this course, passing well N of O'Mallybreaker, until Gaddymore (6m high) is identified. Waypoint ⊕*OM* 53°38'·4N 9°59'·5W is 3 cables N of O'Mallybreaker and 1M W of Gaddymore. Steer 099° from here on the transit of the beacons on Doonee and Inishbarna to clear all dangers to the entrance to Killary Harbour.

Inshore passage round Rinvyle Point

In settled weather with no swell, it is possible to make the passage S of Illaunananima and between Freaghillaun N and Crump Island. Leaving Mweelaunatrua 2 cables to starboard, alter course for Illaunananima when Rinvyle Point shows N of Inishbroon. When the N side of Freaghillaun comes in line with the S side of Shanvallybeg, 089°, turn to starboard and steer on this transit, which leads close N of **Puffin Rocks** (dry 0·5m) and across the bar between these rocks and Illaunananima in a least depth of 3·7m. As soon as the depth increases to 6m or more and Rinvyle Castle (a square ruin near the shore) bears SE (long 10°02'·6W), steer for Corweelaun West (1·9m high), to avoid the rocks extending NW from Freaghillaun North. Cleggan Point over the E point of Inishbroon 233° leads clear

of these rocks. When 3 cables from Corweelaun West, with Freaghillaun abaft the beam, close the shore of Crump Island to pass NE of **Tom's Anchor** (dries 1·6m, marked as "Thos. Anchor" on the chart). Give Shanvallybeg a berth of 2 cables to port. When Blake's Point comes in line with Rinvyle Castle 253° (waypoint ⊕*SV* 53°36'·9N 9°59'·3W) steer 073° with this transit astern; this leads clear of all dangers to the entrance to Killary Harbour.

The following additional transits are available to clear O'Mallybreaker: Tully Mountain over the E point of Crump Island 191° leads E of it; and Tully Point touching the E side of Shanvallybeg 150° leads SW of it.

From W of Inishturk, the SW side of Inishdalla in line with the tower on the summit of Inishturk 321° astern leads W of Pollock Shoal. Stay on this line until the Doonee and Inishbarna leading beacons line up 099°. Alternatively, set a course between Gaddymore and Frehill Island, with Inishdalla directly astern and the Doonee beacon in line with the SW side of Inishdegil More 116°. This leads N of Pollock Shoal, S of Blood Slate Rocks and **Breaker Rock** (dries, 4 cables SW of Frehill Island), and N of **Thanybegnadrusk** (dries 0·6m, 5 cables E of Gaddymore). When 5 cables from Inishdegil More (in long 9°56'·0W) alter course S to clear the 1·8m

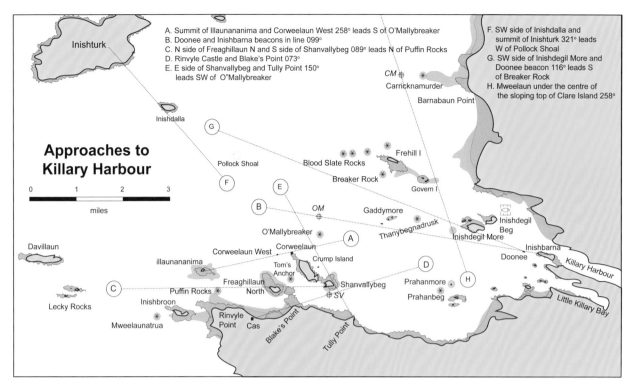

A. Summit of Illaunananima and Corweelaun West 258° leads S of O'Mallybreaker
B. Doonee and Inishbarna beacons in line 099°
C. N side of Freaghillaun N and S side of Shanvallybeg 089° leads N of Puffin Rocks
D. Rinvyle Castle and Blake's Point 073°
E. E side of Shanvallybeg and Tully Point 150° leads SW of O'Mallybreaker

F. SW side of Inishdalla and summit of Inishturk 321° leads W of Pollock Shoal
G. SW side of Inishdegil More and Doonee beacon 116° leads S of Breaker Rock
H. Mweelaun under the centre of the sloping top of Clare Island 258°

Approaches to Killary Harbour

sounding W of Inishdegil More.

The 6m-high white beacons in the entrance to Killary Harbour can often be picked out clearly from a distance. They lead between and close to John Keneally's Rock (11m) and Conolly's Rock (10m). In a heavy sea or swell, keep well S of the leading line at this point.

AC2706 has a sketch of the view along the line of the beacons. There are also two distant transits for the gap between O'Mallybreaker and the Carrickgaddy Rocks: Leenaun Hill (616m high, shown on AC2420) in line with the N fall of Aillachoppal 112°, or Achill Head (AC2420) seen between Caher Island and Ballybeg astern 334°. These transits may be obscured by low clouds or poor visibility. However, once Gaddymore is identified, Gaddy Beg (0·4m high) will be seen and course may be set to pass 2 cables W of it to avoid a rock which dries 0·9m, 1 cable to the W of Gaddy Beg.

From the N, bring Mweelaun, 19m high, under the centre of the sloping top of Clare Island 341° astern; waypoint ⊕*CM*, 53°41'·3N 9°57'·3W, on this line, also leads W of **Carrickamurder** (dries 1·1m, 7 cables W of Barnabaun Point). The transit line passes E of Frehill Island, but over the 1·8m patches E of Govern Island and W of Inishdegil More; keep more to the E and W, respectively, passing these two points. Roonagh Head (8M N) just open E of Govern Island 011° leads E of

Thanybegnadrusk. There is a fish farm close N of Carricknaglamph, NE of Inishdegil Beg.

In heavy weather, approach W of Caher Island and close E of Inishdalla to avoid Middle Ground.

Little Killary Bay (Salrock)
⊕*LK* 53°37'·2N 9°53'·8W
AC2706 and Plan
The head of this inlet is a fine anchorage which can be entered in any weather and provides good shelter; no swell reaches the anchorage, although it appears on the chart to be open to the NW. The shores of the inlet slope steeply, the S side tree-clad and the N bare and rocky.

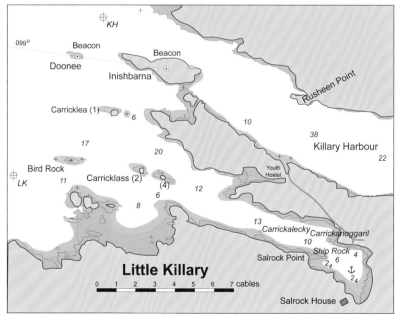

Little Killary

Killary Harbour from the W: Black Rocks bottom L, Inishbarna centre, Doonee lower R centre, with Carricklea and Carricklass beyond;Little Killary Bay to R

Directions

From the W, the sandy bays just W of the entrance are conspicuous. Prahanbeg (dries 0·9m, 1M W of Culfin Point) is the only hidden danger in the approach. All the rocks in the immediate approach show at HW and may be passed on either hand. Note, however, that Carricklea is foul all round, and rocks extend 1 cable E and W of Bird Rock. Illaunmore should be left 1 cable to starboard. **From the N** and Killary Harbour, pass between Inishbarna and Doonee and follow the shore round, staying E of mid-channel between Carricklea and the mainland point to the E. Note that Carrickalecky (dries 2·1m), on the S side, appears further N than charted. Care must be taken at the 0·5 cable wide passage between Ship Rock, (the extension of Salrock Point) and Carrickanoggaril, opposite (Carrickanoggaril is not named on AC2706). Anchor in 2 to 4m, soft mud, on the SE side of the pool E of Salrock Point. The holding has been reported suspect, and in strong winds a second anchor should be used. No facilities ashore.

up the inlet and makes the anchorage at Leenaun uncomfortable. The entrance, between Doonee and Black Rocks (1m high), is straightforward. The shores are clean to within 0·5 cable. There are fish farms in the Harbour.

Constant +0018 Galway; MHWS 4·1m, MHWN 3·1m, ML 2·3m.

Anchorages

* About halfway up on the S side off Dernasliggaun Lodge, in 2 to 4m. The house (now known as Killary Lodge) is an Adventure Centre. There is a small pier to lie alongside at HW. Water on the pier. Visitors' moorings may be available.
* On the N side off Bundorragha, S of the perch in 5 to 7m. A rock was marked on the old charts 70m W of the perch, but its existence is doubtful. Landing at the drying quay which is approached along the W shore.
* At the head of the Harbour in 2 to 3m about 3 cables NW of Leenaun Quay, which dries. Hotel, shop, PO, filling station at Leenaun.

Killary Harbour

⊕*KH* 53°37'·9N 9°53'·2W

This spectacular inlet, 7M long, with mountains falling steeply to the water's edge on either hand, has some of the most remarkable scenery on the coast, and a visit to its head is well worthwhile. In unsettled weather, however, any W wind funnels

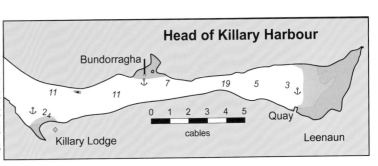

Inishturk pier from the SE

Direct passage – Inishbofin to Clew Bay

In good weather, pass 2 cables S of Lyon Head and leave Carrickmahoy and Lecky Rocks to starboard, then pass 5 cables E of Davillaun and steer 038° to clear Pollock Shoal and Roonah Head (with **Black Rock** to the W of it), and pass E of Meemore. If there is any uncertainty in position, steer closer to Caher Island and within 1M of Mweelaun (19m high, W of Roonah Head). Refer to the directions below for rounding Roonah Head. In heavy weather, avoid Middle Ground altogether; steer close E of Innishdalla, and W of Caher Island and Mweelaun.

Coast – Killary Harbour to Clew Bay

AC2706, 2667

The coast between Killary Bay and the entrance to Clew Bay consists of 6M of sandy beaches broken at intervals by rock outcrops. A number of groups of rocks, reefs and shoals extend up to 1·5M out from the beaches and beyond these groups the depths are irregular up to 4M offshore. The beaches are exposed to the W and are subject to nearly continuous surf. The coast should be given a berth of 1·5M in fine weather. In bad weather, the whole coast E of a line joining Mweelaun to Caher Island becomes a mass of irregular breakers and should be avoided.

Meemore

⊕ 53°46'·2N 9°56'·7W (3 cables N)
AC2667

Meemore, 1·75M E of Mweelaun, dries at low springs and usually breaks. It is a dangerous rock owing to the ease with which it can be confused with **Black Rock** which dries 3·2m and lies 1M off Roonagh Head. Note that the coast from Roonagh Head to Oldhead is open from near Meemore and closed from near Black Rock. A useful clearing mark to keep N of Meemore is the summit of Croagh Patrick (761m) N of the summit of Carrowmore Hill (170m), 2M E of Roonagh Head.

Inishturk

⊕ 53°42'·2N 10°05'W (2 cables SE of the pier)
AC2706, 2667

Inishturk, 188m high and 2·25M long, is the most isolated inhabited island on the W coast. It is, in general, steep-to except at the SE corner where **Floor Shoals** with 6·7m least water extend for 8 cables. There is anchorage, well sheltered from winds between SW and NNW, in Garranty Harbour on its E side, off the pier in 3 to 6m, sand, good holding but somewhat exposed to swell. Shop, PO, pub and restaurant. Ferries to Cleggan and Roonah Quay.

Caher Island

53°43'N 10°01'W
AC2667

Caher Island, 57m high, lies 1·5M E of Inishturk. It has steep, high cliffs at its NW end. There are boat landings at Portatemple on the E and Portnacloy on the W, usable in settled conditions only.

Ballybeg and Caher Islands (foreground) with Clare Island in the distance and Mweelaun between (centre R)

Clare Island

⊕ 53°48'·1N 9°56'·6W (3 cables E of the pier)
AC2667

This magnificent island has superb cliffs on its NW side, beneath which there are a few isolated rocks close in. Between Calliaghcrom and Lecknacurra, the N point of the island, there is a 7m rock which breaks in gales. There are fish farms E and NE of the island.

Anchorage

There is a reasonable anchorage in winds between SW and NW in 3 to 6m, sand, N of the pierhead; in other winds the bay is uncomfortable or untenable. The pier is subject to swell and an alongside berth is not recommended. There are visitors' moorings.

There is a temporary anchorage on the NE side of the island in up to 6m, sand, off the beach which has a small pier and slip at its W end. The bottom further W is rock.

Constant +0015 Galway; MHWS 4·1m, MHWN 3·1m, ML 2·3m.

Facilities

Pub at the harbour, shop and PO at Portnakilly, 1·5M. Ferry to Roonagh Quay.

CLEW BAY

AC2667

Clew Bay lies E of Clare Island, and is about 6M wide and extends 12M E from Roonagh Head and Achillbeg. There is no shelter in the outer part of

Clare Island harbour from the SE; Granuaile's Castle ("Grania Wael's" on the chart) is near the root of the pier. Achill Head on the horizon

Clare Island from the E

the bay but its head is filled with many small islands and there are several good anchorages behind them. There are also tidal channels to Westport Quay and Newport. The inner part of the bay offers fascinating day-sailing in a shallow-draft yacht or a dinghy. The S side of the bay is dominated by the cone of Croagh Patrick (756m) with a chapel on its summit. The coast from Roonagh Head to Oldhead is foul for 6 cables offshore. Oldhead, 146m, is conspicuous and surrounded by trees. There is a pier E of the head which dries, with clean sand bottom along its inner side; to clear the rocks close E and S of the pier approach it near HW on a bearing of 190° and round the pierhead fairly close. There is a temporary anchorage NE of the pier, holding poor and subject to swell.

Passage between Clare Island and Roonagh Head

In all normal summer weather this is the usual approach to Clew Bay from the S. Mweelaun (19m high) provides a conspicuous mark for clearing Meemore safely. However in heavy weather, the uneven bottom, with patches down to 8m, together with a SW going tide of 1·5 kn, creates a high and confused sea. In such conditions the deeper and cleaner channel N of Clare Island is to be preferred.

Passage between Roonagh Head and Meemore
53°45'·5N 9°56'W
AC2667 essential
This is a useful short cut in good weather and is easy to identify when leaving Clew Bay, less so when

approaching from the SW. The passage lies between **Black Rock** (dries 3·2m), 6·5 cables off the shore between Roonagh Head and Emlagh Point, and Meemore Shoal, 7 cables WNW of Black Rock. The key to the passage is the identification of Black Rock, as there are no convenient leading marks in either direction. Black Rock has a distinctive low appearance like a whale's back; covered at HW, it is almost invariably marked by a breaker. Give it a berth of 2 or 3 cables, no more, so as to stay well clear SE of Meemore.

Roonagh Quay, near Roonagh Head, has leading lights for the Clare Island ferries but is not accessible to a yacht.

Approaches to Westport
⊕ *WP 53°49'·6N 9°41'W*
AC2667, 2057, Imray C54 and Plan
From the SW, from a position 1M N of Roonagh Head, leave Dillisk Rocks buoy to starboard. From the NW, leave Cloghcormick buoy to port. Inishgort lighthouse is backed by a conspicuous white wall. In rough weather, approach the lighthouse on a bearing between 080° and 100°. Leave Dorinish buoy close to starboard. The entrance can be rough with wind against tide.

Lights and Marks
Leckanvy Jetty (53°47'N 9°41'·3W), green pole beacon Fl G 5s
Dillisk Rocks buoy, SHM Fl G 5s
Inishgort, white tower L Fl 10s 11m 10M
Dorinish buoy, SHM Fl G 3s
Starboard Bar buoy, SHM Fl(2) G 10s, 3 cables

ESE of Dorinish buoy

Inishlyre buoy, PHM, Fl(2) R 10s
Inishlaghan buoy, PHM Fl R 4s
Inishimmel buoy, SHM Fl G 5s
Inishgowla buoy, PHM Fl R 4s
Inishraher NE buoy, SHM Fl(2) G 5s
Finnaun buoy, PHM Fl R 6s
Corrillan beacon, SHM Fl G 5s
Carricknamore beacon, SHM Fl G 3s
Green Island NW beacon, PHM Fl R 3s
Green Island SW beacon, PHM Fl R 6s
Green Island SE buoy, PHM Fl R 3s
Annagh West buoy, SHM Fl G 5s
Carricknacally beacon, PHM Fl R 6s
Pigeon buoy, PHM Fl(2) R 5s
Illanroe buoy, SHM Fl(2) G 5s
Monkelly's buoy, PHM Fl R 2s
and lateral buoys and beacons to Westport Quay:
Port hand beacons, red perches (1) Fl R 4s, (2)
Fl(2) R 6s, (3) Fl R 4s, (4) Fl R 5s, (5) Fl(2) R 5s,
(6) Fl(2) R 5s
Starboard hand beacons, (1) green perch Fl G 2s,
(2) stone bn Fl(2) G 10s, (3) green perch Fl(2) G 5s
and (4) green perch Fl G 3s

Anchorages among the islands *(see Plan)*

• **Dorinish Harbour,** SW of Inishlyre. Anchor 2
to 3 cables off Dorinish More and W to NW of
the Inishlaghan buoy in 2 to 3m, good holding.
Dorinish Bar covers at HWS but still breaks the
sea.

• **Inishlyre Harbour.** This natural harbour E of
Inishlyre gives good shelter from W and SW
winds. Enter midway between the NE point of
Inishlyre and the SW point of Collan More, then
turn S and anchor in 2m, 1·5 cables N of the SE
point of Inishlyre.

• **Collan More Harbour,** E of Collan More
Island, gives the best all-round shelter and
offers the easiest access to the mainland.
Approach from between Inishlyre and Collan
More as above, with the S end of Inishgort in
line with the N point of Inishlyre. When the SW
point of Collan More comes abeam, bring the N
point of Inishlyre in line with the wall N of the
lighthouse. This leads over a bar with 1m and
N of the drying rock NW of Inishtaggart. The
sailing club sometimes has a racing mark just
to north of this rock; keep to the north of the
mark. The entrance, between Collan More and
Rosmoney Point is 1 cable wide between the
HW marks but the shore on either side is foul
and the navigable entrance is only 45m wide.
Enter in mid-channel in 1·7m; the deepest part
is NNE of the narrows. Submarine electric and
telephone cables and a water pipe are laid across
the narrows. There is an uncharted drying rock
about 120m off the Rosmoney shore, shown
on the Plan. The quay, which dries, is on the S
side of the harbour near the Mayo Sailing Club.
Anchor in 2·6m. Glenans Sailing School has
a base on Collan More, with a members' bar
which welcomes visitors.

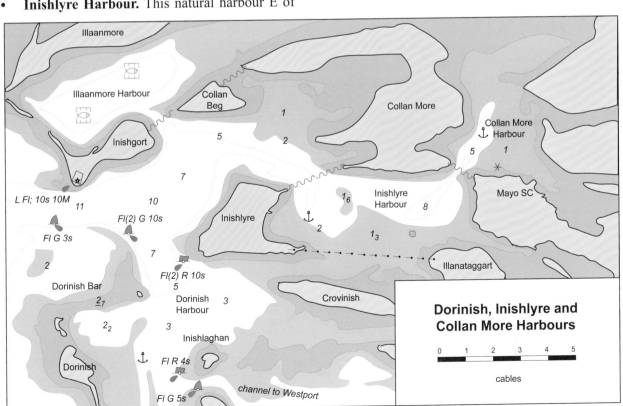

**Dorinish, Inishlyre and
Collan More Harbours**

cables

Approaches to Westport, from the WNW. Inishgort lighthouse, bottom L, with Inishlyre beyond; Dorinish, R

WESTPORT

AC2057 essential

The channel to Westport has a least depth of 0·1m near the quay, and the quay itself mostly dries but with a clean mud bottom.

Directions

From Dorinish Harbour, the channel passes between Inishlaghan and Inishimmel and then N of Inishraher. Follow the marked channel. There should be 1·8m of water at the quay 2 hours either side of HW. The best berth is just E of the tide gauge on the N side. Sea angling boats use the quay. Constant +0020 Galway; MHWS 4·5m, MHWN 3·4m, ML 2·5m.

There are shellfish beds surrounding Carricknacally Rock. Do not anchor or take the ground in this area.

Facilities

Supermarket, shops, pubs and restaurant at the quay. Westport, 1·5 km from the quay, has all the facilities of a sizeable town. Supermarkets, shops, PO, pubs, restaurants, doctors. Train and bus connections to Dublin. Chandlery 098 28800, divers 098 41236.

NEWPORT

⊕*NP 53°51'·6N 9°40'·9W*

AC2667 and Plan

Newport, in the NE corner of Clew Bay, lies behind a labyrinthine maze of low islands and narrow channels which – in moderate weather – offer some fascinating pilotage to the adventurous sailor. The approach channel is marked and lit, but the creek leading to Newport dries at LW. W of the islands, and N and W of the Cloghcormick buoy, is an area of shallow water and irregular bottom which makes the approach from seaward hazardous in heavy onshore weather or a high swell. The main approach passes N of Inishoo and S of a line of rocks and shoals extending 2·5M W from Illanmaw, and comprising the drying rocks **Carrickachorra, Carricklahan, Carrickachaash South, Carrickachaash North** and **Larbaun**, and below-water rocks with 1·4m, 1·7m and 2m.

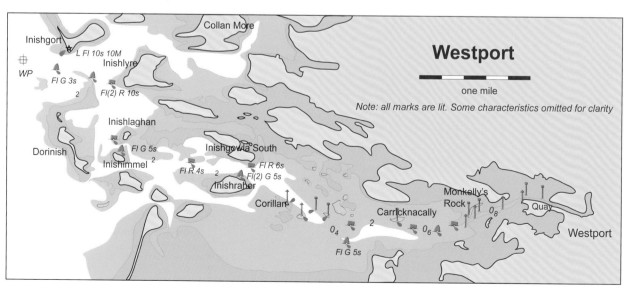

Westport from the W

All the islands are fringed by boulder shoals, so aim always to keep in the centre of the channels. It is important also to keep a careful tally of the islands, most of which are very similar in appearance. Illanascraw is of distinctive shape (rather like the bows of a ship) when seen from seaward. Rosmore Point has a near vertical face, the only one in that vicinity.

Lights and marks
Inishoo beacon, SHM Fl(2) G 6s
Illanmaw buoy, PHM Fl(2) R 5s
Taash buoy, SHM QG
Illanascraw beacon, SHM Fl G 4s
Rosmore Point buoy, PHM Fl R 5s
Rabbit Island buoy, SHM Fl G 5s
Rosmore South buoy, PHM Fl(2) R 10s
Rosnambraher buoy, SHM Fl(2) G 10s
Milcum Quay beacon, SHM Fl G 5s

Newport from the E

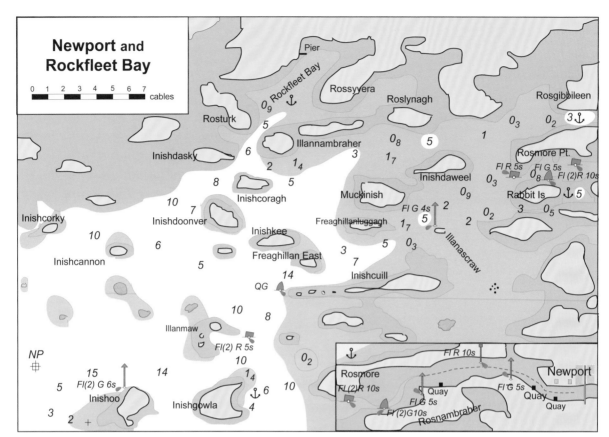

Rosmore East beacon, PHM Fl R 10s
Newport Entrance beacon, SHM Fl G 5s

From the W, approach with the N sides of Inishoo and Inishgowla in line. **From the S**, leave Cloghcormick buoy close to starboard and steer 051° to pass 3 cables NW of Inishoo. Then follow the marked channel. Note that beyond Muckinish there are patches with least depth 0·3m.

Newport itself is accessible above half tide; the channel to the quay 0·25M below the village dries 1m in places.

Anchorages

The following anchorages have sufficient water to lie afloat at LW but can only be reached above half tide.

- S of the E tip of Rabbit Island, in 3m or more. A careful mid-channel course must be kept between Rabbit Island and the island and peninsula to the S of it. Dinghy access to Newport across the spit E of Rabbit Island.
- N of Rosmore Point in the narrows S of Rosgibbileen, with over 3m in midchannel, mud on sand; more exposed in W and SW winds and further from Newport by dinghy than the S anchorage.
- E of Rosbarnagh Island. Note the rocks 2 cables W, SW and S of Illanascraw.

Facilities

Water, shops, pubs, garage at Newport.

Inshore Passage North from Westport

AC2057

There is an inshore passage among the islands from Inishgort to Inishgowla, offering a short cut from Westport for the smaller yacht above half tide, with great care and continuous use of the echosounder. The channel leads NW between Inishgort and Collan Beg, then between Collan More and Clynish, where the least depth (it just dries) is found. Pass between the rocks SE of the E point of Clynish and leave the point 0·5 cable to port. Then follow the channel S of Moneybeg Island and pass either side of Carrigeennafrankagh (dries 4·2m). This leads to the anchorage E of Inishgowla, and the channel to Newport and the other anchorages among the islands.

Moynish More

⊕ *MM* 53°52'·7N 9°43'·2W

AC2667 and Plan

Moynish More is the W'most island on the N shore of Clew Bay. There is anchorage close E of it in settled weather and offshore winds. The dangers in the approach are **Larbaun**, a drying rock 9 cables S of the island, and a 2·9m patch 3·5 cables NW of this rock. **From the S**, steer 001° from Cloghcormick buoy towards Rosturk Castle to leave Larbaun 2 cables to port. **From the W**, a bearing of 078° on the summit of Roeillaun (28m high) leads between Larbaun and the 2·9m patch. When the E side of Moynish More opens up, turn N and leave Moynish Beg a cable to port.

Anchor opposite the first pile of stones on the island, a cable offshore in 3m, sand.

Rockfleet Bay

Rockfleet Bay, 3·5M E of Moyish More, is a good anchorage sheltered in all winds, accessible from Newport between the islands but only accessible from seaward in settled weather. **From the W**, follow the above directions for Moyish More but pass 1 cable S of Roeillaun, then head between Inishcorky and Inishcannon and between Inishdasky and Inishcoragh. When Inishcoragh is abeam head 030° between the next islands 2 cables NE, then steer towards Rockfleet Castle, an old stone tower. Anchor in 2m, very soft mud, W of Rossyvera Point.

Going in by the main channel to Newport, or going up to it from Westport entrance, after passing Illanmaw, head NW to join the above entrance; or leave Freaghillanluggagh (close S of Muckinish) to starboard and Inishcoragh to port.

ACHILL SOUND

53°51'·8N 9°56'W

AC2667 and 2704, Imray C54 and Plans

Achill Island is connected to the mainland by an opening bridge, which was replaced by a new one in 2008. Pipes and power cables have been rerouted underwater and the headroom restriction has been removed. The channel to the bridge is shallow and strongly tidal, but the marks have been upgraded (see plan). However no recent quantitative data on depths is available, and caution is advised. At the time of writing, arrangements for bridge opening have not been finalised, but will be published on www.irishcruisingclub.com as soon as they are available; or for the latest information phone Mayo County Council 098 41169. The S end of the Sound also offers the only sheltered anchorage on this part of the coast, and is well marked and lit. Care is however required in dealing with the strong tides in the channel.

The entrance is E of Achillbeg Island, easily identified by its diminutive lighthouse. The bar, with 1·5m patches, breaks in SW gales. With offshore winds or in calm weather it is possible to anchor temporarily just SW of the bar to await slack water for entering.

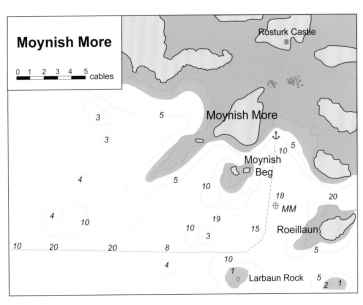

Tidal Streams – Achill Sound

The tidal stream in the S entrance runs at 3 kn at springs, increasing to 4 or 5 kn in the narrows off Darby's Point. Slack water lasts for about half an hour; the tide turns N at –0550 Galway and S at +0100 Galway. The N-going flood sets strongly across the shallows NW of Gubnacliffamore, on which it breaks; the S-going ebb sets strongly across Carrigin-a-tShrutha. The Sound fills through both N and S entrances, and the streams meet S of the bridge. At the bridge, the S-going flood starts about –0450 Galway and the N-going ebb about +0200 Galway. At the Bull's Mouth, the N entrance to the Sound, the tide turns S at –0550 Galway and N at +0100 Galway, and runs at 5 knots at springs, reaching 8 knots in places.

Lights and Marks

S of the bridge (from seaward):

Achillbeg Island, white tower Fl WR 5s 56m 18M, R 262°–281° W 281°–342°, R 342°–060° W 060°–092° R(unintens) 092°–099° W 099°–118°. Shows red over the shoals in the outer approaches to Newport, white over the deep water NE of Clare Island, red over Clare Island and white to the W, with a narrow unintensified red sector over the Bills Rocks.

Achillbeg East, red beacon Fl R 2s 5m

Carrigin-a-tShrutha, red beacon Q(2) R 5s, 2 cables S of Darby's Point

Achill S Sound ldg lts 330° Oc 4s, front 5m rear 6m

Gubnacliffamore, green beacon Fl G 3s

Darby's Point, red beacon Fl R 5s

Gubnaranny buoy, SHM Fl(2) G 6s

Lifeboat Station beacon, PHM Fl R 10s

Kildavnet beacon, PHM Fl(2) R 6s

Glassillaun buoy, SHM Fl G 5s

Achill Sound from the S; Achillbeg foreground, the narrows between Darby's Point and Gubnacliffamore beyond

Dareens beacon, PHM Fl R 3s
Ship Rock beacon, PHM QR
Shraheen's Point beacon, PHM Fl R 2s
Dorrary Point beacon Fl(2) R 6s

N of the bridge (S to N):
Achill Sound, red beacon QR
Saulia Pier, green col Fl G 3s 12m
Carrigeenfushta, green concrete beacon, Fl G 3s
Inishbiggle, red concrete beacon QR
Ridge Point beacon, Fl 5s 21m 5M

Directions – South end of Achill Sound

Enter on the leading line with the pier W of Darby's Point bearing 330°; this leads close to the rocky NE point of Achillbeg, clear between Gubnacliffamore and Achillbeg East port-hand beacon and E of Carrigin-a-tShrutha beacon. Follow the W shore round until past Darby's Point, and head for the ruined tower of Kildavnet Castle, close to the W shore 3 cables N of Darby's Point. Continuous use of the echosounder is recommended. Anchor in 2 to 3m, on the W side of the channel, off the castle; anchorage further NE is reported untenable in strong wind-over-tide conditions. There are visitors' moorings, and a pontoon alongside the quay. Constant +0030 Galway; MHWS 3·6m, MHWN 2·9m, ML 2·1m.

Transit of Achill Sound

The transit should be made above half tide, and ideally commencing on the last hour of the flood, at approximately HW Galway. The

Admiralty charts are based on surveys carried out in 1850 and 1900, and no longer accurately represent the sandbanks in the Sound. The Plans show the general trend of the channel as it is today, but no recent soundings are available and the greatest

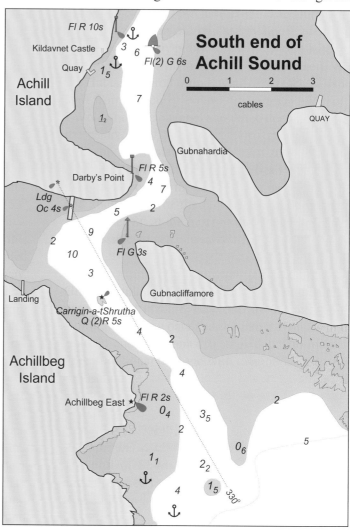

caution is advised, with continuous monitoring of the echosounder.

The channel from Kildavnet to the bridge is marked by six port-hand perches and two starboard-hand buoys; these are lit, but a stranger should not attempt the passage by night. There is a pool close SE of the bridge where temporary anchorage might be available. N of the bridge is a red port-hand beacon, which should be left to starboard when heading N, since the conventional buoyage direction changes at the bridge. At the time of writing the N part of the Sound is not so well marked; there are beacons on Saulia Pier and Carrigeenfushta Rock. Give Carrigeenfushta a berth of 0·5 to 1 cable to avoid the drying Shejoge Rocks opposite, to the E. Steer 010° for the mid-channel of the Bull's Mouth to avoid the rocks SW of Inishbiggle Point and maintain a N'ly heading until Slievemore Point (4M W) is open of Ridge Point (in lat 54°02'N) before turning NW.

Entry from the N should also be made close to slack water, steering 190° until 3 cables past the Bull's Mouth. Anchorage is available 1 to 2 cables S of Carrigeenfushta beacon keeping it in line with Dooniver Point; the deeper water in the channel to the E has a rocky bottom. The anchorage is tidebound and is exposed to a fetch of 1 to 2M, so may be uncomfortable in fresh winds between SE and S.

CLEW BAY TO BLACKSOD BAY
Offshore passage
This rugged coast is subject to the full rigours of the weather. Between Achillbeg and Clare Island there may be a confused sea on the SW-going tide, and there is a rough and confused sea close W of Achill Head in

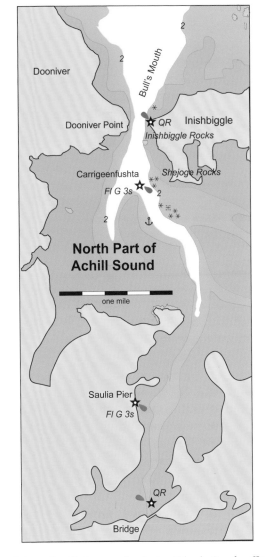

all but the lightest of winds. Black Rock, 6M NW of Achill Head, once had the dubious distinction of marooning its lighthousekeepers more often than any other station in Ireland. Blacksod Bay offers fine anchorages in one of the remotest parts of the mainland of Ireland.

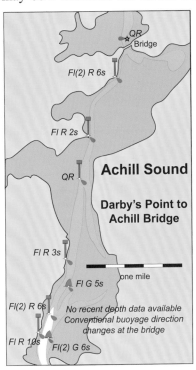

N part of Achill Sound from the SW. The bridge is the old one, now replaced. The Bull's Mouth, top L

Dangers

Drying ledges 0·5M off shore, 2M NW of Achillbeg

Dysaghy Rocks (dry 3m), 5 cables S of Keem Bay

Drying and underwater rocks extending 2 cables S from Achill Head

Rock with 2·9m, in mid-channel between Achill Head and Carrickakin

Lights and Marks

Purteen leading lights Oc 8s

Purteen pier, QR

Black Rock, white tower Fl WR 12s 86m W20M R16M, W 276°–212° R 212°–276°. Shows red to E and NE over

Keem Bay from the ESE

Duvillaun and the Inishkeas, white elsewhere

Blacksod Point buoy, E Card Q(3) 10s

Blacksod Pier ldg lts 180°, orange triangles on posts Oc 5s 3M, front 5m rear 9m

Blacksod Pier, Fl R 3s 6m 3M

Blacksod Point, white tower Fl(2) WR 7·5s 13m W12M R9M, R 189°–210° W 210°–018°. Shows red over Carrigeenmore and close E of it, white elsewhere

Carrigeenmore perch, E Card VQ(3) 5s 3M

Saleen Pier leading lights 319°, Oc 4s 5M

Saleen Pier, 2FG vert

Bills Rocks

The Bills, 5·5M S by W of Keem Bay, are steep-to and 38m high; they are only 1M E of the line from Inishbofin to Achill Head, and though conspicuous by day are unlit and dangerous at night. They lie in a narrow red sector of Achillbeg light.

Gubalennaun Beg (Purteen)

53°57'·6N 10°05'·5W

There is a small harbour at Purteen, N of Inishgalloon.

The outer part, subject to swell, has about 1·3m at LWS along the W quay. Keel village, 2 km, has shops, pubs and filling station.

Keem Bay

53°57'·8N 10°10'·8W

Keem Bay, 2·5M E of Achill Head, is an impressive amphitheatre surrounded by steep slopes rising to 300m cliffs on the seaward side. It offers a convenient passage anchorage in offshore winds but is subject to swell and heavy gusts off the slopes. The beach shelves suddenly; anchor in not less than 5m, sand.

Achill Head

AC2704

In heavy weather give the Head a berth of at least 2M, but in moderate conditions it is sufficient to pass 2 cables W of Carrickakin, and the magnificent spectacle of the Achill cliffs may compensate for any discomfort on the passage. In calm weather, it is possible to make the passage of the channel between Carrickakin and Achill Head, giving the S side of

Achill Head from the N; Carrickakin R, the Bills top centre and Clare Island top L

the Head a berth of 2 cables to clear the drying rocks there, and then staying E or W of mid-channel to avoid the 2·9m rock in the middle. This rock breaks heavily in bad weather. The Priest Rocks, above-water stacks close W of the Head, are steep-to on their W side.

Black Rock

Black Rock (82m high) is 6M NNW of Achill Head and has a light showing red over the Mullet Peninsula and the Inishkeas and white elsewhere. There are rocks above and below water up to 1·25M W and SW of Black Rock, other rocks close S of it and a clean 12m-high rock 0·5 cable E of it. At night or in heavy weather, it is safest to pass E of Black Rock.

Achill Sound, North Entrance

⊕ *AN* 54°00'·6N 9°55'·3W
AC2704, Imray C54 and Plan
For directions, see *Transit of Achill Sound,* above. Note that there are low overhead power cables across the tidal sounds separating Inishbiggle and Annagh and the shore to the E, and across the mouth of Bellacragher Bay to the SE.

BLACKSOD BAY

⊕ *BS* 54°05'·2N 10°01'·3W
AC2704 and Plan
Tidal Streams – Blacksod Bay
The tide sets fairly N and S at the entrance, turning at HW by the shore. The rate is 1 kn at springs.

Blacksod Bay is accessible by day or night in any weather. A 14m shoal 1M S of Duvillaun Beg breaks heavily in gales but is easily avoided. From the S and Achill Head, steer to pass 5 cables W of Saddle Head, and leave Blacksod E Card buoy to port. **From the N,** give Turduvillaun and Duvillaun More a berth of 3 cables to port. In settled conditions with little swell, Duvillaun Sound, between Duvillaun Beg and Gaghta Island, offers a passage in 7m with the beacons on Inishkea South in line 317°; the rear beacon is on the skyline but the front beacon near the shore is not easily seen.

Anchorages
• In the bay NW of Blacksod Pier, close NW of Blacksod Point, about halfway between the pier and Doonbeg Point, outside the moorings in 3m, sand. The pier consists of an L-shaped extension of about 50m from the original stone quay, and has a narrow dredged area alongside with enough water to lie afloat. Shop, filling station and PO, 2 km.
• Elly Bay, 3.5M N of Blacksod Point, is the most sheltered anchorage. Give the shore NW of Ardelly Point a berth of 2 cables, head W towards the moored boats and

Map

Erris Head

Eagle Island
Fl(3) 10s

Portnanalbanagh
Portnafrankagh

Annagh Head
+
Edye Rock   p245

Belmullet

Inishglora

Carrickmoneagh

Usborne Shoal
+

Saleen Bay

p244

Elly Bay

p243

Inishkea North

Blacksod Bay

Inishkea South

Blacksod Point
Fl (2)WR 7·5s

⊕ BS

Black Rock
Fl WR 12s

Duvillaun More

Ridge Point
Fl 5s

Slievemore Point

⊕ AN

Croaghaun
·664m

Achill Island

Achill Head

Keem Bay

Purteen

*Dysaghy Rocks

Achillbeg to Erris Head

0 1 2 3 4 5
miles

Bills

Achillbeg
Fl WR 5s

NW coast of Achill Island: the 664m cliffs of Croaghaun are the highest in Ireland, and the British Isles

anchor outside them. Water and showers at the Adventure Centre 097 81488. Pub. Garage and shop at Drum House, 2 km.

- Elly Harbour, W of Barranagh Island, is usually more liable to swell than Elly Bay but is calmer in N to E winds. Anchor off the middle of the bay.

- Saleen Bay, N of Barranagh Island, offers anchorage sheltered from SW to E, in 3m, sand, in the middle of the bay.

Constant +0030 Galway; MHWS 3·9m, MHWN 2·9m, ML 2·2m.

Passage W of the Mullet Peninsula
AC2704, 2703

There is a clear channel inside the islands, partly sheltered from the swell, easily navigable in daylight.

Dangers
Pluddany Rocks (dry 1·8m), 5 cables E of Inishkea North
Usborne Shoal, 2·1m, 2M N of Inishkea North
Carrickmoneagh (1m high), 2M SW of Inishglora
Edye Rock, 2·6m, 1M WSW of Annagh Head

Light
Eagle Island, white tower Fl(3) 15s 67m 19M

Directions
Pluddany Rocks extend 6 cables E from Inishkea North; there is no passage between their drying heads and the island. To clear the rocks to the E, keep Turduvillaun below the Ears of Achill 198°. The Ears are two prominent summits 7 cables E of Achill Head *(see photograph)*. Heading N, it is useful to keep this transit astern until the small islands to the N are identified. Duffur Rock (17m high), with its vertical cliffs, is more prominent from

Blacksod Bay from the SW; Elly Bay, foreground, with Elly Harbour and Barranagh Island beyond. Claggan Point visible over the spit joining Barranagh to the shore

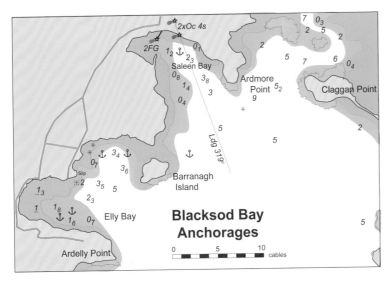

Blacksod Bay
Anchorages

North and South Inishkea

⊕*IK* 54°07'·3N 10°11'·1W

AC2704

These islands have a fascinating history and are well worth a visit. A Norwegian whaling station was set up on Rusheen in 1908, and the rusted remains of equipment may still be seen on the island. The people of North and South Inishkea took opposing sides in the troubles following independence in 1921, and some of the consequential incidents now seem comical, but a drowning tragedy in 1927 claimed the lives of ten islanders, and the islands were finally evacuated in 1939.

a distance than the Carricknaronty Rocks (2m and 3m high) SE of it. Inishkeeragh slopes gently to the sea. Inishglora has ruined cottages on its E end. Heading N, before Inishkeeragh comes abeam, bring Leacarrick just open of Inishglora and then steer to pass close E of Leacarrick as the Mullet side is foul 5 cables offshore. In bad W weather the sea breaks right over Leacarrick and the passage E of it may be covered with foam.

If passing between the Inishkeas and Inishglora, note the **Usborne Shoal** and also **Carrickmoneagh** (1m high), SW of the Inishglora group.

Anchorages *(see Plan)*

- The bay N of Rusheen Island is the best anchorage. It is sheltered from S through W to N but is subject to swell, which can roll in through the narrow sound between the Inishkeas.
- Anchorage is also available in the bay SW of Rusheen Island.
- In NE winds better shelter may be found off North Inishkea SW of the 22m sandhill, between the outer ends of two reefs which extend 1·5 cables SW from the shore. The little bay thus formed has more reefs at its head.

Saleen Bay from the W; Ardmore Point centre L with Claggan point beyond.

Passage inside the Inishkeas, from the N; Pluddany Rocks and North Inishkea, R, with Turduvillaun below the Ears of Achill in the distance

South and North Inishkeas, from the E

Inishglora

54°12'·1N 10°06'·9W

Inishglora has a hallowed place in Irish legend as the resting place of the Children of Lir. There are ancient monastic remains on the island. Anchorage, in settled weather, is available off the SE end of the island.

Inishglora to Erris Head

AC2703

From Leacarrick steer for Annagh Head, on which there is a hut; keep clear of Edye Rock with 2·6m on it. In fine weather pass inside Cross Rock, but there is always a bad sea in this channel, and if at all rough it is better to go outside Eagle Island. Do not pass close to Carrickhesk, and give Erris Head a berth of 5 cables.

Portnafrankagh (Frenchport)

⊕*PF* 54°15'·0N 10°06'·4W

AC2703, Imray C54 and Plan

This inlet, immediately N of Annagh Head, is a favourite port of call for yachts sailing round Ireland as it involves no detour from the direct route. It provides safe shelter, but is subject to swell and should not be attempted in heavy onshore weather, when there are breakers at the entrance. There is a rock drying 3·7m, 1 cable off the inlet on the S side of the entrance; Parson's Rock, awash at LAT, is 0·5 cable off the N point of the entrance. Enter in mid-channel and anchor off the S shore beyond the narrows in 4m, sand. The head of the inlet dries.

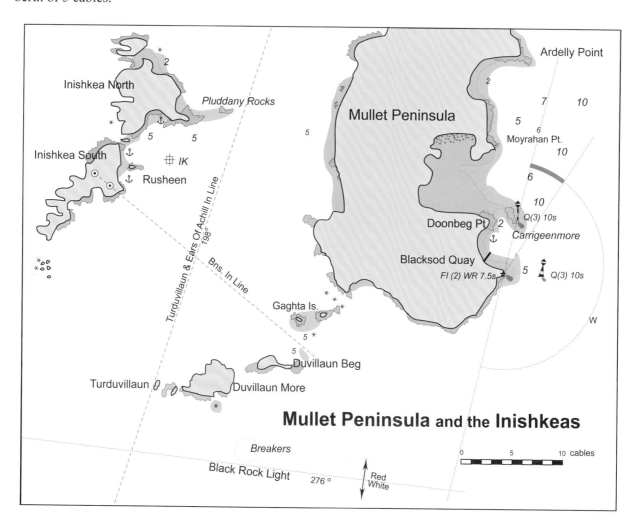

*Inishkeeragh (lower L) from the S, with Inishglora and Leacarrick beyond. On the mainland side, Corraun Point, R,
Annagh Head (upper L centre) and Eagle Island beyond*

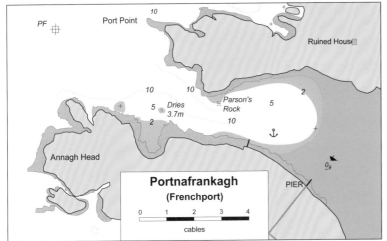

Portnanalbanagh (Scotch Port)

54°15'·5N 10°05'·3W

Scotch Port, just S of its eponymous rock on the chart, is a clean narrow inlet with rocky sides and a steep beach at its head. It provides an interesting temporary anchorage in settled offshore weather.

Portnafrankagh from the SW; Annagh Head, foreground

NW coast of the Mullet Peninsula, from the W; Eagle Island L, Annagh Head and Portnafrankagh R

Chapter 8

Erris Head to Bloody Foreland

The Rosses, west Donegal; Falchorrib Point at the narrows of Trawenagh Bay, lower R, with Aran Sound and its islands in the distance. Aranmore Island, upper L, Burtonport upper R with Owey Island beyond

The north coast of Mayo has some of the most spectacular cliffs in Ireland, backed by a Gaeltacht area with sweeping moorlands and remote communities. Between Broad Haven and Killala, 24 miles to the east, there are no good harbours, but this coast has some of the oldest known human settlements in Ireland – at the Ceide Fields, near Belderg, a complete Neolithic village has been discovered beneath the peat.

The eastern side of the bight has three large sandy inlets leading to Ballysadare, Sligo and Donegal Town, and a stretch of rocky coast with the fascinating offshore island of Inishmurray and the harbour of Mullaghmore. This is Yeats Country, the homeland of Ireland's greatest poet, who is buried in Drumcliff churchyard "under bare Ben Bulben's head". The great fishing port of Killybegs has one of the best natural harbours in the country. Aranmore Island lies two miles across a shallow

and rock-strewn sound from the mainland shore of the Rosses – a dramatic coast of pink granite, with the little fishing harbour of Burtonport tucked away among the boulders. Ireland's north west corner is like nowhere else on the island. Windswept and remote, breaking the pattern of cliffs and sandy bays with moonscapes of boulders and dunes, there is perhaps no stretch of coast with such variety in a short distance.

Charts

AC2725 Blacksod Bay to Tory Island is the largest scale chart which shows the passage from Erris Head to west Donegal, and should be carried if passage-making around the coast. The medium-scale charts AC2703, 2767, 2702 and 1879 and the larger scale 1883 cover the whole coast described in this chapter, and are also essential, except that 2702 need not be carried if simply crossing from Mayo to

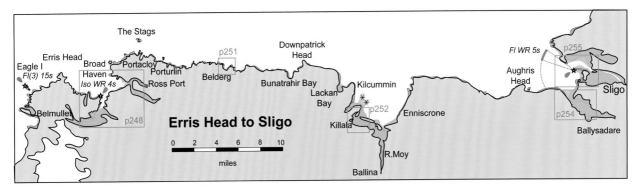

west Donegal. The large-scale AC2792 is marginally useful for detail of Teelin, Killybegs and Church Pool, but is essential if spending time exploring the Sound of Aran and Burtonport. AC2715 is essential for Killala and Donegal Harbours. AC2852 is essential for the port of Sligo, but 2767 covers as far E as the yacht club's anchorage at Rosses Point. The Imray chart C53 Donegal Bay to Rathlin Island may be worth carrying but is no substitute for the Admiralty charts.

Tidal Streams

On this part of the coast HW occurs between +0035 and +0110 Galway. Spring tides rise between 3·7 and 4·1m and neaps between 2·7 and 3·0m above LAT. Offshore between Erris Head and Rathlin O'Birne the tidal set is negligible. From Rathlin O'Birne to Bloody Foreland the tide outside the islands turns S

at +0300 Galway and N at –0300 Galway with a rate of 0·8 to 1 kn. Inshore it turns 1 to 2 hours earlier, and so is in effect running S during the ebb by the shore and N during the flood. Near the salient points the rate reaches 1·5 to 2 kn at springs.

BROAD HAVEN

⊕ *BH* 54°16'·6N 9°52'·7W
AC2703, Imray C54 and Plan
Broad Haven is a safe harbour in most summer winds, but a bad NW or N gale can cause the entrance to break right across. The approach across Broad Haven Bay is clear of all dangers except for **Slugga Rock** (1m high), on the E side, with a rock (drying 0·3m) 1 cable NW of it, and **Monastery Rock** on the S side, also drying 0·3m. The first 1·5M of the inlet is clean, but further S the channel leading to Belmullet lies between extensive shallows and is

Broad Haven from the NW; Gubacashel (foreground), Gubaknockan and Ballyglass Pier (centre R), Inver Point (centre L) with Inver hamlet bay beyond. The long inlet (upper L), leading to Barnatra, dries.

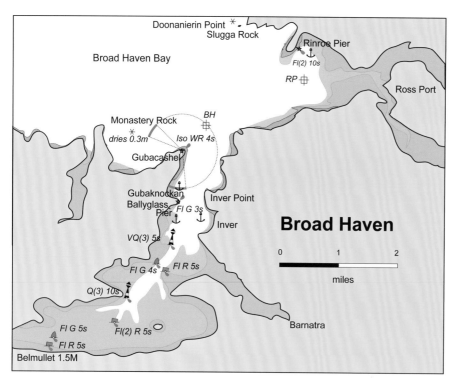

marked by buoys. The tide runs at up to 1·5 kn past the anchorages. Constant +0045 Galway; MHWS 3·7m, MHWN 3·8m, ML 2·1m.

Lights and Marks

Broad Haven

Gubacashel Point, 15m white tower Iso WR 4s 27m W12M R9M, R 110°–133°, W 133°–355°, R 355°–021°. Shows red inshore to the NW, and to the S over Gubaknockan Point and close E of it, and white elsewhere

Ballyglass beacon, green pillar Fl G 3s.

Channel to Belmullet

Barret Point Cardinal buoy, E Card VQ(3) 5s

Barret Point Lateral buoy, SHM Fl G 4s

Fox Point buoy, PHM Fl R 5s

Shanaghy Point buoy, E Card Q(3) 10s

Inishderry buoy, PHM Fl(2) R 5s

Moyrahan East buoy, SHM Fl G 5s

Atticonaun buoy, PHM Fl R 5s

The channel to Belmullet is then marked by a further 3 port- and 7 starboard-hand buoys.

Broad Haven Bay

Rinroe Pier, Fl(2) 10s

Ross Port leading lights, Iso 4s

Anchorages in Broad Haven

• In 3·5m about 2 cables N of Gubaknockan Point with Gubacashel Point in line with the W side of Kid Island. This is the most convenient anchorage, out of the main stream, with good shelter in winds from SW to NW, and accessible

at night.

• Ballyglass Pier is a cable SW of Gubaknockan Point; note that between the Ballyglass starboard-hand beacon and the shore there is an overhead cable with only 2m headroom. Anchor not far beyond the pier in 3m with its outer end bearing 035°. This anchorage is somewhat more exposed to the SW, but sheltered from the N. There are visitors' moorings. The pier has 2m alongside and is well fendered. Water on the pier and diesel by tanker. RNLI all-weather lifeboat. PO.

• In strong E wind the best shelter is in 3·7m, close to shore about 1 cable S of Inver Point, opposite Ballyglass. For convenient landing, anchor further S in 3m about 2 cables offshore in Inver Hamlet Bay. Small shop at Inver; filling station, PO and shop at Barnatra, 5 km S by road and at least partly accessible by dinghy at HW.

All the above anchorages are somewhat subject to swell.

Belmullet

The channel to Belmullet, in the SW corner of Broad Haven, is buoyed and lit, but dries at LW and is not recommended for visiting yachts. There is no convenient berth in Belmullet. The buoyage is provided principally for the safety of small fishing craft, which take shelter in Belmullet when moorings at Ballyglass become untenable in winter gales from the S. Belmullet has supermarkets, shops, PO, pubs, restaurants, doctors, and is best reached by taxi from Ballyglass.

Broad Haven Bay

In moderate weather or with wind N of W there is a convenient anchorage on the NE side of the bay, E of Rinroe Point. Give the point a berth of 1·5 cables and anchor E of it in 3 to 4m, off the pier. This is a handy place to wait for the tide on the bar to Ross Port. Shop, PO at Carrowteige, 1·5 km.

Corrib gas field

At the time of writing (2008) works are in progress to install a pipeline from the offshore Corrib field to a processing plant in NW Mayo. The pipeline will be buried in an excavated trench in the seabed and will come ashore in 54°17'N, close S of the entrance

Ross Port from the W; Sandy Point L, Rossport House top R

to Ross Port. While these works are continuing, pay close attention to radio navigational warnings and give a good berth to all vessels involved in the construction project. These activities may at times restrict access to Ross Port inlet.

Ross Port

⊕*RP* 54°17'·4N 9°50'·4W
AC2703 and Plan
This narrow creek inside the sandbanks offers a feasible anchorage, but it has strong tides. The outer entrance across a bar with 0·3m at LAT is exposed to the swell, and is navigable only in settled conditions

and in daylight. Note that the area on the W side of the narrows, marked on the chart as "Sand Dunes", has suffered erosion and now consists of a high drying sandbank and several grass-topped heads above HW *(see photograph).*

Directions

Recent survey information on the channel at Ross Port is lacking, so judicious use of the echo sounder is required in entering and in choosing an anchorage. The entrance channel is narrow. There are two white leading marks on the W-facing coast of the peninsula N of the houses at Ross Port, but their enduring reliability and their lights should not be taken for granted. Once over the bar turn slightly to port and head towards Sandy Point, 078°. When off the N shore keep about 25m from it. When Sandy Point is abeam turn to starboard and head 147° towards the middle of the narrows between the E shore of the inlet and the grassy sand islets off the W shore. Beyond the narrows and past the slip keep close to the E shore.

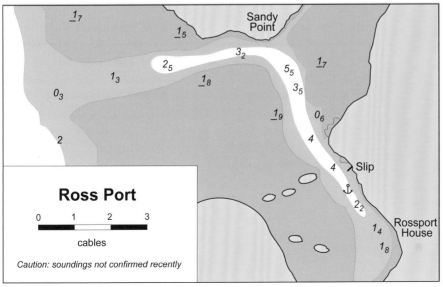

Ross Port

0   1   2   3

cables

Caution: soundings not confirmed recently

The Stags of Broadhaven from the S

Anchorage

Anchor 1 to 1·5 cables to the S of the slip. There is depth further S but the channel becomes narrow, with sandbanks extending from the W shore, and it may be necessary to moor to two anchors. Do not go further S than the old Rossport House.

Facilities

Shop, pub and PO at Ross Port on the E side; pub at Pollatomish further in on the W side and accessible by dinghy. Dooncarton stone circle and megalithic tomb, 1·5 km along the road towards Barnatra on the W side of the inlet, are worth a visit.

Caution

GPS chart plotters should not be implicitly relied upon in the shallow areas of Broad Haven and in Ross Port due to the age of the survey data and the likelihood of changes in the channel and sandbanks. It is essential to maintain good traditional pilotage with continuous use of the echo sounder.

The Stags of Broad Haven

The Stags of Broad Haven are a spectacular group of four rocky islets 70 to 92m in height, with deep water all round. There is a clear passage 1M wide between the Stags and the mainland coast.

BROAD HAVEN BAY TO KILLALA BAY

The 24M stretch from Broad Haven Bay to Killala Bay is high, rugged and spectacular, with cliffs up to 300m and offlying stacks, and in most conditions should be given a good berth; there is no good anchorage, no shelter from the usual swell, and often fierce gusts off the cliffs. The coast is sparsely inhabited. There are five coves or bays, each with a small slip on its W side, where a landing might be effected in settled weather or in moderate S winds. Portacloy and Belderg are the best of these, and offer possible passage anchorages, though somewhat subject to swell. SE of Conaghra Point, the Ceide

Fields visitor centre, a conspicuous pyramidal building on the hillside, is a useful landmark.

Lights – Porturlin

Carrickduff beacon, PHM Fl R 5s 3M
Glassillaun beacon, SHM Fl(2) G 5s 3M
Harbour Rock beacon, SHM Fl G 10s

Portacloy

54°20'·7N 9°46'·3W
AC2703

This bay is close E of the Buddagh, 78m high, a straight-sided tower-like column of rock which presents a steeply sloping grass top to the N; and may also be identified from close inshore by a small lookout hut on the head at its W side. The inlet is about 1·5 cables wide and has clean rock shores and a beach at its head; sand bottom, good holding. It is sheltered from winds from E through S to W although fresh to strong S winds funnel down the inlet. A few lobster boats work out of here. The pier has 0·4m near its outer end.

Porturlin

54°19'·7N 9°42'·2W
AC2703 and 2767

Porturlin is 2·5M E of Portacloy. Pig Island, 5 cables W of the entrance, has a cave right through and appears as part of the mainland though only about half as high. Glassillaun is capped with grass and from NE appears as part of the shore of the W entrance until very close; it has a starboard-hand perch. Carrickduff, off the NE of the entrance, is a bare rock with a port-hand perch. The skyline behind the port is low and the white houses show up well from seaward off the entrance. There are a number of moorings in the inlet, S of the Harbour Rock starboard-hand perch. The holding is reported poor.

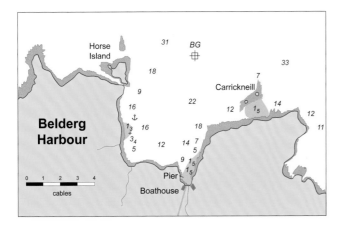

Belderg Harbour

⊕*BG*   54°19'·5N 9°33'·2W

AC2767 and Plan

Belderg is at the E end of the high cliffs stretching E from Broad Haven Bay. E of Belderg the coast is lower though still impressive, with 30m cliffs backed by gentle grass slopes, and the overhanging cliff of Downpatrick Head (35m) is conspicuous. Illanmaster, 103m high with a domed grassy top, is a good mark 3M W of Belderg. Horse Island, on the the W side of the entrance, is comparatively low. Carrickneill, E of the entrance, covers at HW except for two small heads. The disused boathouse shows up well from due N but is obscured from NE and NW. A newer and similar building stands E of it, at the SE corner of the rocky gut; this gut is too narrow for anchoring, but has a breakwater and a slip for dinghy landing. Anchor in less than 10m off the inner half of the W shore of the bay, good holding on sand. PO, pub and shop at Belderg village, 1·5 km.

Bunatrahir Bay

54°18'·7N 9°22'·7W

Bunatrahir Bay has less formidable surroundings but the bottom is rock and provides poor holding. Hotel on W side of the bay; shops, pubs and PO at Ballycastle, 2 km.

Lackan Bay

54°17'·6N 9°14'W

Lackan Bay is exposed and subject to swell. Rathlackan Pier, on its W side, is not normally suitable for alongside berthing. No facilities ashore. In most winds, Kilcummin offers better shelter.

KILLALA BAY

54°15'·5N 9°08'·4W

AC2715 and Plan

The small fishing port of Killala lies behind a bar with 0·3m, in the SW corner of Killala Bay, 5M wide between Kilcummin Head and Lenadoon Point and exposed to the N. The River Moy empties into the SE corner of the bay.

Dangers

Unnamed rocks with 1·6 and 1·8m, 1 cable offshore E and SE of Kilcummin Head.

St Patrick's Rocks, a drying reef extending 1M N and 9 cables E of Ross Point, has two principal heads in **Bone Rock** (dries 3m) and **Carrickpatrick** (dries 1·5m). The E side of the bay is foul up to 5 cables offshore for 2M S of Lenadoon Point.

Killala from SW; Bartragh Island centre and River Moy entrance top R. The training walls are visible, L centre. The Round Tower, lower R

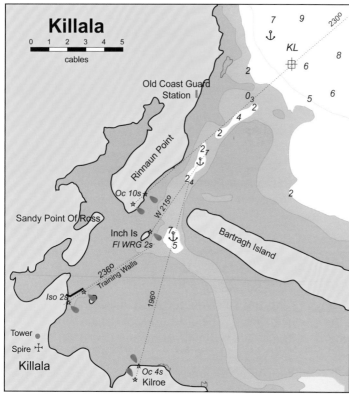

Lights and marks

Bone Rock perch, N Card Q
Carrickpatrick buoy, E Card Q(3) 10s
Killala buoy, SHM Fl G 6s
Rinnaun Point ldg lts 230°, Oc 10s 5M, front 7m, rear 12m
Inch Island, grey tower Dir WRG 2s 6m 3M, G 205°–213° W 213°–217° R 217°–225°. Shows white over the approach channel, green to W, red to E
Inch Island lower leading beacon, unlit
Kilroe ldg lts 196°, white towers Oc 4s 2M, front 5m, rear 10m
Killala Pier ldg lts 236°, white diamonds Iso 2s 2M, front 5m, rear 7m.

Kilcummin and Creevagh Heads in line 308° lead NE of St Patrick's Rocks. Killala Round Tower bearing 221° just open SE of Ross sandhills leads SE of them.

Kilcummin Roads
54°16'·3N 9°12'·2W

This passage anchorage on the W side of Killala Bay 1M S of Kilcummin Head gives a surprising amount of shelter in winds from SW through W to N. Approaching from the NE, the location of the pier may be identified by a conspicuous square concrete section of sea wall against the clay cliff immediately SW of it. Anchor S of the pier, which has 0·6m at LAT alongside. Pub above the pier.

Killala
⊕*KL*　54°14'·2N 9°10'·7W
AC2715 and Plan

The bar should not be attempted with a fresh NE wind, and is best negotiated on a high and rising tide. **From the N or NE**, head for Carrickpatrick buoy, then steer 210° past Killala buoy and identify the white-painted leading beacons on Rinnaun Point. Steer across the bar on the leading line of these beacons 230° until the Inch Island beacons come in line bearing 215°. Hold this course for 2 cables, then turn on to the line of the Kilroe beacons on the S shore, 196°. This line leads close W of the steep beach on Bartragh Island; when immediately S of the W tip of the island, identify the leading beacons on the pier and steer on their line, 236°. The channel to the pier is bordered by old training walls which cover at HW but are clearly marked by poles.

From the W, give Bone Rock beacon a berth of 5 cables. It is normally possible to pass up to 3 cables W of Carrickpatrick buoy, but Carrickpatrick Rock is dangerous if it is not showing up by breaking.

Anchorage
Anchor in 5 to 7m, sand, in Bartragh Pool, 1 cable SW of the W tip of Bartragh Island. Tidal streams here are strong and the sandbanks steep-to, so adequate swinging room must be assured. Anchorage further down the channel inside the bar is possible, but be sure to show an anchor light. The bay to the N of the bar offers a feasible passage anchorage but is very

Killala; Inch Island and its leading beacons, from the S; one of the poles marking the training wall, R. Rinnaun Point, beyond

subject to swell.

Harbour

A depth of 1·5m at LWS is available only at the N end of the pier; if there are fishing boats alongside, raft up to the outermost trot with permission, but in any case be prepared to move at short notice. There is a wide slipway on the NW side of the pier. The S and E parts of the harbour are shallow.

Facilities

Water on the pier. Diesel by tanker. Shops, pubs, PO, restaurants and laundry in Killala village, 1 km. Constant +0045 Galway; MHWS 3·8m, MHWN 2·7m, ML 2·1m.

River Moy

The River Moy has a shallow and hazardous bar at its mouth, but good locally-maintained marks in the channel as far as Ballina Quay (5M from the entrance), and is used routinely by local small craft. However rapid and continuing movement of the sandbanks around the bar has been reported (2005), which makes up-to-date local knowledge essential. Unfortunately no reliable directions can be provided for a stranger. For pilotage assistance phone 096 22183.

Enniscrone (Inishcrone on the charts)
54°13'·2N 9°06'·2W

The village is a seaside resort and is conspicuous in the SE corner of Killala Bay. The breakwater runs out 280° and its S side is a quay 130m long, but a yacht can only go alongside at or above half tide when the depth near the outer end just beyond the steps is 2m. Two concrete pillars in line mark the S end of the channel to the slip. The quay is subject to swell.

East side of Killala Bay

This coast is bordered by extensive flat drying reefs. For 3M N of Enniscrone it should be given a berth of 3 cables and between Pollacheeny and Lenadoon Point a berth of 8 cables. **Pollacheeny Harbour,** named on AC2715, is just a gap between the drying rocks and offers little shelter. For entry (in winds between NE and SE, and no swell) identify the slip from 3 cables out and approach between 085° and 090° to avoid rocks on either side.

Coast between Killala Bay and Sligo Bay

From Lenadoon Point to Aughris Head, 11M further E, the coast is fringed by rocky ledges and should be given a berth of at least 5 cables. Pollnadivva Harbour in Dromore Bay is not recommended even in calm weather; it dries with a rocky bottom alongside. The pier shows a light Fl G 5s 3M. There are no facilities ashore. Aughris Head ends in an overhanging cliff; rocks awash at HW extend 1·5 cables seaward from it. **Cooanmore Bay**, inside **Temple Rock** 1M E of the conspicuous tower at the mouth of the Easky River, offers temporary anchorage from winds from SW through S to SE. Shops and pubs at Easky village, 1·5 km.

SLIGO BAY
AC2767, 2852

The entrance is 4M wide between Aughris Head to the SW and **Seal Rocks** (1m high) to the NE. Midway between these points is **The Ledge** (8m) which breaks with a high swell, when it is simplest to pass S of it. Within the points of the bay are off-shore anchorages in Aughris Hole and Brown Bay. The principal sailing centre is Rosses Point in the entrance to Sligo.

Aughris Hole
54°16'·9N 8°44'·5W

Aughris Hole, on the E side of Aughris Head, provides shelter in winds from SE to SW. At LW a ridge of rock protects the anchorage from the E. Below-water rocks extend halfway from this ridge towards the W shore. Having given Aughris Head a suitable berth the shore is clean to the quay, off which there is anchorage in 2·7m, sand and stones. In W wind, a swell rolls in, particularly with the flood tide. The quay gives no protection from this and a yacht should not attempt to go alongside.

Facilities

Pub 400m, shop 1·5 km.

Ballysadare Bay
⊕ *BB* 54°16'·3N 8°38'·7W
AC2767 and Plan

This large enclosed bay is mostly occupied by drying sandbanks. No recent information is available on depths in the channel, although there are moorings in current use off The Hut. The directions printed in previous editions of this volume are reproduced below but should not be taken as definitive. The buildings referred to as landmarks may not be as conspicuous as they once were, although The Hut is in good repair as a dwelling-house and the slipway there is in usable condition. Note that AC2767 is based on a survey carried out in 1852.

Entrance

The entrance 3M S of Raghly Point and 4M E of Aughris Head can be approached in any moderate

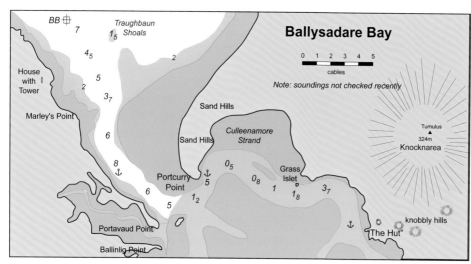

Ballysadare Bay

Note: soundings not checked recently

it Benbulben Mountain with a 45° slope beneath its vertical brow. When the Golf Club building comes under the centre of this slope, turn on to this transit line (038°) which leads between Portcurry Point and the sandbank E of it.

Anchorage

The best anchorage is E of Portcurry Point, close to the shore. There is about 3m at LAT opposite the high sandhill behind the NE corner of the point. The beach is very steep-to. There is good shelter in W and NW winds. It is easy to go ashore and there are some facilities (including the airport) at Strandhill, 3 km – walk across Culleenamore Strand to the road running N to Strandhill. There is also a possible anchorage near the moorings SE of Marley's Point, although the tidal stream here is strong. There is nowhere suitable to anchor in the branch of the channel extending S from Portcurry Point. The Hut, SW of Knocknarea, is an old two-storey house on a point just above the only public slip in the bay; a lane runs up from it to the main road. The anchorage NW of the Hut is sheltered from E winds. To reach this spot, start from Portcurry Point 2 hours after LWS, or at LWN, when the channel should be deep enough but the banks still visible. Steer 114° towards The Hut until the grass islet is abeam, then steer 090° until the point E of it is abeam; then head NE to avoid the rocky N end of the bank. When past it, steer SE, and anchor NW of the Hut. Ballysadare village is 5M further SE at the head of the drying bay, and is inaccessible by sea.

Caution

GPS chartplotters should not be implicitly relied upon in Ballysadare Bay due to the age of the Admiralty survey data and the likely changes in the channel and sandbanks. It is essential to maintain good traditional pilotage with continuous use of the echosounder.

SLIGO

⊕ *SO* 54°18'·7N 8°38'·8W
AC2852, Imray C54 and Plan

The port of Sligo is used by small cargo vessels and is reached by a channel S of Raghly Point and Rosses Point and N of Oyster Island. Sligo YC is

weather but should not be attempted by a stranger in a swell from the NW. The passage over the bar in 3·7m is narrow, so reliable power and good visibility are necessary. Entry near LW is simplest, as the banks and rocks then show, but the directions below lead over a 1·2m patch S of Portcurry Point.

Tidal Streams

The stream in the entrance turns at HW and LW by the shore. The flood has a spring rate of 1 kn on the bar, 3 kn N and NE of Portavaud Point and 1 kn in the inner channels; but the corresponding rates on the ebb are 2·5 kn, 5 kn, and 1·5 to 2 kn inside. Constant +0105 Galway; MHWS 3·9m, MHWN 3·0m, ML 2·2m.

Directions

From the N and Sligo, avoid **Traughbaun Shoals** by staying N and W of a line of bearing 210° on the house with a small tower on its N end, situated on the W side between Derkmore and Marley's Points. When about 2 cables from the shore steer 153° for the E extremity of Portavaud Point, which is inconspicuous, low and flat with bent-grass; on this bearing it is below Carricknasheeogue, an isolated rock like a tooth on the skyline of the hills 5M away, which is conspicuous unless hidden by cloud. This course of 153° clears stony spits extending more than a cable from Marley's Point. When just past Marley's Point, and before it bears W, alter course to 180° until within a cable of the HW mark of the W shore, and then continue in at that distance off. When Portcurry Point comes in line with the N slope of Knocknarea bearing 062°, steer 096° towards the knobbly hills S of Knocknarea. When Black Rock lighthouse (at the entrance to Sligo) closes behind the W side of the sandhills N of Portcurry Point steer 073° towards the middle of Knocknarea. Here it may still be 1·2m deep at LAT. The Golf Club building N of Culleenamore Strand is visible, and beyond located at Rosses Point.

Tidal Streams

In the narrows between Rosses Point and Oyster Island the tide runs at 5 to 6 kn springs.

Dangers

The Ledge, 8·5m, 2m NE of Aughris Head (breaks in gales)

Wheat Rock, dries, 4 cables SW of Raghly Point

Raghly Ledge, dries 0·3m, 3 cables SE of Raghly Point

Drumcliff Spit, 4m, extending SW to a point 6 cables SE of Raghly Point

Black Rock, dries, 1·2M SE of Raghly Point, with

The Cluckhorn, drying boulder ridge running E to Coney Island

Bungar Bank, 1·5m, 5 cables NNE of Black Rock

Blennick Rocks, drying, 2 cables E of Oyster Island

Lights

Wheat Rock buoy, S Card Q(6)+L Fl 15s

Lower Rosses, white hut on piles, Fl(2) WRG 10s, G over Bungar Bank to 066°, W 066°–070°, R 070° – Drumcliff bar. Shows white over the approach from the WSW, green to the S, red to the N

Black Rock white tower, black band, Fl WR 5s, W 130°–107° R 107°–130°. Shows red over Wheat Rock, white elsewhere

Bungar Bank buoy, N Card Q, marks the N side of the bank.

Leading lights 125°, Fl(3) 6s, front on **Metal Man**

Rocks, rear on **Oyster Island**, lead from Bungar Bank buoy and between Deadman's Point and Coney Island. Metal Man Rocks are marked by a pillar surmounted by a statue of a sailor in 19th-century uniform, with an outstretched arm pointing up the channel to the port of Sligo, and are to be left to starboard.

No 2 (YC West) perch, PHM Fl R 1·5s 2M

No 4 (YC East) perch, PHM Fl R 3s 2M

Lifeboat beacon, PHM QR 2M

No 1 (Oyster NE) beacon, SHM Fl(3) G 4s

No 6 (January) beacon, PHM Fl(2) R 6s

No 8 (Blennick Rock West) beacon, PHM Fl R 2s

No 10 (Blennick Rock East) beacon, PHM Fl(4) R 10s

No 3 (The Pool) buoy, SHM QG

No 5 (Old Seal Bank) beacon, SHM Fl G 1·5s

No 7 (Start Wall) beacon, SHM Fl G 3s, marks the outer end of the training wall. From there to Sligo town the channel is marked by a further 9 starboard- and 6 port-hand beacons and two port-hand buoys.

Coney Island Pier, Fl 5s 2m 2M

Directions – Rosses Point

From the N, keep 2 cables W of Seal Rocks and leave Wheat Rock buoy to port. **From the W** in fine conditions it is simplest to head towards Black Rock lighthouse until Wheat Rock buoy is visible and then head for it. If there is appreciable swell, avoid **The Ledge** by keeping 1M off Aughris Head and continuing E for 2M before heading for Wheat Rock buoy; to pass N of The Ledge the N end of Coney Island should be just N of Black Rock

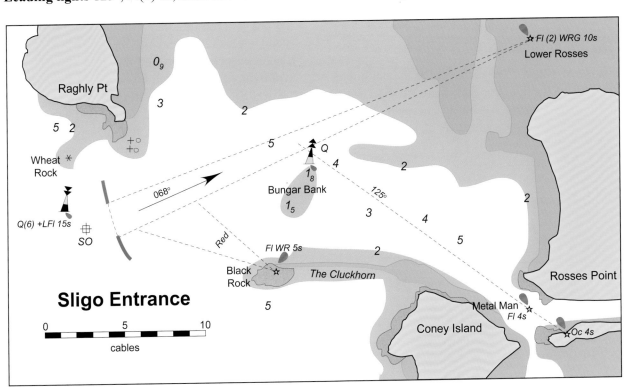

Coney Island (foreground) and Rosses Point with the Metal Man R centre, the channel to Sligo upper R

lighthouse bearing 098°. From 2 cables S of Wheat Rock buoy, head for Lower Rosses beacon or (if it is not identified) steer 068°. Leave Bungar Bank buoy to starboard and bring the Metal Man and Oyster Island beacons in line. Follow this line, and when 0·5 cable from the Metal Man, turn to pass close NE of him and leave the two port-hand perches on the N shore to port.

Coney Island, which shelters the harbour from the W, is connected to the S shore by a causeway running 1·3M SE across the drying sandbank. The causeway covers at HWS. There is a pier on Coney Island opposite the Metal Man.

Rosses Point
AC2852 and Plan
This is a less-than-ideal anchorage as the holding is poor in sand, the tide strong and there is a short, steep chop in a fresh wind. Anchor in line with the local moored yachts, or just outside them, taking care not

to obstruct the shipping channel. A temporary berth may be available at the head of the pier, where the tide is not so strong. In quiet weather a temporary anchorage on sand is possible off the Yacht Club at Deadman's Point. RNLI inshore lifeboat. Shops at Rosses Point village, showers and bar at the YC, 071 9177168.

Rosses Point to Sligo
AC2852 essential
The channel to Sligo runs for 4M E and SE from Oyster Island, and for all but the first mile is bounded by training walls. It is well marked by lit perches and buoys. From the perch on the E end of Oyster Island steer 120°, leaving the beacons marking Blennick Rocks to port and the Pool buoy and Old Seal Bank and Start Wall beacons to starboard. For the next 2M the training wall should be left close to starboard. The training wall on the port hand begins where the channel turns SE for the last 1M stretch to the town.

Pontoon
There is a 60m pontoon with 2m depth alongside on the S side of the river at Sligo, with water, shore power and security gate. Contact HM 071 911 1237, mobile 086 089 0767. Sligo has all the facilities of a large port town including medical services, train

Rosses Point (map)

Deadman's Point
Sligo YC
125°
2
Fl R 1.5s
5
5
Fl(3) 6s
Metal Man
PIER
Fl R 3s
7
6
5
QR
2
2
0₉
1₂
Fl(3) G 4s
1₇
Pier
Fl(3) 6s
Oyster Island
0 1 2 3 cables

Rosses Point from the W; the Metal Man, lower centre, with Oyster Island beyond. Coney Island Pier, bottom R; Deadman's Point and Sligo YC clubhouse, bottom L. Sligo town, top R

Sligo Harbour from S

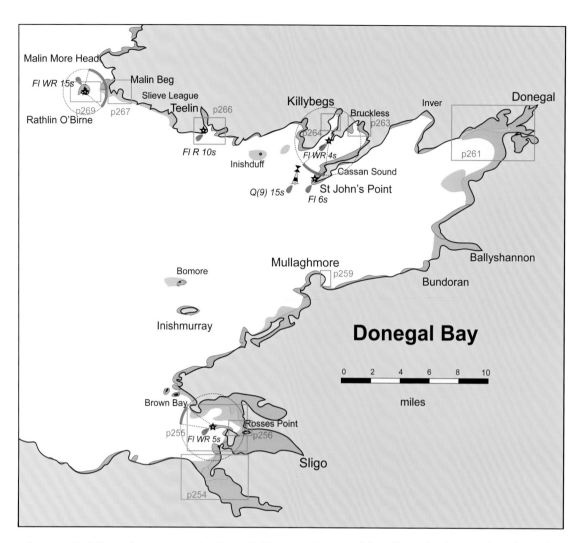

connections to Dublin and an airport (at Strandhill, N of Ballysadare Bay). Sailmaker, Sunset Sails 071 91 62792. Constant +0050 Galway; MHWS 4·1m, MHWN 3·0m, ML 2·3m.

SLIGO BAY TO MULLAGHMORE
AC2702

From Sligo Bay to Mullaghmore Head the coast should be given a good berth in any height of sea from the W; a course halfway between the shore and Inishmurray is a safe one. **Black Bull Rock**, drying 1·2m, is 7 cables offshore 3M NE of Ardboline Island, and there are rocks 1M offshore at Milk Harbour. Along this coast a good lookout should be kept for lobster pots which are often set very far out.

Brown Bay
54°20'N 8°40'W

Brown Bay, between Seal Rocks and Raghly Point, provides reasonably good anchorage and shelter from swell in winds from NW to E, at least 2 cables off the beach in 5m, sand. No facilities ashore.

There is a small drying harbour on the E side of Raghly Point, 6 cables NE of the Wheat Rock buoy.

Approaching from the buoy, give the point a berth of 3 cables to avoid Bird Rocks and Raghly Ledge

Inishmurray
54°25'·5N 8°39'·7W

Inishmurray has been uninhabited since 1950 and is well worth a visit, weather permitting, to see the remarkable and unusually well-preserved 6th century monastic buildings. In profile the island somewhat resembles an old-fashioned submarine. This led to an attack with torpedoes by a warship in 1915, but fortunately the only damage was done to Naval dignity. Clashymore Harbour on the S side is a rocky gut, off which, in perfectly calm weather only, a yacht may be anchored in 7m, weed over rock. Use a tripping line on the anchor.

On the E side of the gut there are natural quays, and mooring rings where local boats go alongside near HW, when it provides good dinghy landing. This is more difficult at LW. With any sea, or at LW, the shoal patches close E and NE of the island must be avoided. **Bomore Rock** (7m high) and its outliers, 1·5M N of the island, should be given a wide berth.

Raghly Point from the SE, with Brown Bay beyond and Horse and Ardboline Islands top L. Raghly Point Harbour, lower R

Mullaghmore
54°28'N 8°26'W
AC2702, Imray C53 and Plan
Mullaghmore is a bustling holiday village, rivalling Rosses Point as the principal sailing centre in Donegal Bay. The bay, on the SE side of the headland, offers secure anchorage in winds from SE through W to N, and the inner harbour is completely sheltered for a yacht that can dry out. Approaching from the W, the headland should be given a berth of 2 cables to avoid rocks to the N. The breakwater end shows Fl G 3s 3M. There are many moorings in the bay, so care is required if approaching after dark.

Harbour
Immediately inside the breakwater is a pontoon 20m in length with 0·6m alongside. The inner harbour mostly dries except for a small pool with 0·5m between and immediately inside the pierheads. There is also a drying shoal in the harbour entrance, one-third of its width from the S pier; so when entering, keep close to the N pier. Local bilge-keel and centreboard yachts are berthed in the harbour, and yachts up to 10m can conveniently dry out alongside the N pier. The pontoon is reserved for embarking and disembarking. The Yacht Club has visitors' moorings in the bay – call 087 257 4497 for availability. The best anchorage is off the harbour mouth in 2m but there is plenty of room N or SE of this in 2 to 3m. If bad weather threatens, a yacht should not remain anchored at Mullaghmore but should take refuge in Killybegs or Sligo. Constant +0040 Galway; MHWS 3·7m, MHWN 2·9m, ML 2·1m.

Facilities
Water on pontoon, diesel from the boatyard but no petrol. Shops, hotels, restaurants, pubs, Mullaghmore YC Clubhouse, sailing school. Rodney Lomax Boatyard – hull, mechanical and electrical repairs 071 9166124.

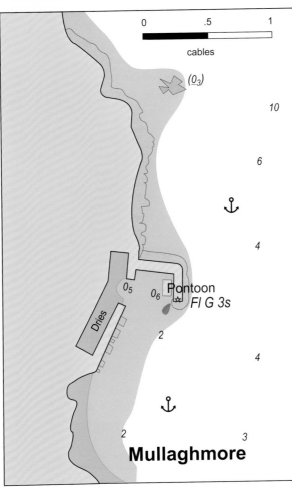

Mullaghmore

Bundoran
54°29'·2N 8°18'W

There is a boat pier at the SW end of the town with about 0·6m LAT where the RNLI inshore lifeboat is stationed. The approach with rocky shoals extending a cable to seaward is shallow, tortuous and not recommended.

Ballyshannon
54°31'N 8°16'·9W

Ballyshannon was a commercial port long ago but has not been used since 1940. It is essentially inaccessible to a stranger. The shallow exposed bar is hazardous, and from it to the town a partially marked narrow channel meanders across a wide expanse of drying sand. The pier at Creevy, 7 cables N of Kildoney Point, offers alternative access to Ballyshannon town. There is a hotel at Creevy.

In settled weather and with a local pilot, it is however possible to reach the old town quay at Ballyshannon, where there are deep and perfectly sheltered pools. Vessels up to 18m in length can moor within a cable of the quay. For pilotage phone 087 222 4854.

At the time of writing (2008) statutory sanction has been granted for buoyage of the channel into Ballyshannon, in connection with a major project to link the inland Shannon-Erne Waterway system with the open sea at Donegal Bay.

Donegal Harbour
54°36'·7N 8°14'·6W
AC2702 (AC2715 essential above Green Island): see Plan

Donegal Harbour is seldom visited by yachts. However the estuary provides fair access, and sheltered anchorages beyond Green Island are in pretty surroundings. Strangers should approach on a rising tide. The entrance is exposed to W and SW and is subject to swell which can sometimes break in apparently safe conditions. It is advisable to approach only in calm conditions or with an offshore wind.

Caution
No recent information is available as to the visibility of the buildings used as marks in the following directions. They should therefore be used with caution.

Marks
Doorin Rock, 70m, a flat-topped hill surrounded by trees, stands above a low cliff NW of Rock Point. Ball Hill, 59m, is conical with fields and hedges and shows up very well. Bell's Island (S of Murvagh Point) and St Ernan's Island are wooded. The steep defile of Barnesmore Gap on the skyline 11M to the NE is unmistakable if visible. Note that **Doorin Rock, Rock Point, Black Rock** and **Blind Rock** are all in a line. Barry's House is large, white and 3-storeyed, just SE of the plantation on Mountcharles Hill and at the NW end of the village. Furey's Shed is W of a terrace of white cottages and its sheeted roof is conspicuous. Tigin Bawn is a very conspicuous white bungalow with a slate roof, on the shore 3·5 cables W of Salt Hill quay. Salt Hill House, above the quay, is visible from seaward but not conspicuous, being covered with creepers. Green Island is no longer even a tidal island as on the chart (see photograph).

Directions – Salt Hill
Stay within 2 M SE of Doorin Point to avoid **Carrickfad Rocks**. A reasonable approach is with Barry's House (or Mountcharles) in transit with Rock Point until within 5 cables of the latter, or stay 3 cables off the shore when within 1·25M of Rock Point. When Doorin Rock is still well left of Rock Point, bring the NW

Donegal Harbour; Salt Hill Point (bottom L), Green Island and Murvagh Point (top R)

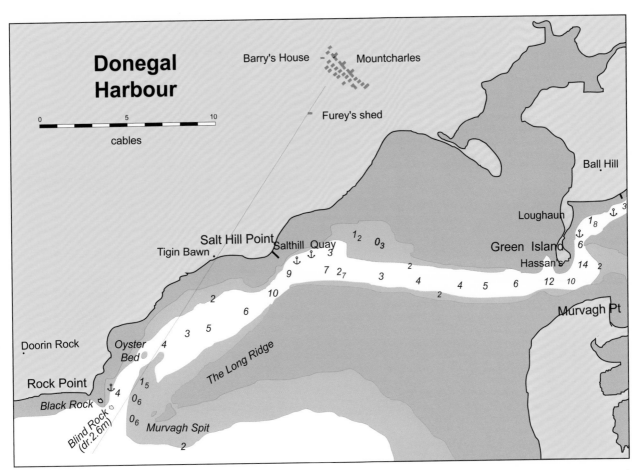

gable of Furey's Shed just open to the right of Tigin Bawn, and on this line go in past **Blind Rock**, which covers at half tide. When not quite 1 cable in from Blind Rock steer 057°, towards Barnesmore Gap, if it is visible. When Tigin Bawn bears N, steer to pass 70m off Salt Hill quay; this clears the stony bank extending 1·5 cables out from Salt Hill Point. The least depth on this track is 1·5m, between Blind Rock and Tigin Bawn.

Anchorages

*   It is possible to anchor in the lee of Black Rock. Buoy the anchor, for as well as any visible moorings there are the remains of old ones around the bottom. This place is exposed to S to E winds.
*   SE or E of the end of Salt Hill quay outside moorings in 2 to 5 m on sand, good holding, but exposed above half tide from SW through S to E. The quay is in good repair, except for broken-off wooden fenders. It dries about 0·5m at the outer steps on the E side.

Directions – inner anchorages

From a position off Salt Hill quay, steer straight for the gap between Green Island and Murvagh Point, with Salt Hill Point dead astern. Pass about 80m S of Green Island, then turn a little N of E. The tide here

runs up to 5 kn at springs and the ebb sets towards Green Island from the Mullanasole channel to the S. The banks off Murvagh Point are steep-to, and if visible can be approached very closely. Once E of Green Island turn to port, steering 353° to pass close E of Loughaun. The deep channel just E of Green Island is only 40m wide. Beyond this either head NE towards the slip and the Youth Hostel (the building above the slip), or anchor as soon as Donegal Hill (2M beyond the town) is open of the steep N side of Ballyboyle Island. This anchorage is on sand in 2·5m, well sheltered but in a strong tide. A yacht can go in only a further 5 cables, beyond which the channel to the town is very shallow and dries in places. Anchor S of the slip not less than 0·5 cable from the shore in about 3·5m. The anchorage further E, 1·5 cables SW of Ballyboyle Island, is better sheltered in E or SE wind; it is just a little SW of the anchorage symbol on the chart and has about 4m.

Donegal Town

The town can be reached by dinghy, preferably before half flood. To pass between **Lug Rock** and Ballyboyle keep the Youth Hostel in line with the two storeyed house with two chimneys, NE of it. There are two quays on the S side.

Donegal Harbour; Green Island (centre), Murvagh Point and Mullinasole Channel (centre R), Ballyboyle Island and Donegal Town (top L)

Facilities
Shops, filling stations, hotels, restaurants, pubs, PO, doctor.

South Channel to Mullanasole
This is pretty at HW but not recommended for keel boats. The tide runs very strongly W of Rooney's Island so the channel is unsuitable for anchoring.

COAST BETWEEN DONEGAL AND INVER
Doorin Point and the coast for 1M each side of it should be given a good berth as reefs project up to 4 cables seaward from the bottom of the cliffs.

Inver Bay
54°37'·2N 8°19'W

Inver Bay is exposed to the SW but provides sheltered anchorage in offshore winds. The chart shows a line to clear **Menamny Rock** which dries only at very low springs and lies 3 cables off the NW shore with foul ground inside it. It is about halfway between Ballyederlan Point and the ruined CG station. The **Whillins**, SW of Inver Port, is a dangerous rocky area, parts of which dry. Inver church in line with the left hand sandhill of Drumbeg, 046°, clears both Whillins and **Rock of the Port** (both dry 2m), as

also does Ballyederlan Point in line with St John's Point. The chart also shows a line to clear the rocks on the E side of the bay N of Doorin Point. The bay has numerous fish farms.

Inver Port
Inver Port, 1M SW of Inver village, has a drying pier and an anchorage S of it. A stranger should not approach in darkness as the lights on the pier are confusing. Approach steering due N, keeping the pierhead in line with the left hand end of a prominent short sandstone wall above the road and just to the left of a green roofed bungalow. This leads W of **Rock of the Port** where there is a mooring and room for a visitor to anchor near the line. N of this the water shoals. Local boats take the ground in the lee of the pier. A keel boat should not dry out alongside the pier because the sand is irregular with soft spots. A small twin-keel yacht could lie aground and afloat in absolute security in any weather well up in the bight towards the wall, where there are trees to which lines may be made fast.

Inver Roads
Inver Roads, at the head of the bay NE of Inver Port, provides safe anchorage in 3 to 5m, well sheltered

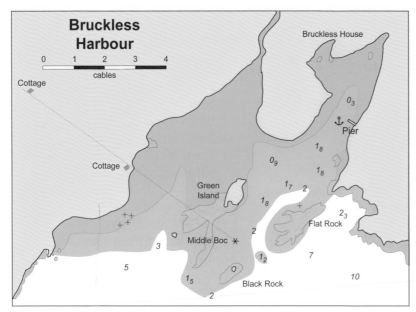

Bruckless Harbour

0 1 2 3 4
cables

Cottage

Cottage

Bruckless House

Green Island

Pier

0_3

1_8

0_9

1_8

1_7 2

1_8

2_3

Flat Rock

2

3

Middle Boc

1_2

5

1_5

Black Rock

7

10

2

in offshore winds, but without convenient landing nearby. However, it is reported blocked by fish farms to the E.

Eany Water

Eany Water runs out across drying flats at the head of the bay. It would provide anchorage for a twin-keel or centreboard yacht, and a shallow draught yacht might lie afloat at the Old Church corner. There is also a small pool with 1·8m LWS right up at the bridge, but with many drying patches on the way up to it. However, after heavy rain with the river in spate, neither of these anchorages would be tenable.

Cassan Sound
54°35'N 8°25'W
AC2702, 2792 Killybegs inset
This open anchorage is 1·5M NE of St John's Point and just N of another bay off which is the dangerous **Black Rock** which dries 2·3m. The bay to the S has a rocky bottom and a bright yellow beach. Cassan Sound has a small stony beach beneath a 3-chimney cottage and should be approached bearing NW or W to avoid Black Rock. Anchor in 3·5m close inshore between the end of the little breakwater and the shore N of it. The anchorage is unsafe in any swell, but sheltered in winds between W and N, and has a handy slip for landing.

Bruckless
54°37'·2N 8°23'·8W
AC2702 and Plan
This pretty creek, with trees down to the water's edge, lies at the head of McSwyne's Bay and is well sheltered (except from due SW) but is now so encumbered with fish cages and mussel rafts

as to be essentially unavailable as an anchorage. Bruckless is hardly anywhere deeper than 1·8m. Green Island, 10m high, is prominent, especially at LW when the extensive reefs on which it stands are uncovered. **Black Rock** (locally known as the Round Rock) stands out well and never covers. Coming in, **Flat Rock** is not easy to see; it covers completely only at very high springs but the small reefs projecting about 20m from its W side cover at half tide. **Middle Boc** is a small isolated rock which dries 1m and lies between Green Island and Black Rock. The marks for it are two white thatched cottages on the W side, one low down near the shore, the other near the top of the first ridge inland from the shore. Middle Boc lies on the transit of the SW gable of the upper cottage with the NE gable of the lower one.

Directions
Leave Black Rock 18m to starboard and steer 038° for the head of the pier, with Pound Point dead astern. This line passes less than 45m SE of Middle Boc. Anchor (if space is available) in mid-channel just short of the pier, bottom soft mud. The pier dries out to the head at LWS and sometimes covers at HW. A large square roofless shed near the root of the pier indicates its position if covered. A bilge-keel boat could take the ground in safety in the W bight of the harbour, which dries out.

Facilities
Shop, PO and fuel at Bruckless village, 1 km NW. Restaurant 800m S of pier.

KILLYBEGS
54°36'·8N 8°26'·9W
AC2702, 2792, Imray C53 and Plan
In terms of landed tonnage, Killybegs is the largest fishing port in the British Isles, and it also has a significant seaborne trade in processed fish and miscellaneous cargo. However the fishery is mid-water pelagic and is essentially confined to the months of September to April; there is relatively little activity in summer. The port is one of the best natural harbours in Ireland, accessible by day or night in any weather, and offers all services including hull, engine, electrical and electronic repairs, but not sailmakers; however sail repairs are available in Sligo. Yachts up to the very largest are welcome and can be accommodated in Killybegs although there are at present no specific facilities

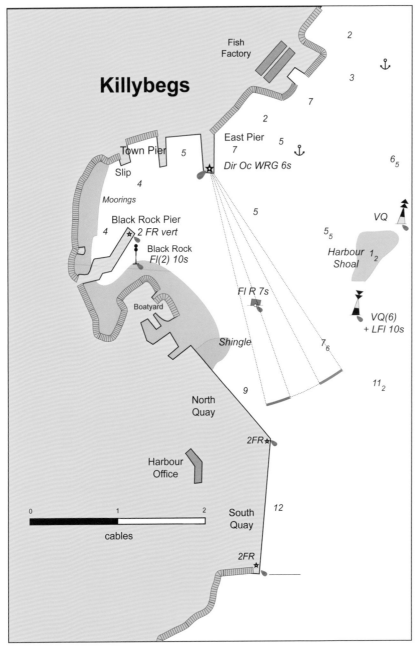

336°–340° AltWR 340°–342° R 342°–348°

South Quay, 2×2FR vert
North Quay, 2×2FR vert
Black Rock Pier, 2FR vert
Smooth Point buoy, PHM Fl R 7s
Black Rock beacon, Isolated Danger mark, Fl(2) 10s
Town Pier, 2FR vert
Killybegs Outer buoy, S Card VQ(6) + L Fl 10s
Killybegs Inner buoy, N Card VQ

Approach by day from W
In bad conditions pass 2M S of Muckros Head and head E till the E side of Drumanoo Head bears NE, then turn to port and give the coast NE of Drumanoo Head a berth of 2 cables. This course leads midway between Ellamore Shoal and the 14·3m shoal 1·5M W of it, both of which can break in gales. For an inshore passage from the W keep fairly close to Muckros Head and then steer into Fintragh Bay well N of **Manister Rock** which is always covered. When **Black Rock** is seen (it only covers at HWS) steer to leave it close to starboard and then pass 2 cables from Drumanoo Head to clear **Horse Head Rock**. Approaching from Teelin or close inshore at Muckros Head, a bearing of 309° on Slieve League summit or Dundawoona Point leads clear SW of Manister Rock.

for them. Call "Killybegs Harbour" on VHF Ch 16 (working channel 14), 24h. The Harbour is managed by the Department of Communications, Energy and Natural Resources.

Lights and marks
St John's Point, white tower Fl 6s 30m 14M.
Rotten Island, white tower Fl WR 4s 20m W15M, R11M, W 255°–008°, R 008°–039°, W 039°–208°. Shows red to the SSW over Bullockmore and St John's Point, white elsewhere
Bullockmore buoy, W Card Q(9) 15s
Rashenny Point buoy, SHM Fl G 2s
Walker's buoy, SHM Fl G 6s
Lackerabunn beacon, PHM Fl R 3s 5m 2M
Killybegs port entry light, white lattice tower Dir Oc WRG 6s, G 328°–334° AltWG 334°–336° FW

Approach by day from S
Leave Bullockmore buoy (1·5M W of St John's Point) 1·5 cables to starboard and steer for Rotten Island. Alternatively, the NE peak of Crownarad (490m) well W of Drumanoo Head bearing 349° leads clear W of St John's Point shoal and E of **Bullockmore** (2·1m). Stay on this heading till St John's Point bears SE, then head for Rotten Island.

Approach by night from W
Steer for St John's Point light keeping it bearing not more than 108° until Rotten Island light bears 039° (W edge of red sector), then steer in on this bearing and leave Rotten Island light to starboard.

Approach by night from S
Steer to pass 1·5M W of St John's Point, identify

Killybegs from the SW; Town Pier centre, North and South Quays bottom R. Note the projecting shingle bank at the NW end of the North Quay (Dept of Communications, Energy & Natural Resources)

Bullockmore buoy and pass W of it, then steer for Rotten Island as above.

Entrance

Keep mid-channel past Rashenny Point, leave South and North Quays and Smooth Point buoy to port and Harbour Shoal (Killybegs Outer) S Card buoy to starboard. Beware the drying spit extending NE from the inner end of North Quay. Constant +0045 Galway; MHWS 4·1m, MHWN 3·0m, ML 2·3m.

Anchorage

The best anchorage, clear of traffic and moorings, is E of the East Pier and S of the fish factory, as shown on the plan, in 2 to 5m; anchorage may also be available in the small bay between the Town Pier and Black Rock Pier, although this area has many moorings, and traffic at both piers may be heavy. The holding ground in Killybegs is excellent, but the chain and anchor must be thoroughly rinsed on weighing, since the bottom mud tends to have a fairly pungent odour.

An alongside berth may be available on one of the piers; contact HM by VHF (Ch 14,16) or by phone 074 9731032 for advice and instructions. The piers are open-piled and a fenderboard is advisable. The slipway W of the Town Pier is used by sea-angling boats but is a convenient place to land by dinghy.

At the time of writing (2008) there are proposals for a marina betwen Black Rock Pier and the Town Pier.

Facilities

Diesel by tanker on piers, or cans from filling station, 1 km. Petrol from filling station. Bottled gas. Water on slipway W of Town Pier. All amenities, shops, hotels, pubs and restaurants, banks, hospital. Ship chandler; Mooney Boats (074 9731152) mechanical, electrical and electronic supplies and repairs, 75t travelhoist (the largest in Ireland). Atlantic Marine, electrical and electronic supplies 074 9731440. Buses to Donegal Town and Sligo.

Walker's Bay

Walker's Bay, on the E of the entrance, is a pleasant overnight anchorage. It is well sheltered in SW or W winds and Killybegs offers an easy alternative if the wind veers NW. The area with suitable depths

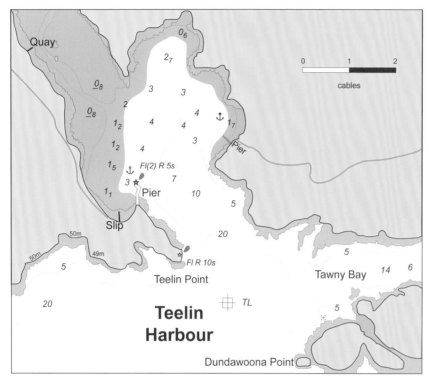

Teelin Harbour

shortly after MLWS. Possibly scout with a dinghy to enter this quiet and beautiful anchorage.

Teelin Harbour
⊕ *TL* 54°37'·2N 8°37'·5W
AC2702, 2792, Imray C53 and Plan
Teelin is a picturesque natural harbour suitable for a night at anchor in reasonable weather. It is exposed to S and SW swell. In NW winds very severe squalls can come down off the mountain. Some fishing vessels use the anchorage.

Approach
The entrance is hard to discern until fairly close. From the E, it does not open up until Dundawoona Point is abeam; from the W, Tawny Bay, the inlet E of Teelin, is conspicuous from a position close inshore E of Carrigan Head. The entrance, which faces SE, is 2 cables wide and steep-to on both sides.

is narrow and it shoals quickly inside. Anchor in 5 to 8m, NW of the slip, but keep clear of local moorings.

Port Roshin, on the W side opposite Rotten Island, has minimum depth 2m. The entrance is only 20m wide at LAT and is not difficult; however, care should be taken to avoid rocks to the S which cover

Lights
Teelin Point, the W side of the entrance, shows Fl R 10s from a red structure which is inconspicuous by day. The **pier light** shows Fl(2) R 5s.

Teelin Harbour from SW. The inner bay (upper L) largely dries

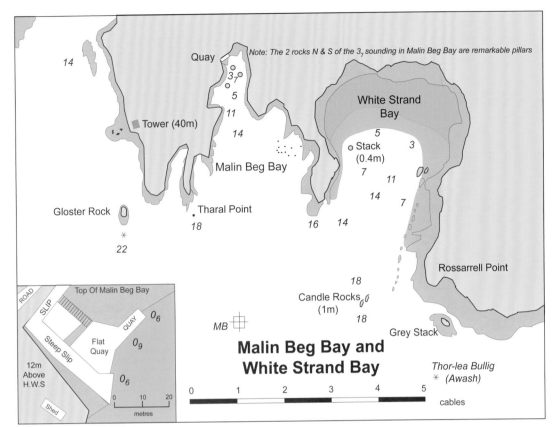

Note: The 2 rocks N & S of the 3, sounding in Malin Beg Bay are remarkable pillars

Quay

White Strand Bay

Tower (40m)

Malin Beg Bay

Stack (0.4m)

Gloster Rock

Tharal Point

Rossarrell Point

Candle Rocks (1m)

Grey Stack

MB

Malin Beg Bay and White Strand Bay

Thor-lea Bullig ✳ *(Awash)*

Top Of Malin Beg Bay

ROAD

SLIP

QUAY

Steep Slip

Flat Quay

12m Above H.W.S

Shed

metres

cables

Anchorage
Off the moorings on the W side, depth 3 or 4m, not too far N of the pier as there is more swell further N. The end of the pier has 3m at LAT and offers excellent shelter alongside. The E side of the bay is foul with discarded moorings and fish farms and is not recommended.

Facilities
Water on pier. Diesel by tanker or at Carrick village, 5 km.

COAST FROM TEELIN TO GLEN HEAD
The coast between Teelin and White Strand Bay, 6m to the WNW, presents a fine spectacle, with the cliffs of Slieve League sweeping 597m almost sheer to the sea, the second highest cliffs in Ireland.

The coast is clean to within 3 cables of the shore and there are several tempting beaches accessible only from seaward, but survey data is scanty and conflicting, and the only prudent advice to a stranger is to admire the view from a safe distance.

White Strand Bay
⊕ *MB* 54°39'·3N 8°47'W
See Plan
White Strand Bay offers temporary anchorage in N winds in about 5m, sand, in pretty surroundings. From the E, stay 5 cables offshore, identify **Candle Rocks** and continue until the W point of the bay is open W of Candle Rocks before turning N, to avoid **Thor-Lea Bullig,** which uncovers only at very low springs. Anchor in the middle of the bay E of the **Stack,** which covers at HW.

White Strand and Malin Beg bays from the SW; Candle Rocks (breaking) bottom R, Malin Beg village, top L

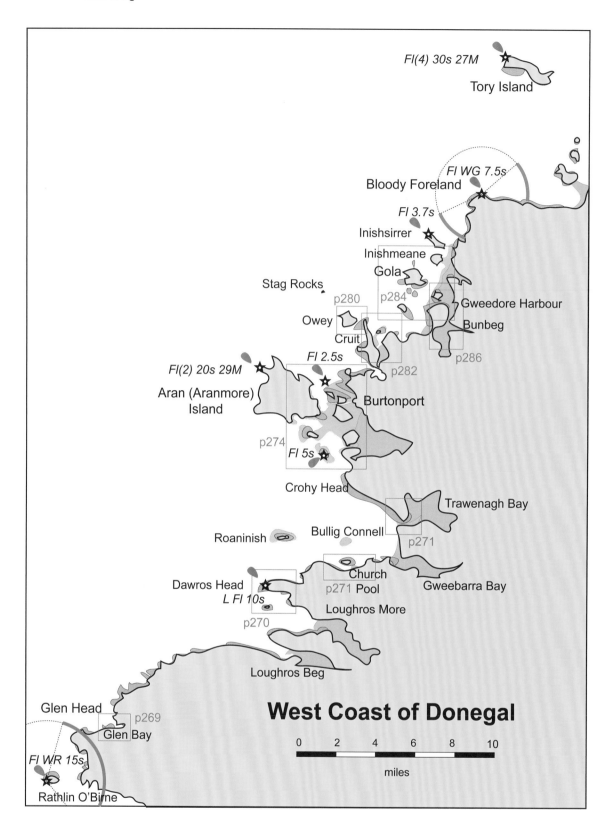

Fl(4) 30s 27M
Tory Island

Fl WG 7.5s
Bloody Foreland

Fl 3.7s
Inishsirrer

Inishmeane

Gola

p284

Stag Rocks

p280

Owey

Cruit

Gweedore Harbour

Bunbeg

p282

p286

Fl 2.5s

Fl(2) 20s 29M
Aran (Aranmore)
Island

Burtonport

p274

Fl 5s

Crohy Head

Trawenagh Bay

Roaninish

Bullig Connell

p271

Church
Pool

p271

Gweebarra Bay

Dawros Head
L Fl 10s

Loughros More

p270

Loughros Beg

West Coast of Donegal

Glen Head   p269

Glen Bay

0   2   4   6   8   10

miles

Fl WR 15s

Rathlin O'Birne

Malin Beg Bay

⊕ *MB* 54°39'·3N 8°47'W

See Plan

Malin Beg Bay has a slip and a small quay with about 0·4m alongside. A yacht should enter only in really fine weather as the head of the bay is less than 0·5 cable wide with three rocks, the two left ones being remarkable pillars. Temporary anchorage is available just beyond the first rock; with sufficient rise of tide an alongside berth is possible at the quay. Malin Beg, 400m, has shops and PO.

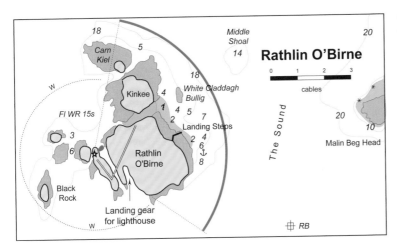

of **White Claddagh Bullig** (dries 1·2m) which extends further S than would appear. It is best to anchor NE of the SE corner where the holding is better than off the landing steps. There is no anchorage or landing off the S shore, where a crane is positioned to service the lighthouse.

Light
Rathlin O'Birne, white tower Fl WR 15s 35m W18M R14M, Racon (O) 13M, R 195º–307º, W 307º–195º. Shows white to seaward and red inshore between Carrigan Head and Malin More Head.

Rathlin O'Birne Sound
⊕ *RB*   54°39'·4N 8°48'·7W
See Plan

Rathlin O'Birne is 1M offshore, and the clear passage 5 cables wide through the sound is nearer the island as rocks extend 4 cables from Malin Beg Head. The tide runs N at 1·5 kn at springs for 9·25 hours, starting at –0200 Galway. The S going tide is very weak. The streams may be strongly affected by N or S winds.

Rathlin O'Birne Island
Rathlin O'Birne Island is worth a visit on a calm day. The best landing is at the whitewashed steps on the E side. Beware

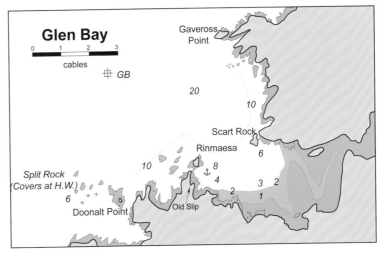

Loughros More bar, from SE; Roancarrick and Dawros Head, top L

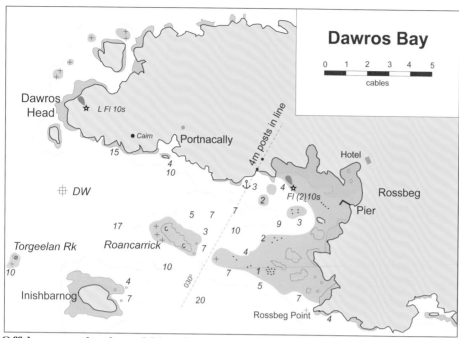

Dawros Bay

0 1 2 3 4 5
cables

Dawros Head L Fl 10s

• Cairn **Portnacally**

15

4

10

⊕ *DW*

5   7   7

17   3   10

Torgeelan Rk   **Roancarrick**   7

10   4

10   7   1

4   5

7

Inishbarnog   20

Rossbeg Point

4m posts in line

3   4

2   Fl (2)10s

Hotel

Rossbeg
Pier

9   3

2

030°

Offshore weather buoy M4, yellow, Fl(5) Y 20s, is moored 45M WNW of Glen Head in position 55°N 10°W.

Glen Bay

⊕ *GB* 54°43'·0N 8°45'·8W

AC1879 and Plan

Glen Bay provides temporary anchorage in winds from NE through SE to S. Anchor close to Rinmaesa Point in 7m, sand. The bay is dangerous in winds between SW and N.

COAST FROM GLEN HEAD TO CROHY HEAD

AC1879

N from Glen Head there are spectacular cliffs and stacks. The coast is most impressive, but foul up to 5 cables offshore. Close S of Toralaydan there is a small pier, but its approach is strewn with rocks and it should be avoided by a stranger. The only feasible overnight anchorage on this stretch of coast is Church Pool, while in heavy weather the nearest safe anchorage is Aran Road, entered from the N after going west-about Aranmore Island, 28M from Rathlin O'Birne.

Loughros More and Beg Bays

54°47'·5N 8°34'W

These bays are not normally accessible, with dangerous bars that almost always break near LW. Older editions of this volume included a plan of Loughros More, surveyed prior to 1902, and some directions. However in the absence of recent survey data the only possible advice to a stranger is to avoid the area.

Dawros Bay from the SE; Rossbeg Point centre L, Dawros Head and Roancarrick top L

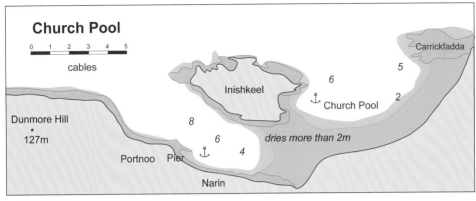

Church Pool

0 1 2 3 4 5

cables

Carrickfadda

Inishkeel

Church Pool

Dunmore Hill

127m

Portnoo Pier

Narin

dries more than 2m

Dawros Bay

⊕*DW* 54°49'·2N 8°33'·9W

AC1879 and Plan

Dawros Bay provides temporary anchorage in calm sea conditions with N or E winds. The bay is best entered from the W; the approach from the S is on the line of two 4m posts, 030°. The continued visibility of these posts is not guaranteed. However the easiest anchorage is also on this line near the shore. The pier dries at LW and is too difficult for a stranger to approach at HW. The beacon 2·5 cables WNW of the pier is a black pole with red bands and shows Fl(2)10s 5m 3M. Hotel and PO; small shop 800m SE.

A shallow draft yacht might visit Portnacally, just W of the bay, a delightful little inlet, the entrance being W of the island with rocks outside it. **Dawros Head** shows L Fl 10s 39m 4M from a square white column.

Boylagh Bay

54°51'·5N 8°30'·2W

AC1879, 2792

There is a string of shoals and rocks stretching into the bay from **Bullig More**, 11m, 4M NW of Dunmore Head. These should all be avoided though some of them are dangerous only in a big sea or swell. **Roaninish**, 4·6m high, is clean on its S side but has reefs extending up to 7 cables N and W. Landing on Roaninish is possible at the gut N of the W end of the island; the bottom all along the N side is foul. The innermost danger in Boylagh Bay is **Bullig Connell**, 0·3m, 8 cables N of Inishkeel. The flood tide sets strongly into Boylagh Bay.

Approach

From the S, give Dawros Head a berth of 3 cables and stay within 5 cables of Dunmore Head and Inishkeel, to avoid the rocks close NW of Dawros Head and Dawros Island, and the shoals in

Boylagh Bay to the north. The approach **from the N** is trickier, with no good leading lines. From Crohy Head, steer 160° towards the rocky shore at Carrickfadda, E of Church Pool, with Illancrone beacon astern so as to pass well E of Bullig Connell; the chart shows clearance marks to pass E or W of this rock.

Caution

The Gweebarra River, in the SE corner of Boylagh Bay, has a dangerous and very shallow bar and should be avoided.

Anchorages

• Church Pool, E of Inishkeel, offers excellent shelter in winds from SE through SW to WNW, and good holding in about 3m, sand. A tripping line is recommended since the bottom is fouled by the ground chains of the former trot of visitors' moorings. There does not seem to be any reduction of depth now as mentioned on AC2792.

• Portnoo, SW of Inishkeel, is more exposed to swell than Church Pool. However it provides better shelter in NE wind and in really calm conditions it is a pleasant place to stay overnight. Anchor 0·75 cable E of the end of the pier in more than 2m, or further out in less than 5m.

Hotel, shops, PO at Portnoo.

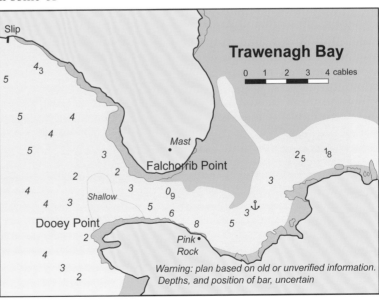

Trawenagh Bay

0 1 2 3 4 cables

Slip

Mast

Falchorrib Point

Dooey Point

Shallow

Pink Rock

Warning: plan based on old or unverified information. Depths, and position of bar, uncertain

Trawenagh Bay
54°53'N 8°24'W
AC1879 and Plan

This inlet at the NE corner of Boylagh Bay has a narrow entrance marked by a tall thin mast on Falchorrib Point. Most of the bay dries out, and no recent survey data is available. The following directions are reproduced from previous editions of this volume and should not be taken as definitive.

The entrance is narrow and exposed to the W, and should only be approached in swell-free conditions and near HW. The bar had a reported depth of 2m which may now be reduced. Approach from the NW staying a little less than 1 cable offshore when approaching and abeam Falchorrib Point. The shoal N of Dooey Point does not now dry as shown on the chart. Continue SE till over the bar, then keep the S shore close aboard till the shoreline turns slightly

SE. At this point you may see a small square rock up on the shore, painted pink, which is a useful mark for going out. Head up about 060° and anchor in about 3m, not more than 2 cables up.

Caution

GPS chart plotters should not be implicitly relied upon in Trawenagh Bay and approaches due to the age of the survey data and the likelihood of changes in the channel and sandbanks. It is essential to maintain good traditional pilotage with continuous use of the echo sounder.

CROHY HEAD TO BLOODY FORELAND
AC1883, 2792, Imray C53

The coast from Illancrone, 2M S of Aranmore, to Bloody Foreland is sheltered by a string of islands, some of which have permanent communities.

Approaches to Aran Sound from the S; South Sound, foreground; Illancrone and its offlying reefs centre L, Middle Sound, Inishkeeragh, Chapel Sound and Aranmore top L, Crohy Head bottom R, Wyon Point centre R, Inishfree Upper and Rutland top R, Owey in the distance.

The largest and most populous of these is Aran, usually known as Aranmore (the lifeboat station, almost uniquely, spells it *Arranmore*). The islands sheltering Burtonport have summer residents; and others including Owey and Gola, are seasonally occupied. The coast – part of the region known as The Rosses – has a number of excellent anchorages and harbours amid beautiful scenery, with some splendid sandy beaches, and is a most attractive cruising ground. The islands give a useful amount of shelter for coastwise passages, and the pilotage, while interesting and challenging, is not unduly difficult. This is a Gaeltacht area and Irish is widely used as an everyday language.

Offlying dangers – passage W of the islands
Leenon More, 2M W of Inishkeeragh, has 8m at LAT but breaks with a heavy swell. The **Stag Rocks,** 1·25M NW of Owey, consist of three rocks 9m high and one, SW of these, which dries 1·2m. **Bullogconnell Shoals,** locally called **the Blowers,** are 1M NW of Gola and are the most dangerous. A small portion of the N shoal dries 1·4m and the middle and S shoals have depths of 2m and 3m. They break heavily and should be given a wide berth. Keeping Bloody Foreland closed behind Inishsirrer, 045°, leads between them and Gola, and also NW of **Rinogy Rock** N of Gola. To pass outside the shoals keep Cluidaniller, the summit of Aranmore Island, open W of Owey. At night the secondary light on Aranmore lighthouse (Fl R 3s, vis 203°–234°) shows over all these dangers, and they may be avoided by staying W of the arc of visibility of this light.

In gales from SW through W to NW the whole coast is subject to very heavy swell and the sea state can be high, confused and dangerous, especially close W of the islands and salient points. If making the passage around the coast in such conditions it is prudent to stand several miles out to sea.

ARANMORE ISLAND AND SOUND
The W side of Aranmore has some of the finest cliff scenery in Ireland. In the Sound and between the islands within it there is a wide choice of anchorages. The North Sound of Aran has good depth and provides the safest access to Aran Road and Burtonport. The South Sound of Aran has a least depth of only 0·3m and many dangerous rocks; it should be attempted only in suitable weather and in daylight with an adequate rise of tide. There are many beacons and leading marks inside Aranmore, most of them with lights, but as these may not be absolutely reliable, visiting yachts should not attempt to use the channels after dark.

Caution
Nomenclature can be a little confusing on this coast. Distinguish between **South Sound,** which is the channel between Illancrone and Wyon Point, and the **South Sound of Aran,** the shallower and rock-strewn channel between Cloghcor Point and Rutland Island. The general term **Aran Sound** is here used to describe the entire passage between Aranmore Island and the mainland. Distinguish also between **Bullig Connell** in Boylagh Bay and **Bullogconnell Shoals** NW of Gola, and between **Rinogy Rock,** N of Gola, and **Rinnagy Rock,** N of Aran Sound (note also that on AC2792, Rinnagy Rock is spelt *Rinnogy*). The major island is here referred to as Aranmore, which is also the name favoured by the Commissioners of Irish Lights for the lighthouse.

Lights and Marks
Aranmore (Rinrawros Point), 23m white tower Fl(2) 20s 71m 29M. Auxiliary light Fl R 3s 61m 13M, vis 203°–234°.
S Approaches to Aran Road and Burtonport:
Illancrone, 3m square white tower Fl 5s 7m 6M. A small stone hut on Illancrone may be more conspicuous by day than the beacon, particularly from the N.
Wyon Point, 5m square white tower Fl(2)WRG 10s 8m W6M R3M; vis G shore–021°, W021°–042°, R042°–121°, W121°–150°, R150°–shore. Shows white over the approach from SW, green inshore to the S and SE, red over Illancrone and Middle Sound, white to the NW and over Inishkeeragh, and red over Turk Rocks, Aileen Reef and the South Sound of Aran to the N
The Clutch, unlit beacon 4 cables S of Aileen Reef beacon.
Turk Rocks, 9m green tower Fl G 5s 6m 2M.
Aileen Reef, 9m square red beacon QR 6m 1M.
Leac na bhFear, square white tower Q(2) 5s 4m 2M, 2 cables W of Aileen Reef beacon.
Aphort, unlit beacon 1·5 cables NW of Leac na bhFear beacon.
Carrickbealatroha Upper, 5m square white tower Fl 5s 3m 2M.
Corren's Rock, 6m square red tower Fl R 3s 4m 2M.
South Rutland, unlit conical beacon 0·5 cable N of Corren's Rock.
Yellow Rock, unlit beacon on the E side of the channel E of Rutland Island.
Teige's Rock, 5m white tower Fl 3s 4m 2M.
Chapel Sound (Cloghcor) leading lights Iso 8s 2M 048·5° from black and white banded bns NE of Chapel Bay
Rossillion Bay (Aphort) leading lights Oc 4s 308·5°

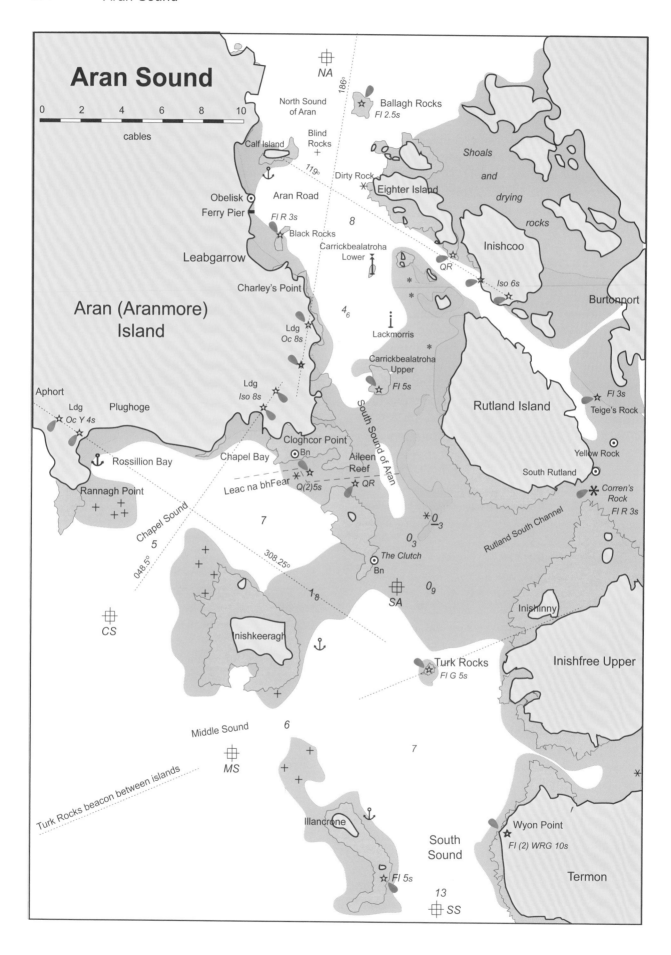

Aran Sound

0 2 4 6 8 10
cables

NA

North Sound
of Aran

Ballagh Rocks
Fl 2.5s

Blind
Rocks
+

Calf Island

Obelisk
Ferry Pier

Aran Road

Dirty Rock

Eighter Island

Shoals

and

drying

rocks

Inishcoo

186°

119°

8

Fl R 3s

Black Rocks

Carrickbealatroha
Lower

QR

Iso 6s

Burtonport

Leabgarrow

Charley's Point

4 6

Aran (Aranmore)
Island

Lackmorris

Ldg
Oc 8s

Carrickbealatroha
Upper
Fl 5s

Rutland Island

Fl 3s

Teige's Rock

Aphort

Ldg
Iso 8s

Plughoge

Ldg
Oc Y 4s

Cloghcor Point

Bn

Chapel Bay

Aileen
Reef

Yellow Rock

Rossillion Bay

Leac na bhFear

Q(2)5s

QR

South Rutland

Corren's
Rock
Fl R 3s

Rannagh Point

+
+ +

Chapel Sound

5

048.5°

308.25°

7

0 3

0 3

South Sound of Aran

Rutland South Channel

The Clutch
Bn

0 9

SA

Inishinny

CS

1 8

Inishkeeragh

Inishfree Upper

Turk Rocks
Fl G 5s

Middle Sound

6

MS

7

Turk Rocks beacon between islands

Illancrone

South
Sound

Wyon Point
Fl (2) WRG 10s

Termon

Fl 5s

13

SS

from black and white banded bns N of Rannagh Pt.

N Approaches to Aran Road and Burtonport:

Ballagh Rocks, conspic 10m conical beacon, white with black band, Fl 2·5s 13m 5M

Black Rocks, red column Fl R 3s 3m 1M.

Carrickbealatroha Lower, stayed perch W Card, unlit.

Lackmorris, stayed perch Isolated Danger mark, unlit.

South Channel red PHM perch, unlit, 2 cables E of Lackmorris.

Aran leading lights Oc 8s 3M 186° from bns S of Charley's Point. Front 8m black with white band, rear 17m black.

Carrickatine red beacon, No 2, QR 6m 1M.

Inishcoo leading lights Iso 6s 1M 119·3° from bns on Inishcoo Island. Front 6m white with black band, rear 11m black with yellow band.

Inishcoo red beacon, No 4, QR 3m 1M.

Rutland leading lights Oc 6s 1M 137·6° from bns on Rutland Island. Front 8m white with black band, rear 14m, black with yellow band.

Nancy's Rock, green beacon, No 1, QG 3m 1M.

Edernish Rock, red beacon, No 6, QR 3m 1M.

Burtonport leading lights FG 1M 068·1° from bns above harbour. Front 17m, grey with white band, rear 23m, grey with yellow band.

Burtonport Pier Channel, conical stone bn, white with black band, unlit.

APPROACHES TO THE SOUTH SOUND OF ARAN

54°55'·4N 8°29'W

AC1883, 2792, Imray C53 and Plan

Between Crohy Head (on the mainland) and Rannagh Point (the S point of Aranmore Island) are three channels: Chapel Sound, Middle Sound and South Sound. Of these, only South Sound can be recommended to the stranger.

Marks

The rounded height and 30- to 45m cliffs of Crohy Head, and the 243m hill Croaghegly, with low-lying ground for some miles N and S of it, are very distinctive. The tower on Crohy Head is not easily discerned from seaward, but the beacon on the low promontory of Wyon Point, one mile further N, is more conspicuous. Illancrone is low-lying and has a single stone shelter about the middle of the ridge, and its light beacon on the rocks to the SE. Inishkeeragh, which is also low-lying and flat, is best identified by its single row of roofless houses.

South Sound

⊕*SS* 54°56·1'N 8°28'W

From the SW, identify Crohy Head and the beacon on Wyon Point. Approach with Roaninish astern and Wyon Point beacon bearing 032°; this leads clear E of **Bullig-na-naght** (3m) and **Carrickgilreavy** (dries 2·7m) and W of **Leenon-rua** (dries 0·9m).

South Sound of Aran from the SW; Inishkeeragh foreground with Chapel Bay on Aranmore Island, L; The Clutch and Aileen Reef centre R; Eighter and the channel to Burtonport, upper R; Owey at top

Carrickgilreavy is often marked by breakers, and **Meadalmore**, the S extremity of Illancrone, covers only at very high spring tides. When Illancrone beacon is abeam, turn N, leaving the beacon 3 cables to port. Identify Turk Rocks beacon, one mile N, and steer to pass 2 cables W of it. The transit of Carrickbealatroha Upper and Ballagh Rocks beacons, 354°, leads clear W of Turk Rocks.

Note that these directions lead over Middle Shoals, with a least depth of 5·5m, and which break in heavy weather or a high swell. However in such conditions a yacht should not in any case attempt the approach to Aran Sound from the S, but should proceed outside Aranmore Island.

Middle Sound

⊕*MS* 54°56·9'N 8°30'W

Middle Sound is scarcely more than a cable wide between rocks extending from the islands on each side. It is only navigable in settled conditions, and from seaward only with judicious use of GPS. For a vessel bound S out of Aran Sound it may provide an attractive option: the leading line is Turk Rocks beacon astern in line between Inishfree Upper and Inishinny. The beacon 069° in line with the S end of Inishinny gives a least depth of 5m but leads close

S of a 0·6m rock; the beacon 066° in line with the W point of Inishinny gives a least depth of 3m but a slightly greater margin for error on each side. It is essential to establish the identity and continued visibility of the leading marks before commencing the passage.

Chapel Sound

⊕*CS* 54°57'·7N 8°31'·2W

Chapel Sound is 1·5 cables wide between dangerous rocks and has a shoal with 2·4m at its SW end. The leading beacons NE of Chapel Bay lead through it, but for the stranger, it is to be approached from seaward only in clear visibility and with judicious use of GPS. Outward bound, the leading marks must be clearly identified to begin with, and must remain visible.

Anchorages S of Aranmore

- 1·5 cables NE of Illancrone in 3m, sand.
- Between 1·5 and 2·5 cables E of Inishkeeragh in 2·5 to 3·5m, sand.
- Rossillion Bay (Aphort, 54°58'·3N 8°30'·8W) is sheltered from winds between W and NE and may be reached by crossing the shoal between Inishkeeragh and the Clutch Beacon

Arranmore lifeboat heading E from Aileen Reef towards Chapel Sound. The lifeboat has left Aileen Reef beacon (bottom R) close to port and is heading for Leac na bhFear beacon (centre). Aphort beacon is just visible above and to the right of Leac na bhFear. Rossillion Bay (Aphort) top L

North Sound of Aran from the SW; Leabgarrow foreground, Calf Island centre, Ballagh Rocks upper R centre, Owey top L and Bloody Foreland Hill in the distance. Entrance to Burtonport S of Eighter Island, middle R

in a least depth of 1·8m keeping Turk Rocks beacon bearing 128° and the leading beacons in line 308°. Anchor in 2m, sand, clear of the moorings in the bay. The pier and slipway just N of Rannagh Point has 1m alongside and room for a 10m yacht to tie up for a short visit. Pub at Plughoge, 400m.

- Chapel Bay (54°58'·3N 8°29'·7W) is well sheltered between NW and NE. Anchor one third of a cable S of the 2m-high rock in 4·3m, or SW of this position in 2·7m. Small pier.

All these anchorages are somewhat exposed to swell.

SOUTH SOUND OF ARAN
⊕*SA* 54°57'·7N 8°28'·4W
AC2792
The South Sound of Aran, N of Turk Rocks, is navigable by a yacht only above half tide and in reasonably settled weather. Leaving Turk Rocks beacon not less than 1 cable to starboard, bring Carrickbealatroha Upper beacon in line with Ballagh Rocks beacon 354° to leave Clutch beacon 1·25 cables to port. Keep on this line until Cloghcor Point, the SE corner of Aranmore Island, comes abeam, then steer 325° for the N of the two leading beacons on the Aranmore shore S of Charley's Point. When the S leading beacon comes abeam, turn to starboard and head N, giving Charley's Point

a berth of two cables to avoid the rocks off it.

South Sound of Aran to Chapel Bay
54°58'·2N 8°28'·6W
The sound SW of Aileen Reef and W of Aileen Reef beacon is not recommended for deep keeled yachts. Shallow draft vessels using this channel should leave Aileen Reef beacon close to port and Leac na bhFear beacon close to starboard, then turn to starboard to head towards Aphort beacon. When half a cable from the Aphort beacon, turn on to a course of 250° until Chapel Bay opens up. The photograph opposite shows the lifeboat using this channel.

Caution
Note that (unusually) the navigable channel lies **between** Aileen Reef (to the N) and the Aileen Reef port-hand beacon. There is foul ground S and E of the beacon.

NORTH SOUND OF ARAN
⊕*NA* 55°00'·2N 8°29'·1W
AC1883, 2792 and Plan
This is the normal approach to Aran Road and Burtonport. It is safe in almost any weather, the exception being NW gales; a prolonged NW winter gale can cause the entrance to break right across.

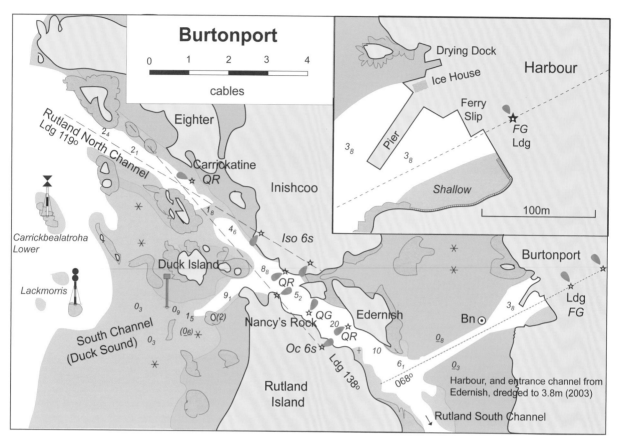

Directions - North Sound to Aran Road anchorage

The entrance is marked by the 9m high **Ballagh Rocks** beacon, a dominating feature of the sound, which should be approached from NNW so as to leave **Rinnagy** (dries 2·4m) and **Bullignamirra** (dries 3·7m) well to port. There are two alternative leading lines. **Lackmorris** perch a little to the left of **Carrickbealatroha Lower** beacon 161° leads W of **Leenane na Mallagh**, a 5·5m patch which breaks in heavy weather. The leading beacons on the Aranmore shore S of Charley's Point in line 186° lead over Leenane na Mallagh. Both lines lead close E of **Blind Rocks** (0·9m), E of Calf Island.

Approaching from the N: once past Ballagh Rocks, borrow a little to the left of the leading lines to give a good berth to Blind Rocks, and as Calf Island comes abeam identify the Obelisk on the Aranmore shore. Do not turn to starboard until the peak of Moylecorragh (162m) comes in line with the Obelisk, 241°; this leads S of Blind Rocks and N of **Calf Island Shoal**, which has a least depth of 3·4m. There is however no harm in continuing southwards until the Obelisk bears W before turning in to the anchorage.

Anchorage

The best area is NE of the Obelisk and S of Calf Island. There are a good many moorings there, but room to anchor outside them. This is a safe anchorage, usually comfortable in settled or W weather, but sometimes subject to swell. There is also plenty of room to anchor E of the Obelisk but it is probably more exposed to swell there. Stackamore quay is just W of the Obelisk with a slip and FY light. There is 0·7m alongside at the steps and a little less along the inner half. The ferry pier and slip are 1·5 cables S of this quay. The ferry pier has deep water alongside and is a handy place for a short visit to pick up stores.

Yachts should anchor so as to leave ample room for the ferry to manoeuvre. A tripping line is recommended since the bottom is fouled by the ground chains of a former trot of visitors' moorings. The bay close to the old drying pier further S at Leabgarrow is encumbered with rocks and unsuitable for anchoring.

Facilities

Water at ferry pier. Diesel (in cans), contact Aranmore Co-op. Small shop, restaurants, pubs, PO. Doctor. Car ferry to Burtonport. RNLI all-weather lifeboat station.

BURTONPORT

AC2792, Imray C53 and Plan
54°59'·5N 8°29'W

Burtonport (Ailt an Chorráin) is the principal mainland harbour on this coast and the ferry port for Aranmore. The islands in the approach were once the centre of a major fishery enterprise. Around 1784, the local landowner William Burton Conyngham built docks, houses and boatyards on Edernish, Inishcoo and the large island to the south, Inis Mhic an Doirn, which he renamed Rutland in honour of the Duke of Rutland, who was Lord Lieutenant of Ireland at the time. The enterprise was short-lived, but fascinating relics are still to be found, including an unexpected row of Georgian terrace houses on Edernish.

Burtonport today has a small fishing harbour managed by Donegal County Council. The harbour offers excellent shelter in all weathers. Yachts are welcome on the understanding that the Aranmore ferries and the fishing boats have priority. In particular the ferry must be allowed room to manoeuvre.

Yachts should avoid the former anchorage at Rutland Harbour on account of the ferry and fishing boat traffic to Burtonport. The former Black Hole anchorage and the old quays on West Edernish Island are no longer available due to private developments and fish farming activities.

Burtonport has been identified by Donegal County Council as a future location for marina development.

Main approach – Rutland North Channel

Rutland North Channel is well lit and beaconed. The passage should be made under power only, due to the presence of ferry and fishing vessel traffic in this narrow channel. **Dirty Rock**, 0·5 cable W of the W end of Eighter Island, is particularly dangerous since it is close to the channel, covers at HW and in calm weather does not break. From S of **Blind Rocks**, the transit of **Carrickbealatroha Lower** and **Lackmorris** perches leads clear W of **Dirty Rock**. On this transit, pick up the **Inishcoo** leading beacons, 119°, which lead in and very close S of **Carrickatine** beacon (QR). Immediately beyond this, the leading line of the **Rutland** beacons, 137°, must be followed closely, in particular erring nothing to starboard. Then steer for **Nancy's Rock** beacon (QG), leave it close to starboard and **Edernish** beacon (QR) close to port. Keep to the Edernish side of the channel until the **Burtonport** leading beacons line up. Turn on to the leading line steering 068° and proceed up the dredged channel leaving the pier channel beacon to port. Steer for the conspicuous ice house on the NW side of the harbour until the entrance is well abeam, then turn in.

There is a conspicuous wind turbine on the shore 1 cable S of the harbour.

Burtonport Harbour from the N in 1997. The area of reefs and islets to the right of the picture has since been reclaimed and fronted with rock armouring facing the harbour, and a wind turbine stands to the right of the large sheds, top R

Burtonport Harbour

The SE part of the harbour is shallow and encumbered by small craft moorings; the NW part, with both sides of the pier, and the approach channel, is dredged to 3·8m. Yachts should raft up to fishing boats against the pier but must be prepared to move as required. In settled weather it is possible to lie against the outer (NW) side of the pier. A fenderboard would be required if lying directly against either side of the open-piled pier. The E wall of the harbour, SE of the ferry berth, is available as a temporary berth at high tide. To the N of the root of the pier is a small drying dock with up to 4m at MHWS and a clean, gently shelving concrete bottom. This is available for emergency repairs.

Harbour dues may be levied. The harbour office monitors VHF Ch 16, working channel 12. Contact HM for advice on berthing and facilities. Constant +0050 Galway; MHWS 3·9m, MHWN 2·9m, ML 2·2m.

Facilities

Supermarket, pubs, restaurants, PO, mechanical and electrical repairs. Bottled gas. Water and diesel (by hose) on the pier. Petrol at filling station, 800m Buses to Letterkenny, Fintown and Dublin. Airport at Carrickfin, 13 km. Car ferry to Aranmore.

South Channel or Duck Sound

54°58'·9N 8°28'·3W

This channel, between Duck Island and the N tip of Rutland Island, should not be confused with Rutland South Channel. Pilotage of Duck Sound is tricky and it is simpler and safer to use the N channel for access to Burtonport. The narrow and shallow part of Duck Sound is just SE of the South Channel red perch, where there is 0·9m. Approaching through the South Sound of Aran, and with sufficient rise of tide, turn to starboard when Cloghcor Point is abeam and head for a point midway between Lackmorris and South Channel perches, leaving Carrickbealatroha Upper beacon 0·5 cable to port. Pass 40m S of the South Channel perch and head E towards a small rock W of Rutland. When the Inishcoo rear leading beacon is in line with the N point of Rutland steer towards it and pass close to the point after which you are soon in the main channel. If turning N wait until Nancy's Rock beacon is visible; this avoids a rock extending ESE from Duck Island. Going out, use the same line until the NW corner of Duck Island bears N when turn to pass 40 m S of the red perch.

Rutland South Channel

54°57'·8N 8°27'·6W

This channel is extremely hazardous on account of the many unmarked rocks and the strong tidal stream, which runs on to the reefs N of Inishfree at up to 6 knots. Strangers are strongly advised to use the North Channel in preference. Directions are given here for the sake of completeness but should be used only by shallow draft vessels with sufficient power to overcome the current. The passage should only be attempted around HW as there are patches, including the narrows, with as little as 0·3m at LAT. The channel at the narrows is only 30m wide.

Start the approach from near Illancrone at HW Galway or 15 minutes later (the same time is about right for leaving Burtonport). Leave Turk Rocks beacon to starboard and head for the middle of Rutland Island; if it is more convenient to leave Turk Rocks to port, head N until on the first transit. This involves identifying Corren's Rock beacon and S Rutland conical beacon to the left of it, both off the SE point of Rutland. Bring S Rutland beacon in line with a church on the skyline 057°; the church has a slate roof and is towards the right of a group of buildings. When nearly halfway along the S shore of Rutland, if the distinctive conical Errigal Mountain is visible, bring it in line with S Rutland beacon 071°. When the beacons are equidistant steer midway between them. If Errigal cannot be seen and if there is difficulty in getting the exact bearing on the beacon, it is better to steer for the tip of Rutland Island and turn to leave both the beacons to port when Corren's comes abeam. After passing the beacons continue E for 0·75 cable before heading due N for Yellow Rock beacon. Approaching Yellow Rock alter course to leave it 65m to starboard, then

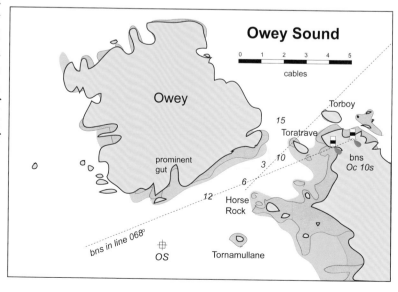

Owey Sound

0 1 2 3 4 5
cables

Owey

prominent gut

Torboy

15

Toratrave

Horse Rock

10

3

6

12

bns Oc 10s

bns in line 068°

OS

Tornamullane

steer to leave Teige's Rock Beacon 20m to starboard and from it steer W to the Rutland shore where there is a slightly prominent boulder. When the shore is just 40 m away turn towards the S point of Edernish Island, which means continuing close to Rutland at the start of the passage.

Going out, steer from Yellow Rock beacon for a group of houses on Inishfree. When passing between the pair of beacons steer well over towards Rutland to get the conical beacon bearing 071° as soon as possible.

OWEY
AC1883
Owey Island is free of offlying dangers except on the SW side where a number of rocks terminate in Tornagaravan, 9m high, and on the SE where a spit extends part of the way across the sound. Red granite cliffs with many caves on the W and N sides make impressive scenery. There is no secure anchorage but in settled sea conditions there can be good shelter in W wind on the SE side of the island off the village in 5m. There is a good boat landing

at a small quay in the deep, narrow gut just N of the E point. The island has occasional summer residents but no facilities.

Owey Sound
⊕ *OS* 55°02'·7N 8°27'W
Owey Sound presents no difficulty except in high swell or strong SW or N winds, but cannot be used at night. It is however possible to go through in strong W winds when it would be particularly unpleasant W of the island. Heading straight from Aran Sound identify **Tornamullane Rock**; if it does not show up well, the gut on the SE coast of Owey is conspicuous and makes a good mark. Do not err to the E of a bearing of 190° on **Ballagh Rocks,** in order to avoid **Bullignamirra** (dries 3·7m) and **Rinnagy Rock** (dries 2·4m) and the area S and SE of them, which is incompletely surveyed. Approaching Owey Sound, leave **Tornamullane Rock** 1 cable to starboard and then steer N until the black and white banded leading beacons near the N point of Cruit Island come in line 068°. Steer on this transit until the sound is well open to the N, then turn to port

Cruit Bay from SW; Corillan and Gortnasate Point centre R, Inishillintry upper L; Inishfree, Gola and Inishmeane top centre, Bloody Foreland Hill top R

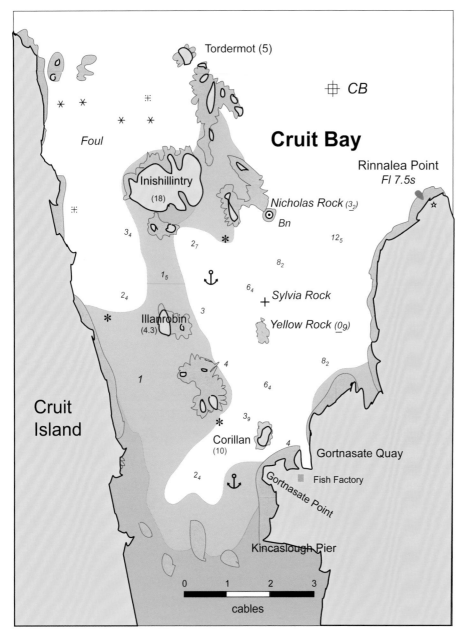

Tordermot (5)

⊕ *CB*

Cruit Bay

Rinnalea Point
Fl 7.5s

Foul

Inishillintry
(18)

Nicholas Rock (3₂)

Bn

3₄

2₇

12₅

1₅

8₂

⚓

6₄

+ *Sylvia Rock*

2₄

Yellow Rock (0₉)

⚹

Illanrobin
(4.3)

3

⚹

4

8₂

1

6₄

3₉

Corillan
(10)

4

Gortnasate Quay

2₄

⚓

Gortnasate Point

Fish Factory

Cruit Island

Kincaslough Pier

0   1   2   3

cables

Lights and Marks

Rinnalea Point, the N extremity of Mullaghderg, shows Fl 7·5s 19m 9M visible only between 132° and 167°. The light is on a 2·5m tower which is inconspicuous by day as it is the same colour as the rocks behind it. On **Gortnasate Quay** there is a light Fl R 5s. The tower in ruins standing at a height of 48m on the level ridge of Mullaghderg is conspicuous from all directions and an unmistakable daymark.

Approach

From Owey Sound or the W there are no offlying dangers apart from the **Stag Rocks,** well offshore. There is a rock 1·5 cables NE of the N point of Cruit Island. The sound W of Tordermot and Inishillintry should not be mistaken for Cruit Bay. Leave Tornamuldoo, Tordermot (5m high) and Illannanoon (9m high) a cable to starboard. Leave **Nicholas Rock** beacon to starboard and steer straight for **Corillan**, 10m high and rocky. To pass well E of the unmarked **Sylvia** and **Yellow Rocks** keep the E side of Corillan in line with Gortnasate Point. Passing W of Corillan, stay within 0·5 cable of the island to avoid a drying rock less than a cable to the WNW. Approaching from the N, give the shore S of Rinnalea Point a berth of a cable. The ebb tide runs out strongly.

and hold mid-channel between **Toratrave** (13m) and Owey. A spit with 3m extends 2 cables SE from Owey; it is safe to make the turn to port off the leading line once the NW points of Toratrave and **Torboy** (2 cables NE) come in line. The lights, Oc 10s, on the leading beacons are reported unreliable.

CRUIT BAY

⊕ *CB* 55°02'·8N 8°24'W
AC1883 and Plan

Cruit Bay is a good anchorage, easy of access and secure in all summer winds. However, swell in N winds makes it uncomfortable at times, and much of it is encumbered with moorings. The channel to the W of Inishillintry has more rocks than are shown on AC1883 and is not navigable by yachts. A stranger should not attempt to enter Cruit Bay at night.

Anchorages *(all on sand)*

- The best anchorage is S of Corillan in 2m.
- The area a little more than 2 cables SW of Corillan has many moorings; it is possible to anchor just N of them.
- With careful pilotage it is possible to reach an anchorage S of Inishillintry. Enter close SE of Nicholas Beacon and keep the beacon bearing between 045° and 055°. This leads between two rocks and beyond them there is an area about 3m deep and good room to anchor. The best sheltered part is reported to be NW away from

View NE over Gola North Sound. Go Island foreground, Gola centre, with Portacrin L and Gubnadough R; Inishmeane and Inishsirrer top centre and Bloody Foreland in the distance

the rocks with Nicholas Beacon bearing 065° and Gortnasate Quay bearing between 150° and 156°. There is also an entrance to this anchorage from Corillan keeping Gortnasate Quay bearing 151° and heading towards the right hand of two rocks just S of Inishillintry's S point, passing through a 0·5 cable gap between Yellow Rock and the rocky area SW of it.

Gortnasate Quay
55°02'·2N 8°24'·3W
On the E side of a narrow inlet E of Corillan is a 100m-long quay, with a road connecting it to Kincashla village 1 km to the SE. The quay has deep water alongside and there is a fish factory at the head of the inlet. Water is available at the fish factory; shops and PO at Kincashla. The disused Kincashla pier ("Kincasla" on the chart), just SE of Gortnasate Point, dries.

Carnboy Channel
⊕*CC* 55°03'N 8°21'·6W
AC1883, and Plan of Gola Sound
Carnboy Channel is the passage between the mainland and the rocks to the S and SE of Inishfree. From the S, **Rabbit Rock**, which always shows, should be left close to port. The main challenge lies in negotiating the 1-cable-wide gap between (on the E) the rocks extending 2 cables out from Carnboy Point and (on the W) **Bullignagappul** (dries 0·3m) and **Bullignamort** (0·3m). A stranger should not attempt this passage in poor visibility or at night due to the difficulty of identifying the leading marks. The summit of Inishmeane, 3M to the N, just open of Gubnadough, the E extremity of Gola, 012°, leads through the gap, as do the leading beacons on Mullaghdoo Point, 184°. The F Or lights on these are reported unreliable, and the beacons themselves are hard to pick out by day.

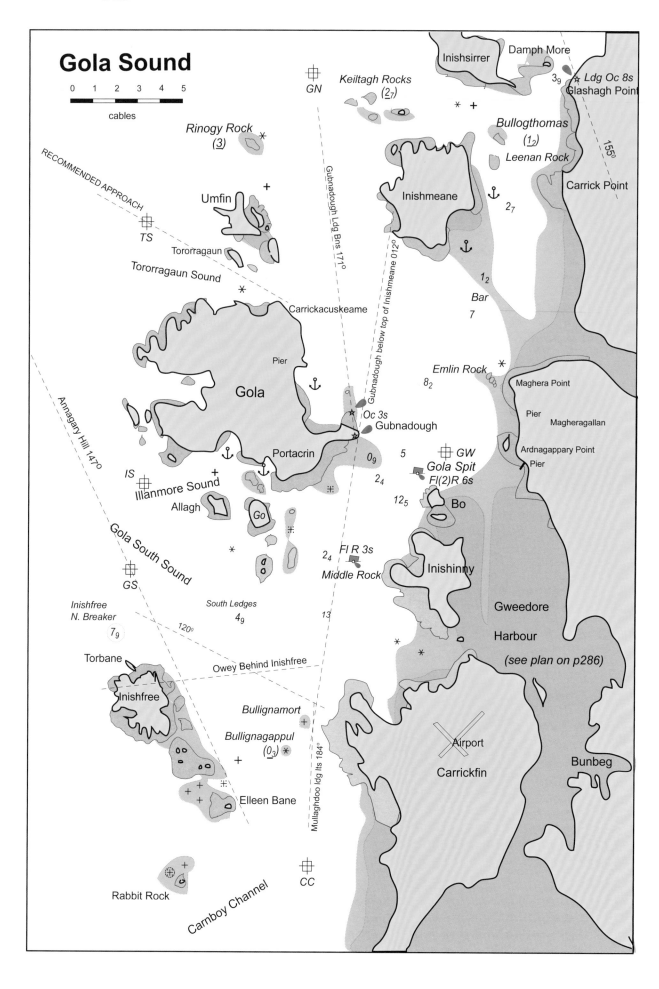

Gola Sound

0 1 2 3 4 5

cables

RECOMMENDED APPROACH

GN

Keiltagh Rocks (*2₇*)

Inishsirrer

Damph More

3₉ ☆ *Ldg Oc 8s* Glashagh Point

Bullogthomas (*1₂*)

155°

Rinogy Rock (*3*) ✳

Leenan Rock

Carrick Point

Umfin ✛

Inishmeane

⚓

2₇

TS

Tororragaun

Tororragaun Sound ✳

1₂

Bar

7

Carrickacuskeame

Gubnadough Ldg Bns 171°

Gubnadough below top of Inishmeane 012°

Emlin Rock

Maghera Point

8₂

Pier

Pier *Magheragallan*

⚓

Gola

⚓

☆ *Oc 3s*

☆ Gubnadough

Ardnagappary Point Pier

Portacrin

⚓

0₉

5

GW Gola Spit Fl(2)R 6s

Annagary Hill 147°

2₄

12₅

Bo

IS

Illanmore Sound ✛

Allagh

Go

Inishinny

✳

Gola South Sound

2₄ *Fl R 3s*

Middle Rock

Gweedore

GS

South Ledges

4₉

13

Harbour

Inishfree N. Breaker (7₉)

120°

(see plan on p286)

Torbane

Owey Behind Inishfree

Inishfree

Bullignamort

Bullignagappul (*0₃*) ✳

Airport

Mullaghdoo Lds lts 184°

Elleen Bane ✛

Carrickfin

Bunbeg

⊕ ✛

Rabbit Rock

Carnboy Channel

CC

Once N of Carnboy Point, identify Middle Rock buoy at the S end of Gola Roads and steer to leave it close to port.

GOLA ISLAND AND SOUND
55°04'·7N 8°21'W
AC1883 and Plan

Approaches to Gola Anchorages, Gweedore Harbour and Bunbeg

There are many dangers N and S of Gola and several channels inside the island. None of the approaches is simple for a stranger and in bad weather and especially in poor visibility a yacht coming from the S would be safer to make for Cruit Bay or Aran Road. Coming from the N in good visibility it is safe to go in through Gola N Sound. There are leading lights on Gubnadough, Oc 3s 2M, front white pillar with black band 9m, rear black pillar with white band 13m, leading 171°.

Gola lost its permanent population in the mid-1960's but has several houses maintained in good repair, a small number of residents in summer, and a tourist boat from Magheragallon and Bunbeg.

Gola South Sound
⊕ *GS* 55°04'·4N 8°23'·1W

Rocks and breakers extend almost a mile south of Gola. In settled weather it is safe to give Torbane and the N side of Inishfree a berth of 1·5 cables, but in heavy weather or any appreciable swell it is advisable to stay well outside Inishfree North Breaker, 2 cables NNW of Torbane. Approach with Annagary Hill bearing 147°, open left of Innisfree, until 2 cables N of Innisfree, then steer 120° until Owey Island is just shut in behind the height of Innisfree. Then steer 085° until Gubnadough is below the top of Inishmeane, and turn to port leaving the two red buoys – Middle Rock, Fl R 3s and Gola Spit, Fl(2) R 6s – to port.

Illanmore Sound
⊕ *IS* 55°04'·9N 8°22'·9W

Illanmore Sound is the most direct passage from seaward but has several hazardous rocks. To avoid **Passage Rock**, in the middle of the channel N of Allagh Island, first identify **Torroe** off Gola at the entrance to the

Sound. Leaving Torroe 0·5 cable to port, turn to port towards the large bay on Gola. When off the middle of the bay turn to starboard and head towards the NW point of Go Island. Give Go Island a berth of 50 to 80m to starboard, then keep the N point of Allagh Island just open of Go Island so as to pass N of **Leonancoyle Rock**. Continue on this line until Gubnadough (the E point of Gola) is in line with the top of Inishmeane before turning to port.

Tororragaun Sound
⊕ *TS* 55°06'·2N 8°22'·8W

Tororragaun Sound is the gap between the N side of Gola and **Tororragaun Rock**, 19m high. It is easy to identify and in fine weather is the shortest and simplest route from Owey to Gola Pier. It is probably dangerous in any swell as there is a ridge of rocks right across it, with less than 1m and two drying rocks in the S half, but with 4·6m least charted depth on the N half. Enter just 50m off the SW of Tororragaun, which is steep-to, and then steer for the NE point of Gola, labelled Carrickacuskeame on the chart.

Gola North Sound – Approach from the N
⊕ *GN* 55°06'·9N 8°21'·5W

The entrance lies between **Keiltagh Rocks** (dries 2·7m) to port and **Rinogy Rock** (dries 3·0m) to starboard. The line of the leading beacons on Gubnadough, 171°, leads midway between these dangers. If the beacons cannot be distinguished, steer towards the N point of Umfin Island until Inishsirrer light beacon bears 050° and Gubnadough

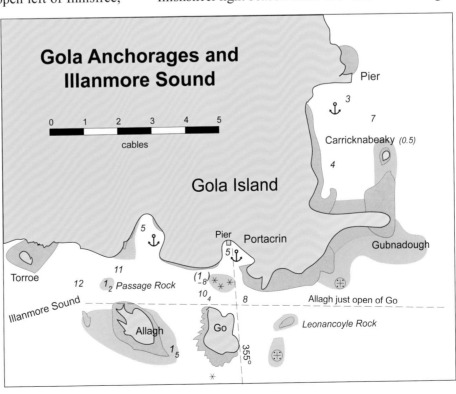

Gola Anchorages and Illanmore Sound

171° (Illancarragh just open of Gubnadough), then steer direct for Gubnadough.

Gola Anchorages
AC1883 and Plan

- S of the pier on the E side of the island, in 3m, sand. May be subject to swell. The pier has sufficient depth alongside towards HW to offer a temporary berth in swell-free conditions.
- In winds from NW through N to E, the bay on Gola N of Allagh Island is a very suitable anchorage and easy to enter using the directions for Illanmore Sound. Anchor in 5m staying more than 0·5 cable from the W side and giving the NE side a fair berth as well.
- The anchorage off the pier at Portacrin, N of Go Island on the S side of Gola, is smaller and more difficult to enter but offers good shelter and is convenient for going ashore. Approach from the NE point of Go Island and head 355° towards the pier with a long single-storey house in transit above it. The channel is very narrow so it is simplest to enter near LW when the rocks show clearly. Anchor in 4·5m in line with the pier and opposite the other possible entrance from the W.

A ferry runs from the pier on the E of the island to Magheragallan Pier or Bunbeg on the mainland. There are no facilities on the island.

GWEEDORE HARBOUR AND BUNBEG
⊕*GW* 55°05'N 8°20'·2W
AC1883, Imray C53 and Plan
The entrance to Gweedore Harbour crosses a shallow bar, and the channel requires care and has strong tidal streams, but it is well marked and leads to a secure and attractive anchorage. The harbour at Bunbeg is used by a diminishing number of fishing boats and the Tory Island ferry, and yachts are welcome.

Lights and marks
Bo Island shows Fl G 3s, **No.1** and **No.5** QG, **Nos.2, 4** and **6** QR. **No.3** is unlit. A stranger should not, however, attempt to enter in the dark.

Caution
GPS chartplotters should not be implicitly relied upon in Gweedore Harbour and its approaches due to the age of the survey data and the likelihood of changes in the channel and sandbanks. It is essential to maintain good conventional pilotage with continuous use of the echosounder.

Directions
The entrance lies between Bo Island and Ardnagappary Point, and has a reported depth of 1m at LAT. The best depth is close to the rocks

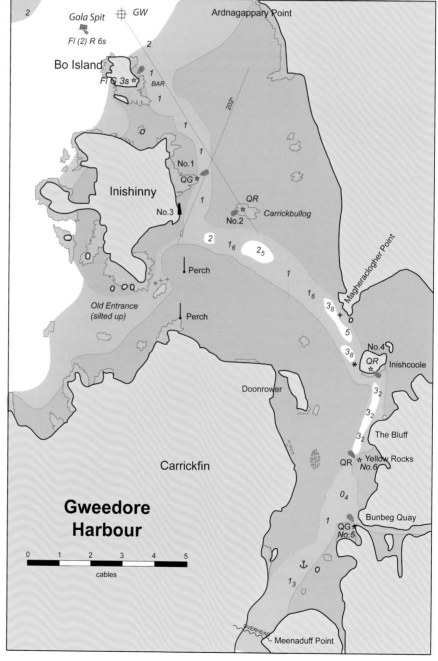

Gweedore Harbour from the NE; Inishinny, centre R, with Inishfree, Cruit and Aranmore top R

extending E of Bo; these can usually be seen below water. As soon as the E end of Bo is abeam, steer towards Carrickbullog, and when E of the NE point of Inishinny turn S to pass just 12m E of No.1 beacon. From here steer 202° and when abeam of No.3 beacon (on the E point of Inishinny), turn SE for about 60m, then turn to pass 120 to 150m S of No.2 beacon on Carrickbullog. When the E of Carrickbullog is abeam turn on to 140°. Give Magheraclogher Point a berth of 100m to clear the submerged **rock** about 50m off it, then stay 70m W of Inishcoole to clear the rock there, which just dries; the tidal current may indicate its position. When past the rock keep a little nearer to the island and follow its S shore round to clear a spit extending E, just to the S of Inishcoole. Then head past The Bluff, which is steep-to, and W of No.6 beacon. This beacon is on a **rock**, and all the area to the E of it dries. The channel between here and No.5 beacon, at the entrance to Bunbeg, now has at least 0·4m and does not dry as shown on AC1883. From No.6 beacon head for the mid-channel between Meenaduff Point and the shore opposite.

Anchorages

Anchor 2 cables SW of No.5 beacon, 1·5m, sand. Tidal streams here are still significant, so a second anchor may be advisable. Anchoring in the channel N of Bunbeg entrance is not recommended because of the ferry traffic. Constant +0055 Galway; MHWS 3·8m, MHWN 2·9m, ML 2·2m.

Caution

A power cable with a clearance of 6·4m crosses the channel at Meenaduff Point, 5 cables S of Bunbeg entrance.

Bunbeg

55°03'·5N 8°19'W
See Plan
Bunbeg Harbour occupies the inlet between steep rocky shores at the mouth of the Clady River, E of the No 5 beacon in Gweedore Harbour. It is used by the Tory Island ferryboat and some small fishing vessels, but yachts are welcomed. It offers excellent shelter. Leave the No 5 beacon 10m to starboard on entering. The quay, on the N side of the inlet, is 300m in length and has a reported depth of 2m alongside. There is limited but adequate turning room between the quay and the shore on the S side. The ferry's berth is near the centre of the quay, where the crane is positioned, and should be left unobstructed. The tiny bays on either side of the islet opposite the quay are shallow; the W one has some small-boat moorings

Bunbeg from the S at LW; Yellow Rock and the No.6 beacon, L centre. Inishmeane, Inishsirrer and Bloody Foreland Hill in the distance

in it and the E one, known as the Shingles, dries out. The old harbour further up the creek also dries.

Facilities

Water on the quay. Diesel by tanker. Restaurant and bar at the harbour. Shops, pubs and PO at Bunbeg village, 1 km. This is the nearest harbour to the airport at Carrickfin, on the W side of Gweedore Harbour.

Magheragallan

55°05'·2N 8°19'·8W

There are two small concrete piers on the coast at Magheragallan, S of Maghera Point. The more N'ly, from which a ferry runs to Gola, would provide a possible temporary berth for a yacht above half tide in settled weather.

Inishmeane

55°05'·7N 8°20'W

AC1883

Passage between Inishmeane and the mainland is straightforward in swell-free conditions with sufficient rise of tide. Heading N give Maghera Point a berth of 3 cables to clear Emlin Rock, then hold mid-channel to find the deepest water. There is a small pier on the E side of Inishmeane, and anchorage is available either ESE of the island, south of the bar, or just N of its E point, N of the bar, taking care to stay well clear of Leenan Rock.

Inishsirrer

Locally known as Inishutter, the island has occasional residents in summer. There is a slipway at its SE end. A white concrete tower on the NW end of the island shows Fl 3·7s 20m 4M.

Inishsirrer Strait

55°06'·6N 8°19'·4W

AC1883

A safe and simple passage except in strong onshore wind or high swell when it should not be attempted. **Damph More** always shows, but all the other rocks SW of it and E of the anchorages cover. From the S, enter the strait with E side of Damph More bearing 000° to pass between the spit E of **Damph Beg** and the reefs SW of Glashagh Point. Then steer 030° to leave Damph More 0·5 cable to port. Two black and white banded concrete beacons Oc 8s 12m and 17m 3M on the shore N of Glashagh Point, in line 137·25° lead NE of the small rocks N of Damph More and SW of **Bunaninver Shoal**, so in bad weather keep a bit nearer to Inishsirrer. In settled conditions it is however possible to head N for Bloody Foreland as soon as the leading beacons come in line; this takes a yacht inside Bunaninver Shoal.

Anchorage

At the SE of Inishsirrer there is a good anchorage sheltered from WNW through S to ENE. It should be approached with the prominent kelp store building (just inside the W of the quay) in line with the W side of Inishmeane 233°. When **Damph More** comes abeam to port steer for the summit of Inishmeane. This leads to an anchorage in 3·5m, sand, E of the kelp store.

Bunaninver Port
55°07'·4N 8°18'·7W
AC1883
Bunaninver Port is a pleasant temporary anchorage in good weather. The entrance breaks right across in any rough sea. Keep well outside until you can head in exactly 134° to the inner end so as to avoid the outer rocks on either side. Anchor outside the narrower part. There is a slip on the N side.

BLOODY FORELAND
Bloody Foreland Hill, 315 m high, slopes down gradually to the low point of the headland from which reefs extend for 1 cable. Swell is apt to run high off the point, so it should be given a berth of at least 5 cables. However the headland is not as savage as it sounds; the name is derived from the glorious pink hue which the sunset lends to the granite rocks.

Lights
Bloody Foreland, 4m white beacon, Fl WG 7·5s 14m W6M G4M W 062°–232°, G 232°–062°. Shows green over the islands and rocks to the SW and NE, white elsewhere (including over Tory Island)
Tory Island, black tower, white band, Fl(4) 30s 40m 27M, Racon (M) 12-23M

INSIDE PASSAGE SOUTH FROM BLOODY FORELAND
AC1883 and 2792, and see also Plans of Gola Sound and Aran Sound
If there is sufficient height of tide to pass inside Inishmeane, steer from Bloody Foreland towards the NW end of Inishsirrer until the leading marks on Glashagh Point come into line, then head in on this line 155° until **Damph More** is well abeam. Turn SSW, giving Carrick Point a berth of 2 cables, and hold mid-channel between Inishmeane and the mainland. Give Maghera Point a berth of 3 cables to clear **Emlin Rock**, then leave the two red buoys in Gola Roads close to starboard. With Gubnadough under the summit of Inishmeane, 012°, pass inside **Bullignamort** and identify **Elleen Bane** and **Rabbit Rock** to the SW. Leave each of these a cable to starboard, and once round Rabbit Rock head for the N end of Owey.

When Owey Sound opens up, leave Torboy close to port and hold mid-channel between Owey and Toratrave until the leading beacons S of Torboy come in line, 070°. Turn to starboard on this line steering 250° until **Ballagh Rock** with its conspicuous light beacon, at the entrance to the North Sound of Aran, is identified. When Ballagh Rock bears 190°, steer to pass close W of it, erring nothing to port in order to avoid **Rinnagy** and **Bullignamirra** and the incompletely surveyed area S and SE of them. Approaching Ballagh Rock bring the leading marks on Aran in line 186° and steer on this line. This passes very close to **Blind Rocks**, 2 cables SW of Ballagh Rock, so in a swell it may be advisable to borrow a little to the left of the line, but beware of **Dirty Rock** to the W of Eighter Island. Keep **Carrickbealatroha Lower** beacon slightly to the right of **Lackmorris** beacon, then leave Carrickbealatroha Lower to port and turn to starboard to pass 1·5 cables W of Lackmorris and **Carrickbealatroha Upper** beacons. Once past Carrickbealatroha Upper beacon, turn to port to bring it in line with Ballagh Rock astern, and steer 174° on this transit to pass W of **Turk Rocks** and out through South Sound.

For detailed descriptions of the marks in the Sound of Aran, refer to the main text.

Appendix 1

CHARTS AND ADMIRALTY PUBLICATIONS

Admiralty (UK Hydrographic Office) Charts:

No	Title	Plans	Scale 1:	Pub date
1123	Western Approaches to St George's Channel and Bristol Channel		500,000	Dec-06
1787	Carnsore Point to Wicklow Head		100,000	Nov-91
1772	Rosslare Europort and Wexford Harbour with Approaches	Rosslare	30,000	Jul-05
2049	Old Head of Kinsale to Tuskar Rock		150,000	Feb-95
2740	Saltee Islands		25,000	Aug-76
2046	Waterford Harbour, New Ross and Dunmore East	New Ross, Dunmore East	25,000	Sep-06
2017	Dungarvan Harbour		15,000	Nov-98
2071	Youghal Harbour		12,500	Oct-91
1765	Old Head of Kinsale to Power Head		50,000	Jun-05
1777	Port of Cork, Lower Harbour and Approaches		12,500	Mar-05
1773	Port of Cork, Upper Harbour		12,500	Mar-05
2424	Kenmare River to Cork Harbour		150,000	Feb-95
2053	Kinsale Harbour and Oysterhaven		12,500	Aug-04
2081	Courtmacsherry Bay		25,000	Nov-77
2092	Toe Head to Old Head of Kinsale	Glandore Harbour	50,000	Sep-93
3725	Baltimore Harbour		6,250	Nov-91
2129	Long Island Bay to Castle Haven		30,000	Feb-02
2184	Mizen Head to Gascanane Sound		30,000	Feb-02
2423	Mizen Head to Dingle Bay		150,000	Dec-81
2552	Dunmanus Bay	Dunbeacon Cove, Kitchen Cove, Dunmanus Harbour	30,000	May-80
1840	Bantry Bay - Black Ball Head to Shot Head	Castletownbere	30,000	Oct-79
1838	Bantry Bay - Shot Head to Bantry	Whiddy oil terminal	30,000	Jun-02
2495	Kenmare River	Dursey Sound, Sneem, Ballycrovane, Ardgroom & Kilmakilloge, Upper Kenmare River	60,000	Nov-81
2125	Valentia Island	Valentia Harbour	30,000	Nov-78
2789	Dingle Bay and Smerwick	Smerwick	60,000	Nov-02
2790	Ventry and Dingle Harbours, Blasket Islands	Blaskets at 1:37,500	15,000	Apr-94
2739	Brandon and Tralee Bays	Fenit	37,500	Mar-98
2254	Valentia to the Shannon		150,000	Nov-81
1819	Approaches to the River Shannon		50,000	May-06
1547	River Shannon - Kilcredaun Point to Ardmore Point	Kilrush	20,000	Mar-03
1548	River Shannon - Ardmore Point to Rinaleon Point		20,000	Dec-86
1549	River Shannon - Rinaleon Point to Shannon Airport	Foynes	20,000	Jun-01
1540	River Shannon - Shannon Airport to Limerick		12,500	Jun-81
1125	Western Approaches to Ireland		500,000	Jan-85
3338	Kilkee to Inisheer		50,000	Apr-80
2173	Loop Head to Slyne Head		150,000	Jul-84

No	Title	Plans	Scale 1:	Pub date
3339	Approaches to Galway Bay and the Aran Islands		50,000	Aug-05
1820	Aran Islands to Roonagh Head		75,000	Mar-84
1984	Galway Bay		30,000	Aug-05
1904	Galway Harbour	New Harbour	10,000	Mar-05
2096	Cashla Bay to Kilkieran Bay	Rossaveal	30,000	Mar-05
2709	Roundstone and Approaches		30,000	Nov-83
2420	Aran Islands to Broad Haven Bay		150,000	Jul-84
2708	Ballyconneely Bay to Clifden Bay with Slyne Head		25,000	Nov-83
2707	Kingstown to Cleggan Bays and Inishbofin to Inishturk		25,000	Nov-83
2706	Ballynakill and Killary Harbours and Approaches		25,000	May-82
2667	Clew Bay and Approaches	Newport	50,000	Feb-83
2057	Westport Bay		15,000	Aug-05
2725	Blacksod Bay to Tory Island		200,000	Oct-99
2704	Blacksod Bay and Approaches		50,000	Nov-81
2703	Broad Haven Bay and Approaches	Portnafrankagh	50,000	Feb-80
2767	Porturlin to Sligo Bay and Rathlin O'Birne Island		75,000	Dec-79
2715	Killala and Donegal	Donegal 15,000	25,000	Jul-77
2852	Approaches to Sligo	Sligo Harbour	20,000	Aug-06
2702	Donegal Bay		60,000	Oct-79
2792	Plans on the North West Coast of Ireland	Teelin, Church Pool, Killybegs, Sound of Aran and Burtonport	various	Oct-05
2723	Western Approaches to the North Channel		200,000	Dec-05
1879	Rathlin O'Birne Island to Aran Island		75,000	Oct-79
1883	Crohy Head to Bloody Foreland including Aran Island		30,000	Nov-81

The above are all available in electronic format via the Admiralty Raster Chart Service (ARCS). Up-to-date information on chart availability, both paper and electronic, is obtainable on www.ukho.gov.uk.

Standard Caution on Accuracy

The following Note, issued in 2007, appears on many of the charts of this coast:

"Owing to the age and quality of some of the source information, the charted detail may not be positioned accurately with respect to the horizontal datum, and therefore positions obtained from Global Navigation Satellite Systems such as GPS should not be relied upon when using this chart.

"Mariners are advised to use other methods to determine their position, particularly when navigating close to the shore or in the vicinity of dangers."

Admiralty Small Craft Folios

These Folios comprise charts in a 600 by 420mm format displaying all the coastal detail from the relevant individual charts and also selected areas from the smaller-scale charts. SC5622 Waterford to Kinsale and SC5623 Bantry Bay to Kinsale (both published Sept 2006) have 16 and 17 charts respectively. GPS positions may be plotted directly on these charts; there is no offset in horizontal datum.

Other Admiralty Publications

Irish Coast Pilot, NP40, 17th edition 2006
Published annually:
Admiralty Tide Tables, NP201 Volume 1 UK & Ireland
Admiralty List of Lights, NP74
Admiralty List of Radio Signals, NP281 Maritime Radio Stations

Admiralty List of Radio Signals, NP282 Aids to Navigation
Admiralty List of Radio Signals, NP283 Maritime Safety Information Services

Agents for Admiralty Charts and Publications

*   Windmill Leisure and Marine Ltd, 18A The Crescent, Monkstown, Co.Dublin, 01 460 0345, www.windmillleisure.com
*   Todd Chart Agency Ltd, Navigation House, 85 High Street, Bangor BT20 5BD, Northern Ireland, 028 9146 6640, fax 028 9147 1070, admiralty@toddchart.co.uk; www.toddchart.com
*   Union Chandlery Ltd, Penrose Quay, Cork, 021 427 1643
*   Galway Maritime, Lower Merchants' Road, Galway, 091 566568

Imray Charts

C57 Tuskar Rock to Old Head of Kinsale, 1:167,000, with plans of Kilmore Quay, Dunmore East, Waterford, Dungarvan, Youghal, Cork Lower Harbour, Crosshaven and Kinsale

C56 Cork Harbour to Dingle Bay, 1:170,000, with plans of Kinsale, Courtmacsherry, Glandore, Castle Haven, Baltimore, Schull, Crookhaven, Castletownbere, Glengarriff, Bantry, Ardgroom, Kilmakilloge, Sneem, Portmagee, Valentia and Dingle

C55 Dingle Bay to Galway Bay, 1:200,640, with plans of Dingle, Fenit, the Shannon, Kilrush, Foynes, Limerick, Galway Bay, Galway Harbour and Cashla Bay

C54 Galway Bay to Donegal Bay, with plans of Roundstone, Clifden Bay, Inishbofin, Cleggan Bay, Westport, Achill Sound, Portnafrankagh, Broad Haven and Sligo

C53 Donegal Bay to Rathlin Island, 1:191,200, with plans of Killybegs, Teelin, Sound of Aran and Burtonport, Gweedore Harbour and Approaches.

Appendix 2

CUSTOMS AND IMMIGRATION REQUIREMENTS

We are obliged for the following to the Revenue Service of Ireland

Yachts arriving in the Republic of Ireland from other countries of the European Union are normally required to report to Customs only if they have on board persons who do not have right of residence in the EU. This requirement is, however, waived in the case of voyages between the United Kingdom (including Northern Ireland and the Isle of Man) and the Republic of Ireland, since there are normally no immigration formalities between the two jurisdictions. Yachts arriving from outside the European Union must report to Customs on arrival. Yachts with goods to declare, or carrying restricted items such as firearms, must also report. The report should be made by telephone to the nearest customs office to the port of arrival: there are offices at Rosslare 05391 61310, Waterford 051 862145 or 087 642 6753, Cork 021 432 4444, Bantry 027 53210, Tralee 066 716 1000, Limerick 061 488000, Galway 091 536000, Sligo 071 914 8600 and Letterkenny 07491 69400. In the event of difficulty the report may be made at the nearest Garda station or by telephoning 1800 295 295. Harbourmasters can also provide advice. Yachts required to report should fly flag Q until clearance is obtained. Yachts being permanently imported from outside the State are also required to notify Customs within 3 days of arrival.

Under international law, the Customs authorities of a state have the right to examine any yacht within the territorial waters of the state, and in exceptional circumstances (such as suspicion of illegal goods on board) in international waters as well.

Yachts owned by EU residents should carry proof of VAT-paid status at all times. For further information see www.revenue.ie.

Appendix 3

MARITIME SAFETY INFORMATION

WEATHER FORECASTS

The principal sources of weather forecast information are the Coastguard Radio stations, national and local public broadcast radio stations, Met office phone and fax weather services, and the Internet.

Coastguard Radio Stations

Garda Costa na hÉireann, the Irish Coastguard Service, has its headquarters and Marine Rescue Coordination Centre at Leeson Lane, Dublin 2, and Sub-Centres at Valentia Island, Co. Kerry and Malin Head, Co. Donegal.

Dublin Coastguard Radio (phone 01 662 0922, 01 662 0923 and 01 678 2324) also operates stations at Carlingford, Wicklow Head, Rosslare and Mine Head.

Valentia Coastguard Radio (phone 066 947 6109) also operates stations at Cork (Roche's Point), Mizen Head, Bantry (Bere Island), Shannon (Loop Head) and Galway.

Malin Head Coastguard Radio (phone 074 937 0103) also operates stations at Clifden, Belmullet, Donegal Bay and Glen Head.

All these stations maintain a 24-hour listening watch on VHF channel 16 and working channels, and Valentia and Malin Head also listen on 2182 kHz MF. Weather forecasts and navigational warnings are broadcast at regular intervals on working channels, following a DSC alarm call and a SECURITÉ announcement on Ch 16 and 2182 kHz (Dublin uses VHF only). Working channels are as follows:

Carlingford VHF Ch 04
Dublin VHF Ch 83, MMSI 002500300
Wicklow Head VHF Ch 02
Rosslare VHF Ch 23
Mine Head VHF Ch 83
Cork VHF Ch 26
Mizen Head VHF Ch 04
Bantry VHF Ch 23
Valentia VHF Ch 24, 1752 kHz MF, MMSI 002500200
Shannon VHF Ch 28
Galway VHF Ch 04
Clifden VHF Ch 26
Belmullet VHF Ch 83
Donegal Bay VHF Ch 02

Glen Head VHF Ch 24
Malin Head VHF Ch 23, 1677 kHz MF, MMSI 002500100

Forecasts from Met Éireann, the Irish weather service, are provided for the coastal waters of Ireland up to 30M offshore and the Irish Sea, updated four times daily, valid for 24 hours and including an outlook for the following 24 hours. The forecast information is given clockwise around the coast, with the whole area divided into between one and four forecast areas, depending on the weather, using major coastal features as boundaries. The features used are shown on the chart below. Weather reports are given for six shore stations and six weather buoys; the positions of these and of the radio stations are also marked below.

Broadcast media

RTÉ1 broadcasts the sea area forecast for the coastal waters of Ireland and the Irish Sea four times daily on 88–90 MHz FM. Broadcast times are 0602, 1255, 1657 and 2355. The RTÉ broadcast includes the reports from the shore stations but not the weather buoys.

Some of the local radio stations, notably Radio kerry (88-90 and 95 MHz FM), also broadcast the sea area forecast.

BBC Radio 4 (198 KHz AM in Irish waters) broadcasts the shipping forecast for all the sea areas around the British Isles four times daily, at 0520, 1200, 1755 and 0048. Sea area Fastnet covers Carnsore Point to Valentia, Shannon covers Valentia to Slyne Head, and Malin covers Slyne Head northwards. Sea area Rockall is immediately offshore to the northwest of Slyne Head.

Navtex

Portpatrick and Malin Head are Navarea 1 Navtex stations, and transmit both Irish and British forecasts and navigational warnings.

Forecasts by phone and fax

Met Éireann operates a premium-rate telephone service providing the latest sea area forecast on 1 550 123 855. For faxed information, dial 1 570 131 838 and follow the voice instructions. For the text of the current sea area forecast the code is 0021, for

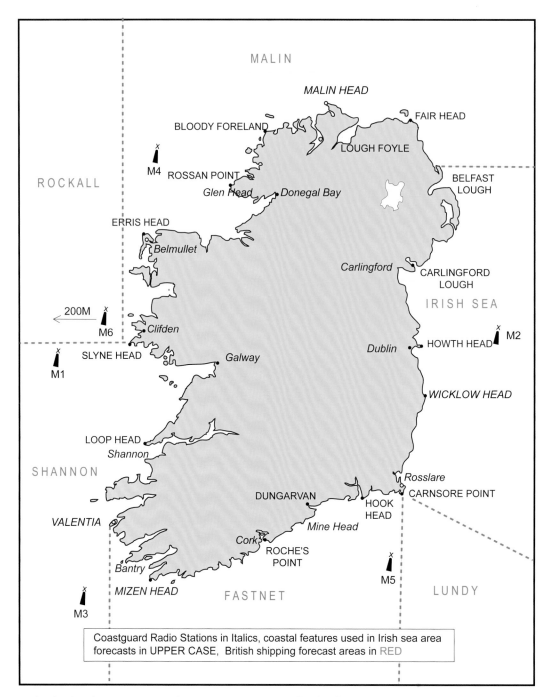

Coastguard Radio Stations in Italics, coastal features used in Irish sea area forecasts in UPPER CASE, British shipping forecast areas in RED

the current isobaric chart 0015 and for the 24 hour forecast isobaric chart 0016.

Internet

Sea area forecasts and isobaric weather charts are available on many websites. The principal ones are those of Met Éireann (www.met.ie/forecasts/seaarea) and the British Met Office (www.met-office.gov.uk). The European Centre for Medium-range Weather Forecasting (www.ecmwf.ie) is also reliable, as is www.theyr.net. Several clubs and voluntary organisations also have excellent websites with links to forecast sources; any of the standard search engines will reveal those currently active.

NAVIGATIONAL WARNINGS

Navigational warnings for the coastal waters of Ireland and for the the Irish Sea are regularly broadcast by the Irish and UK Coastguard Radio stations on their working channels.

MANDATORY SAFETY EQUIPMENT

In the Republic of Ireland it is mandatory for every vessel, regardless of size, to carry a lifejacket or personal flotation device for every person on board. Young persons under 16 must wear these, when on deck, when the vessel is under way. On a vessel under 7m in length, lifejackets must be worn by everyone on board.

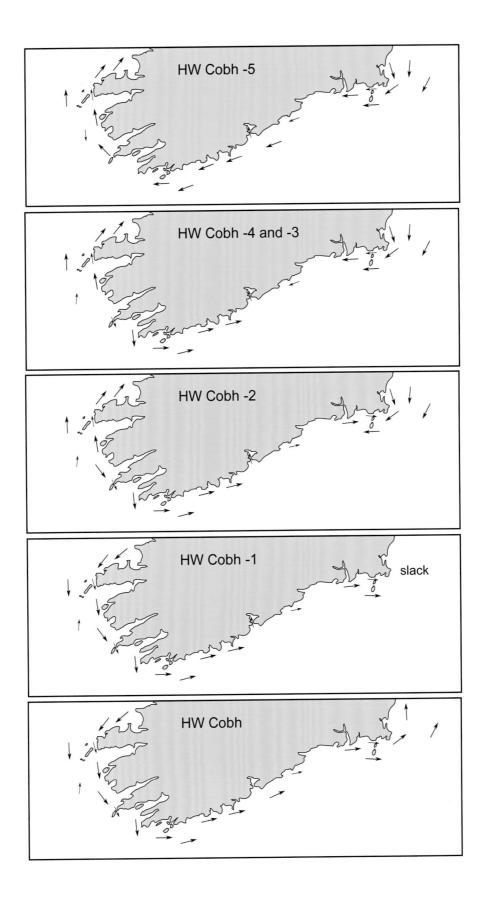

Appendix 4

TIDAL STREAMS

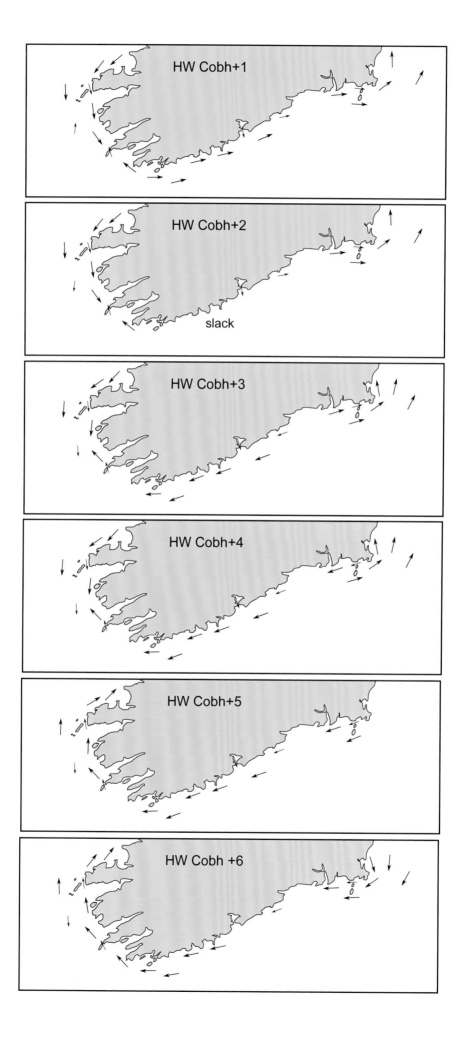

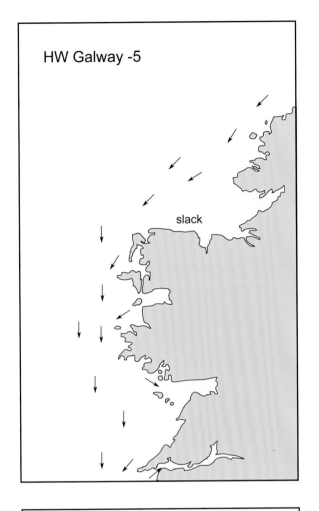

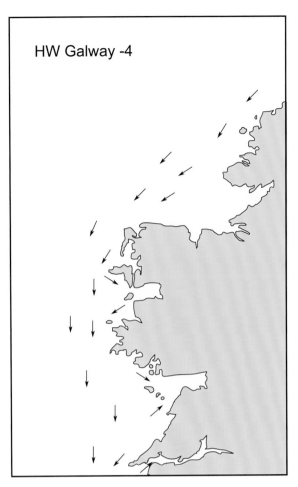

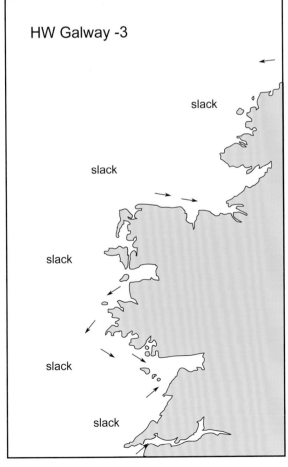

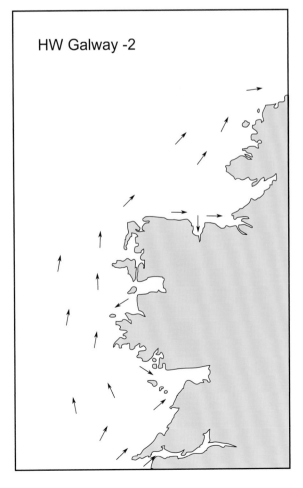

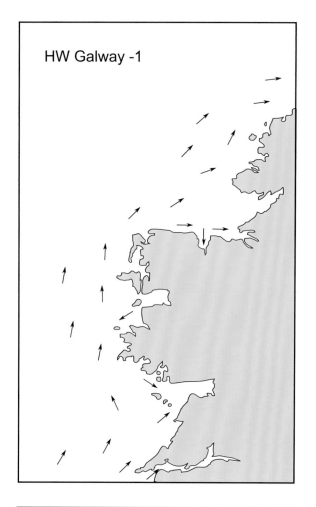

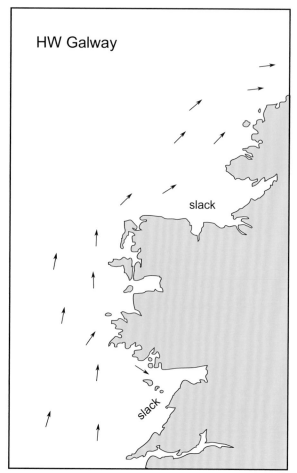

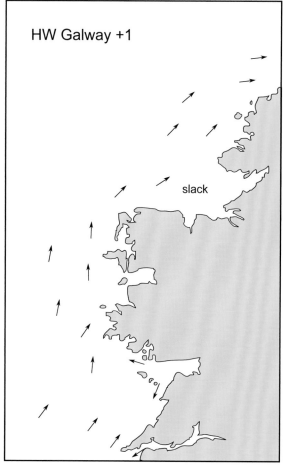

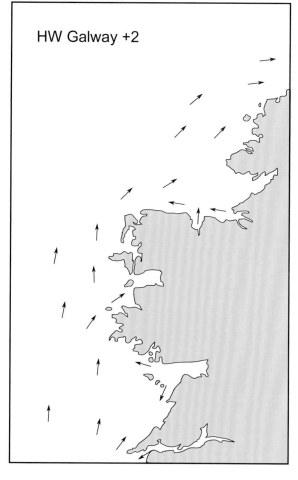

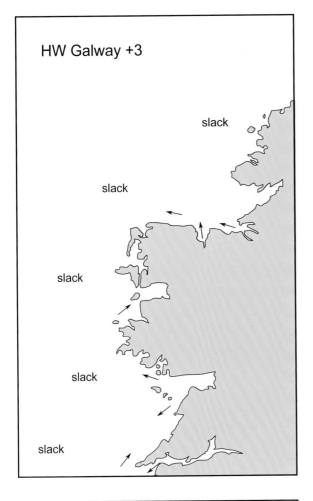

HW Galway +3

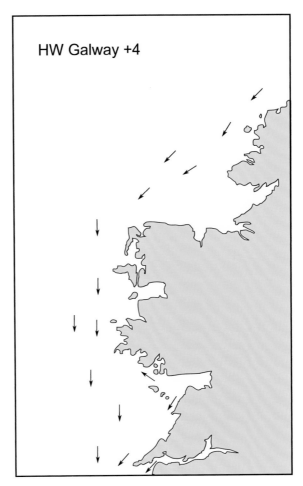

HW Galway +4

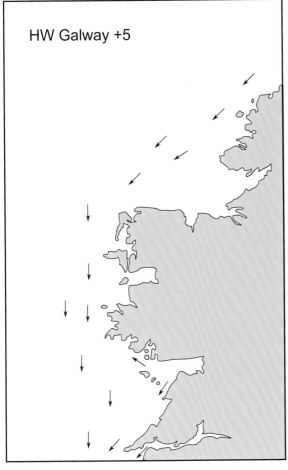

HW Galway +5

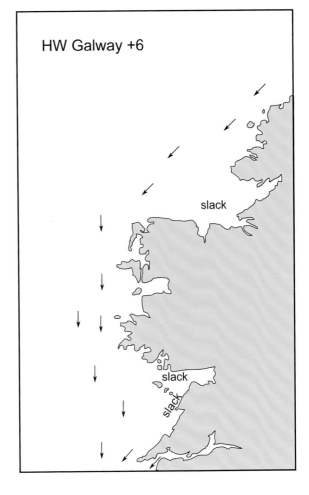

HW Galway +6

Appendix 5

TABLE OF DISTANCES

nautical miles

	Carnsore Point	Dunmore East	Helvick	Youghal	Ballycotton	Crosshaven	Oysterhaven	Kinsale	Courtmacsherry	Glandore	Castle Haven	Baltimore
Cape Clear	128	105	87	73	64	67	46	46	38	20	16	8
Baltimore	125	102	83	70	61	54	42	42	34	16	12	
Castle Haven	116	93	75	61	52	45	34	34	25	6		
Glandore	114	91	73	59	50	43	32	32	23			
Courtmacsherry	98	75	57	43	34	27	15	15				
Kinsale	88	65	47	34	25	17	5					
Oyster Haven	84	61	44	30	21	14						
Crosshaven	78	55	38	24	15							
Ballycotton	65	43	25	11								
Youghal	58	35	18									
Helvick	45	22										
Dunmore East	25											

	Baltimore	Schull	Crookhaven	Kitchen Cove	Dunbeacon	Berehaven	Glengarriff	Bantry	Sneem	Kilmakilloge	Derrynane	Ballinskelligs	Portmagee
Valencia	62	58	53	52	55	42	57	57	35	36	23	20	11
Portmagee	56	51	46	45	48	35	50	50	28	29	16	13	
Ballinskelligs	48	43	38	37	40	27	42	42	18	19	6		
Derrynane	44	39	34	33	36	23	38	38	14	15			
Kilmakilloge	52	47	42	41	44	31	46	46	4				
Sneem	51	46	41	40	43	30	45	45					
Bantry	42	37	32	28	31	17	6						
Glengarriff	43	38	33	29	32	18							
Berehaven	32	27	21	19	21								
Dunbeacon	36	31	25	4									
Kitchen Cove	32	27	21										
Dunmore East	14	8											
Schull	9												

	Valentia	Dingle	Blasket Sd	Smerwick	Brandon Bay	Fenit	Loop Head	Carrigaholt	Kilronan	Galway	Cashla Bay	Kilkieran	Roundstone
Slyne Head	97	95	85	75	70	72	54	67	30	50	32	24	15
Roundstone	94	93	82	77	70	72	52	65	22	40	23	15	
Kilkieran	93	91	81	75	67	70	48	62	14	35	15		
Cashla Bay	94	92	82	74	66	66	48	58	10	24			
Galway	103	101	91	84	75	77	57	68	25				
Kilronan	85	83	73	66	58	58	38	53					
Carrigaholt	58	56	46	38	27	26	11						
Loop Head	48	45	36	28	19	20							
Fenit	46	44	34	25	15								
Brandon Bay	34	32	22	15									
Smerwick	22	20	10										
Blasket Sd	12	10											
Dingle	13												

	Slyne Hed	Inishbofin	Clare Island	Westport	Achill Head	Elly Bay	Portnafrankagh	Broad Haven	Killala	Sligo	Killybegs	Teelin	Rathlin O'Birne	Burtonport
Bloody Foreland	139	128	119	131	103	101	86	80	64	61	53	45	35	12
Burtonport	128	117	108	120	92	90	75	69	54	51	43	35	25	
Rathlin O'Birne	103	92	83	95	67	67	50	48	29	26	18	10		
Teelin	110	99	90	102	74	74	57	54	33	23	9			
Killybegs	116	105	96	108	80	80	63	62	38	26				
Sligo	108	97	88	100	72	72	55	53	23					
Killala	92	81	72	84	56	56	40	37						
Broad Haven	67	58	48	61	31	30	13							
Portnafrankagh	55	46	37	50	20	19								
Elly Bay	53	38	32	44	16									
Achill Head	36	25	16	28										
Westport	44	29	15											
Clare Island	28	16												
Inishbofin	13													

Appendix 6

ABBREVIATIONS

AC	Admiralty Chart	kHz	kilohertz	Q	quick-flashing
AIS	Automatic Identification Systems	kn	knots		
Alt	alternate	L (in captions)	left	R	red
		LAT	Lowest astronomical Tide	R (in captions)	right
Bn	beacon	Ldg	leading	RoRo	roll-on, roll-off
		L Fl	long flash	RWVS	red & white vertical stripes
Card	cardinal	lt	light		
CG	Coastguard	LW	low water	S	south
Ch	channel	LWM	low-water mark	s	second(s)
col	column	LWN	low water neaps	SC	sailing club
		LWS	low water springs	SHM	starboard-hand mark
Dir	directional				
		m	metres	t	tonne
E	east	M	miles	TSS	Traffic Separation Scheme
		MF	medium frequency	twr	tower
F (wind)	Beaufort force	MHWN	mean high water neaps		
F (light)	fixed	MHWS	mean high water springs	unintens	unintensified
Fl	flashing	MHz	megahertz		
		ML	mean level	vert	vertical
G	green	Mo	Morse	VHF	very high frequency
				VQ	very quick flashing
h	hour(s)	N	north		
HM	Harbour Master			W	west
hor	horizontal	obsc	obscured	W	white
HW	high water	Oc	occulting		
HWM	high-water mark	Or	orange	Y	yellow
HWN	high water neaps			YC	yacht club
HWS	high water springs	PHM	port-hand mark		
		PO	post office		
Iso	Isophase				

Appendix 7

IRISH LANGUAGE GLOSSARY

The following table lists some of the placename elements found in the area of this book, with their Irish Gaelic word origins and English translations. Also included are some of the Irish words commonly met with on signs, particularly in Gaeltacht areas.

English rendering	Gaelic	English translation	Examples of derived placename/ expression
	abhaile	homewards	Slán abhaile! - Safe home!
	aerfort	airport	
agh, agha	achadh	field	Aghada - long field
ail-, alt-	ailt	ravine	Ailroe - red ravine
	aimsir	weather, season	
aird-, ard-	ard (noun)	height, top, highest point	Ardmore - the high headland
	aire	notice, attention	Pobal ar Aire - Neighbourhood Watch Area
-ane, ana, anna	éan	bird	Illauneana - bird island
anna, annagh	eanach	marsh	Annagh Point
ard-	ard (adjective)	high, (of a person) chief	
ass-, assa-	eas	waterfall	Easky
	baile	town, townland	
bad, vad	bád, bhád	boat	CarrickavReenavade - boat pointaud - boat rock
bal-, bally-	baile	town, townland	Ballynakill - Churchtown
bal- , bel- , val-	béal	mouth, entrance	Bealadangan - fortress entrance
-ban, -bane, -van,-vane, bawn	bán	white, fair	Trawbawn - white beach
ban, ben	bean (pl mná)	woman	Mná - Ladies
barnog		barnacle	Inishbarnog - barnacle island
barra	barra	bar, sandbank	Kinvarra - head of the bank
beg	beag	small	Inishbeg - little island
bo	bó	cow	Inishbofin - white cow island
boher	bothair	road (literally, cow path)	
brack, breck	breac	speckled, dappled	Illaunbreck - speckled island
bradan	bradán	salmon	
breel	broigheall	cormorant	
brock	broc	badger	Illaunbrock - badger island
	bruscar	litter	
bullig-	bolg	bulge, blister; hence underwater rock, breaker	Bulligmore - the big breaker
bun-	bun	base, bottom, (of a river) mouth	Bunbeg - the little river mouth
bwee, boy (suffix)	buí	yellow	Illaunbweeheen - little yellow island
	comhairle	council	
caher	cathair	fort	Cahersiveen - the fort of little Sive
cairn, carn	carn	heap, mound, cairn	Carnboy - yellow cairn
camus	camas	bay, cove	
can-, ken-, kin-	ceann	head	Canduff - black head
carrick, carraig	carraig	rock	Carraig Fada - long rock
	ceol	song, music	ceol agus craic - songs and laughter
claddagh	cladach	rocky shore	
clogh, cloy	cloch	stone	
cloon	cluain	meadow	
colleen	cailín	girl	Colleen Og Rock - young girl's rock
	comhairle	council	Comhairle Chontae Chorcaí - Cork County Council

English rendering	Gaelic	English translation	Examples of derived placename/ expression
cool, cul, cole	cúl	back, corner	
coon	cuan	haven, harbour	
coor, cuar, cour	cur	foam	Couraghy - foamy place
corran, corraun	corran	crescent	
	craic	fun, jokes, laughter	ceol agus craic - songs and laughter
dangan	daingean	stronghold	Dingle - the fortress
	deas	south	
	deoch	drink	
derg	dearg	red	Belderg - the red river mouth
derry, darry	doire	oakwood	Derrynane - oakwood of the birds
dillisk	duileasc	dulse, edible seaweed	Dillisk Rock
doo, duff, duv	dubh	black	Carrickduff - black rock
	droichead	bridge	
drum-, drom-	druim	ridge	Dromadda - the long ridge
dun, doon	dún	fort	Dunboy - yellow fort
dysert	díseart	hermitage	Killadysert - the hermitage church
	gobhar	goat	
-een	-ín	little (diminutive suffix)	Carrigeenboy - little yellow rock
	gaoth	wind	Bunagee - river-mouth of the wind
fad, fadda, adda	fada	long	
	fáilte	welcome	Bord Fáilte - the Irish Tourist Board
fer, var	fear (pl fir)	man	Fir - Gents
fin	fionn	white, fair	Carrickfin - white rock
freagh, free	fraoch	heather	Freaghillaun - heathery island
gall	gall	stranger	Donegal - fort of the stranger
gar-	gearr	short	Garinish - short island
garve, garriff	garbh	rough, rugged	Glengarriff - the rough glen
glas, glass	glas	green	Glassillaun - green island
glinsk	glinn uisce	clear water	
gola, gowla	gabhlóg	fork	Inishgowla - forked island
gore, gower	gobhar	goat	
gorm	gorm	blue	
	go mall	slowly	on the roads in Gaeltacht areas
gub	gob	point, promontory	Gubacashel - castle point
gwee	gaoth	wind	Carrigwee - windy rock
	machair	grassy plain	
	iar	west	Iarthair Chorcaí - West Cork
illan, illaun, illane	oileán	island	
inish, innis, ennis	inis	island	Inishmore - big island
inver	inbhir	river mouth	Derryinver - rivermouth of the oakwood
	mullan	hillock	
keel, kill, kyle	caol	strait, narrows	
keeragh, cooragh	caorach	sheep	Carrigieragh - sheep rock
kil-	cill	church, monk's cell	
kil-, -kilty	coillte	woods	Clonakilty - fort of the woods
knock-, crock-, croagh	cnoc	hill	Croagh Patrick - St Patrick's Hill
lack- lackan	leaca	stony slope	
lahan	leathan	broad	
league, legaun		pillar, pile of stones	
leck, lick	leac	slab, flat rock	Doolick - black slab
lee, lea	liath	grey	Ringlea - grey point
lenan, leenan		weed-covered rock	

English rendering	Gaelic	English translation	Examples of derived placename/ expression
letter			
lis-	lios	ring fort	
long	long	ship	LE=Long Éireann - Irish Ship, a naval service vessel
	sean	old	
maan	meán	middle	Inishmaan - midddle island
mac, mic, vic-, vick-	mac, mhic-	son of	Macdara's Island - island of the son of Dara
maddy, vaddy	madaidh	dog	
magher, maghera	machair	grassy plain	
mara	mara	of the sea	
meal	meall	lump	Mealbeg - little lump
more, vore	mór, mhór	big	
muck	muc	pig	
mullagh	mullach	summit	Mullaghmore - big summit
mullaun	mullan	hillock	Mullauncarrickscoltia - split hillock rock
murren, murrisk		low seashore	
mweel	maol	bare	
oge	óg	young	
oir	oir	east	
ooey, owey	uaimh	cave	Owey - island of caves
owen-, own- avon-,	abhainn	river	Owenboy - yellow river
pool	poll	pool	
portan, partan	portan	crab	
rannagh, ranny, rin	rinn	promontory	
reen, ring, rin	rinn	point, promontory	Rineanna - bird point
	rogha	choice	rogha bia - choice of food, menu
ron	rón	seal	Carrignaronemore - big seal rock
roo, row, roe	rua	red	
ross	ros	promontory	
scolt	scoilt	split; cleft	Mullauncarrickscoltia - split hillock rock
shan-, shen-	sean	old	an Sean Cheann - the Old Head of Kinsale
shoonta	siunta	cleft, crevice	Carrigashoonta - cleft rock
skellig	sceilg	steep rock, crag	Skellig Michael - St Michael's crag
	slán, sláinte	health	slán abhaile - safe home. Sláinte! - Cheers!
slieve	sliabh	mountain	Slieve League - pillar mountain
stack, stag	stac	pinnacle rock	The Stags of Broad Haven
tear-, tyre-	tir	land	
ti-	teach, tí	house	
tober	tobar	well	
tooskert	tuaisceart	north	Inishtooskert - north island
tor, tur	tor	clump, tower	Turduvillaun - black island tower
tra	trá	beach, shore	Tralong - ship beach
turk	torc	boar	Inishturk - boar island
wheelaun	faoilean	seagull	Carrickaweelaun - seagull rock

Index

For Helen, and a big
thank you to Adélie
for her help
A.S.

First published 2013 by Nosy Crow Ltd
The Crow's Nest, 14 Baden Place
Crosby Row, London SE1 1YW
www.nosycrow.com

ISBN 978 0 85763 115 2

Nosy Crow and associated logos are trademarks and/or registered
trademarks of Nosy Crow Ltd
Text © Nosy Crow 2013
Illustrations © Axel Scheffler 2013

The right of Axel Scheffler to be identified as the illustrator
of this work has been asserted.

A CIP catalogue record for this book is available from the British Library.

Printed in China

Papers used by Nosy Crow are made from wood grown in sustainable forests.

7 9 8

Pip and Posy

The Bedtime Frog

Axel Scheffler

Posy was going to
stay at Pip's house.

She packed up her suitcase very carefully.
She didn't want to forget anything.

Then she got on the bus.
She was very excited.

Pip was really happy
to see Posy.
"Hi, Posy!" he called.

"Hello, Pip!" giggled Posy.

Pip and Posy had lots of fun.
They played with Pip's cars.

They played with the farm.

And then they played a game called 'pirates in hospital'.

They ate
spaghetti.

They had a
bubbly bath.

They brushed
their teeth.

And they read
a funny story.
After that, it was
time for bed.

"Night-night, Posy," said Pip,
as he cuddled up with his piggy.

"Sweet dreams, Pip," said Posy.

They switched off their lights.

Pip was very nearly asleep
when he heard a voice.
"Froggy!" said the voice.

It was Posy.
"I've forgotten Froggy," she sniffed.

"I CAN'T SLEEP WITHOUT MY FROGGY!!"

Pip turned his light back on again.
"Would you like this teddy, Posy?" he said.

But Posy did not want Pip's teddy.
"It's not green," she said.
"My frog is green."

"Would you like my dinosaur?" said Pip.
"He's green."

"No!" said Posy.
"That dinosaur
is too big and too scary!"

"What about my frog money box?" said Pip.

"No!" said Posy,
"That is the WRONG FROG!"

Posy cried and cried and cried.

Oh dear! Poor Posy.

Pip thought for a moment.
Then he did a **very difficult** thing.

"Would you like Piggy, Posy?" he said.

Posy stopped crying.
Piggy was an extremely nice pig.

"Yes, please, Pip," she said.

Soon Pip was asleep.

And so was Posy.

And the next day, when Posy
went home to her house,
she found her frog . . .